081 1TT

D1426515

UNIVERSITY OF WESTMINSTER

Failure to return or renew ~
borrowing rights at all

~r

26 0059751 9

WORK, GENDER AND FAMILY IN VICTORIAN ENGLAND

STUDIES IN GENDER HISTORY

Recent years have shown that the study of gender has proved to be of too great an importance to be ignored. By challenging long-accepted approaches, categories and priorities, gender history has necessitated nothing less than a change in the historical terrain. This series seeks to publish the latest and best research, which not only continues to restore women to history and history to women, but also to encourage the development of a new channel of scholarship.

Published titles

Karl Ittmann
WORK, GENDER AND FAMILY IN VICTORIAN ENGLAND

Jutta Schwartzkopf
WOMEN IN THE CHARTIST MOVEMENT

Lillian Lewis Shiman
WOMEN AND LEADERSHIP IN NINETEENTH-CENTURY ENGLAND

Clare Taylor
WOMEN OF THE ANTI-SLAVERY MOVEMENT

Cornelie Usborne
THE POLITICS OF THE BODY IN WEIMAR GERMANY

Series Standing Order

If you would like to receive future titles in this series as they are published, you can make use of our standing order facility. To place a standing order please contact your bookseller or, in case of difficulty, write to us at the address below with your name and address and the name of the series. Please state with which title you wish to begin your standing order. (If you live outside the UK we may not have the rights for your area, in which case we will forward your order to the publisher concerned.)

Customer Services Department, Macmillan Distribution Ltd
Houndmills, Basingstoke, Hampshire, RG21 2XS, England.

Work, Gender and Family in Victorian England

Karl Ittmann
Assistant Professor of History
University of Houston

INFORMATION RESOURCE SERVICES
UNIVERSITY OF WESTMINSTER
HARROW IRS CENTRE
WATFORD ROAD
NORTHWICK PARK
HARROW HA1 3TP

MACMILLAN

© Karl Ittmann 1995

All rights reserved. No reproduction, copy or transmission of this publication may be made without written permission.

No paragraph of this publication may be reproduced, copied or transmitted save with written permission or in accordance with the provisions of the Copyright, Designs and Patents Act 1988, or under the terms of any licence permitting limited copying issued by the Copyright Licensing Agency, 90 Tottenham Court Road, London W1P 9HE.

Any person who does any unauthorised act in relation to this publication may be liable to criminal prosecution and civil claims for damages.

First published 1995 by
MACMILLAN PRESS LTD
Houndmills, Basingstoke, Hampshire RG21 2XS
and London
Companies and representatives
throughout the world

ISBN 0–333–60479–2

A catalogue record for this book is available
from the British Library.

10   9   8   7   6   5   4   3   2   1
04 03 02 01 00 99 98 97 96 95

Copy-edited and typeset by Povey–Edmondson
Okehampton and Rochdale, England

Printed in Great Britain by
Ipswich Book Co Ltd
Ipswich, Suffolk

To my father Beverly Ittmann (1931–84), my mother Leonore Ittmann, and the Reverend Clayton Garland

Contents

List of Tables and Figures

Tables

Figures

Acknowledgments

This book began as a dissertation at the University of Pennsylvania and received financial assistance from a number of sources along the way. The University of Pennsylvania gave me a Pennfield Fellowship and the Department of History provided additional travel and research funds, while the Council of European Studies at Columbia University awarded me a Pre-dissertation Fellowship. Princeton University supported my work with a summer faculty research grant. While at the University of Houston, I have received both a Research Initiation Grant and two Limited Grants in Aid to assist in the completion of my manuscript.

In England I benefited from the assistance of the staff of a number of library and archives. I would like to thank the staff of the University of Leeds Archives, the Huddersfield Polytechnic Library, the West Yorkshire Record Office in Wakefield, the British Library and the Public Record Offices at Chancery Lane and Kew for their patience and kindness. I would like to thank Elvira Willmott and the staff of the Bradford Central Library for their assistance. I owe the greatest debt to David James and his staff at the Bradford District Archives. David is both a remarkable archivist and scholar and a wonderful human being. His knowledge and skill allowed me to fully explore the rich sources available in Bradford. I would also like to thank Jack Morrell, Keith Laybourn and Tony Jowitt for sharing their knowledge of the West Riding and Bradford with me.

A number of people have offered advice and encouragement over the years. At Michigan State, Peter Vinten-Johansen, Anne Meyering and David Loromer pushed me toward graduate school. My graduate advisor at the University of Pennsylvania, Lynn Lees, gave generously of her time and provided invaluable assistance in the completion of the dissertation and the manuscript. I would also like to thank my committee members Jack Reece and Walter Licht for their help. While at Penn several members of the Population Studies program provided advice and suggestions, including Doug Ewbank, Susan Watkins and Mike Strong. I also owe a great debt to my friends Steve Ruggles and Miriam King, who helped me with the data gathering and analysis. At Princeton, Phil Nord, Reid Mitchell and Peter Mandler made my stay both challenging and enjoyable. I wish to thank my University of

Houston colleagues Sarah Fishman, Jim Jones, Ken Lipartito, Jim Martin and Steve Mintz for their help and suggestions. Martin Weiner, Richard Price and Michael Haines read all or part of this work and offered their suggestions. I, of course, remain responsible for all errors and omissions.

Finally I would like to thank my friends and family for their moral (and financial) support over the years. My brothers and sisters Mike, Pat, Mary and Steve all followed this project with interest and concern, My friends in the USA and England gave me great aid and comfort as this project moved forward and without their help it could not have been completed. In particular I wish to thank the Garlands, James Vaughn, Danny Wooley, Jeff Regeczi, David Blackburn, Peter and Carol McCaffery, John McGranahan, Brett Gary, Ken Straus, Jay Lyall, Richard Soderlund, Susan Marrs and Terry Lohrenz, as well as the many I lack the space to name.

KARL ITTMANN

Introduction

In 1844 George Weerth, a German businessman and political radical, traveled to Bradford, West Yorkshire for the first time. Of his travels in the Pennine hills outside the city he observed,

> Bradford lies, as I have already remarked, in one of the most beautiful parts of the county of Yorkshire, surrounded by hills, small woods, splendid meadows in a narrow valley which merges into the hills on three sides.[1]

He contrasted the beauty of the local countryside with the smoke-filled valley that surrounded Bradford

> Oh, I still retain the first impression, fresh in memory that this terrible-wonderful town made upon me. I wouldn't have felt differently if I had been taken straight to hell. Every other factory town in England is a paradise in comparison to this hole . . . In Bradford . . . you think you have been lodged in no other place than with the devil incarnate.

For Weerth, as for many others in the nineteenth century, the contrast between the vast clouds of smoke that choked the valley and the clear air and sunshine of the hills formed the overwhelming impression of Bradford. The ability of industry to overwhelm nature struck many with a mixture of awe and fear at its power. Today, the smokestacks and church steeples that dominated the nineteenth-century skyline remain perched on the hillsides, but the air is clear, for the factories are empty shells, wasted products of a vanished age in a post-industrial landscape. Bradford survives as a relic, a theme park of the industrial revolution for the tourists the local council tries to lure to the north to revitalize an economy in painful decline. In between these two moments lies the modern history of Bradford, a time in which the 'worstedopolis' became a world city, the center of a vast trade in woolen goods that spanned the globe. To understand that history is to understand much of what happened to England and the rest of the Western world in the course of the Industrial Revolution.

If Bradford was transformed by the rise of industry, so too were the lives of its inhabitants, most of whom lived there because of the

1

possibilities for work in the mills. Bradfordians of the mid-nineteenth century lived during the first generation of the industrial age and their life experiences created much of what we today consider characteristic about English working-class culture. The pub, the friendly society, the football match and the factory are all products of this era of rapid change and accommodation.

Many feared the consequences for society of such rapid change. Often these fears focused upon the family and its transformation by industrialization. The greater economic and social role of women, the changing relationship between parents and children, the decline of masculine power all played a role in the perceived crisis of the family. The results could be seen in crime, infanticide, abortion, poverty and the use of birth control. In 1881, the Bradford Medical Officer of Health noted that the 'gradual diminution of births and marriages since 1876 mark an epoch of bad trade, from which . . . there seems to be no revival'.[2] By calling attention to the decline of the birth rate in Bradford, the Medical Officer of Health noted a trend which would continued unabated for the next sixty years and would have revolutionary implications for family life.

The deliberate limitation of family size became a general phenomenon by the late nineteenth century in most of Europe and the United States and the uncoupling of sexuality and reproduction sent shock waves through western societies that still resonate today.[3] The freedom to choose parenthood changed the meaning of child bearing forever. The unprecedented decision by millions of men and women to control their fertility despite legal sanctions and moral disapproval has fascinated historians and social scientists. Beginning in the 1940s, the theory of the demographic transition provided the primary explanation for this change.[4] Transition theory argued that family limitation represented the final stage in the process of modernization, which changed the value of children as economic actors and which created new social incentives for smaller families. These included the decline of the extended family, higher incomes, increased education, the higher status of women, greater individualism and rationality, the rise of urban life and the fall in infant and child mortality. Demographers and historians attempted to link modernization and family limitation by using aggregate measures of social change, such as the percentage literate or levels of infant mortality, and comparing them with levels of fertility at the national or regional level.[5]

While this approach succeeded in establishing the broad outlines of population history in western Europe and the United States since the eighteenth century, much of the historical process remained obscure. The severe functionalism of transition theory, as well as its reliance on quantitative studies, struck many historians as reductive and ahistorical. The belief that rational choice models could explain the complex behavior of families across several hundred years and many countries ignored new ideas about family life and gender developed by historians since the 1960s, while the insistence that family limitation trickled down from the upper classes to the lower classes failed to explain the social relationships that created such unprecedented uniformity of behavior.

Several new historical studies of family limitation call transition theory into question.[6] While these studies cover a variety of geographic areas and chronological periods, they share the belief that fertility should be studied at the level of the family, not the region or the nation. The reliance on individual and family-level data requires intensive collection of information and virtually dictates a small-scale approach.[7] The popularity of local or regional studies also reflects a belief that the specific context of family limitation needs to be understood before the motives and values of ordinary people can be grasped. With rare exceptions, most families and individuals left little information about themselves and even less about intimate decisions such as reproduction and sexuality. Ultimately, the historian must infer motivation from behavior and context. For most recent students of family limitation, a local study informed by a sense of the broader structures of society offers the best hope for accomplishing a reasonable understanding of these issues.

This book examines the beginning of family limitation in a single town, Bradford, West Yorkshire, England from 1850 to 1914. It builds on two linked arguments. One is that it is possible through a close reading of local history to recreate the web of material and social forces that shaped the decisions of working men and women about family life. Second, the analysis of family limitation in a city like Bradford can tell us a great deal about that process elsewhere in England and western Europe.

Bradford, West Yorkshire stands out as an appropriate case for a number of reasons. Its place as the center of the world's worsted trade made it a product of the industrial revolution in its classical phase. Despite it own peculiar history, the city formed part of the leading edge of social and economic change in the nineteenth century. What Patrick Joyce has said of Lancashire is equally true of Bradford and the West Riding of Yorkshire.

If Lancashire was not the England of the capital, of the ports, of the 'traditional' manufacturing towns, least of all the England of the land and the county town, then it was the new England of town and industry, and these forces transformed England.[8]

Bradford exemplifies the forces that shaped much of the history of nineteenth-century England. The new patterns of work and life produced by the rise of modern industry first appeared in areas like Bradford. The uneven and incomplete process of economic change made Bradford a leader, but eventually much of the country came to resemble the new towns of the north, in social composition, if not architecture. As the sixth largest city in Great Britain, Bradford represents the emergence of urban life as a dominant force on the national scene. By 1911, 41 per cent of the English population lived in large conurbations like that of the West Riding and many more lived in their orbit. Although no one area can hope to represent all the experiences of a country, Bradford underwent many of the most important changes of the long nineteenth century that stretched from the Napoleonic Wars to the First World War.

Bradford represents an early case of the spread of family limitation, one that tells us a great deal about the larger issues of English population history. Contemporary observers in England focused on the outstanding feature of the initial stages of family limitation – the differential fertility of social classes.[9] The more rapid decline of the birth rate among the wealthier and more highly educated raised fears of 'race suicide' and social disorder.[10] In the words of Ethel Elderton, a eugenicist and early student of family limitation, 'any . . . differential fertility means racial degeneration'.[11] Although eugenicists and other commentators decried the trend toward smaller families, especially among the well-to-do, the birth rate continued to fall into the 1930s.[12]

Most population historians see differential fertility and its disappearance in the twentieth century as evidence that family limitation began among the middle classes and spread downward through society through a process of 'social capillarity'.[13] Demographers assume that this process reflected an increasing uniformity of values and beliefs as middle-class attitudes diffused throughout society. Yet, although the birth rate declined more rapidly among wealthier families, a wide range of social groups began to practice family limitation at roughly the same time.[14] Textile workers showed evidence of family limitation in the late nineteenth century, despite the fact that their experiences differed quite radically from the those of middle-class families that began to control their fertility in the same period. Textile workers earned relatively low wages and textile regions generally suffered from poor environmental conditions, high infant mortality and low levels of education. The idea that declining child labor, in combination with rising levels of women's work, transformed the family fails to account for the experience of areas like Bradford, which exhibited consistently high levels of both throughout the nineteenth century.[15]

The inability of transition theory to explain the experience of textile workers raises some larger questions of social theory and causality. By assuming that all people in English society practiced family limitation for the same reasons, demographers discount the importance of social class in the nineteenth century. Yet the late nineteenth century saw a heightened awareness of class differences in England. This awareness took the form of discussions of the 'condition of England question' or concern over the growing militancy of trade unions.[16] This era saw the emergence of new class-based political and cultural movements that must be accounted for in any explanation of working-class fertility.[17]

In order to analyze the decline of fertility in Bradford, this study uses four samples of Bradford's population from the 1851, 1861, 1871 and 1881 censuses, comprising some 28,000 people. The sample allows us to examine the evolution of family life and work and to link these changes to patterns of family limitation. Rather than relying upon regression analysis to relate quantifiable social and economic trends to fertility, this study builds an explanation based on a close reading of local experience in the Victorian era. Using a variety of sources helps address the central question of why families had fewer children. This question cannot be answered directly, for workers in Bradford did not leave us any diaries or other materials that reveal why they had fewer children. Instead, we must build on our understanding of the interaction between the family and the local social and economic environment. Patterns of leisure and association, work and politics all played a role in this change.

The unifying themes of this study differ dramatically from those of transition theory. The emergence of industrial capitalism transformed working-class families as they adapted to the new circumstances, but not in the ways demographers assert. The older communal structures of village life, in so far as they still existed in the early nineteenth century, disappeared by the 1850s, but they were not replaced by the isolated nuclear family, seeking to make its own way in the world. Instead new communal organizations emerged, based on ties of workplace and residence, that offered many of the same support systems and exercised their own forms of surveillance and control. The working-class community's demand for the 'respectability' of its members proved as important as earlier social norms and values in regulating the behavior of community members.[18]

At the same time, the meaning and content of family ties changed as new ways of life dissolved the old patriarchy of the proto-industrial and agrarian villages of Yorkshire. The disappearance of domestic industry, the increasing importance of child labor, the decline of patriarchal supervision of labor and the ability of women to earn independent incomes turned the family on its head. 'Manliness' and other notions of gender and age relations were redefined to accommodate the new realities of work and daily life. The family became a contested ground, in which conflicts over authority and resources undercut the dominance of a single actor in the family. Complicating our picture of family relations is the nature of birth control in this era. Two of the primary methods – coitus interruptus and abstinence – required men and women to cooperate.[19] In these circumstances, family limitation had to serve the differing interests of men and women.

Shifts in family and community took place in the shadow of the reshuffling of life by industrial capitalism. Successive waves of economic and social reorganization forced the family and the working-class community to adjust to new ways of life and work. The expansion of domestic labor in the early nineteenth century gave way to the rise of the mill, which in turn began to change under the impact of increasing world competition in the late nineteenth century. Far from being a haven from the demands of the outside world, the family was subjected as never before to the pressures of the marketplace, which put family members in a new relationship to each other and the outside world. In these circumstances, the logic of uncontrolled reproduction fell apart and family limitation emerged as a way to stabilize life in face of new forms of production and wealth.

The book examines each of these issues in turn. Chapter 1 deals with the growth and structure of the worsted wool textile industry that dominated the economic life of Victorian Bradford. Chapter 2 looks at the patterns of work created by the worsted trade and their effect upon working-class men and women. Chapter 3 focuses on the political system that characterized mid-Victorian Bradford for clues to how issues of work, poverty, gender and power came to be expressed in local politics. Chapter 4 details the emergence of two separate class cultures in this era and the implications this had for family life. Chapters 5 and 6 discuss the changing nature of gender and family life in the period. Of particular concern in these chapters is the perceived impact of industrialization upon the family and how that perception shaped the discourse of family life. Chapter 7 sets out the dimensions of fertility decline and the material and social forces that lay behind the adoption of family limitation.

While the major structures of working-class life – family, community and work – placed limits on the behavior of working-class individuals and families, such structures did not produce a unitary response to the problems of life. Some families, for whom the material logic of family limitation was strong, may have chosen for personal, moral or religious reasons not to control their fertility. In the end, part of the significance of family limitation lies in its ability to illuminate the human side of the process of change, to suggest the possibilities that ordinary men and women grasped or ignored as they moved through their lives. These men and women experienced their lives not as a linear process of modernization, but rather as a complex, seemingly discontinuous series of events. Our reading should restore this aspect of historical experience to a central place, for it recreates the vision and the uncertainty that lay behind family limitation.

1 The Worsted Trade and the Development of Bradford

When Daniel Defoe toured the West Riding of Yorkshire in the late eighteenth century, he paid little attention to the village of Bradford, though he noted the impact of the worsted trade upon the Yorkshire countryside, where the cottages dotted the hillsides.[1] Seventy years later, Bradford filled the valley,

> its hundred streets stretching their wide arms for miles; filled with an overflowing population of busy merchants and manufacturers, artizans and operatives; and the immense products of its stupendous mills – where thousands of clanking power looms, and whirring spinning frames din the ear.[2]

This dramatic transformation resulted from the rise of the worsted wool industry, which defined the modern history of Bradford. Nineteenth-century observers frequently invoked the special relationship between the industry and the city. Edward Collinson in his history of Bradford written in the 1850s said: 'The increase of the population has been progressive in a ratio corresponding with the extension of the worsted manufacture in this important district.'[3] John James, a nineteenth-century historian of Bradford, referred to it as the 'Metropolis of the Worsted Trade . . . raised to a proud eminence among the manufacturing towns of the kingdom'.[4] James saw the worsted industry as the foundation of society, the base of the pyramid that supported the city and its people.[5]

Despite the boosterism of these nineteenth-century writers, they offer us the proper starting point for the study of mid-Victorian Bradford. The story of Bradford in the nineteenth century is one of ceaseless change and the ways in which people tried to adapt to this change. The prime mover in this process was the worsted industry. Bradford's role as the center of the world's worsted textile trade allowed it to grow from an oversized village of some 13,000 in 1801 to a city of 200,000 by 1901. This chapter traces the rise of domestic industry in the West

Riding, the emergence of the factory and mechanized production and the maturity of the trade in the second half of the nineteenth century. Two key issues need to be addressed. One is how the worsted industry achieved and sustained its enormous growth. The second is why the industry failed to continue to develop, a failure which ultimately led to the decline of both the trade and the city it built. Both of these issues are crucial to understanding the ways in which the industry shaped the lives of Bradfordians in the nineteenth century.

The rise of industry in the West Riding of Yorkshire moved work from the home to the factory and provided wealth for some and a livelihood, often precarious, for the rest. The expansion of cities like Bradford gave rise to an entirely new way of life. These changes in work and daily life helped transform the values and experiences of the ordinary people who lived through them. In order to recreate the reasons why couples began to limit their families, we must first understand the nature of these changes and how they affected the family.

The process by which Bradford became the leading center for worsted production can be divided into three stages. The first, roughly 1700 to 1830, saw the transfer of the production of long wool goods from Norwich and the West Country to the West Riding and its expansion, first through domestic putting-out and then through the factory system. In the second stage, 1830 to 1873, the creation of new products and mechanization revolutionized the worsted trade and created the preconditions for forty years of expansion. The third stage, 1873 to 1914, saw the worsted trade falter in the face of new competition and foreign tariffs and begin its long, slow decline. Each of these stages brought corresponding changes to the city of Bradford and the people who depended upon the industry and city for their livelihood. The first two stages created the city, and helped lay the groundwork for a particular way of life. The third undermined that way of life and led to a variety of efforts to stabilize life in the face of change.

THE RISE OF THE WORSTED INDUSTRY, 1750—1850

Bradford has been a woolen area since the Middle Ages. Originally traditional woolen goods such as kerseys dominated production, but in the late seventeenth century this began to change. Merchants from the

West of England sought to escape high labor costs and conflicts over the dilution of skill by moving into new areas, away from the controls of artisan guilds.[6] The West Riding of Yorkshire offered a haven for worsted merchants, for it contained a large population familiar with hand techniques, but outside the traditional guild structure. As in most other areas of Yorkshire, farmers combined home industry with subsistence agriculture in order to supplement their incomes from the soil. In the Bradford area the process of enclosures created a split between a small group of substantial yeoman farmers and a much larger group of cottagers and small farmers. This latter group provided the labor force for the expansion of the putting-out system in the West Riding.[7]

Worsted manufacturers dealt with an international market in America and Europe and thus stocked a wider range of materials than other woolen merchants, who often specialized in a single product for the home or foreign trade. They also had to maintain sufficient labor and equipment to meet any sudden changes in demand. Due to these factors and the longer production time of worsted fabrics, the worsted trade required greater capital investment than the woolen trade, even in this era of relatively low entry costs. This led to the domination of the industry in the eighteenth century by a small, wealthy group of merchant-manufacturers. These men purchased raw wool and sent it out to be combed, spun, and woven in villages throughout the West Riding. After weaving, the merchants finished, dyed and marketed the cloth. These final stages took place in the expanding West Riding cities of Leeds, Halifax, and Bradford and represented the first step in the progressive centralization of the industry.[8]

These merchants drew upon a number of sources for their capital. Most important were the personal resources of the merchant and his friends and family. Loans and the mortgaging of assets, primarily land, provided the basis of most enterprises. In addition, local gentry, banks, and wealthy individuals in fields such as mining and milling backed the fledgling industry. These sources of capital placed a premium on local connections, for such ties proved vital in raising the necessary funds. In its early stages, therefore, local men with preexisting social networks controlled the Bradford trade.[9]

For most of the eighteenth century, the putting-out system remained adequate for the needs of the manufacturers. Yet a number of problems in the domestic trade led to a more centralized method of production near the end of the century. The high cost of distributing and collecting the materials from the scattered villages and farms of the West Riding and the difficulties of controlling labor lay behind this trend. Without close supervision, the cottagers and their families worked at their own pace, one dictated more by their own financial and personal circumstances than the needs of the manufacturers. In addition, theft and diversion of raw materials could not be controlled easily in the putting-out system. Domestic workers saw the waste products of their work, such as noils of wool left from worsted spinning, as their due.[10] They also adulterated goods by adding sand or water to increase their weight to disguise embezzlement of materials. These practices led Bradford manufacturers to set up the Worsted Committee in 1777 and to obtain an act of Parliament which gave them the power to investigate and prosecute incidents of theft as well as the right to enforce contracts.[11] Despite their efforts, the Committee and its inspectors failed to solve the problems of labor discipline within the domestic system.

Although the problems with the domestic putting-out system favored a more centralized method of production, it took the perfection of machine spinning to set the process of centralization in motion. The factory system in the West Riding grew out of a marriage of the needs of manufacturers for lower costs and better labor control with the technical innovations of the late eighteenth century. The process went farther in cities like Bradford because of the relative weakness of artisan and trade union barriers to the introduction of machinery and the ability of Bradford's manufacturers to obtain sufficient capital to invest in the new techniques.

The first water-powered mills in the worsted industry appeared in the 1780s and the first mill in Bradford opened in 1801 with the construction of Fawcett's Mill. The lack of adequate water power in Bradford meant the new mills had to be steam powered. This initial handicap became an important advantage in the next thirty years, as steam proved to be the major source of power in the industry. Although Bradford lacked sufficient water power, it possessed a more than adequate supply of coal and a native iron industry capable of producing the necessary machinery for steam power. In the thirty years following the first mill in Bradford, a number of improvements in spinning occurred. The development of the slay and the perfection of the throstle frame gave spinners the ability to spin high quality yarn at greatly reduced prices.[12] The number of spinning mills in Bradford grew from five in 1810 to thirty-four in 1833. A turning point in the establishment of the factory system in Bradford came in 1825. In that year the combers and weavers struck for higher wages and union recognition. After a bitter strike lasting several months, they returned to work on the masters' terms. From that point onward, the workers of Bradford lost control over the introduction of machinery into mills and offered little resistance to the mechanization of the industry.[13]

The slow build-up of the industry bore fruit in the 1830s as a series of innovations radically altered the products and techniques of the industry and transformed the city into the world center for worsted goods. From the mid-1830s, Bradford manufacturers began to turn out pieces that had cotton wefts and wool warps, and which contained new fibers such as alpaca and mohair. These mixed fiber goods resembled more expensive all-wool pieces, but cost considerably less due to the lower price of cotton. This opened up new markets for Bradford merchants, particularly in women's clothing. They came to dominate not only the traditional lower quality markets, but also the better quality markets previously closed to worsteds. Along with these new products, and essential to their success, came a method for dyeing these mixed fabrics while in the piece. This technique, pioneered by the Bradford dyers Ripley and Sons, made mixed fabrics commercially feasible.[14]

In addition to these innovations in products, the actual processes of production underwent considerable alteration from 1830 to 1850. The last two important areas of hand work, weaving and combing, became machine processes in this era. The need to feed the mills with combed wool and to weave the machine made yarn at first increased the demand for hand labor. Even after the successful introduction of the power loom in the late 1820s, a large number of hand weavers found employment, albeit at steadily decreasing wages. Most manufacturers took advantage of a mixed system of production to lower their capital costs, supplementing their production in good times by using hand weavers and cutting back in bad times by letting them go.[15]

Combing proved a more difficult step to mechanize, but with the invention of the Holden and the Lister machine combs and their mass production in the late 1840s, machine combing rapidly replaced hand combing. Combing, once a highly skilled and highly paid occupation in the early nineteenth century, became a sweated trade even before mechanization.[16] Many hand weavers and new immigrants, particularly the Irish, flocked to the trade as the only alternative to complete destitution. The competition with machines only intensified this process and machine combs displaced as many as 10,000 hand combers in the decade following 1845.[17]

These innovations dramatically affected the industry. With the mechanization of combing and weaving, the worsted trade completed its evolution into a factory industry. Manufacturers could now centralize production and closely supervise their workers. Mechanization, by reducing the physical strength and skill necessary for spinning and weaving, allowed women and children to become the majority of the factory work force.[18] The number of mills in the city increased from 34 in 1833 to 67 in 1841 to 128 in 1850. At the same time, these firms began to expand in the size and scope of their operations. The average number of spindles per firm increased over 60 per cent from 1839 to 1856. In 1850, forty-one firms combined spinning and weaving in a single mill and the total number of spindles in use jumped from 165,120 in 1839 to 268,653 in 1850.[19] In 1836 manufacturers employed only 2,768 power looms in all of the West Riding; by 1850 there were 12,896 in Bradford alone. The number of operatives directly employed in textile production quadrupled from 6,022 in 1835 to 25,872 in 1850.[20]

Despite its dramatic growth in the first half of the nineteenth century, the worsted industry suffered from a number of sharp downturns prior to 1850. As an industry dependent upon foreign markets for survival, it proved vulnerable to larger fluctuations in the world economy. Thus from 1815 to 1819, 1825 to 1826, 1829 to 1830, 1837 to 1841 and 1845 to 1848, the trade and the city of Bradford experienced considerable hardships.[21] The depression of 1845 to 1848 proved to be the most severe, throwing thousands out of work and onto the relief rolls.[22] These downturns did not alter the overall progress of the trade and by 1850 Bradford formed the heart of the world's worsted industry, the 'worstedopolis', as its boosters referred to it.

BRADFORD'S ECONOMY IN THE MID-VICTORIAN ERA

The stabilization of political life after 1848 and the general buoyancy of the European economy gave the Bradford industry further impetus in the 1850s and 1860s. Manufacturers had a clear field and little competition and they expanded their capacity rapidly. From 1850 to 1872, the number of power looms in the Bradford district increased by almost 120 per cent and the number of spindles by over 140 per cent and entrepreneurs constructed more than 1000 mills and warehouses in the borough.[23] The mid-Victorian era was a golden one for textile manufacturers. Between 1856 and 1867, the level of assessed profits in Bradford shot up 250 per cent.[24] The prosperity of the worsted industry did not eliminate the problem of trade cycles, and there were slumps from 1854 to 1855, 1856 to 1857 and 1867 to 1868. These downturns, however, never attained the proportions of those of the 1840s. The American Civil War and the Franco-Prussian War created new opportunities as Bradford's traditional rivals in textile production, the Lancashire cotton industry and the Continental wool producers, suffered from the dislocations of war just as the demand for textile products increased. As a result, the worsted industry doubled its output from 1850 to 1873. Worsted manufacturers expanded their exports to two-thirds of the total exports of woolen goods by the early 1870s and it is likely that they duplicated this success in the home market.[25]

Bradford enjoyed a more diversified economy than other textile cities. The growth of the city and the worsted industry provided new opportunities in a variety of trades. The need to supply houses, mills and warehouses stimulated the construction industry. The native stone trade of Bradford boomed and Archibald Neill, a contractor, estimated that over 6,000 men worked in the stone cutting and getting trades in Bradford in 1873.[26] The demand for both iron and machinery stimulated expansion of the engineering and metal industries. Employment in engineering, mining and metal work was highly concentrated in Bradford. Two firms, Hodgson's, which made power looms, and Knowles, a manufacturer of dyeing and finishing machinery, provided the majority of jobs in engineering.[27] Two foundries, Low Moor and Bowling, located on the southern edge of the city, occupied the same position in metals and mining. Because of their location, the foundries existed almost as a separate village within the borough. Their physical separation from the crowded inner city districts continued until the construction of Ripleyville, the housing estate connected with the Bowling Dye Works, in the 1860s. Begun in the 1790s and specializing in high quality iron, these foundries employed about 7,000 miners and iron workers in the 1880s.[28] By the late 1870s however, changes in the demand for high grade iron undermined this trade, leading to a steady decline in output and employment.[29]

The preeminence of Bradford as a site of production gave Bradford merchants and bankers the opportunity to solidify and expand their role in marketing and finance. Bradford emerged as the principle mercantile center for the industry, replacing Halifax and Leeds. The new Exchange Building replaced the old Piece Hall in 1828 to facilitate the increasing volume of trade. This was in turn replaced in 1867 to accommodate an even greater expansion in mercantile activity. Through the efforts of its merchants, the city became completely integrated into the British railway network by 1850. The number of merchants based in the city increased from twenty-four in 1834 to two hundred fifty-two in 1873. Many of these were foreigners who wished to move closer to the center of the industry and the designation of the warehouse district as 'Little Germany' showed the importance of Germans in the export and warehousing trades.[30]

OCCUPATION AND CLASS IN MID-VICTORIAN BRADFORD

The development of Bradford's economy created a characteristic form of occupational and class structure. Like most English industrial cities, Bradford was overwhelmingly working class.[31] In 1851, only 7.2 per cent of the city's adult men were engaged as white-collar workers, shopkeepers or capitalists. Despite the growth of the service sector, by 1881 these upper strata encompassed only 11.7 per cent of adult men.[32] In 1851 only 6.7 per cent of Bradford's households employed servants and only 6.9 per cent of the female labor worked as domestic servants.[33]

The upper level of the social structure divided into a number of smaller groups. At the top were the merchants, bankers and manufacturers involved in the worsted trade, as well as a few landowning families.[34] Men like Titus Salt and S.C. Lister became enormously wealthy in the worsted industry and stood out as examples of the possibility for riches for those from modest middle-class origins. Below this level stood the professionals and small capitalists who flourished as the city and the worsted trade grew.

The growth of Bradford also created opportunities for white-collar workers, as the retail and commercial sectors expanded. The number of clerks, primarily in the worsted industry, tripled from 1851 to 1881.[35] The new lower middle class of Bradford took advantage of the expansion of marketing and managerial functions as the industry matured. Young men could parlay education and social connections into an office position, where they kept books, checked orders and mailed and received samples.[36] Many of the more adventurous found employment as commercial agents and travellers. Some of these agents represented Bradford firms at home and abroad, while others served the interests of foreign companies doing business in Bradford. Men as diverse as Frederick Delius, the composer, and George Weerth, the German radical, found employment in this field.

Alongside these newer trades stood the more traditional retail and artisan trades, which employed 10.7 per cent of the adult male workforce in 1881. As small property owners with connections to the working class, they straddled the class lines in the city. Many depended upon working-class customers for their trade, a point emphasized by the consumer boycotts of the Chartist era. Master artisans and other tradesmen possessed a more direct connection to the laboring population by virtue of their training and daily work.

For the rest of the city's population, the factory loomed large. By 1861, over half of the working population earned its living directly through employment in the textile industry.[37] The worsted industry dominated employment in mid-Victorian Bradford, providing the largest single source of jobs for all groups. In 1851 68 per cent of the adult women (over age twenty at work) and over 46 per cent of the adult men earned their livings in the textile industry or related work such as dyeing and warehousing. For females and males under twenty, the percentages were 88 per cent and 64 per cent, respectively. Yet, despite the dominance of the worsted trade in an absolute sense, its relative importance declined after 1851.

There was a three-tiered hierarchy within the worsted industry. At the top stood the overlookers and skilled workers, who enjoyed relatively high salaries (20s. to 40s. per week) and job security, as well as some control over their labor.[38] Women and children involved in the two primary stages, spinning and weaving, formed the second, and by far the largest, group of operatives. Poorly paid and unorganized, these operatives gave Bradford manufacturers their cost advantage through cheap, productive labor. At the bottom of the hierarchy combers, rough sorters, and laborers performed unskilled tasks for wages of 10s. to 20s. per week. These men constituted the excess labor pool created by mechanization and the replacement of adult male labor in the worsted trade.

For the rest, the opportunities for work often depended upon the prosperity of the industry. Construction workers, iron workers and coal miners all relied upon orders generated by the expansion of the staple trade. A change in the routine of the mills, such as the granting of the Saturday half-holiday in the 1850s, could produce an alteration in the pattern of life of Bradford as a whole. The emergence of a more mature industrial economy in Bradford expanded employment outside the worsted trade. Skilled men in the construction trades, mining, and the local iron and engineering industries enjoyed their own boom period in the years 1850 to 1873, which allowed them to successfully organize trade unions and to press for both higher wages and better conditions.[39] By 1871, the building trades or related fields employed over 15 per cent of the adult male labor force, while about 10 per cent worked in engineering and metals. Skilled workers in metals and engineering, who were more highly unionized than their counterparts in the worsted industry, enjoyed higher wages and more stable employment. The wages of ironmoulders, boiler makers and ironfounders averaged over 30s. per week in the 1870s, while planers, smiths, pattern makers, fitters and turners made 24s. to 28s. weekly. Stone masons, who formed the elite of the construction trades, earned from 30s. to 90s. per week.[40] (See Table 1.1.)

In addition to these better paying, more highly skilled jobs, a significant sector of the adult labor force remained confined to the unskilled and casual labor markets. Despite the growth of new opportunities both within and outside the worsted industry, many men failed to find new jobs after 1851 and left the city. As a result the number of adult men declined between 1851 and 1861. For those who remained, the expansion of the worsted trade led to an increased demand for unskilled laborers of all types, both within and outside the factory, to supply the muscle power necessary to business. The need to transport and store the worsted industry's products as well as the provisions of a growing population provided new jobs in carriage and warehousing. In 1881 about 20 per cent of adult males could be classified as casual workers, facing all the problems of unemployment and low pay that plagued these workers elsewhere.[41]

The arrival of thousands of Irish migrants in the 1830s and 1840s added an ethnic dimension to the occupational structure of the city. Lacking formal training, networks and sometimes the necessary language skills, the Irish formed the bottom of the social ladder. Segregation and discrimination magnified these disadvantages. The Irish found work at first in the hand trades of the worsted industry, especially hand-combing and also the hawking and peddling trades. Packed in the slums of Silsbridge and White Abbey in the northwestern sector of Bradford township, the Irish constituted 10–12 per cent of the population by 1851.[42]

In addition to skill and ethnic divisions within the working class, there also existed significant age and gender distinctions. The importance of young people in the worsted trade created numerous opportunities for these workers. During the mid-Victorian period, the

Table 1.1   Employment in Bradford, 1851–81 (percentages)

	Boys	*Men*	*Girls*	*Women*
Textiles				
1851	26.3	46.8	36.7	32.8
1881	15.0	26.9	23.8	31.9
Building				
1851	2.5	11.7	0.1	0.2
1881	1.9	13.6	0.1	0.2
Heavy industry				
1851	5.1	10.1	0	0
1881	1.8	9.1	0.2	0.4
Laborer				
1851	0.8	4.1	0	0.4
1881	0.6	5.8	0	0.1
Domestic				
1851	0.1	0.2	2.5	6.9
1881	0.4	0.8	3.1	8.8
Consumer				
1851	3.6	13.7	2.1	6.4
1881	3.4	15.9	1.6	6.2
White collar				
1851	0.6	3.3	0.2	0.4
1881	1.1	5.4	0.2	0.6
Capitalists				
1851	0.1	1.5	0	0.2
1881	0	1.6	0	0.8
Unemployed				
1851	0	0.1	0.1	0.1
1881	1.3	5.5	0.8	2.0
School				
1851	22.9	0	20.3	0
1881	41.4	0	40.5	0
Home/spouse				
1851	11.4	0.2	12.7	18.7
1881	0.2	0.3	0.3	7.4
Blank				
1851	24.7	0.6	25.0	31.7
1881	28.2	0.2	28.6	38.7

passage of the Factory Acts and the growth of subsidized and mandatory education reduced the proportion of young people below the age of fourteen at work. As was the case with adult males, higher productivity reduced the need to expand the younger labor force in the worsted trade and thus made the shift away from work to school for younger children possible.

Women experienced less dramatic changes in employment after 1851 and they were concentrated in fewer areas of work than men throughout. Only about half the women above twenty worked outside the home. Paid employment peaked between the ages of fifteen and thirty for women in Bradford and decreased steadily with age. It is not known to what extent part-time work or work within the home replaced work outside the home, since the census imperfectly measured these categories.[43] Unmarried women constituted the majority of the paid female labor force, but married women in Bradford worked outside the home more than women in non-textile areas.[44] The textile industry employed the most women, followed by domestic service and the clothing trades. Despite the increase in domestic service after 1851, Bradford had a far lower percentage of servants than most cities in England, due to the limited size of the middle-class population and the lure of higher paying factory jobs.[45]

MANAGEMENT AND THE PROBLEM OF COSTS IN THE WORSTED TRADE

The dramatic expansion of the worsted trade in the mid-Victorian period rested upon a set of technical achievements that allowed for a steady increase in productivity and quality. Equally important, however, were the talents of Bradford's merchants and manufacturers. These entrepreneurs managed an industry that included most of the world and required constant attention to shifting conditions in far-flung markets in raw materials and finished goods. Success depended upon the ability of businessmen to accommodate change. In its prime, the Bradford trade reflected this need for flexibility in its organization and daily operations.

The key to understanding the worsted industry lies in the market conditions that shaped the trade. Unlike the cotton industry, which initially favored higher quality cloth, the Bradford trade produced lower-cost goods that substituted for more expensive all-wool goods, particularly those of the French woolen industry.[46] This portion of the woolen market expanded rapidly after 1835 and manufacturers invested heavily in mixed-goods production.[47] The worsted trade (and to an extent the woolen trade) relied upon markets in England, Europe and the United States, which while richer, were more competitive and more difficult to maintain.[48] These markets were quite sensitive to price differences and manufacturers constantly struggled to remain ahead of their competitors in price, design and quality.[49]

A steady rise in the relative price of wool made this situation more difficult.[50] The high price of wool and the burden of carrying expensive stocks of raw and finished materials represented a crucial problem for the industry.[51] While the use of cotton and other materials such as alpaca and mohair allowed worsted manufacturers to offset this trend, in the end they could not control a major cost in their industry.[52] The cost of materials could represent about 60–70 per cent of a firm's turnover in a year and often a firm invested the majority of its capital in goods rather than machinery.[53] Firms tried to reduce their costs by speculating in wool to take advantage of price swings, but ultimately they remained a prisoner of the market.[54] The limited supply of wool kept the market tight, despite the efforts of the Chamber's wool supply committee to increase the production of colonial wool.[55]

To counter the problem of material costs, firms aimed for high turnover, mainly through price competition, for the key to the 'Bradford system' was high volume and low unit cost. To keep prices low, manufacturers looked to lower the cost of production. Labor, which constituted 20–25 per cent of the total cost of a finished piece, represented one potential area of savings.[56] To reduce labor costs, manufacturers increased work loads and invested heavily in new machinery. According to Eric Sigsworth the use of larger and faster looms and the practice of minding more than one loom raised weaving output about 70 per cent per loom after 1851. In spinning, productivity increased at least 25 per cent due to the introduction of cap frames and the requirement that each spinner mind two frames rather than one.[57] Spindles became faster, going from 1,400 to 1,800 r.p.m. in 1825 to 2,800 r.p.m. in 1850. By the 1870s, cap frames achieved a speed of 6,000 r.p.m. and the frames grew from 38 spindles a side to 144 or even 200 per side.[58] In 1872, one worker claimed that three to four frames per worker had become the norm and another believed the improvement in productivity to be over 100 per cent in spinning due to the increased speed and size of spinning machinery.[59] In 1861 Henry Ripley estimated that machine combing substituted the labor of 2,000 men for that of 21,900 and that the dyeing trade experienced a 40–50 per cent reduction in labor requirements over the previous ten years.[60] These productivity gains allowed the manufacturers of Bradford to reap considerable increases in output without having to dramatically expand their work force.[61]

The intense competitiveness of the industry can be measured in part by the survival rate of firms. Robert Baker estimated that only 127 out of 318 firms in the Yorkshire trade as a whole survived from 1836 to 1846. Sigsworth and Blackman found that half of the worsted firms in the West Riding failed from 1870 to 1875 and that only 9 per cent survived from 1870 to 1912.[62] This competitiveness helped produce the other key characteristic of the worsted industry, its diversity, which took two forms. One was a subdivision of the industry into firms that specialized on a single stage of the productive process – combing, dyeing, weaving or spinning. The other was an intense focus by manufacturers of yarn and finished pieces on a particular niche in the market.

A unique combination of market conditions, machinery and firm structure characterized each step in the process of producing worsted pieces. This diversity makes it difficult to generalize about the entire trade, but all these stages shared a common desire to lower costs and remain competitive. The initial stage in the process was combing. The mechanization of combing in the 1840s led to the creation of large specialty firms like Holden's, which combed wool in Bradford and France. Combers produced tops, or slivers of combed wool, which they sold to spinners in England and abroad. The role of the comber overlapped with that of the topmaker, who appeared in the 1870s. These entrepreneurs purchased and sorted wool, sent it out to commission wool combers and then sold the tops. This led to the proliferation of small, specialty combing shops that worked wool for a fixed payment.[63]

Dyeing and finishing represented the final step in the production process. The technique for dyeing mixed goods had been invented in Bradford and by 1872 forty dyeing firms operated in the city. According to the census reports for Bradford these firms employed almost 900 adult men in 1871 and about 1,800 males of all ages by 1881. This underestimates the size of the dyeing trade, for in evidence given in 1854, three dyeing firms, Smith's, Armitage and Ripley's, reported some 950 operatives between them.[64] In 1870, four firms, including Ripley's, but not Armitage or Smith's, claimed to employ over 1,500 workers.[65] Unlike manufacturers, who had a sense of demand for months in advance, dyers' orders varied week to week and even day to day, according to the needs of merchants who placed the orders. Sudden changes forced dyers to work virtually full time to finish a rush order or risk the loss of the contract. There were two busy seasons, which lasted six to eight weeks, in spring and fall and the work week varied between forty-six and sixty hours per week, depending on the season.[66]

In the later nineteenth century, parts of the dyeing and finishing process began to be spun off as separate enterprises in order to lower the costs of production. Commission mending firms appeared in this era to undertake the laborious process of preparing dyed pieces for market by correcting flaws by hand.[67] This fragmentation mirrored that of other parts of the industry. In dyeing, however, cartelization accompanied the streamlining of the trade. The Bradford Dyers Association, formed in 1898, tried to regulate prices and negotiate with skilled unions. An attempt to organize the combing trade in a similar fashion in 1900 proved less successful, though eventually a cartel emerged.[68]

Historians have emphasized the uniqueness of the worsted trade and its structures, but in fact the worsted and cotton industries developed along similar lines after 1850. In both cotton and worsted, firms that combined spinning and weaving declined after the 1850s, as the increasing competitiveness and diversity of products led to specialization in a single process or even a single product within that process. In the worsted trade, the decline after the 1870s of the industry's one mass market, women's mixed goods, accelerated this fragmentation.[69]

The weaving sector of the cotton industry developed at about the same time as mechanized weaving in the worsted trade, in the 1830s. Cotton weaving firms, like those in worsted, tended to be small and highly specialized and relied upon the same rental and second-hand arrangements made by worsted weaving firms.[70] In cotton spinning the establishment of the great Oldham Limiteds in the second half of the nineteenth century created a more impersonal, corporate form of management and ownership.[71] By contrast, worsted firms tended to be family owned or partnerships. As late as 1912, less than 30 per cent of worsted firms made use of limited liability.[72]

Despite the general trend toward specialization and smaller size, a number of large firms thrived. Salt's Mill with 1,200 looms and John Priestman's with 1,800 looms, as well as combing and spinning equipment, were considerable enterprises, while Manningham Mills, owned by Samuel Lister, employed as many as 4,000 operatives.[73] The Rivers Pollution Commission's survey of worsted concerns in 1870 listed 17 firms with more than 100 employees that employed an average of 390 operatives. In the West Riding worsted industry as a whole, average firm size reached 193 operatives by 1868 and 259 by 1904.[74] By 1909, twelve firms, nine of them limited liability, owned 40 per cent of the spindles, while 77 firms operated the remaining 60 per cent.[75]

Larger firms coexisted with a multitude of smaller enterprises. Commission combing shops and tiny weaving and spinning concerns began business on minimal capital. They found equipment on the second hand market and rented space and power from larger firms.[76] These small capitalists, often former overlookers or managers, depended on the credit extended to them by merchants and banks.[77] Their chronic shortage of capital led to the overuse of credit or the writing of overdrafts, followed by a quick departure from town when the debt became too much to support.[78]

The merchants tied together this diverse industry. They bought and sold raw materials, semi-manufactured goods like tops and yarn and pieces in the grey, which they then finished. Formerly based in the Bradford Piece Hall, by the 1850s most merchants operated from their own warehouses. These establishments combined storage, processing areas for sorting and the commercial offices of the firm. In order to purchase materials and market their goods, merchants relied upon domestic and foreign commercial agents. Successful merchants mastered not only markets in materials and finished goods, but also kept abreast of currency and economic fluctuations worldwide.[79]

Merchants operated through commission and direct sales. Commission merchants took goods on acceptance, paying for a portion of the goods they received, with the balance paid upon final sale, minus a five to ten percent commission and costs of storage and transport. They were associated with speculative marketing, particularly in the American and Far Eastern trades and many manufacturers preferred not to deal with them.[80] Other merchants bought directly from manufacturers and then sold on their own account. Manufacturers received a lower price, but did not have to wait to receive their funds or rely upon discounting to survive. A large number of foreign nationals entered this branch of the trade and established their own firms in Bradford. These merchants came to dominate the marketing of goods in the second half of the nineteenth century. Their superior contacts abroad allowed them to better manage the difficult task of marketing goods.[81]

Given the scarcity of bank credit and the rarity of limited liability, merchants functioned as a major source of credit for the industry and access to credit through banks was a precondition for mercantile success. Merchants who specialized in raw wool, known as woolstaplers, generally gave material on loan, with interest charged on the outstanding balance. The period of the loan varied, but the common period was ninety days. The increasing pace of production made this period too long and merchants tried to reduce this period after 1850.[82] Merchants who dealt in worsted pieces or yarn also advanced money to manufacturers by giving them bills for a portion of the goods' value, which they could then sell on the discount market to obtain ready cash.[83] This role as de facto bankers gave merchants considerable influence over the course of trade and led to resentment among manufacturers. Businessmen complained about credit arrangements and the Chamber of Commerce of Bradford tried to implement a system of uniform credit to prevent failures caused by what it termed 'vicious credit'.[84] Complicating this was the appearance of a number of speculative wool buyers who displaced the long-established wool staplers and who had little incentive to follow the custom of the trade.[85]

The highly competitive nature of the industry forced many firms to engage in a variety of questionable practices. In good times, mills ran overtime, often working at night. This continuous operation, coupled with the overuse of machinery, the purchase of used steam engines and the substitution of cheaper oils, could lead to boiler explosions or mill fires.[86] In bad times, firms stocked up, producing goods in the hope of higher prices in the future. Manufacturers relied on credit to bridge the gap and would sell below cost to forestall bankruptcy. Rich merchants preyed upon these firms, buying their stocks at bargain prices, thus forcing down the general price level. This reduced the profitability of the trade in a weak market and could produce a ripple effect of collapsing prices and business failures in a recession.[87] These problems were most acute among the smaller concerns in the trade and most bankruptcies affected such firms.[88]

Competition also gave rise to practices that degraded the quality of goods. The constant pressure to compete led to a widespread cheapening of goods. Rather than commissioning their own designs, Bradford manufacturers produced copies of French designs, adapting their machinery to the new tastes.[89] One manufacturer complained of

> the perpetual deterioration of our manufactures – the decreasing width and substance, the practice of what is called 'cutting' – and the inveterate and discreditable habit of copying a brother manufacturer's styles and designs, and producing the same continually, in an inferior cloth.[90]

The practice of 'cutting' was widespread, particularly in dyeing. Henry Ripley argued that the key consideration in dyeing was the saving of money in production through the use of cheaper dyers and less colorfast materials.[91] Oates and Ingham, another dyer, resisted efforts by merchants to reduce the cost of dyeing, explaining that the end product would only be an imitation.[92] Merchants, who usually purchased goods in a grey, unfinished state and then dyed and finished them, came under attack from critics for hurting the trade through such practices.[93]

Observers of the industry such as the *Textile Manufacturer* complained of the obsessive secrecy that competition brought to the trade. Unlike the cotton trade, no general agreements on wages or prices could be reached among manufacturers.[94] Henry Mitchell, a prominent Bradford merchant and politician, noted that the desire of each manufacturer to fully exploit his designs made it impossible to publicly display patterns.[95] Another spoke of the fear of the 'ruinous piracy' of designs and styles on the part of merchants and manufacturers.[96]

The atmosphere of competition and secrecy bred corruption. Ministers of religion noted the prevalence of dishonest practices in the worsted trade. J.H. Lewis, in a sermon in 1878, excoriated the practices of the industry, attacking the connivance of the many in the dishonesty in dealing of the few.[97] Accusations of corruption came from many sources and dealt with a number of activities. Both French customs officials and the US Consul in Bradford complained about the systematic evasion of customs laws by Bradford traders, who undervalued their goods and packed them elsewhere to disguise their origin.[98] The Consul came under pressure from manufacturers in Bradford for exposing such behavior and a group of them approached a US Senator in an effort to intimidate the Consul.[99] Letter writers to local papers brought the problems of adulteration of goods, slow deliveries and incorrect or fraudulent weighings to public attention.[100] The Chamber of Commerce acknowledged the validity of these issues and from its formation in 1851 attempted to mediate in disputes between businesses. The majority of cases dealt with disagreements over the quality and length of pieces, but the Chamber also sought to help the general reputation of the trade by exposing dishonest practices such as the adding of foreign material to wool to increase its weight. Despite these efforts, the Chamber admitted that the commercial reputation of Bradford was poor.[101]

In response to such charges, businessmen cited the need to remain competitive with other producers, an argument they extended to the laws and regulations that affected the industry. These concerns became more pressing during the depression of the later nineteenth century, but they formed an integral part of the political efforts of Bradford's industrialists throughout this period. During the hearings held by the Commission on the Pollution of Rivers and Streams in 1867, manufacturers stood united in their opposition to any effort to control the dumping of industrial wastes in the Bradford Beck or to force them to clean up their works. Joseph Ingham threatened to close his dye works if required to clean up its liquid wastes. Both the Town Engineer and the Town Clerk argued that the burden of paying for pollution control had to be equalized over all firms to ensure that no firm suffered a competitive disadvantage.[102] Industrialists continued their opposition to pollution control into the 1870s, when they fought efforts to create an authority with the power to control the river basin of the Aire–Calder and regulate the dumping of liquid refuse.[103] Attempts to control smoke pollution floundered for the same reason; manufacturers objected to the increased costs.[104] Likewise, mill owners successfully opposed efforts to require the fencing of all shafting in mills in the 1850s and resisted attempts to change employer liability for injuries.[105]

Because of the importance of child labor, Bradford manufacturers also opposed any new legislation for the worsted industry.[106] In the 1850s and 1860s the Chamber of Commerce and other businessmen sought to prevent the extension of the Factory Acts to warehouses and dyeing establishments. Dyers like Ripley fought any attempt to regulate their works and the Chamber helped organize a public meeting in 1864, with the participation of skilled workmen, to protest the possible application of the Factory and Workshops Act to warehouses. Employers threatened to stop employing women and children if forced to reduce hours and submit to inspection.[107] Manufacturers also renewed their overt opposition to the Factory Acts, which had been quieted by the passage of the Ten Hours Bill and the prosperity of the 1850s. In the early 1870s, the Chamber of Commerce led the fight against the extension of the educational provisions of the Factory Acts. Manufacturers testified against the proposal to raise the age of work to ten and to require the fourth standard to begin full-time work and lobbied Parliament to delay the imposition of the Factory Act of 1874. They also stood at the forefront of efforts to stop the introduction of the nine-hour day.[108]

It was this combination of circumstances which shaped the Bradford entrepreneur. Bradford entrepreneurs enjoyed a reputation as sharp dealers, 'very sleuth hounds in search of money'.[109] A Methodist hymn in the eighteenth century referred to Bradford as a place 'Where Satan keeps his seat.'[110] 'Bradford men' inhabited a certain terrain in the business world, and combined sharpness with thrift and austerity. Clare Delius, sister of Frederick Delius and daughter of a worsted merchant, described her father's disgust at the shabby dress and uncultured ways of even the richest men.[111] J.B. Priestley, the Bradford-born writer, recalled the disdain of such men for non-business pursuits and their thrift, which extended to buying their own cloth, rather than accepting that of their tailor.[112] George Weerth referred to 'strange energy and awesome endurance' of Bradfordians, saying that 'these people work like horses, from morning till night, indefatigably, without ever allowing themselves a moment's rest and respite.'[113] Those who could not endure the rough and tumble of such a life were labeled not 'up to sample'.

The intense focus of Bradford's merchants and manufacturers upon business earned them a reputation for philistinism. Men one or two generations removed from the workshop rarely dedicated themselves to civic or cultural pursuits, preferring instead to spend their money on conspicuous consumption. Bradford entrepreneurs drew the rebuke of Ruskin in his famous speeches of 1859 and 1864 for their worship of 'The goddess of getting on'.[114] Later generations may have abandoned the austerity of their fathers, but usually left Bradford to pursue the good life.[115] The emigrant merchant community, particularly the Germans who came to the city in the mid-century, provided a counterbalance to the rough and simple men of Bradford. They endowed charities and cultural institutions to fill the void in civic life. Julius Delius, father of the composer, supported the local symphony and the Bradford Children's Hospital, while Jacob Behrens played a key role in numerous local charities. These men, however, seemed perfectly capable of adjusting to the quick pace of business and prospered in their new environment.

THE END OF PROSPERITY—THE SLUMP OF THE 1870s

The aggressiveness and flexibility of Bradford entrepreneurs fueled the mid-Victorian expansion of the worsted trade. The industry founded its growth on a particular arrangement of production and a style of management that emphasized low cost goods as the key to competing in world markets. Yet the entrepreneurs who founded this system could not respond to the challenge of new competition in the later nineteenth century. Faced with the steady decline of their staple trade, Bradford manufacturers failed to alter their ways of business to accommodate the realities of the marketplace. The failure of the worsted trade marked the end of mid-Victorian stability and the beginning of an era of testing and reorientation in all areas of life – from the work place to the family .

The prosperity of the Bradford trade collapsed with the financial panic of 1873 and a resultant decline in prices and exports. The worsted industry's exports fell about 20 per cent from 1867–69 to 1877–79, a figure supported by the impressionistic statements of businessmen.[116] Robert Jowitt, a Bradford merchant, complained of slow trade and idle mills in his private letter book.[117] In 1879, the *Textile Manufacturer*, the trade's primary journal, noted that 'the chief articles of manufacture are in as little demand as they have been for a long time, nor does there appear to be any indication of a different state of things'.[118] As late as 1881, it reported that the majority of firms in the trade were running short-time.[119]

Considerable disagreement existed at the time over the nature and dimensions of the downturn. Jacob Behrens argued that profits and prices rather than total output were the primary victims of the slump and that consumption per capita increased from 1860–64 to 1880–84.[120] Henry Mitchell, a prominent merchant and political figure, noted that various sectors of the trade fared differently. The 1870s marked a shift toward greater specialization in the industry and greater reliance upon sales of yarn or semi-manufactured products such as tops or noils by Bradford manufacturers.[121] Yarn exports, men's coatings and some specialty product lines such as velvet fared better during the slump. For large numbers of firms in the Bradford trade, however, the depression brought lower prices and profits and long periods of short-time or complete cessation of work.

The manufacturers of the bright, lustrous goods that made up the bulk of the lower-class trade in worsteds suffered the most and their markets failed to fully recover from the downturn of the mid-1870s. An increased supply of colonial wools suited to all-wool goods allowed French manufacturers to undercut Bradford products. The difficulties of mixed-goods manufacturers resulted in a sharp rise in business failures, leading to fears of a general collapse of the trade. In all of the West Riding woolen trade from 1866 to 1870 there were an average of 15 failures per year; in 1879 in Bradford alone, at least 67 firms filed for bankruptcy.[122] These bankruptcies appear to have been concentrated among the smaller firms in the industry.[123]

The income tax schedules reflected the impact of both prosperity and depression upon the city. The total amount collected under schedules D and E of the income tax increased 42 per cent from 1871 to 1881, despite the raising of the lower limit of taxation from £100 to £150 in 1876. Between 1877 to 1881, however, over 600 persons subject to taxation on Schedules D and E (roughly 11 per cent of those subject to taxation) dropped out of the Bradford rolls.[124] These figures suggest that the impact of the depression was not uniform and that some firms and individuals continued to prosper, while others fell down the social ladder.

What was different about this slump was not the unemployment or business failures it generated. As many argued, earlier downturns, especially that of the mid-1840s, produced far greater hardship in an absolute sense. The unique feature of the crisis was that it forced many in the worsted industry and the city to reexamine their trade and admit that changing conditions had undermined their normal way of doing business. In the words of the *Textile Manufacturer*

> The condition of the Bradford trade excites very gloomy apprehensions in the minds of thinking men, and unless the causes of the present depression are clearly understood, and effectual steps are taken to remove them, it certainly appears that trade will become worse and worse.[125]

Many in the industry and the town argued the slump resulted in part from the great prosperity of the 1870s that harmed the trade through an overextension of production and the abandonment of good business practices. Andrew Byles, son of the editor of the town's main paper, stated, 'Let it never be forgotten that times like those of 1872, 1873 are altogether abnormal.'[126] The *Textile Manufacturer* spoke of the need for 'a balance between supply and demand' to allow prices and wages to recover.[127] Some believed that the depression could actually serve a useful purpose by weeding out 'overconfidence and negligence' and getting rid of those unsuited to business.[128]

These claims formed part of a larger argument about the solution to the problems of the trade. Many focused on the cost advantages of foreign, especially French, manufacturers. In part these advantages resulted from the tariff barriers faced by the Bradford trade. The protectionist policies of the French Republic, the German Empire and the United States hit hard at the traditional markets of the English worsted industry. While most in the city agreed on the harmful effects of these tariffs, they could not agree on the solution. Some in Bradford advocated 'fair trade' or retaliatory tariffs, but most defended free trade. In any event, the efforts of Bradford industrialists could do little to affect this problem in the short-run.[129]

The other area of costs lay more in the control of Bradford manufacturers – the wages and hours of operatives. Manufacturers saw lower prices as the best method for ending the slump, which meant that workers had to concede longer hours and lower wages. As one 'manufacturer' argued,

> longer hours must be worked; and if we are to maintain our hold of the neutral markets of the world, wages will have to be yet further reduced . . . I know it will be a difficult task to adapt ourselves to a much lower scale of living, but I see no alternative.[130]

W. Farrar Ecroyd, a worsted spinner and MP for Preston, stated that workers should sacrifice the fifty-six hour week and return to sixty hours a week in order to restore prosperity. Foreign competition could only be met by a new commitment on the part of manufacturers and their employees. People had to return to the values of hard work and sacrifice that had formerly characterized the industry. As he put it,

> No doubt the sudden flush of excessive prosperity in 1871–72 produced an unhealthy inflation, and to a certain extent demoralized all classes by encouraging carelessness, idleness, and extravagance. But these bad habits will be checked by the wholesome discipline of adversity, and wages and prices of all kinds will find their necessary level here as in other countries.[131]

The *Textile Manufacturer* reported 'almost general agreement that the workpeople work such short hours and are paid so highly in comparison with their continental confreres that fair competition is impossible'.[132] Observers linked the need for longer hours and lower wages to the argument that prosperity spoiled the working class and made them selfish. Andrew Byles, noting the improved diet of working-class families, stated, 'Ham and eggs are the favorite luxuries of the working class and those in no sense can be termed necessary articles of diet.'[133] The US Consul agreed, recalling that oatmeal and vegetables used to suffice for workers. He went further and attacked the Education Acts and the reduced hours of workpeople for producing laziness and discontent with their station in life. Workers had become greedy and sought easy labor and high wages, which led to improvidence and drunkenness.[134] James Ford, a minister, saw only evil coming out of higher wages and shorter hours, 'The people are found to have become more effeminate, less content with simplicity of life, and less able to endure severity of circumstance.'[135]

The manufacturers tried to convince the operatives of the necessity and justice of these measures. Local businessmen commissioned a series of studies of the French industry to establish its advantages in hours and wages, but these studies failed to document decisively the claims of manufacturers. One found a 25 per cent advantage in labor costs, but its authors admitted that this translated at most into a 6.5 per cent cost advantage and perhaps even less, depending on the proportion of total cost represented by labor.[136]

Workers remained skeptical about the claims of merchants and manufacturers. Local trade union leaders disputed the accuracy of Behrens' and Mitchell's testimony before the Commission on Depression of Trade and Industry, arguing that they understated the extent of unemployment and short-time.[137] The *Textile Manufacturer* acknowledged that workers resisted any attempt to lengthen hours or reduce wages.[138] In deference to such feelings, the Bradford Chamber of Commerce declined to endorse an 1879 petition by Huddersfield manufacturers that called for longer hours.[139] Many of the arguments of manufacturers first appeared during the dispute over the nine-hour day that flared up in the early 1870s. Then workers had fiercely abused mill owners for selfishness and unwillingness to consider the interests of operatives.[140] The resistance of workers made attempts to lower the general wage level likely to produce social conflict and unrest. Since wages constituted at most 25 per cent of the cost of a finished worsted piece, no reasonable wage reduction could create a drop in prices sufficient to revive the demand for mixed goods. One member of the Bradford Chamber of Commerce questioned the value of 'chimerical schemes for lessening the price of English labour, or for reintroducing longer hours'.[141]

Conflicts between workers and employers also emerged over the issue of technical education. Originally promoted by Henry Ripley, the dyer, in the 1860s, technical education reemerged with a new vigor in the mid 1870s as the Bradford trade lost ground to the French. Many argued that the lack of competitiveness of the worsted industry was due in large part to the poor training of supervisory and other skilled workers. Prominent businessmen such as Jacob Behrens, Henry Mitchell and M.W. Thompson, a brewer and former MP, as well as the Bradford Chamber of Commerce, gave their support to the idea of technical training. In an article on the setting up of a weaving school in Bradford, the *Textile Manufacturer* commented,

> Now, however, that the condition of trade has brought it [technical education] into prominence, and those who in the hurry of business passed it aside as an unnecessary subject, at last feel that if idle looms are once more active, technical education must receive undisputed attention.[142]

These supporters moved quickly to establish technical education in Bradford and in 1882 the Prince of Wales came to inaugurate a new Technical College with its own separate facilities.[143]

Despite the success of proponents in setting up a Technical College, many proved resistant to the idea of technical education. Henry Mitchell admitted that 'the great body of manufacturers have not yet taken a great interest in it'. He explained the difficulty,

> Many think that as our trade has developed very largely under the old system, we had better keep to our traditions . . . Others, I imagine, are afraid we shall raise up a superior body of men, both as managers, overlookers, and manufacturers, and thus have a keener competition. And others are afraid that we shall train a considerable number of young men who will go out to America and other countries, and that those countries will get the benefit of the instruction which we give them.[144]

Others echoed this conservatism and fear of competition. One letter writer to the *Textile Manufacturer* insisted that the greatest problem in managing a firm was not the supposed shortage of overlookers, but the unwillingness of employers to train a man in his job for fear of losing trade secrets.[145]

An ambivalence about the purposes of education plagued technical education in Bradford.[146] While Alfred Harris, head of the Scientific Department of the Mechanics' Institute and a friend of John Ruskin, spoke of technical education as a way of elevating the nature of work and restoring its ennobling qualities, others took a more hard-headed view.[147] F.H. Bowman, writing in 1867, supported technical education not only as a way to increase the efficiency of workers, but also as a method of lessening their resistance to continued mechanization.[148]

This had clearly been the thrust of an earlier experiment with a building trades technical school attached to the Mechanics' Institute. The school was set up in 1868 ostensibly as a joint project of workers and employers, but the masters tried to use it to weaken the building trade unions, particularly the stone masons, who had vigorously (and successfully) resisted mechanization.[149] According to the *Bradford Review*, the new school served as a way around the apprenticeship regulations and the strict work rules imposed by the unions.[150] While the school was only a partial success, it pointed out the potential dangers for skilled workers of technical education.

Such experiments provoked one writer to question the motives of employers who supported technical education:

> The other evening at the soiree held in the Mechanics' Institute, he [Henry Ripley] spoke on the necessity of a technical education being given to the working classes. Why? Because then they would become more profitable to their employers. The cleverer the workman the better the work, the better the work the better the trade, the better for trade the better for the manufacturers' and merchants' pockets.[151]

The poor education provided for the majority of workers in the textile mills proved to be a major obstacle. Proponents of technical education admitted the insufficiency of elementary education and pointed out that most workers would not be able to take advantage of the new training schemes.[152] Henry Mitchell put it this way:

> The great benefit would be to those who are placed in responsible positions, such as managers, and overlookers and manufacturers; but to the ordinary artisan who does his work mechanically I do not think it will be of much benefit.[153]

The instruction in weaving, dyeing, design and cost calculations offered at the Technical College was intended to broaden the purely empirical training of skilled workers in textile mills. The *Bradford Observer* argued 'we should turn out an improved class of designers, overlookers and dyers . . . Its [the Technical College] intention is to supply theoretical training'.[154] The tasks of the overlooker, for example, required a certain level of experience and intelligence, but no real imperative kept such training in the hands of the overlookers themselves. The skills of an overlooker could be taught in a classroom, if backed up by some work experience.

Thus, the new technical school aimed directly at the privileges enjoyed by skilled workers in the textile trade, who despite their lack of union militancy, exercised a fair degree of power over hiring and training. Potentially technical education could end the job control enjoyed by workers' societies and lead to its replacement by a system controlled and managed by a federation of employers of labor. 'Overlooker', writing to the *Bradford Observer*, stated this fear directly.

> I can also say that the action of various employers during the few years trade had been depressed in forcing down the wages of skilled workmen, and valuing them at less than the unskilled labourer, has caused the Technical [College] to be viewed with a great amount of jealousy, through the fear that it was only supported by the employers so that they could glut the market and thereby depress the value of skilled workers.[155]

As another worker put it,

> The only result of the new movement as at present time framed will be to cheapen the labour of really competent men. . .Every good workman knows what to expect when he sees the approach of such lame cattle. He knows that the process of cheapening his labour is about to be attempted.[156]

As a result, Bradford's trade unions remained reluctant to cooperate and the Bradford Trades Council boycotted the opening of the Technical College.[157]

Resistance to wage cuts and suspicion of technical education involved more than just a disagreement over wages or hours, it also involved a critique of how manufacturers attempted to deal with the crisis in the worsted trade. One worker, writing under the pseudonym Timothy Tappitnose, argued that wages cuts and technical education would not solve the problems of the trade.

> If it were possible for us to compete with the long hours, cheap labour, and daylight of the French, where is the trade in high class fancies that will make any perceptible difference to the almost countless looms and spindles of Bradford.[158]

Thomas Illingworth, a local writer, expanded upon this criticism in his pamphlets.[159] He attacked what he considered to be an oligarchy of wealth that ruled the community and failed to consider the interests of working men.

I wonder if it occurs to English and foreign capitalist manufacturers that if they pay three-quarters of the population the lowest possible wages and work them half their living hours, and for those depressed wages and hours get an ever-increasing production of goods, the question must sooner or later be answered, who is going to consume the goods produced?[160]

For Illingworth the problem was a 'capitalists', not an artisans', question.'[161] Bradford manufacturers, previously successful in the cheap goods market, failed to react to the new market for all-wool goods. Technical education or new tariffs would not address this problem, which resulted from of a 'want of adaptation'.[162]

This criticism echoed the comments of many in the trade. Much of the debate focused on the uncertain response of Bradford manufacturers to changing market conditions. While manufacturers recognized the shift toward all-wool goods on the part of consumers, they disagreed on the permanence of this change. Many in the trade were reluctant to invest in new machinery and products to suit what one termed 'the vagaries of fashion'.[163] Another spoke of the expense involved in reequipping 'at the caprice of fashion which must change'.[164]

The Bective movement of the early 1880s brought the issue of fashion and design to public notice. Named after its founder, the Countess of Bective, the movement sought to promote the use of English wool and fabrics by encouraging fashionable women to wear English clothing. Some, like William Forster, Bradford MP and manufacturer, welcomed the movement toward 'patriotic fashion'.[165] Others, however, saw little merit in the initiative. The *Textile Manufacturer* labeled it 'foolish twaddle'.[166] It went on to observe,

Year after year some Bradford manufacturers have plodded on, making the same class of goods and ignoring the changing tastes of consumers, and then when business naturally becomes slack, they attribute to others rather than themselves the causes of their misfortune.[167]

Many in Bradford focused on the problems of adapting to the changes in fashion. The move to all-wool goods specialized in by the French required Bradford spinners to shift from ring spinning to mules. Henry Mitchell stated that one manufacturer estimated the cost at over £30,000.[168] The change over to mules required more than capital, it also demanded an entirely new system of production and the retraining or replacement of operatives and skilled workers.

While some cited the high cost of reinvestment in new machinery as the chief obstacle to the revival of the trade, others in the trade believed that manufacturers refused to face facts and make the changes required by new tastes. John Waugh believed 'We have too much affection for old machinery, engines and boilers included.'[169] Although firms like W. Ramseden and John Smith and Sons made the transition, most stayed with ring spinning.[170] In the end, most Bradford manufacturers remained committed to the traditional worsted production techniques, while seeking new markets in men's coatings and semi-finished products.[171]

For many in Bradford, no solution seemed forthcoming, and a new note of pessimism crept into discussions of the future of the trade. John Waugh, like many others, saw the problem as a dramatic one, arguing, 'When the disease is dangerous, the remedy must be searching.'[172] Some believed that the trade was overstocked and that only a reduction in numbers would solve the oversupply of worsted goods and workers. For some this meant a policy of guided emigration to reduce the numbers of hands available.[173] To Samuel Lister,

> Our population is rapidly increasing, and although I have no wish to be a prophet of evil, still I have a very strong conviction that in the future workmen are going to increase faster by far than they can be, by any possibility, profitably employed.[174]

This pessimism about the future stands in stark contrast to the boundless optimism that marked the first seventy-five years of the century. How widely felt this pessimism was is hard to gauge, but the sense of declining opportunity and of an overabundance of labor in a stagnant market was widely shared. Ironically, Lister's fears of overpopulation never came to pass, for at the same time that he wrote, the steady and dramatic fall in the birth rate began to alter the balance between population and work. The rise and decline of the worsted industry played a key role in two respects. First it created a particular arrangement of work in Bradford that shaped the working-class community. Second, its decline forced that community to seek new solutions to problems of subsistence and family life in order to stabilize itself in the face of yet another round of change. We now turn to the world of labor created by the worsted trade and the ways in which this affected family and social life.

2 Work and Its Discontents

In mid-Victorian Bradford, as elsewhere in England, the rise of industry forced people to find a new vocabulary to express what was new and distinctive about their world.[1] Bradfordians, fascinated by the machine and the factory, repeatedly used mechanical analogies to describe both social relations and social structure.[2] Often this took the form of parallels between the factory and daily life. The Reverend Benjamin Wood felt no embarrassment when he compared the social order to a weaver's shuttle, or Saint Paul to an overlooker in his 1868 sermon to working men, for he spoke in a familiar idiom. The notion of the community as a factory or a mechanism frequently appeared in public discourse. Reverend Charles Robinson put it this way:

> Every community may be compared to a vast machine, in which every wheel is dependent on some other, so that the derangement of the smallest portion of it is fatal to the efficiency of the whole.[3]

The comparison of the social order to the machine expressed a vision of society as an interdependent whole. The belief in a mutual dependence that functioned automatically to ensure social cooperation was a powerful one that found its most common expression in the belief in the market and its beneficial invisible hand.[4] Yet the image of society as a machine revealed a certain ambivalence about the emerging industrial order. Part of this ambivalence stemmed from the transformation of life by the rise of the factory. The physical transformation of Bradford, which led to its sprawling growth and pollution caused many to doubt the benefits of change. As Jonathan Glyde, a prominent local minister, noted, 'some may . . . wish that greatness had never been thrust upon them and that wealth and smoke were equally unknown.'[5]

Similar doubts arose over the impact of industry upon work. Many considered the demise of domestic industry and the large-scale employment of women and children as a potential source of moral and social evil.[6] Such doubts found expression in the campaigns for factory regulation and political reform in the 1830s and 1840s. From this perspective, the use of mechanical analogies revealed the darker side of industrialization, which threatened to reduce the value of the worker to no more than a part in a machine, identical and replaceable. One letter writer to the *Bradford Observer* in the early 1870s spoke of the 'human machine' that tended to the textile machinery.[7] Another argued that manufacturers believed that 'The workman is a sort of machine, "improve him as you have improved other machinery, lest we who profit by his handicraft be behind in the chase after wealth." '[8]

The assimilation of the human to the machine spoke of the triumph of the mechanical over the natural and how the factory helped create a new set of ideas about labor and its value and purpose. Older models of society that argued for an equal association of artisans, secure in the possession of their trades and masters within their own homes, no longer described the reality of increasing numbers of workers in Bradford and England as a whole. This loss of identity required that new beliefs about labor had to accompany the rise of the factory.[9]

In mid-Victorian Bradford, labor played a critical role in the redefinition of society and individual identity. The common experience of work created a shared set of values and ideas among members of the working class. To the extent that workers shared common grievances about labor, work helped foster a mutuality and consciousness of difference reflected in the struggle over wages and conditions and the emergence of a distinctive working-class society. At the same time, the factory and the larger Victorian social structure rested upon the unequal rewards given to those who possessed 'skill'. These hierarchies of work created a series of dividing lines in the mill and the working-class community based on age, ethnicity, gender and income.

Work also involved cooperation across class lines. Skilled workers obtained their authority and security within the industrial system by cooperating in the organization and control of the mill. This fostered a belief in the mutual interest of workers and employers. At their height, these beliefs took the form of elaborate paternalistic schemes such as the model village and mill, Saltaire, located near Bradford.[10] The set of circumstances that produced this cooperation proved volatile however. The need for Bradford manufacturers to compete led them to engage in a number of practices that harmed the interests of workers – speed-up, changes in the number of looms and spindles minded, cutbacks in employment and unsafe working conditions. Bradford's manufacturers, who fought to contain both government regulation of the work place and labor organization, blocked efforts to address these issues. The owners of the worsted mills used blacklisting and the Worsted Acts to suppress not only labor mobility and turnover, but also attempts to organize unions and strikes among weavers, combers and dyers. Although skilled workers and their trade societies received a grudging acceptance of their right to organize, other groups did not receive this privilege. These unorganized workers expressed their discontent in a number of ways – frequent changes of work, theft and wildcat job actions – that left little permanent record, but which did challenge the legitimacy of the status quo.

The difficulties of the worsted industry in the 1870s intensified these trends. They also brought attempts to reorganize the trade that threatened the prerogatives of skilled workers. Whether in the form of technical education, deskilling or the introduction of new machinery and products, these efforts undermined existing arrangements and investments in skill. This pressure on skilled workers occurred not only in the staple trade, but in other industries hit hard by the slowdown in worsted production. Wage reductions and unemployment undermined the position of less skilled operatives who had begun in the late 1860s to enjoy some benefits from the mid-Victorian expansion of trade. The erosion of the productive compromise of the mid-Victorian era provoked a reorganization of social and political institutions along more class-oriented lines.[11] In Bradford this led to a resurgence of militancy in the 1880s and 1890s in the form of general unionism and socialism.[12]

LABOR PROCESS IN THE WORSTED INDUSTRY

Historians have devoted considerable attention to links between the organization of labor and the larger outlines of social and political life in the Victorian era. Two key issues stand out in this work. One is the development of a new working-class culture in the late nineteenth century. The other is the relationship of this culture to the political and social order. In the context of mid-Victorian history, historians wish to explain the gradualism of working-class organizations after 1848. The relative political calm that lasted until the 1880s stands in marked contrast to the radicalism of the first half of the nineteenth century and that of the early twentieth century.

Beginning in the 1950s, the work of Eric Hobsbawm and a generation of labor historians focused on the role of the labor aristocracy. Hobsbawm argued that the peculiar characteristics of the English working class could be explained in part by the emergence of a group of highly paid, skilled male workers in the nineteenth century. This group, which constituted 10–20 per cent of the working class, enjoyed greater security and authority at work. While most historians agreed on the existence of a tier of higher paid-workers in Victorian England, controversy centered on the impact of this group on the social and political life of the working class. Hobsbawm and other writers argued that this group dominated the working-class community and sought to make its values and interests identical with those of the community as a whole. This led to a valuation of skill and independence as key features of both personal and social identity. This in turn created layers of status within the community and a distinctive form of consumption and behavior that came to be understood as 'traditional' working-class life.[13]

The aristocracy of labor combined a militant defense of their privileges with an acceptance of capitalism and its reorganization of the work place. The ascendancy of the labor aristocracy within unions and political organizations explained the curious combination of militancy with a lack of revolutionary organization within the English working class. Deprived of leadership, the English working class remained within the boundaries of a distinctive culture, which while separate from that of the middle and upper class, never fundamentally challenged the legitimacy or survival of capitalism.

The most detailed attempt to apply this concept to the mid-Victorian textile industry came in the work of John Foster. Foster argued that the collapse of political militancy in the 1840s and the subsequent mid-Victorian calm could be explained by the acquiescence of a stratum of skilled workers to the capitalist division of labor in exchange for greater authority within the mill. This power translated into status within the working-class community and the labor aristocracy stood out as a separate, self-perpetuating group within the working class.[14]

A number of scholars criticized Foster's work and the theory of the labor aristocracy in general. Many argued that it exaggerated the revolutionary potential and coherence of England's working class in the 1830s and 1840s and thus attempted to explain a non-event, the betrayal of the revolution by a self-interested elite. Still others dismissed the term labor aristocracy as too broad and vague in its application. Labor aristocrats were no more united in their views of the world than any other spectrum of the population and any attempt to link these disparate groups to the larger political events of the period floundered on a lack of evidence about how they felt and what motivated them to act as they did.[15]

Patrick Joyce, one of the most influential critics of Foster, turned the notion of the labor aristocracy on its head in his work. Joyce argued that the distinctive feature of the mid-Victorian textile industry and society in general, was not conflict, but rather cooperation between capitalists and workers. Joyce believed that both shared in the benefits of modern technology. Paternalism shaped the social relations of production associated with that technology, as owners asserted a model of society in which everyone participated in the family of work and community life. The acceptance of paternalism by workers created an ingrained consent to the existing order that radiated into all areas of life. Social and class relations focused on this paternal link, even in times of conflict, and sought to establish its reality when threatened.[16]

Joyce examined the process of generating consent in two arenas. In the mill, the triumph of mechanization subjected operatives to the demands of machinery in their work routines. This real subordination contrasted with the formal subordination of the earlier era, when the workers' mastery of handicraft skill gave them control over the work process and employers relied upon disciplinary schemes and the law to maintain order.[17] Outside the mill, mill owners sought to increase their control over the work force and repair the ties loosened by industrialization by building a new community based on the ties of work and the paternalistic institutions of the factory town. These paternalistic activities, from mill outings to friendly societies, gave workers rewards for their cooperation and tied the community together in a range of shared experiences.[18]

Joyce argued that the cotton textile areas of Lancashire and the woolen textile areas of Yorkshire differed in their social and political environments because of the more advanced nature of cotton textile production, which created a more advanced system of industrial relations. By contrast, slower and less complete mechanization in woolen textiles produced a fractured system of industrial relations and consequently more social and political conflict and tension.[19] The growth of large textiles firms in Lancashire allowed paternalism to flourish, while their relative absence in Yorkshire meant that paternalism remained underdeveloped.[20]

The connection between work and life in Joyce's work makes it essential to examine the work process in some detail to ascertain the aptness of his characterization of both the Lancashire cotton industry and the woolen industry of the West Riding. Joyce believed that earlier and more complete mechanization in Lancashire subordinated spinners and other skilled trades to the manufacturers, who could replace them. But this picture is an incomplete one. As William Lazonick and others have shown, the persistence of craft control by minders in cotton spinning and the slowness of the trade to introduce new work arrangements or technology prior to the First World War stemmed in part from the relations of production within the industry. Spinners maintained a strong bargaining position even after the invention and improvement of self-acting mules obviated any strictly technical need for the minder-piecer system in the cotton spinning industry.[21]

This strong bargaining position stemmed in part from the structure of the cotton trade and the market conditions faced by spinning capitalists. Cotton spinners produced for a buoyant world market, one increasingly oriented to the less developed world. They also enjoyed a steady decline in the relative cost of their main input, cotton, until the late nineteenth century. When faced with increasing competition, they shifted toward new markets in Asia and Latin America, rather than engaging in fierce competition with Western textile producers.[22] Lancashire's entrepreneurs focused on the maintenance of high output and sought to avoid disruptions in production that could disadvantage them in their internal competition. The result was the rise of mule spinners' unions and the wage and price lists, a cooperative strategy that favored at least some of the workers in the industry. While such arrangements proved beneficial over the short and medium term, they inhibited the technological modernization of the cotton industry and ultimately led to its decline in the twentieth century.[23]

The outcome of the struggle for control of the labor process in cotton was a mixed one. Cooperation and conflict characterized labor relations in the cotton industry and neither side possessed full freedom of action. Workers remained constrained by the relative weakness of unions outside of spinning and the potential of technology to eliminate their position in the mill.[24] On the other hand, capitalists could not simply reorient their systems of production without facing tremendous costs. Joyce exaggerated the freedom of maneuver enjoyed by owners in their choice of productive systems. Spinners, like workers, faced severe constraints. The costs of equipment, the disruptiveness of change and the resultant lost opportunities limited capitalists in their choice of technique.

Joyce overstated the power of employers in the labor process in cotton and fails to note the ways in which these limits came to cripple the trade. He also exaggerated the technological differences between the cotton and the woolen industries. Joyce failed to adequately distinguish between the woolen and worsted sections of the woolen industry.[25] In the woolen trade, the use of the mule and the survival of small scale hand production resembled the picture painted by Joyce for the woolen trade as a whole.[26] The worsted trade of the West Riding, however, mechanized far earlier than the woolen trade.[27] The use of ring spinning displaced men from the basic production process and reduced operatives to machine minders. Adult men never entered spinning in large numbers in the worsted trade because mechanization made their labor unnecessary and because manufacturers chose to use women and children. Unlike the cotton and woolen spinning industries, the worsted trade relied on the *exclusion* of adult men from the process of production for the most part and their cooptation in the skilled and supervisory grades. In addition, Joyce ignored the weaving sector of the cotton industry, which mechanized completely only in the 1840s, about the same time as worsted weaving and which was characterized by a more fragmented and small-scale system of production.[28]

The differences in labor organization between cotton and worsted resulted not from differences in technology, but rather from the market conditions encountered by entrepreneurs in the two industries. Worsted capitalists, unlike those in cotton, suffered a steady rise in the cost of their primary raw material, wool. At the same time, they struggled to remain competitive in the more developed markets of Europe and the United States. Caught in this double bind, worsted entrepreneurs looked to control the one area of costs in their grasp – labor. Worsted manufacturers could not afford the agreements reached by cotton spinners, for they needed to shave costs through mechanization and labor substitution to remain competitive with foreign producers as well as each other. This, rather than technology or firm size, produced the characteristic form of labor organization in the industry. As a result, the impact of mechanization upon the division of labor in the worsted trade was far more profound than in Lancashire and manufacturers realized more of the cost-saving possibilities of machinery.

As in the cotton industry, the pursuit of lower costs and competitive advantage led Bradford capitalists to make a series of decisions about machinery and personnel; decisions which dictated the path of the industry long after market conditions undermined their original utility. The worsted trade rested on a sexual and age-based division of labor in which women and children constituted the majority of factory operatives, while adult men filled both the upper stratum of the factory work force and the lowest levels of the unskilled. Low wages, speed-up and increased casualization characterized the worsted trade in the mid-Victorian era, despite its tremendous prosperity. Cheap labor and mechanization remained crucial for the success of the trade and this militated against a paternalist style of management.

The intense competitiveness of the worsted trade made it difficult to maintain an aura of paternalism. Observers decried the penchant for speculation and the greed for quick profits that obsessed the new capitalists, a generation removed from the heroes of the age of industrialization. It became a common complaint that the new circumstances degraded the former good feeling between worker and master. *The Voice of the People* attacked the new entrepreneurs as a group of 'Jews and Germans, an a lot o'petty cigar smoking puppies', guilty of driving honest employers from the trade and forcing down wages.[29] On the level of the shop floor, these complaints reflected the grievances that simmered beneath the surface. Accidents, physical brutality, sexual harassment and low wages all produced discontent. Worsted employers used the law and the legal process to regulate labor relations well into the 1870s. The reliance on legal means to repress unions and limit labor mobility demonstrated the limits to real control of the labor process even after the mechanization of the industry.

Joyce dismissed the importance of such conflict in the work place, but in fact this reflected his sources on factory life.[30] Joyce cited few accounts from those actually at work in the mills, or their supervisors or inspectors. Instead, he relied upon writers and newspapers to document the culture of the factory. These accounts tell only part of the story, for they leave out the day-to-day details of factory life. For example, Joyce cited James Burnley's optimistic account of mill life in Bradford to point out how the pace of work still left time for socializing and play.[31] Yet he failed to note that Burnley's role as a local writer appealing to middle-class audiences put him in a far less independent position than doctors and other observers who painted a more grim picture of factory life.[32]

With the onset of the slump, the problems of the worsted industry intensified. Investment decisions after 1850 followed the original line of development of the industry, and in the wake of a slowdown, the manufacturers of Bradford became reluctant to pour more money into the trade.[33] Investment in new equipment like spinning mules required a complete reorganization of productive relations, not simply the purchase of machinery. Few manufacturers were bold enough to take the risks involved in such a dramatic step. Instead they heightened the trend toward casualization and intensification of work as a stop-gap measure, while floating schemes for the reorganization of the trade. Such trial balloons alienated skilled and supervisory workers, already afraid of deskilling and unemployment.[34] The failure of worsted manufacturers to respond to changes in the marketplace ultimately led to the decline of the trade.[35]

The worsening of labor relations in the worsted industry in the last quarter of the nineteenth century flowed from this failure and the costs it imposed upon workers. The desire for control over the work place undermined the familial rhetoric of the period and created new forms of working-class organization that challenged the legitimacy of paternalism as a social form and questioned the mutuality of the factory. The emergence of general unionism and socialism after 1890 grew out of a convergence of interests between skilled workers and factory operatives in the worsted trade, as speed-up and lower wages impacted the entire industry.

The decline of paternalism as a preferred form of labor relations should not obscure the severe limitations it encountered before this period. Manufacturers in the West Riding and elsewhere invoked the image of the factory and the community as family to defend the legitimacy of the industrial order, but this image remained problematic. As we will see, the notion of family could be used against textile employers because of their reliance upon women's and children's labor. The perceived violation of older norms of work and domesticity by such practices undermined the claims of capitalists to head an extended family based in work.[36]

The problematic nature of family rhetoric gave paternalism an important role in the discourse about gender in this era. Sonya Rose and other feminist scholars point out that paternalism built upon assumed ideas about the roles of women and men in Victorian England.[37] Skilled workers and manufacturers could agree on the regulation and marginalization of women's and children's labor as part of a larger paternalistic order. They justified this role as the extension of women's 'natural' inclination toward domestic pursuits. Employers also built on gendered notions of work and life when they created institutions to control the leisure time of young factory women and to train them in domestic skills.[38]

The belief in the employer as a patriarchial figure assumed a level of knowledge and interaction unlikely to occur on a regular basis. The larger size of firms in the second half of the century, even in the more fragmented worsted trade, made personal contact between workers and employers unlikely. A stratum of intermediaries came between the ownership and workers, from managing partners to foremen and skilled workers. Titus Salt built the model village of Saltaire, but by employing 5,000 operatives he made a fiction of the idea of personal contact and knowledge. For the capitalists of the mid-century, paternalism reduced itself to a series of symbolic actions and gatherings that occurred a few times a year, rather than a daily process of building relationships.

The paternalism described by Joyce flourished mainly in the small textile cities of the north of England, dominated by a single industry or even a single employer.[39] Similar efforts in the worsted trade, such as Saltaire and Black Dyke Mills in Queensbury, occurred in more isolated rural settings, where employer provision of housing and sponsorship of mutual aid groups proved crucial and where a single employer could wield a dominant influence over the community.[40] In Bradford, no single employer dominated employment or the city. The potential mobility of workers between firms and out of the city or neighborhood made paternalism less important to cementing labor than wages and conditions of labor. It proved more attractive to manufacturers to focus efforts at paternalism outside the mill. Employers supported a range of agencies to aid and moralize the working class, but these stopped at the factory gates. Manufacturers preferred to leave the costs and difficulties of social reform to others and instead to concentrate on the control of labor within the mill.[41]

In a larger city like Bradford, a complete range of self-help organizations existed to serve workers. Workers chose to belong to their own organizations, whether unions or friendly societies, rather than depending upon those created for them by employers. In fact, such self-reliance enhanced their security by providing them an additional means of assistance not directly tied to employment. These organizations formed part of the greater scope for independent action available to workers in larger cities, a trend reinforced by the increasing geographical separation of working-class life in large urban areas. This network of independent organizations proved to be the springboard for challenges to the established power of the manufacturing elite of the West Riding in the late nineteenth century.

SKILL AND THE REORGANIZATION OF THE WORSTED TRADE

The division of labor in the worsted trade can be seen as a marriage of convenience between the need for manufacturers to cut labor costs to a minimum and the desire of skilled male workers to define and maintain a privileged position. The reorganization of textile production in the factory in the 1850s created a new set of hierarchies within the worsted industry. These hierarchies rested upon a marked differentiation of workers based on age, ethnicity and gender.

The mechanization of the worsted industry led to the replacement of adult men by women and children, as well as a slow down in the growth of the overall labor force due to rising productivity.[42] The improvement and spread of the power loom in the 1830s displaced hand-loom weavers, primarily adult males working at home, and fostered the growth of factories staffed by women. As H. S. Chapman noted in his report on the hand-loom weavers in 1838, 'Why then is the power loom complained of? Because hitherto women and girls only have been employed, to the exclusion of men.'[43] In combing an even more abrupt transition eliminated the jobs of 10,000 hand combers after the introduction of power combing.[44] Between 1851 and 1861, the number of adult men employed in the worsted industry declined dramatically, almost entirely due to the decline in hand combing.

In both spinning and weaving, the creation of factory-based industry involved more than simply transferring production and skills from the home to the mill. Spinning and weaving at home involved the worker (or more precisely the worker and his or her family) in the whole range of productive tasks. Once mechanized and based in the factory, these processes came to be subdivided into a variety of tasks. While in the cotton trade, spinning remained a privileged, male occupation, in worsted, both spinning and weaving were defined as unskilled or semi-skilled tasks.[45] The lack of a preexisting craft tradition in either worsted spinning or weaving reinforced this pattern by leaving the field wide open for the creation of hierarchies of work in what were essentially new occupations. The key step in the worsted trade involved the assignment of the labor intensive and rote tasks to the cheapest, most tractable workers (women and children) and the dominance of the more complex tasks by adult males.

Adult men increasingly worked in skilled and supervisory jobs in worsted mills or in preparatory or finishing processes that were not yet highly mechanized, such as wool sorting and dyeing. In addition to the supervisory workers in spinning and weaving, known as overlookers, there existed a variety of skilled trades in the mills. Primarily adult males, they enjoyed higher wages and greater job security. Stuff preparers and warp dressers prepared warps and finished pieces in the mills, while each mill employed its own mechanics and millwrights, responsible for the upkeep of the steam system and the repair of broken machinery beyond the capacity of overlookers to fix. These skilled workers made from 28s. to 40s. per week and along with overlookers constituted about 25 per cent of the adult male work force in the factory.

The reorganization of the worsted industry redefined the nature and meaning of skill. Increasingly within the worsted industry, the notion of machine-based skill supplemented older notions of craft or trade.[46] While trades within the mill revolved around knowledge of machines, most skilled labor involved not machine working, but rather machine upkeep or tasks such as warp dressing that fed into the primary processes of spinning and weaving. The reconstitution of skill was not a neutral process, for it remained the property of adult males and served to set them apart from the rest of work force in and outside the mills.[47] Skilled workers relied upon work rules and union organization to preserve their trades from dilution by women or younger males. This exclusionary definition of skill rested upon intertwined hierarchies of age and gender and drew upon broader understandings of the place of women and young people in mid-Victorian society.[48] Skilled men justified their positions by appealing to common sense understandings of the abilities and proper role of women and children. In warp dressing, male workers argued that the strength required to lift the warp onto the loom prohibited women or young men from entering the trade, despite the fact that many women possessed the strength to lift the beam and that this portion of the job represented only a minor step in the overall process.[49] Machine tenders cited the inability of women to perform mechanical tasks as the reason for the male monopoly among mill mechanics. Such arguments extended even to occupations like weaving, where men received higher pay on the basis of their alleged ability to make do with less assistance from overlookers.[50]

Skilled workers also used the rhetoric of domesticity to justify the low status of women in the trade. Women should not work outside the home, because they competed with men and neglected their role as wives, daughters and mothers. Jobs should be reserved for men who needed to support a family. The assimilation of bourgeois notions of domesticity for the purposes of defending males' prerogatives in the work place became commonplace in this era.[51] Yet it encountered many of the same contradictions inherent in bourgeois versions of domesticity. Whereas middle-class observers felt constrained by the gap between domestic values and the necessity of employing women and children in large numbers, working-class men attempting to exclude or limit the labor of these groups in the name of domesticity failed to acknowledge the reality that such workers were a permanent feature of the worsted industry.

Male operatives argued that women, who often migrated from rural areas, were transients and showed little commitment to work. Young women made frequent moves from mill to mill, unlike skilled men, who frequently worked in a single mill for their entire working lives. Furthermore, they argued that the young women who made up the bulk of operatives would not remain in the mills for long, but would soon marry and quit work.[52] Such arguments confused cause and effect. The internal recruitment procedures of most skilled trades, which favored relatives and close acquaintances, restricted the opportunities for mill hands to move up in the factory hierarchy. Most operatives remained trapped in dead-end jobs, unable to effectively bargain for higher wages or better conditions.[53] Under such circumstances, women had little incentive to remain in one mill for long or to persist in the trade. Despite this, large numbers of women supported their families on the low wages of spinning or weaving.

The ability of some adult men to defend their trade privileges also created a division among male operatives in the worsted industry. Most men found work not as skilled workers, but rather in a variety of unskilled or semiskilled jobs. Mills employed a considerable number of laborers to assist in moving and storing raw and finished goods, as well as to perform maintenance tasks such as fueling boilers. Equally important were the unskilled or semiskilled tasks created by mechanization and the expansion of mercantile activities. In both combing and dyeing, the use of machinery gave rise to a number of machine tending or laboring jobs. Other men found work in warehouses and shipping agencies as laborers. These operatives remained on the fringes of the industry, finding work by the day or week and lacking the security and higher wages of the skilled minority.

THE ORGANIZATION OF LABOR IN SPINNING AND WEAVING

The labor process in the trade can be broken down by the stages of production. First came cleaning, combing (a step unique to worsted production) and preparing the wool, followed by spinning and then weaving. Finally came the dyeing and finishing of piece goods, which merchants at home and abroad marketed. In addition to this classification by process, it is also necessary to examine the various tasks within each process to determine the nature of work done, who did it and the amount of skill considered necessary for the task.

Spinning was the first stage to be mechanized and by the 1820s power spinning replaced home spinning in the West Riding.[54] The worsted trade relied upon throstle frames rather than the spinning mules used in both cotton and woolen production. These frames imparted the necessary tension through drawing and twisting rather than through the action of the mule. During the 1850s, the cap frame began to replace the fly frame as the most common spinning machine, a process virtually complete by the early 1870s.[55]

Walter McLaren, a partner in a West Riding spinning firm, noted in his book on spinning the cost advantages of cap frames over mules. Mules took up twice as much room and did not turn off the same weight of yarn per spindle. Furthermore, the cap and ring spinning machines could spin yarn to a higher count, which allowed the production of inexpensive goods that had the appearance of high quality woolen goods. Finally, young boys and women minded the cap and ring machines, whereas men and boys usually worked the mules.[56]

This latter factor weighed heavily with Bradford manufacturers, for it allowed them to avoid the higher costs of using adult male labor while still enjoying the benefits of mechanization. According to one report,

> in Bradford the children are trained to spin at the flyer or cap frame. To be effectively managed, the mule must be manned by men and boys, who are stronger, more suitably clad, and have more 'staying power' than women.[57]

The cost differential between the two systems could be substantial. According to Lazonick, in the 1870s a pair of mules in the cotton trade employed a minder at 30s. to 34s. per week, a big piecer at 12s. to 14s. and a little piecer at 7s. to 9s.[58] In worsted spinning in 1866, adult women earned between 7s. and 10s. per week, while girls and boys earned from 2s.6d. to 4s.[59] Given the productivity of a cap frame, which produced out of 184 spindles as much as a 500 spindle mule, the Bradford system translated into a lower cost per spindle and per pound of yarn spun when compared to woolen spinning by mule.[60]

Spinning operatives, children or young women paid by the day, minded two sides of the spinning machine, or frame. Each side had anywhere from 60 to 110 spindles and operatives worked in the narrow space between two frames called the gate. They pieced broken threads and made sure the frames kept operating. Doffers and bobbin minders, usually one or two for each frame, assisted them, working in gangs, replacing spindles of raw wool and removing spun yarn. The spinner's job required dexterity and speed, but unlike mule spinners, cap spinners were not considered skilled workers.[61]

Weaving only became mechanized in the 1830s, but by the 1850s, power looms had displaced hand looms. As in spinning, women and the young provided the bulk of the labor force. According to one contemporary observer, women composed two-thirds of the new work force and young men the other third.[62] Plain stuff weavers minded two looms, while those working in fancy stuffs minded one. The weaver kept the loom supplied with material, picked out knots, and fixed broken threads. Shuttle forks, which stopped the loom when a thread broke, facilitated the latter task. Weavers received payment by the completed piece, which varied in quality, length and width.[63]

Wages in the weaving sections varied considerably depending upon the age and sex of the worker, though in general they were on the low end of the scale. Men consistently earned more than women for the same tasks; they averaged four to six shillings more per week than women. Weavers' wages increased from 10s.6d to 13s.6d. per week between 1855 and 1871.[64] These figures fail to account for short-time or deductions for fines, which substantially reduced a weaver's income over the course of a year.[65] Furthermore, such estimates overstate the wage level, because most wage data came from larger firms that paid higher wages. Even then, the figures seem inflated, for while one observer put the wage of women weavers at 14s. to 15s. per week in 1883, weavers on strike at Manningham Mills in 1882 claimed that reductions lowered their weekly wages to 10s. to 12s.[66]

Because of the predominance of women and children in spinning and weaving, factory legislation set the hours of work in those sections of the industry. The Ten Hours Bill limited the work week for women and children to sixty hours. Their day began at six am and went to six or seven in the evening, with time off for meals. In the Bradford area, agitation began in the 1850s for a Saturday half-holiday to allow workers time for domestic arrangements and recreation. The Short-Time Committees managed to establish the principle of the half-holiday, though as late as the 1870s it was not universal. The passage of the Factory Act of 1874 finally made the half-holiday a legal requirement for all practical purposes. The nine-hour day, which prevailed in construction, engineering and metal work in the early

1870s in Bradford failed to make headway in the textile industry, where the ten hour day remained the norm.[67]

The use of children and young women gave Bradford manufacturers a considerable cost advantage over their competitors, both in woolen and cotton goods. As Edward Forster, of the Bradford Chamber of Commerce noted in front of the Labour Commission, 'Of course, it is notorious that the wages (in Bradford) are lower (than in the cotton trade).'[68] Weavers, paid by the piece, and the spinners paid by the day cost less than adult male mule spinners or weavers, yet the system depended on the availability of women and children to work in the mills.[69] Bradford manufacturers attempted to maintain the supply of cheap labor so central to the success of the industry. In addition to opposing extensions of the Factory Acts, firms also sought to actively recruit young persons. Charles Stead, a partner in Titus Salt's firm, argued that the use of throstles (another term for ring spinning) rather than mules made the supply of children crucial to the industry. His firm, one the largest and most modern in the West Riding, employed over 800 children between the ages of eight and thirteen and recruited families from agricultural districts to ensure an adequate supply of labor.[70] During the trade depression of the 1870s, the *Textile Manufacturer* argued that the dearth of children in the worsted industry would force employers to reconsider their support for the emigration of destitute children.[71]

Women and children made up the bulk of a fairly unstable work force in spinning and weaving. In general, young and unmarried persons constituted the majority of operatives, despite the claim that many married women worked in the mills.[72] In spinning, the female workers were usually less than twenty years old. Most young men left the factories after eighteen to seek better employment, except for the few who stayed on as overlookers or skilled workers in other trades, since even laborers were likely to be more highly paid than semi-skilled worsted operatives.[73] This created a career pattern in the trade that differed from that of the cotton trade of Lancashire. Unlike the piecers in mule spinning, operatives in spinning and weaving had little hope of advancement or even earning an adult living wage.[74] As a result, both spinning and weaving experienced a considerable turnover in personnel. Bradford school teachers frequently complained of the habit of young workers leaving one mill to go to another, necessitating a change of schools.[75] The Worsted Committee Inspectors reported that weavers moved from place to place seeking better employment despite the threat of prosecution for neglect of work.[76]

THE ORGANIZATION OF LABOR OUTSIDE OF SPINNING AND WEAVING

A number of preparatory and finishing processes existed in the worsted industry, some carried out in the mills, others set up as separate enterprises. These auxiliary trades expanded as a result of the growth of the worsted industry, creating new niches for adult males outside the confines of the mill itself. The impact of mechanization upon these processes varied widely. In combing, mechanization transformed combers into machine minders, while wool sorting remained a hand trade that relied upon the experience and knowledge of the sorters.

The initial step in the production of worsted goods was the separation of wool into different grades. Housed in sheds attached to warehouses or spinning mills, woolsorters worked over sorting boards with lattice wires in large ventilated rooms. They separated the wool into three to fifteen varieties, depending upon the final product to be made. Each sorter used his own board and, after weighing and packing the wool, sent it on to the washing and combing rooms. A gap opened between two types of sorters, packers who opened bales and perhaps did rough sorting and daymen, who did the finer sorting and oversaw the work of the other operatives.[77]

The steady increase in demand for worsted goods and the use of new materials such as alpaca and mohair gave sorters a strong bargaining position. In the mid-1860s, the daymen made as much as 32s. per week, although the less skilled made as little as 20s.[78] The daymen set up their own trade society in 1838, which regulated apprenticeships and conditions of work and provided sickness and unemployment benefits. Apprentices assisted a sorter for three to seven years before working on their own. A father was allowed to bring one legitimate son into the trade without formal apprenticeship. In addition, the society limited each sorter to one board to prevent unemployment among members.[79] The society enrolled 140 members by the late 1860s.[80]

After sorting, the wool was washed and combed. A few operatives working in a combing shed replaced hundreds of hand combers working at home.[81] Although this ameliorated the domestic condition of the combers, its impact on their work lives proved less beneficial. Combing operatives were casual workers, hired by the day and paid by the weight of wool combed. They tended and maintained the washing, carding and combing machines. Both adult men and women filled these positions and earned 12s. to 17s. a week by 1871. In 1891, males made up 40 per cent of the 3,000 operatives in the trade, women the other 60 per cent.[82] Unlike other branches of the worsted trade the combing mills worked two shifts. The use of adult men for night work allowed combing shops to avoid restrictions on night work for women and children. No set scale of pay or notice for dismissal existed and observers considered the combing trade the final stopping place of broken-down laborers.[83]

The final stage of the production process, dyeing and finishing, reflected the uneven impact of mechanization in the worsted industry. Adult males made up the majority of the dyeing workforce. Women stitched pieces together before dyeing and mended finished materials. Boys under eighteen made up somewhere between 10 per cent to 25 per cent of the work force, usually working as assistants to men in dyeing and finishing.[84] Dyers washed yarn or wool in large vats called Petries wool washing machines in a mixture of human urine diluted with water. Wound upon cylinders, the material was steamed to prevent shrinkage, dried and singed over hot iron and copper plates. The material was then placed in various dye baths and dried in a ventilated room over heated cylinders. Large hydraulic machines pressed completed pieces to provide a finish.[85]

Successful dyeing depended upon the knowledge and experience of the master dyer. The dyeing process could take days and the color and appearance of the material rather than a set schedule determined the end of the process. This gave foremen dyers considerable power, which they vigorously defended. Henry Ripley testified that he reluctantly dismissed two trained chemists from his dyeworks when his master dyer quit in protest of the infringement on His authority.[86]

Skill and pay varied considerably within this sector of the trade, from the highly trained master dyers and stuff pressers who earned 30s. to 60s. per week to the slabs or dyers' laborers, who earned from 15s. to 20s.[87] Slabs, casual laborers who lined up each morning for work, often alternated between the dye-works and other forms of casual labor such as the gas works or combing. Between these extremes resided many semi-skilled and skilled workers such as singers, crabbers, and facesiders, who did more than brute labor, but who could not claim higher status. In 1871, top wages for skilled workers such as finishers stood at about 24s. per week; the rest earned between 18s. and 22s. weekly.[88]

Bradford's importance as a market produced a rapid increase in warehouse activities in the mid-Victorian period. An entire warehouse district, known as Little Germany, sprang up in the 1850s and by 1864,

1,500 to 1,600 workers found employment there.[89] The warehouse, in the words of one writer, 'was an all-male preserve sustained by cheap labor.'[90] A small group of workers, the maker-ups and packers, sorted and graded the various materials stored in the warehouses and enjoyed higher wages and better conditions, earning around 22s. per week. In slack time, they would be kept on to ensure their presence when needed. In fact, cards became known as the 'makers-up game' because of this.[91] For the rest of the employees, warehouse work involved long hours, no set terms of employment and low pay. Because of the lack of a system of apprenticeship, the job was a dead end for the operatives who earned around 15s. per week. Contrary to the claims of skilled workers organized by the owners to protest the possible extension of the Factory Acts to warehouses, the work was dangerous and ill-paid, and the hoists, shafts, and hooking machines presented a threat to life and limb for the unwary.[92]

GRIEVANCES AND WORK CONDITIONS

Despite the variations in work and conditions within the worsted industry, the intensification and mechanization of labor created a series of problems that all workers shared. Grievances that covered a wide range of areas – labor discipline, sexual harassment, accidents, working conditions, wages, piece work and speed-up – emerged in this era. Yet the commonality of grievances failed to produce a unified response. Skilled workers sought to preserve their position *vis-à-vis* the mass of the operatives through their own unions rather than seeking to organize the entire workforce in the industry. Trade unionism and strikes represented only the most visible outbursts among textile operatives in this era. Lacking effective organizations, other operatives often resorted to covert forms of struggle. These alternative forms of resistance, such as theft or leaving work to seek new employment, only emerge from the records of daily life in the factory.

The lack of well-organized unions or strikes did not mean that a culture of deference emerged in the worsted mill. Beneath the ceremonies of paternalism like the yearly works outing or the factory gala, daily conflicts over work occurred and served as a constant reminder of the inequities of the system. Although skilled workers may have possessed the opportunity to structure their work experience and capture some of the benefits of the increasing intensity of work, their privileges rested on the disabilities of others. The young persons and women who made up the majority of the work force lacked this advantage and for them the mid-Victorian era was not an age of improvement. The burden of the increasingly competitive world market fell upon their shoulders through speed up and disguised forms of wage-cutting such as fines and changing payment schemes.[93] The intensification of the existing system of production in the 1870s and 1880s led workers of all skill levels to resist efforts to force workers to bear the brunt of the failure of the worsted trade.

Mill operatives complained most about the increased work load in the period 1851 to 1881. In spinning, the greater speed of spindles, the larger number of spindles per frame and the requirement to tend at least two and perhaps three or four frame sides intensified the work of all operatives in the spinning room.[94] While to a certain extent higher wages compensated for the greater work load, operatives repeatedly voiced their discontent. Because spinning was considered unskilled work, concern focused on the severity of the work, rather than the degradation of skill. Most observers agreed with Henry Mitchell, who argued that the speed of the machinery and the hours of work and not the skill of the worker determined the level of output in spinning.[95]

Considerable disagreement prevailed about the difficulty of spinning. William Cudworth, a publicist for the trade, characterized spinning as an easy job that provided the spinner with time for 'larking with doffers'.[96] Doctors Holmes and Bridges saw spinning in a different light in their report to the Local Government Board in 1873. They visited several factories and concluded that, although the degree of exertion differed between mills, spinning required a great deal of attention and movement on the part of operatives. They also noted complaints about the intensity of work, observing,

> The principal grievance urged by the advocates of shorter time appears to be the great increase alleged to have taken place of late in the number of spindles attended to by each hand. It is contended that the spinner has a greater distance to walk up and down, and a greater strain upon his attention than formerly.[97]

In a series of letters to the *Bradford Observer* in the spring of 1872, operatives supported a nine-hour day by detailing the increasing severity of work. 'A Factory Worker', writing in reply to James Tankard, a spinning mill owner who had attacked the nine hours movement, said, 'Does he [Tankard] deny that operating four to six times as many spindles, running more quickly as twenty years ago, increases the strain?'[98] In another letter, 'A Factory Worker' stated that spinners saw their work load grow from two frames of 72 to 96 spindles to three or four of 144 to 200 spindles. This meant more ends to piece and greater distances to cover for the operative.[99] Another operative estimated that each frame had 30–60 per cent more spindles than twenty years earlier and that these spindles ran 70 per cent faster.[100]

In weaving, the issue of speed-up mingled with a long-standing debate over the issue of skill. While one letter writer in the *Bradford Observer* argued, 'I can state, from close observation, that it does not require a high order of skill to produce well made piece goods by power loom,' others in the trade disagreed.[101] Henry Mitchell believed that weaving should be considered a more skilled occupation than spinning, while a letter writer in the *Textile Manufacturer* claimed that weaving was a skilled job and that manufacturers fought to keep their best workers.[102]

As in spinning, disagreement surfaced over the difficulty of weaving, despite the evidence of an intensification of effort in the mills. Both George Taylor and William Cudworth, contemporary observers of the industry, argued that the job required little manual labor and taxed the weaver's patience more than her strength.[103] Henry Mitchell, however, noted that the speed of looms doubled between the 1840s and the 1880s to 170 to 180 picks per minute.[104] James Wilkenson believed that the increased effort brought by speed-up produced a greater strain upon the operative. By his estimate, a weaver turned out five pieces, thirty-six to forty yards long in sixty hours in 1872 as compared to two pieces the same length in seventy-two hours in 1838.[105] Weavers attempted to resist this trend by preventing operatives from taking on more looms. In October of 1881, police charged two weavers from Silsden with intimidation and assault on a man and a woman who incurred the wrath of fellow weavers by minding three looms instead of the customary two.[106]

For weavers, who worked by the piece, a whole series of specific complaints existed. No fixed system of compensation per piece developed in the Bradford trade and weavers were often unaware of the price for various widths of a piece or the accepted length of a piece. In 1877, 200 weavers at Ramsden & Co. went on strike over the increasing uncertainty of payment as the length of pieces increased from forty-eight to fifty-four or even sixty yards without an increase in piece rates.[107] Witnesses to the Royal Commission on Labour testified to outright fraud in payment on the part of owners through the secret coding of pattern cards.[108] The practice of fining weavers for damaged or short pieces sparked fierce controversy as well. Such fines could not be appealed and the operative could not examine the piece or determine if the machinery itself was the problem. The fact that the damaged piece would be sold anyway proved galling to the weavers. The increased use of the bonus system, where the overlooker received extra pay in exchange for higher output in his section, exacerbated these problems.[109]

Operatives also complained about the conditions at work. Witnesses before the Royal Commission on Labour testified to the primitive and overcrowded sanitary arrangements at most mills. The usual concession to filth, a coat of whitewash, failed to hide the stench of overflowing privies.[110] Workers suffered in disproportionate numbers from lung diseases such as tuberculosis and the clouds of dust raised by sorting, spinning and weaving produced a form of brown lung and a plethora of other lung ailments.[111]

Mill owners steadfastly refused to acknowledge their responsibility for illness in the work place. J.B. Thompson typified this attitude in an article in the *Edinburgh Medical Journal*, in which he asserted that 'In Yorkshire, the better classes frequently send the delicate members of their families to the woolen mills for the benefit of their health.'[112] Yet there was a growing awareness of the health problems associated with the worsted trade. The Medical Officer of Health (MOH) for Bradford devoted a considerable portion of his 1884 report to this issue and cited the poor hygienic quality of factories as a serious health problem.[113]

Despite the MOH's critical assessment of factory conditions, the Inspectors of Factories failed to report a single case of unsanitary conditions in 1884. In part, this reflected the heavy work load of inspectors. By 1869, an inspector was responsible for 800 to 900 factories, compared with 300 in earlier years, a load that expanded to over 2,000 by the 1890s.[114] It also grew out of their lack of medical expertise, which inhibited their intervention in questions of health and disease.[115] Although Robert Baker, the long time Inspector for the Bradford district, was a physician, most inspectors lacked formal medical training. Other doctors, with the notable exception of J.H. Bridges, remained enmeshed in a web of patronage and employment that dictated a more circumspect approach to health issues and the factory. The dominance of worsted employers over the Bradford Infirmary and the middle-class nature of most private practices made activism on health issues risky.[116]

These issues surfaced in the controversy over the most famous work-related illness, 'wool-sorter's disease' or anthrax. The disease first appeared in Bradford in the 1860s among workers in eastern wools such as mohair and alpaca and helped raise public awareness of health problems in the industry. Despite the fact that observers linked the disease to 'fallen' fleeces taken from dead sheep, manufacturers refused to remove suspicious fleeces. Instead they tried a variety of measures to allow them to use contaminated wools. At least 64 workers from three firms died between 1869 and 1880 and many more suffered from milder forms of the disease.[117] Far from taking responsibility for these deaths, manufacturers tried to dismiss them as a result of the general poor health of the sorters. Noting the prevalence of lung ailments among wool sorters, the Saltaire Medical Officer theorized that only 'weak-chested' men suffered from anthrax and blamed vices such as intemperance for the disease.[118]

The debate over anthrax split the medical community of Bradford between those who argued in favor of 'constitutional' theories of disease and those who believed in a germ theory. The Medico-Chirurgical Society formed a Woolsorters' Disease Commission to investigate the disease and the commission eventually adopted a germ-contagion explanation. The key piece of evidence for this view came from the committee's confirmation of Pasteur's work on anthrax.[119] This conclusion received a rather mixed reception among members of the Society, for some refused to accept a report implicitly critical of worsted employers. The Society privately circulated the report and only publicly printed it with assistance from the woolsorters' union.[120] Despite the report and subsequent confirmation by government inquiries, owners continued to evade the new regulations issued to slow the spread of the disease.[121]

Manufacturers took a similar stance when it came to the problem of accidents on the job. They denied responsibility for these injuries and tried to shift the blame onto the operatives. One manager, writing to the *Textile Manufacturer*, argued that accidents resulted from the ignorance of workers about proper maintenance procedures.[122] Manufacturers fiercely resisted attempts to make them liable for work place accidents and for compensating injured employees. Prior to the passage of the Employers Liability Act of 1880, workers and their families possessed no legal means of recovering for injuries and death and even the new law required lengthy and expensive court proceedings to collect.[123]

Injuries inflicted by 'flying shuttles' received the most publicity. The shuttles on a loom frequently came loose and could strike weavers in the head, causing serious injuries or death. In 1876 the Bradford Eye and Ear Hospital devoted a meeting to such accidents. One doctor claimed to have treated eighteen victims of flying shuttles in five years, all of whom lost their sight in at least one eye.[124] Despite the efforts of factory inspectors and others to require the fencing of machinery and shuttle guards, the problem persisted into the 1890s.[125]

Machinery of all kinds menaced factory operatives. Unprotected shafting could catch the clothing or hair of workers and drag them to their death.[126] Defective boilers also injured workpeople; the problem of scalding was particularly acute in dyeing where many tasks required the use of steam.[127] The cramped quarters inside mills led to accidents when operatives stood or leaned on machines while attempting repairs.[128] The general practice of cleaning and fixing machinery while it operated in order to keep up the production of the mill led to numerous injuries to the arms and hands of mill workers.[129] The lack of fire exits and the poor construction of mills also killed or injured workers by preventing escape in the event of a fire or accident.[130]

In addition to complaints about working conditions, there also existed a more personal area of discontent, the sexual harassment of female operatives by fellow workers, overlookers and owners. To earlier radicals such as George Harley, it seemed obvious that millowners preyed on working women and that 'No wed woman or young lass is safe wi' [sic] him [the mill owner].'[131] The question of the sexual misconduct of overlookers formed part of a larger debate over the moral impact of the factory system upon women. While many focused on the debasement of values brought by contact between men and women at work, others saw the problem as one of temptation and power.[132] J.H. Marshall, a local social reformer, called attention to this issue, noting:

> Dressed in a little brief authority; which they know but too well and too often how to abuse, [they] have been known to play a leading, and not infrequent part in the guilty drama [seduction of mill women]. It is of course, unnecessary to add, in passing, that not all, nor perhaps even a majority of the persons here categorized, are thus accused.[133]

Marshall left unstated, but clearly implied, his belief that overlookers engaged in widespread sexual harassment. Incidents such as the conviction of overlooker Samuel Hustler for assaulting Mary Ann Padget, an operative of Northgate Mill to whom he had been 'familiar', represented the rare public side of a mainly secretive problem.[134] Years later, J.B. Priestley noted, 'Managers who were obdurate if mill girls wanted another shilling a week, could be found in distant pubs turning the prettiest and weakest of them into tarts.'[135]

OVERLOOKERS AND THE CONTROL OF LABOR

These grievances highlight the contested nature of mill labor in the mid-Victorian era. As average firm size increased, the ideal of a close relationship between employer and employee proved difficult to achieve. At the same time, the use of semi-skilled women and children in spinning and weaving created the need for a cadre of supervisory workers to control their labor and ensure discipline. In the period after 1850, overlookers increasingly became intermediaries between management and labor. Because of the high turnover among a young, semi-skilled workforce, overlookers and foremen provided the continuity and stability that kept the mills functioning.

Overlookers worked in all branches of the trade, from combing to dyeing, but played their greatest role in spinning and weaving. In spinning, overlookers repaired machinery, inspected the final product and supervised both drawing and spinning room operatives. A senior foreman selected several assistants, who usually began their three to four year apprenticeships between the ages of sixteen and eighteen. Each overlooker in spinning supervised about forty workers.[136] Weaving overlookers performed similar tasks, being responsible for both supervision of workers and the repair and upkeep of machinery. In addition, they inspected the warps for weaving and determined the quality of completed pieces. An overlooker took charge of fifty to one hundred looms, often with a learner.[137]

Weaving and spinning overlookers enjoyed higher wages and more regular employment than the great majority of textile workers. They earned from 25s. to 35s. per week and remained on the payroll even during periods of recession.[138] Overwhelmingly male and recruited from the ranks of factory operatives, they often worked at a single mill for most of their lives.[139] Power loom overlookers chose their assistants and the Overlookers' Society imposed fines on those who took learners without permission and gave benefits to those fired for refusing unapproved learners.[140] Once selected, assistants received empirical training, based on factory practice, from a senior overlooker.

The overlooker, particularly in large establishments, enjoyed a great deal of power to hire and fire. Theoretically, the oversight of managers and owners limited this power, but in practice day-to-day operations remained in the hands of the overlookers.[141] Overlookers ruled through a combination of coercion and cooperation. As former factory workers themselves, they understood the nature of the work and the mentality of their workers. At the same time, they did not hesitate to employ harsher measures. Newspapers carried reports of continued violence in the work place, such as the case of a ten year old boy who died in March of 1857 a week after a beating by an overlooker at Garnett's Mill. In another incident, an overlooker assaulted a young boy in an attempt to prevent him from testifying in the manslaughter trial of a fellow overlooker.[142] The frequency of such violence led the *Textile Manufacturer* to remark in December of 1875 that overlookers seemed to believe that they could treat children as they pleased. It recommended that notices be posted telling overlookers that they could not strike children.[143]

These workers formed the elite of the factory labor force, a so-called 'aristocracy of the operative class'.[144] The elite of Bradford saw this role embracing not only the factory, but also social life, for they believed that the overseers, as enlightened working men, constituted the natural leaders of their class. Overlookers, however, occupied an ambiguous social position in Bradford. Their high salaries and supervisory roles set them apart from the mass of operatives, while their responsibility for enforcing discipline made them the focus of operatives' anger. Many workers believed that overlookers favored the owners in their jobs and imitated the behavior of the upper classes.[145] Both overlookers and employers asserted their mutual interest in the operation of the mill.[146]

Nevertheless, overlookers could not escape their working-class status. In earlier years, overlookers could attempt to set up a small firm to capitalize on the many niches provided by the worsted industry. This path for upward mobility closed to many as the depression of the 1870s devastated numerous textile firms. Fred Jowett, a future Labour MP, was one of many who failed in his attempt to start his own business.[147] Even for their children, the opportunities for escape from working-class life seemed slim. According to Henry Ripley the dyer and an avid supporter of education, the foreman making less than £100 per year could not afford to send his children to school beyond the age of thirteen or fourteen.[148] The new white collar jobs opened by the expansion of trade appear to have gone to the sons of the lower middle class who could afford to receive secondary schooling.[149] The best opportunity for an overlooker's child was to be trained as an assistant foreman or to enter into another skilled trade.

The overlookers' trade societies reflected this dual role as managers and workers. The earliest society, the Managers and Overlookers Society, was formed in 1827. Initially the Society included drawing and spinning overlookers and it admitted carding and combing foremen as their trades mechanized. Three separate societies existed until their amalgamation in 1887.[150] By 1874, they represented 590 overlookers.[151] The weaving overlookers organized a society in 1844 and had 457 members in two branches when they amalgamated in 1881.[152] Both societies began as friendly societies, offering burial, unemployment and sickness benefits. In 1870, members of the Third Society of Spinning Overlookers paid a subscription of 2s. a month.[153] For this injured or sick members got 1s.8d. per day, while unemployed members received 1s.9d. for the first 72 days out of work and 1s. per day afterwards. Power loom overlookers received 10s. per week if injured or unemployed, but received no benefits during strikes or lock-outs.[154]

These friendly society functions mixed uneasily with the other activities of the societies. Although the Managers and Overlookers Society specifically ruled out conducting strikes for its members or supporting strikes by other workers, it and other societies resembled trade unions in many ways. The Power Loom Overlookers acted as a clearinghouse for employment, levied fines on members for working contrary to society rules and enforced apprenticeship regulations.[155] The government considered overlookers' societies trade unions and forced the Third Society of the Managers and Overlookers to register as one in 1885.[156] Most public comment about the overlookers centered on their political activities. Overlookers took the lead in the effort to extend the Factory Acts and shorten the hours of labor as well as the movement for the expansion of the suffrage for men.[157] To the extent that overlookers made common cause with operatives on factory regulation or political rights, they undermined the social order of the factory system.

The ambivalent role of overlookers grew out of their work as well. While relatively privileged compared with other workers, they faced the problems of unemployment and disability and long stretches of illness or loss of work could impoverish them. Overlookers were also subject to many of the same laws and rules that applied to other workers. They could be and were charged under the Worsted Acts for neglect of work or theft. These problems heightened in the late 1870s, as the prolonged trade depression increased unemployment and decreased the funds of the societies.[158] Efforts by employers to introduce new machinery and technical education also undermined the position of overlookers. The problems of unemployment, the use of the bonus system to increase output and the desire to control conditions of employment led overlookers' societies toward trade union status in the 1880s, though in a halting fashion.[159]

THE WORSTED COMMITTEE AND LABOR DISCIPLINE

Within the factory, overlookers and other skilled workers provided the day-to-day management of most tasks. Yet, manufacturers remained surprisingly reliant upon the use of legal sanctions to discipline and control their work forces, even supervisory and skilled workers. To do so they called upon the Worsted Committee, a body set up by Parliament in the late eighteenth century to enforce the Worsted Acts.[160] The Acts regulated relations between owners and employees and gave the Committee the power to pursue cases of dishonesty and corruption. Mill owners used legal sanctions to punish workers and to limit labor mobility into the 1870s. The Committee, initially funded by the drawback on soap and contributions from manufacturers, employed its own staff of inspectors.[161] A smaller group of inspectors, who covered large districts and relied on the rapidly expanding local police forces to arrest offenders, replaced this force in the 1850s. The payment of bonuses for convictions and the sympathy of Bradford and West Riding magistrates, a large proportion of whom were worsted capitalists, ensured vigorous enforcement of the Acts.[162]

The inspectors concentrated on the discovery of embezzlement and theft of materials and the prevention of 'neglect of work' (leaving without adequate notice) by operatives. The Worsted Acts defined the latter offense as a criminal act subject to a fine of several pounds or up to three months in jail at hard labor. Theoretically, the Acts applied equally to owners and employees, but in practice they served the owners' interests. Operatives lacked the resources to prosecute employers for illegal dismissal and the threat of imprisonment and the expense of a trial often forced them to return to work regardless of the merit of the case.[163].

The inspectors relied upon the public prosecution of a few workers who left work without notice to frighten other operatives. This tactic could be used against strikers and trade unionists, as when a strike at Townsend & Sons collapsed after an inspector charged six strikers with neglect of work and threatened them with Wakefield Jail. These practices peaked during periods of good trade such as the early 1870s, when the demand for workers gave them greater choices for employment. Conversely, the problem declined in bad times. As one Inspector wrote,

> I have noticed many who have returned sooner than be summoned – there have not been as many enquiries for my services this quarter as I have usually had, but I attribute that to the bad trade of which complaints are very general.[164]

The other major area of concern for the inspectors, theft and embezzlement, touched upon the customary practices of the hand trades and the survival of old techniques among the new factory workers. While most of the cases of theft dealt with large amounts of material stolen by employees engaged in illicit dealing of wool, a number dealt with the theft of small amounts of materials by operatives for personal use. Workers considered waste products such as noils, fents and ends from warps their own to use.[165] In one case, an inspector found a woman weaver knitting stockings from her warp.[166] Others took waste material for home consumption. Such incidents imply the continued existence of hand spinning and weaving techniques among the population. Knitting remained part of the school curriculum at the insistence of parents, who wanted their children to learn 'useful' skills.[167]

Other workers went beyond personal use to large scale embezzlement. For example, an inspector apprehended a mill watchman and others stealing machine tops from Black Dyke Mills in Queensbury.[168] Even skilled workers and managers could be involved in theft, as in the case of the warp dressers accused by inspectors of stealing cotton to sell to twine dealers.[169] The proliferation of small dealers in textile materials offered ample opportunities to sell pilfered goods and supplement the inadequate incomes of workers.[170] The line between theft and legitimate activity was often a fine one, for many workers were given control over large amounts of material, while they simultaneously pursued their own careers as dealers or worked for other masters.[171] Warehouse owners tried to solve this problem by resolving not to employ men who dealt in woolen goods without their consent.[172]

The Worsted Acts and their successor, the Master and Servant Act, highlighted the quasi-legal status of trade unionism and the hostility of the judicial system to unions.[173] The constant threat of legal action combined with the lack of similar sanctions applied to employers

created considerable resentment and greatly inhibited union organizing. Magistrates refused to intervene to stop blacklisting by manufacturers while the Worsted Inspectors used their powers to prosecute for
neglect of work to attack trade unionism and strikes.[174] These laws
applied to all sectors of the mills and overlookers, managers, warp
dressers and wool sorters all found themselves subject to criminal
prosecution in this era.[175]

TRADE UNIONISM IN THE WORSTED INDUSTRY

Before the advent of the general unions in the 1880s and 1890s, a mass
of non-union weaving and spinning operatives coexisted with small
craft unions in the worsted industry. Trade unionism in the major
branches of the trade, spinning and weaving, confined itself to skilled
male operatives such as warp twisters and dressers.[176] In all the other
major processes but combing, a fairly substantial stratum of skilled
workers exerted varying amounts of control over their work. Trade
unions defined their primary function as the defense of the position of
skilled workers and the provision of a safety net of benefits for sickness
and unemployment.

The greater security and higher wages enjoyed by skilled male
workers in the mid-Victorian period transformed the position of
unions, both within and outside the worsted industry. Prosperity
created new opportunities for union organizing in a variety of trades
and new unions formed in dyeing, warp dressing and wool combing.[177]
Even unorganized workers achieved pay increases despite a reduction
in hours. This took place amid a general upsurge in union activity
among all trades, particularly engineering and construction.[178] These
gains failed to ensure the position of skilled workers in the worsted
trade, as the collapse of the industry in the mid-1870s produced serious
problems of unemployment, speed-up and loss of control over work.
Skilled workers tried to fight back through their trade societies to slow
the impact of the depression, but the existence of a pool of workers
ready to replace skilled workers if possible and the general inability to
mobilize the majority of operatives in the industry hampered these
efforts.

The dyers' union offers a good example of the fate of trade unions in
the worsted industry in this era. The earliest recorded trade union
action among dyers, a general strike in the trade in September 1866,
succeeded in gaining a 2s. increase for a sixty hour week. In the wake of

the strike, a protective society sprang up, which enrolled up to 700 members in two branches before its dissolution in 1870.[179] The boom of the early 1870s permitted more aggressive union activity. A new union, set up in 1871, won a 10 per cent reduction in hours at the same wage rate.[180] However, the collapse of the trade later in the decade brought a worsening of conditions and an effort by employers to lengthen the work week. The union disbanded in 1877 and remained inactive until 1878. Following its failure to prevent a return to the sixty hour week in 1879, union membership fell to 79 men.

The turning point for the dyers' union came in 1880, when it conducted a successful mass strike in the Bradford trade and reestablished the fifty-six hour week. The union began the strike with less than 100 members and faced a federation of employers determined to starve out the strikers. The dyers mobilized the entire workforce of the town's dye works, bringing thousands of strikers to daily meetings. They organized roving pickets that shut down working plants through sheer force of numbers and defied police attempts to break the strike.[181] Despite this victory and the establishment of the union on a permanent basis over the next five years, the situation remained bleak. The difficulties of the worsted industry trade led to greater casualization of the trade.[182] The dyers suffered from irregular hours, lower wages (a 30 per cent nominal decline between the 1870s and 1890s) and the victimization of union men, a situation aggravated by the general labor surplus.[183]

Like the dyers, the woolsorters' control over work eroded in the 1870s. The depression in the staple trade led to increased unemployment among woolsorters; from 1875 till 1881 the unemployment benefits paid out by the Woolsorters' Union exceeded contributions.[184] The expansion of the trade in tops, especially in the export sector, led to a proliferation of small commission combing shops. These shops often failed to follow the custom of the trade and hired any qualified workers, who could be found among the packers or unemployed sorters. These operatives suffered from irregular employment, alternating overtime with unemployment, and received payment by the piece (pounds sorted) rather than the day. The established society excluded these casualized sorters and they formed their own association. Like all the trade unions, the woolsorters complained of the victimization of union men by employers and the use of blacklisting against them.[185]

For unorganized workers, the strikes and unions that appeared proved brief and ephemeral, the product of particular, sharp grievances that galvanized workers, primarily wage reductions. Such wildcat actions come to our attention only when they became widespread enough to shut an entire mill or affected a major firm. For example, in July of 1876 1,200 weavers struck at Saltaire to protest a wage reduction.[186] At Manningham Mills in 1882, in an action that foreshadowed the great strike of 1890–1, hundreds of spinners, drawers and weavers went out over a wage reduction as well as poor working conditions.[187] Before the 1890s, these actions never created a permanent organizational base among weavers and spinners and often faced the hostility of male trade unionists thrown out of work by them.[188]

The failure of trade unions to organize the bulk of the operatives in the worsted industry weakened skilled unions and efforts to negotiate industry-wide agreements on wages, conditions or hours. Many observers cited the isolation of women and children from the rest of the work force and their pattern of early entry and exit from the industry to explain the low level of organization among these workers. Yet these patterns of work were the product of the industry's hierarchy, rather than the inherent nature of women's or children's labor. The cooperation of trade unions with management made it difficult for traditional unions to undertake the task of organizing the industry. Many unions responded to attempts by the semi-skilled to organize by reasserting the exclusiveness of their unions and cooperating with management to keep mills open.[189]

In the 1890s the impetus for organizing general unions came from outside the existing trade union structure. New unions, such as the General Union of Textile Workers, that targeted unorganized workers in weaving, spinning and other trades established themselves. Two factors played a role. One was the greater militancy of textile workers, who were predominantly female. The Manningham Mills strike of 1890–1 inaugurated an era of more aggressive action by female factory operatives. The strength and coherence of the strike showed the possibility for union action on the part of these workers, and laid to rest the myth of their passivity. The roots of this militancy lay in the general deterioration of wages and conditions in the trade since the 1870s, which affected these workers most.[190]

A new generation of leaders, often linked to the emerging socialist movement, most notably the Independent Labour Party, directed the drive for general unionism in the worsted trade. The ILP, founded in Bradford in 1893, embraced the task of organizing the worsted industry as part of its larger political strategy. Led by men like William Drew,

Tom Maguire and Fred Jowett, the ILP recognized the need to advance conditions for all operatives as a precondition for success in the West Riding. For the first time, male operatives began to cooperate with female operatives in organizing the work place.[191]

Despite this new effort, general unionism in the worsted industry achieved only modest success. By 1910, union members comprised 12,000 out of a total work force of 55,000 in Bradford, and in the West Riding as a whole only 10 per cent of the work force belonged to unions.[192] In part, this reflected the difficulties of union organizing in the entire industry. The weakness of the worsted trade made it difficult for unions to establish themselves. In occupations such as weaving and combing, the slowdown of trade created a labor surplus that made it easy for employers to break strikes and victimize union members.[193]

The limited gains of unions among semi-skilled operatives and female workers also reflected serious problems in leadership. The ILP and its associated unions remained ambivalent about the position of female operatives. The dominance of men in the leadership of these unions aggravated the problem. Although some women, such as Julia Varley, a weaver and suffragette, gained prominence, most women occupied secondary roles. The inability of men to understand the unique problems of women workers slowed the organizational efforts of the unions. The only solution most leaders could envisage to the problems created by the double duty of home and work for female operatives was the withdrawal of women from paid employment. As was the case with earlier unions, many in the new unions saw the best strategy as one that aimed to raise male wages and eliminated surplus labor by restricting the opportunities of women and children through legislative action. As a result, before the First World War, unions made only minor inroads among the mass of operatives in the worsted trade.[194]

THE PROBLEM OF LABOR IN MID-VICTORIAN BRADFORD

Skill, gender and ethnicity represented enduring divisions within the working class; divisions expressed to a large extent by differential opportunities for status and advancement. The exclusion of the Irish and women from skilled labor created both occupational and social hierarchies in Bradford's neighborhoods. These hierarchies can be seen, in part, in the gap between respectable and non-respectable workers. For the 'respectable' worker, there existed the chapel, the friendly society, the Mechanics' Institute, and political rights. For the 'rough' workers, the pub, street life and the common pursuits of leisure defined the world outside of work. Gender roles played a large part in this division, for, increasingly, 'respectable' workers asserted their status by insisting that their wives and daughters stay at home and by arguing for a family wage.[195] Similarly, ethnicity contributed to this pattern through the labeling of the Irish as 'rough' and their neighborhoods as slums.

The means used to control labor generated discontent, while the division of the work force by skill, sex and age inhibited collective action to resolve grievances or bring fundamental change. Although operatives shared similar complaints about the factory and the difficulties of work, the privileged position of the skilled workers, and more importantly, the supervisory role of the largest stratum of skilled workers, the overlookers, undermined this common ground. The higher status of skilled workers was in many ways premised on the existence of a mass of poorly paid, low-skill operatives. This meant that gains could not be distributed equally nor could a common strategy for all operatives be easily formulated. Cooperation in areas such as political rights or the limitation of hours could be achieved, but not concerted trade union action or efforts to raise the general wage rate. This fact, coupled with the need for overlookers to enforce labor discipline and the prerogatives of the owners, cut against the attempts of both skilled workers and the bourgeoisie to put forth the upper layer of the working class as the leaders of their class.

At the same time, the continued conflicts between the interests of skilled workers and their employers prevented their easy integration into mid-Victorian society. Manufacturers stood ready to give some workers higher wages and limited authority, but they wished to limit that authority as much as possible. The argument that the upper stratum of the working class filled a key place in the social and economic order cut against the financial and social imperatives of the worsted trade. The trend in the mid-Victorian era was to limit and undermine workers' prerogatives in order to ensure the lowest possible cost of production. Casualization and mechanization both worked to increase the choices open to capitalists, while increasing the discontent of skilled workers with the status quo.[196]

3 Politics in Bradford 1850–1900

In 1853, the Reverend Jonathan Glyde, a prominent Nonconformist minister, expressed what many consider to be the essence of mid-Victorian Liberalism,

> Political reforms must move forward, and although men may cease to expect direct accessions of happpiness and comfort, from the possession of either political or municipal franchises, the principles of equity and freedom must be fully embodied in our institutions.[1]

Spoken only five years after the failure of the last Chartist uprising in Bradford, these words seem a world away from the crisis ridden days of the 1840s. In a remarkably brief time calm had returned to political and social life. A flexible and progressive brand of Liberalism confronted the challenges of the age with great self-confidence and its belief in political reform, laissez-faire and self-help formed the basis of a consensus among the elite and members of the working class. Crucial to this consensus was the assertion by Liberals that they represented the interests of the broader community in the fight for liberty and reform.

This heroic image of the role of Liberalism grew out of the political and economic changes of the previous two decades. The Liberals offered a view of the world in which improvement and reform were possible, in contrast to the more arid and stagnant paternalism of the Tories. The image of Liberals as defenders of the people against 'the cliques of men who have tyrannized equally over them,' gave them a powerful tool to attract working-class support in the mid-Victorian era. As late as 1905, Alfred Illingworth, the embodiment of Bradford Liberalism, could call on working men, even those among the Independent Labour Party, to unite against the aristocratic threat to liberty and good government.[2]

In recent years, historians have sought to understand the relationship between the Liberal party and its working-class supporters and why that relationship frayed in the early twentieth century. Scholars like Patrick Joyce and Eugenio Biagini argue that the ability of Liberals to speak to the concerns of working men about equality and liberty cemented the electoral basis of popular Liberalism. Whether under the title of populism or Radicalism, this ideology called for a democratic society in which everyone enjoyed civic and legal equality and independence from state interference. These beliefs motivated the great campaigns of the mid-Victorian era in favor of church disestablishment, tax reform, the legalization of trade unions and the extension of the suffrage.[3]

The strength of popular Radicalism lay in its relationship to community. As a citadel of advanced Liberalism, Bradford offers us a picture of the strengths and weaknesses of Radicalism at the local level.[4] Radicals dominated the local party structure and even before the 1850s established links with working men to strive for political reform. The shared heritage of Chartism and Radicalism made it possible for these links to grow throughout the mid-Victorian period and for the Liberal party in Bradford to recreate itself as a mass political party. The language of politics also helped construct community by giving weight to certain values and institutions. The centrality of independence, the ability of working men to speak and act for themselves, privileged skilled working men, who possessed the income and education to participate in public life. In order to assert their fitness to participate in public life, working men cultivated an image of sobriety and reason, or respectability. The needs of respectability dictated a certain style of behavior in voluntary associations and forms of consumerism centered around the home, perhaps best symbolized by the front parlour piano and lace curtains.[5]

While popular Radicalism rested on a belief in shared interests within a community, it also defined that community through a process of exclusion as well as inclusion. The unskilled and poor remained outside the bounds of popular Radicalism, excluded from the franchise and from the voluntary associations that dominated the public life of the working class. Of equal importance was the definition of gender through the process of political exclusion. Gender subordination was critical to the stability of the mid-Victorian era. The political rhetoric of popular Radicalism portrayed men as representatives of their families within the community. The dependency of women in the political arena flowed from their economic dependency, which limited their independence. Women's dependency allowed them to create the proper domestic life that reinforced the claims of working men to independence and respectability.

The challenges of the 1870s began to unravel this consensus by opening new divisions among the elite and convincing some members of the working class that the community posited by popular Liberalism no longer functioned. While some historians argue for a continuity between Radicalism and the Independent Labour Party, there were discontinuities as well.[6] A growing awareness of class permeated the social and political life of late nineteenth-century Bradford. Liberalism, as both a cultural and political force, found itself on the defensive, as the universal assumptions of the mid-century disintegrated in the face of economic and political change. The slow death of free trade, the erosion of voluntarism and the challenges posed by a revived Conservative party and an independent labor movement removed the signposts of earlier years.

THE EMERGENCE OF LIBERALISM

In the early nineteenth century, political and social power in Bradford rested in the hands of a small group of local gentry and merchant–manufacturers. They exercised power through a variety of offices, many of which dated back to the Middle Ages. This group included local manufacturers such as the Woods, but it tended to have a land owning and aristocratic ethos and remained closely tied to the Church of England.[7] The emergence of a new class of merchants and manufacturers challenged this older elite. Liberal in politics and Nonconformist in religion, these new men wished to impress their own values and beliefs upon the city. In the 1830s and 1840s, these men displaced the older Tory elite who controlled the institutions of local government and the social life of the West Riding.

The struggle to reform local government provided the central battleground for Liberals and Conservatives before 1850. Local government rested in a variety of institutions. The JPs and the manorial courts controlled the administration of justice and distributed poor relief, while the local parish vestry oversaw the election of church wardens, constables and highway surveyors. The Improvement Commission, set up by an Act of Parliament, was the most important local body. Its fifty-eight members were responsible for the cleaning, lighting, patrolling and clearing of the town's streets. The commission's jurisdiction extended to only a small portion of the future borough and the indifference of the commissioners, selected by cooption, further circumscribed its effectiveness.

Tories and Liberals agreed on the need to deal with the massive social and environmental problems brought by industrialization, but disagreed over the means. Tories favored a continuation of the traditional institutions that exercised power, but with more central coordination. The Liberals stood for a restructuring of local government through the creation of an incorporated borough out of the four distinct townships of Bradford, Bowling, Horton and Manningham, with expanded powers to deal with building, pollution and sanitary improvements.[8] Both parties defined this disagreement in ideological terms. For the Tories, their cause represented a defense of the rights of property and established institutions against the selfish attacks of monied upstarts. The Liberals saw their fight to extend the franchise and reform local government as part of a larger struggle to free society from aristocratic privilege and to open up a new period of prosperity and individual freedom.[9] Each freely accused the other of corruption and self-interest, particularly when it involved efforts to attract working-class support.[10]

The conflict over local government merged with the other political battles of the era. The anti-Poor Law movement, the Factory Agitation and Chartism all found wide popular support in Bradford. Both Liberals and Tories sought to gain the backing of working men by supporting movements for reform. The Operative Conservative Society, founded in 1837 by Matthew Balme and supported by wealthy conservatives, tried to enlist working men to assist Tory candidates. It had over 300 members and was widely credited with helping the Tories succeed in the parliamentary election of 1841.[11] The Tories wanted to establish an alliance with working-class organizations on the basis of a modernized paternalism, one that accommodated the realities of the industrial age. In general, they offered legislative amelioration in exchange for obedience and respect for authority and property. Thus, conservatives supported the efforts of the lower class to overturn the Poor Law in the 1830s, even when such efforts led to disorder. In conjunction with Tories like William Walker and Richard Oastler, working men and women in Bradford set up Short-Time Committees to agitate for regulation of the hours and conditions of factory labor.[12]

The Liberals also sought an alliance with workers, but on different grounds. They presented a vision of the world in which unfettered economic activity combined with individual self-help would produce an era of social harmony and prosperity hitherto unknown. Through organizations such as the Reform Society and the Liberal Party, they offered 'responsible' working men a share of power by expanding the suffrage and bringing them into a more broadly-based local government. They succeeded in splitting the Bradford Political Union by attracting moderate Chartists to the United Reform Club in the early 1840s.[13] They also proved willing to compromise on issues of importance to working-class men and women. The force of opposition to the New Poor Law led the Board of Guardians to soften its implementation and it offered outdoor relief, often in violation of government orders, in times of economic depression.[14]

The twenty five years following the defeat of Chartism represented a period of stabilization in Bradford. The success of incorporation, the final defeat of the Chartists and the return of prosperity marked the end of an era in Bradford's political and social development. The Liberals' belief in laissez-faire, local government and self-help set the tone for the new era. The growth of the municipal franchise before 1860 to over 15,000 (almost five times the parliamentary franchise) meant that many working men possessed the vote. These new voters stood behind the Liberals after a brief flurry of Chartist candidates in the early 1850s.[15] From the beginning, the Liberals dominated the central elective body in Bradford, the city council. Of the first 158 councillors elected between 1847 and 1860, 108 were Liberals. The party also controlled the selection of the city's aldermen, the mayor and the borough magistrates.[16]

A formidable political organization lay behind this dominance. The Liberal party in Bradford organized an electoral machinery in the 1830s to carry on its struggles with the Tories for the control of local government.[17] In the 1850s, the Liberal Electoral Association still dominated the local political scene, nominating candidates and canvassing voters. Along with the Electoral Association, various special interest groups, most notably the Liberation Society, a Nonconformist pressure group, participated in electoral work. The heating up of the suffrage issue in the mid-1860s led to a reorganization of Bradford's political life. Building upon the work of the Reform Union, the Liberals established a permanent party organization. Clubs, set up in each ward of the city, handled electoral matters and a central group, the caucus, ran the party. This organization provided the basis for the continued supremacy of the Liberal party in the wake of the new franchise in 1867.[18]

Business groups like the Bradford Chamber of Commerce fulfilled a quasi-political role. Founded in 1851, and run by the most important manufacturers and merchants in the worsted trade, the Chamber styled itself as the voice of the business community in Bradford. It helped organize the business community in political affairs and led the way on issues such as tariff reform, railway and postal services and the Factory Acts.[19] In the late 1860s, the Chamber began to play a part in labor relations, attempting to set itself up as an arbitrator, a role it already filled for disputes between firms.[20]

As in most mid-Victorian cities, power rested in a mixture of private and public bodies that linked the elite together socially and politically. In Bradford, the textile trade and the Nonconformist chapels formed the base of the Liberal party leadership. The Horton Lane Congregational Chapel supplied five of the first eight mayors of Bradford. This sectarian influence overlapped with that of the textile trade. The mayoralty and aldermanic positions were, in the words of one historian, 'the virtual preserve of the textile trade'.[21] Of the first seven mayors of Bradford, six came from the textile trade. Men such as Alfred Illingworth, a prominent merchant and son-in-law of the inventor of the combing machine, and William Forster, a Quaker manufacturer and MP, controlled the Liberal party into the early twentieth century.

Local journals and newspapers, the most prominent of which was the *Bradford Observer*, tied together the ideas and actions of the elite. Founded by William Byles in 1834, the *Observer* served as the organ of Liberalism throughout its existence and provided a forum for discussions on the leading social and political topics of the day.[22] In the mid-Victorian period, a number of local newspapers such as the *Bradford Review*, a Radical paper, and the *Telegraph*, which supported the Conservatives, challenged the monopoly of the *Observer* in local journalism and a range of specialized publications in trade and religious matters supplemented the reading materials of the elite.[23]

The Liberal party in Bradford, as elsewhere in England, contained a mix of different interests.[24] Moderate Whigs, hard-line Nonconformists, manufacturers and a significant working-class element cohabited in the mid-Victorian party. This mixture of interests held down the strong Radical element in the party prior to 1867. Although Bradford remained a stronghold of advanced Liberalism throughout the nineteenth century, its parliamentary representatives did not reflect that position. The Liberals rarely nominated too advanced Liberals, seeking instead to balance their ticket to include all strands of Liberal thought. In the late 1860s, Edward Miall, the disestablishment Radical, and William Forster, the mainstream Liberal, served together in Parliament. The Conservatives, although active in both local and parliamentary politics, formed a permanent opposition in this period. They accepted the strength of Liberal influence and nominated moderate Liberals such as Henry Ripley or M. W. Thompson in order to frustrate the Radicals.[25] Only a few Tories, such as John Rand or William Walker, sons of Anglican families of long standing, broke through this monopoly and served in city government.

Religion provided one of the central dividing lines in mid-Victorian politics.[26] In this period, religion often functioned as the continuation of politics by other means.[27] In the 1830s and 1840s, the struggle between Liberals and Conservatives often involved religious issues. Nonconformists attacked the traditional role of the Church of England as a supporter of the local Tory elite and as a corrupt established religion.[28] To weaken the Church, Bradford Liberals refused to pay the rates levied to support the local vestry. Despite the arrest of several prominent Liberals in the early 1840s, including Titus Salt, the Anglicans were forced to rely on voluntary payments to support the Church.[29]

The struggle left a heritage of sectarian conflict and religion remained an important rallying point for political disagreement. After 1850, the substance of the church–chapel conflict focused on the rights and privileges of the Established Church in Britain and Ireland. The Nonconformists saw the Church as one of the last great bastions of aristocratic privilege and corruption and thus as an obstacle to the creation of a truly liberal society based on merit and free association. In the words of one minister, 'they sought nothing which they were not prepared to give to the whole human race, namely, to be left free from state patronage and state interference and control.'[30]

For their part, the supporters of the Church of England attempted to portray the Nonconformists, particularly the members of the Liberation Society, as radicals bent on destroying the venerable institutions of England and undermining the Constitution.[31] They argued that the Nonconformists wished to establish a republic and pointed to the problems of the United States, Italy and France as reasons for maintaining the Church.[32] The defenders of the Church made clear their attitude toward attempts to strip the Church of its endowments and privileges. To do so would be 'to commence a revolution in sacrilege and end it most appropriately in communism'.[33] They reminded the Liberals that

when the tenure of property is concerned; the question of justice or injustice depends upon the title, and has nothing whatever to do with numbers . . . In Bradford there are a considerable number of gentlemen who have amassed large fortunes, and a very much greater number who have very little ones. Is it true because Jones or Brown has a very large property and a very large number of persons have nothing, that there is any injustice?[34]

This concern for property rights anchored a world view which rejected democracy as an organizing principle of politics. For Anglicans, there had to be 'fixed institutions, . . . order, subordination, and established faith'.[35]

This point of view appealed to moderate Liberals and others leary of the excesses of the Liberation Society and the Society increasingly found itself in the minority. In the 1860s and 1870s a series of bitter internecine struggles to elect Edward Miall and Alfred Illingworth to Parliament divided the Liberal Party. These struggles set the Liberation Society against both the senior member for Bradford, William Forster, and those manufacturers already drifting toward Toryism such as Samuel Lister and Henry Ripley.[36]

The fissures within the Liberal Party widened in the 1880s. The threat of foreign competition and lower profits brought by the depression of the 1870s called the Liberal consensus into question. The erection of new tariff barriers by Germany, France and the United States convinced some in the worsted trade that the era of free trade was over and that Great Britain had to respond in kind. Under the banner of Fair Trade or Reciprocity, the new protectionists brought their case to the public and in August 1881 they formed a Bradford branch of the Fair Trade Association.[37]

The issue of fair trade proved divisive among Bradford's elite. For fifty years, free trade had been an article of faith with the worsted manufacturers and Liberals. Jacob Behrens, a local merchant, served as a member of Cobden's delegation that negotiated the free trade treaty with France in 1860. The Chamber of Commerce and the business community paid regular homage to free trade's benefits for everyone in the city. The defense of free trade involved more than just tariff policy, for it symbolized the integral values of Liberalism – independence and self-help. In the words of one writer

Protection would stifle mechanical and inventive genius; it would encourage the industrial classes to be perpetually looking to the State for assistance and it would destroy that manly independence which is the birthright of every Englishman, and whose development has been largely due to the fact of every man, every class of man, every town, every trade, has been accustomed to help [itself] instead of being helped by the State.[38]

The Fair Traders' proposals struck at the heart of the Liberal coalition and they hoped to use the issue of tariffs as part of a larger political strategy to realign party politics and gain a mass base for the Conservatives. The Fair Traders called for a new relationship between the individual and the state and the expansion of state power to safeguard England's future.[39] W. Farrar Ecroyd, a worsted spinner and politician, put forth the populist argument for 'fair trade' in a series of letters and speeches in the late 1870s. Ecroyd argued that the new tariffs passed by foreign nations had destroyed free trade and England could no longer act as if it existed. He called for equalized tariffs with other countries in order to maintain price levels. At the same time, imports of food should be subject to tax in order to protect home agriculture and allow Britain to be self-sufficient in food production. Rather than relying upon lower wages and prices, workers and manufacturers should seek to stabilize employment and prices and pay the higher cost of food such a policy entailed.[40]

The protectionists saw the Empire as a neglected asset that could be mobilized by Britain in her competition with the rest of the world. The government should encourage and protect trade with the colonies in order to create a market for British goods and an assured supply of raw materials and food at reasonable prices, instead of treating the colonies on an equal basis with the rest of the world, as in a free trade policy. This policy would enhance national independence and strength in the face of a hostile world:

> If this great question should ever be taken into the domain of party politics, it would be because the benefits he had been endeavoring to describe could only be realized for the working classes of the country, by that Conservative policy which regarded the whole Empire as one, which would bind Great Britain to all her colonies as closely as the States of the American Union were bound to one another, which would give us the same confidence in our resources, and the same power to be independent, if it pleased the rest of the world to treat us badly.[41]

This twin appeal to patriotism and self-interest was the core of the Fair Trade message to working men. Working men and manufacturers

had to band together, however, to realize these benefits. According to
S.C. Lister, a wealthy manufacturer of velvet and silks, it was
impossible to 'protect the labourer without protecting the product of
that labourer'.[42] Lister argued that laws governing conditions and
hours of labor constituted a form of protectionism that cost him and
other manufacturers thousands of pounds per year, therefore they had
a right to call for additional protection for their enterprises. Without
such measures, lower wages and longer hours would be necessary. He
contended 'that foreign competition means low wages, long hours, and
great distress and misery to the British workman'.[43] There would be
some suffering, but the worker would benefit more from full employment than low food prices. Lister, for one, saw no alternative to this
program,

> The Radical Organization will lead them [the workers] in another
> direction entirely. They will clamour for land and strike at property;
> you will see your works in flames, and Broughton Hall inhabited by
> communistic workers, before the working classes join to support you
> of their own accord. You must educate them up to it through their
> own delegates.[44]

Charges and countercharges flew as a result of the rise of protectionist sentiment. In 1877, Henry Mitchell, a prominent merchant and
an early supporter of protection, attacked Behrens and others in the
Chamber of Commerce for failing to press the French for equal tariffs.
He argued that foreign merchants such as Behrens had different
interests than manufacturers and therefore could not be trusted.[45]
The free traders, on the other hand, accused the protectionists of
pursuing their own narrow interests at the expense of the larger
community. Andrew Byles, the son of the *Observer* editor, attacked
the protectionists as self-interested men, seeking to aid the rich at the
expense of the poor.[46] He leveled this charge directly at Lister, whom
he accused of seeking relief for the silk industry regardless of its impact
on the worsted trade.[47]

The debate over free trade benefited the Conservatives in two ways,
despite their failure to revise the tariff policy of Great Britain.
Although working-class organizations showed little interest in supporting proposals to raise the price of food in the midst of a downturn in
trade, the Conservatives used the issue of fair trade as part of a larger
political strategy.[48] The Tories formulated a strategy based on an
appeal to nationalism, imperialism, and concern about unemployment
that gave them the potential for a mass base among the working

class.[49] The success of the Conservative campaign can be measured by their ability to gain control of the Bradford Borough Council in the late 1890s.[50]

At the same time, the fight over fair trade drove a wedge in the Liberal party between some businessmen and conventional Liberals. The call for protection divided the elite of Bradford, though not into equal camps. The Fair Traders themselves split between those calling for outright protectionism and those who believed in reciprocity.[51] Institutions such as the Chamber of Commerce and the *Bradford Observer* remained firmly committed to free trade. The continued difficulties of the worsted trade, however, eroded this support for free trade. By 1904, the Bradford Chamber of Commerce voted for a series of proposals calling for retaliatory tariffs.[52] This was the beginning of the identification of the Conservatives with business interests that was to become a staple of twentieth-century politics.

THE CHALLENGE OF WORKING-CLASS POLITICS

The growing challenge of independent labor politics compounded the difficulties of the Liberal party. Through conflicts with the established Liberal hierarchy, a fledgling labor movement began to form in the 1880s with its own priorities and ideas. This marked a crucial step away from the system of political patronage that had dominated Bradford politics since the late 1840s. The reemergence of independent labor politics harked back to the working-class radicalism of the first half of the nineteenth century, with its combination of political and industrial strife. The transformation of the worsted industry in the early nineteenth century generated a number of responses from workers. Luddism flourished in the West Riding. In the most famous incident in Bradford, a crowd attacked Horsfall's Mill in 1826 in an attempt to destroy newly introduced power looms.[53] The great combers' strike of 1825, an effort to slow down the pace of mechanization of the trade, paralyzed the trade for weeks before collapsing.[54]

The leaders of the strike, men like Peter Bussey, carried the struggle into other arenas. Bradford was a center for both the Factory Agitation and the anti-Poor Law campaign. Working people, supported by paternalist Tories, tried to prevent the seating of the new Board of Guardians in 1837. The first attempt to do so provoked a riot and the final installation of the Board could only be accomplished when a complement of soldiers escorted the Guardians. Many in

Bradford saw the new Board as the embodiment of Liberal insensitivity to the plight of the poor and a threat to the family in its insistence on the use of segregated workhouses.[55]

The heating up of the question of political reform in the late 1820s led to the appearance of groups such as the Bradford Political Union. In the wake of the passage of the Reform Bill, many in Bradford turned to Chartism and from the late 1830s onward, the city became a center of Chartist activity. The Chartists, organized in the Bradford Northern Union, attracted far greater support than the traditional parties. The Chartists drew in excess of 50,000 people to demonstrations and thousands to quasi-military organizations. The most popular leaders, such as George White and Peter Bussey, refused to ally themselves with a single party and attempted to play them against one another.[56] Bradford officials felt so exposed that they requested (and received) the permanent stationing of troops in Bradford Low Moor after 1841.[57] The presence of soldiers failed to deter the Chartists, for in both 1842 and 1848, thousands participated in military drills, riots and processions in defiance of the local authorities. Chartism culminated in two attempted uprisings in 1840 and 1848, which had to be suppressed by military force.[58]

Although this is not the place to undertake a complete examination of Chartism as a political and social movement, many of the issues emphasized by historians of the movement are relevant to an understanding of its local history. Bradford Chartism mobilized an impressive display of support from a varied local population. Traditional craftsmen, hand workers, factory operatives and petty shopkeepers all mingled in Bradford's inner districts. No single set of demands, beyond the call for relief or a push for a wider suffrage, united these groups. As Gareth Stedman Jones has pointed out, the Chartists and their allies lacked a coherent critique of capitalism and a blueprint for a new society. Radicalism focused on the political causes of discontent, the monopolization of power by a small group, rather than the social causes of discontent, the actions of capitalists. The main supporters of radicalism, the hand weavers and combers, represented a dying element in society. Their poverty produced rage and protest, but they disappeared in the next ten years.[59]

Many workers, particularly the new supervisory workers in the mills and well-to-do craftsmen, believed that peaceful accommodation remained possible. As property owners they shared the elite's concern with social disorder and crime and some cooperated with the town's manufacturers to blunt Chartism. In the attack upon Horsfall's Mill, the overlookers and woolsorters defended the mill, as they would in the 1840s during Chartist disturbances. Skilled workers also joined the special constables at the height of the Chartist troubles.[60]

The disunity of working-class politics represented one reason for the failure of Chartism. Another reason lay in the effect such militancy had upon the contentious elites in Bradford. The Tories and Liberals fought one another with a great deal of venom and bad feeling, yet they never split over basic issues. In the face of a challenge to law and order or property, the two factions cooperated to preserve their positions. They served together as special constables, organized relief for the destitute, and endorsed the use of the military when all other options failed. The Tories never contemplated allowing working men to dominate the Factory Movement, nor did Liberals endorse the idea of working-class control over political life, even if universal manhood suffrage became a reality. The threat of a Chartist rebellion, real enough in the 1840s, persuaded the two parties to set aside their differences.[61]

This coming together can be seen in the success of the drive for incorporation. Initial attempts to create a new borough floundered on the resistance of the three smaller townships to the dominance of Bradford, the concerns of small shopkeepers about increased rates and the desire of Tories to maintain the status quo. At first, the Tories combined with the Chartists, who feared the creation of an efficient police force, to block the first petition of incorporation in 1846.[62] This opposition concealed the fact that many Tories, particularly those in the central area of the borough where crime and pollution were most evident, supported Liberal efforts to incorporate. The pitiful performance of the constables in the face of Chartists and the revelation of the horrific conditions of life faced by the majority of the population in the course of the agitations of the 1840s eroded the opposition of many to the Liberal scheme. The second petition of incorporation in 1847 was not opposed in a concerted fashion by the Tories, and many joined with the Liberals in signing the new petition.[63]

The willingness of Bradford's local elite to accommodate at least some of the demands of local working-class radicals helped undermine the picture of an intransigent, self-interested clique advanced by Chartists and others. The mostly middle-class United Reform Club endorsed the idea of an expanded suffrage in the 1840s.[64] Middle-class Radicals also criticized the behavior of the army in its actions against local Chartists as an attack upon the liberty of the English people. This embrace of reform included the Ten-Hours Bill of 1847, which

Bradford manufacturers accepted, although without great enthusiasm.[65] The success of the Ten-Hours Act also consolidated gendered notions of politics shared by working-class men and the advanced wing of the Liberal party. Working men in Bradford gained the right to speak for their larger community in the process of incorporation. This included the belief that women should not be included in any extension of the suffrage. The masculine nature of politics constituted another area of broad agreement between middle-class and working-class men.[66]

After the decline of Chartism in the late 1840s, independent working-class politics suffered a long hiatus, despite the efforts of some former Chartists to keep their program alive.[67] In the late 1850s, the agitation for a Second Reform Bill revived political organization among working men. The Reform Union, a primarily middle-class group, and the Reform League, a working-class organization, cooperated in the agitation for a Reform Bill, with the Union supplying the money and the League the manpower. The passage of the Reform Bill in 1867 transformed the political scene in Bradford. The number of voters tripled and working men constituted about 75 per cent of the post-Reform electorate.[68] About 50–60 per cent of all working men (about 19,000 of 34,000 in 1871) gained the vote and the electorate reached 27,000 by 1880.[69]

After 1867, both established parties stepped up efforts to attract working-class votes. The Tories formed a Church Defence Association and attempted to reestablish the Workingman's Conservative Association to build support for their position.[70] Church of England supporters pointed to the provision of charity and education to the poor as proof of the Church's and Conservatives' commitment to working men. The Bradford Conservative Association, set up to counter the operation of the Liberal Electoral Society, flourished at first, but collapsed in the mid-1870s as support from working men dried up.[71] In addition, a Bradford section of the Volunteers formed in 1859, primarily through the impetus of Bradford Tories concerned about the threat of French power. Shunned by Liberal manufacturers, it attracted some working-class members, many of whom were probably attracted by the prospect of earning a 30s. capitation grant.[72]

The Liberals built their own political machine, but they hoped that their support for reform would bind working men to the party. Liberals invoked the struggle for liberty and equality as the foundation of their association with working men. S. C. Kell, a local Radical, reminded the working class of the Liberals' support for political reform in an attempt to cement political loyalties.[73] The common Radicalism of many Liberals and working men made this appeal more attractive. Men like John Mitchell, a political activist and merchant, shared the local enthusiasm for working-class heroes like Garibaldi and Kossuth, who visited the town, and sympathized with the snub given Palmerston on his 1864 visit to the city.[74] Edward Miall, an MP for Bradford from 1869 to 1874, had supported the Charter during his stand for office in 1845.[75] Men like this could call upon a reservoir of sympathy among many working-class voters for their past actions and present beliefs. Radicalism also built upon the identities of skilled working men as the representatives of their class. While this meant that they stood in for the poor and unskilled, it also implied that married men represented their families, especially their wives. This in turn rested on the assertion of masculine authority and privilege within working-class culture that informed trade unions and voluntary associations. The vote constituted one more affirmation of this authority within the family and the community.[76]

If working men accepted the tutelage of the middle-class leaders of the party, then reform would continue and the suffrage would expand. As Alfred Illingworth argued in 1880,

It is probable that the next generation or the next but one, will see a larger influx of working men in the nation's council to guide our posterity just as the political middle class, the outcome of the Reform Act of 1832, is guiding us at present.[77]

In the meantime, with the assistance of working men, the Liberals would achieve their agenda. As one local politician argued in a letter in September of 1866,

Whether or not you agree with the extent of the Suffrage generally sought by the Working Classes, is not a point to differ about, as it is not likely to be made the basis of a Reform Bill by the leaders of the Liberal Party in Parliament . . . They [the workers who do receive the vote] will assist in securing us those measures necessary to peace, retrenchment and religious equality, which have been so long obstructed by the unpopular side of the House of Commons.[78]

The Liberals believed that the issues of concern to them, such as retrenchment or the position of the Irish Church, would continue to attract support. For many working men, attacks on the Established Church and state expenditure formed part of a larger struggle for equality. As George Potter argued in a speech in 1871,

The Church had been in the hands of an oligarchy, which oligarchy had endeavored to suppress the rights of the people of the country. In the struggle for the abolition of the Corn Laws, in their endeavor to obtain the franchise, and in the endeavor to obtain secular education in the schools, the clergy had been against them.[79]

This rhetoric recalled the days of political struggle in the 1830s. Yet, by the mid-Victorian era, the Liberals found themselves in the unfamilar position of being part of the establishment. The fading of opportunities for social advancement within the worsted trade, the increasing withdrawal of wealthy second-generation entrepreneurs from the city and the trade and the aging of a generation of Liberal leaders all undermined the message of equality.

The fading of the egalitarian ideal can be traced in the language of the Nonconformist churches. No one would be surprised at Edward Dibb, an Anglican, attacking 'the erroneous idea that equality is a thing intended for mankind, or at all attainable by him'.[80] However, when James Campbell, addressing the Horton Lane Chapel, spoke of the 'fraternity of society – a fraternity which is not equality, and which is most beautiful in the absence of equality', he brought into question the commitment of the Nonconformists to the struggle for equal rights for the working class.[81]

The reform impulse within Liberalism often collided with self-interest. The Liberals of Bradford supported reform in Parliament, but never allowed these initiatives to impinge on their own special interests. This limit to reform can be seen in local government. The borough of Bradford had been created in order to give the local government the power to deal with the social and environmental problems of industrialization. Once in place, the council, using the powers granted to it by the central government, set up a series of committees to oversee building, sanitation, the borough police and various other aspects of local government. In the first decade of the corporation's existence, the borough municipalized the water supply, passed new building and sanitary bye-laws and reformed the police. The council passed some reform measures, most notably a series of building bye-laws that forbade the notorious back-to-back houses.[82]

The borough government failed to make full use of those powers. A Local Government Board inspector cited Bradford as one of the worst regulated cities in England in 1872, noting its failure to collect proper statistics, enforce the Lodging Acts, or ensure compliance with the Public Health Act. The council failed to create a Medical Officer of

Health until compelled to do so in the 1870s.[83] The conflict between public and private interest that reappeared throughout the mid-Victorian era limited the drive for reform. Attempts to control pollution of the air and water floundered on the refusal of mill owners to incur the costs necessary to prevent such pollution and the inability of the council to force them to respect the bye-laws.[84] The bye-laws restricting the construction of back-to-back houses passed in the 1860s remained a dead letter and such houses continued to go up in the 1880s.[85]

Many in Bradford questioned the motives for local government actions. A significant faction, both within the council and the city, remained strenuously opposed to the expansion of municipal responsibilities and the increase in rates this implied. Linked primarily with the shopkeeper interest, this faction could not control the council, but it could frustrate council efforts and make life extremely unpleasant.[86] Working-class voters, who bore a heavy burden of rates, often shared these objections.[87] One area of complaint concerned the expansion of the police force. The Bradford police force, reformed in the late 1840s, expanded from 72 constables, officers and clerks in 1847 to 240 men in 1882.[88] The police absorbed a large portion of local expenditure. Of the £21,480 the Sanitary Committte spent in 1851, £5000 went for the police.[89] The attack upon popular pastimes like gambling, the use of police during strikes and their cooperation in the enforcement of the Worsted Acts made the police unpopular with many working-class voters.[90]

As the governing party, the Liberals bore the brunt of discontent about local government. They also faced criticism for corruption and political misconduct. Many involved in Bradford city government used their offices for personal gain and glorification, and charges of personal profit from office were a stable of local elections.[91] The municipalization of the water supply produced a large profit for its politically well-connected owners and an inadequate supply of water for the city.[92] The use of pressure by employers, while difficult to quantify, was not unknown in Bradford. Commentators accused major employers like Henry Ripley, the dyer and John Hardy, the Tory iron master, of using their power to force their employees and local shopkeepers to support them. Ripley, a newly minted Conservative, was stripped of his electoral victory in 1874 for treating and other corrupt practices. Even William Forster, a model Liberal and a supporter of the secret ballot, stood accused of undue pressure on working men in 1868 and 1874.[93]

INFORMATION RESOURCE SERVICES
UNIVERSITY OF WESTMINSTER
HARROW IRS CENTRE
WATFORD ROAD

Many working-class voters chafed under the sectarian focus of Bradford Liberalism and they wished to see questions of concern to them addressed by the party. G. Dalton, a mason, expressed the growing discontent of politically active working men at a trade union rally in 1873.

> They [working men] had privileges to obtain, wrongs to redress which would cost them many a hard fight yet. Like other speakers, however, he could see no hope until they sent their own men to Parliament - the men whose hands were hard with labour and who knew their wants - and paid them while there. Let them be jealous of the local charitable gentlemen, who, while they gave them dinners and trips, robbed them of their independence. No trades unionist must be bamboozled by such means; they at any rate must not be the Essus of politics. Working-class questions were constantly shelved or talked out of the House, while minor questions, or those affecting the privileges and emoluments of the upper classes were pushed to the front and it was in these things that they wanted justice done to them.[94]

This demand for a different agenda for the Liberal party overlapped with a desire to gain greater access to the leadership of the party and to bring forward working men as candidates. Many in the Liberal establishment feared the growing assertiveness of working-class voters. In October of 1867, the Reform League endorsed the platform of the Positivists, who argued in favor of an independent working-class movement.[95] The Positivists' demands for trade union rights, free education, factory legislation, and manhood suffrage attracted wide support among workers in Bradford.[96] After 1867, workers repeatedly voiced their desire to participate in the Liberal Electoral Association.[97]

The Liberals of Bradford faced a dilemma. The party relied upon wealthy manufacturers and merchants in the worsted trade for financial support, while its electoral and organizational strength rested upon working-class voters. The party walked a fine line in order to avoid conflict between these sections. In the late 1860s and early 1870s, the dispute over the legal position of trade unions revealed the weakness of Liberalism's rhetoric of reform and placed the party in the middle of the labor–capital conflict that was becoming increasingly important.

Despite the borough's reputation as a Radical stronghold, many middle-class Liberals in Bradford unequivocally condemned trade unions. In part this reflected the strength of political economy. The doctrine of the wage fund was used to dismiss claims that unions could raise the pay of workers through collective action.[98] The principles of political economy (a higher power as Alfred Illingworth termed it) regulated wages and conditions, and nothing could affect the natural rate of wages set by supply and demand.[99]

Efforts to control working conditions or raise wages interfered with the relationship between master and employee. Unions threatened to take 'away from employers the right of controlling and organizing their servants according to their requirements'.[100] Such behavior inevitably led to coercion. The *Bradford Review*, a Radical journal, commenting on the Sheffield outrages in 1867, stated, 'intimidation, tyranny, injustice, depression are the legitimate fruits of such institutions as at present constituted and conducted'.[101] In another editorial, the *Review* added,

> Again then we assert the members of trade societies, as a rule, do not respect the rights of their fellow citizens, but seek habitually to violate them . . . that we know of no class, that has inflicted more injustice, wrong and cruelty upon the working men than trade societies have inflicted upon the operatives of this country.[102]

From the perspective of the *Review* and its supporters, mutual aid and education formed the only legitimate ends of trade union activity. Restriction of output through the use of work rules or strikes to raise wages constituted illegitimate activities.[103]

The weakness of trade unions in Bradford also informed attitudes toward trade unions. In the 1860s and 1870s, advanced Liberals proposed arbitration as a way around strikes and other industrial conflicts. Several union leaders and businessmen proposed the idea of a council of arbitration for the Bradford trade, and the Chamber of Commerce went so far as to invite Andrew Mundella, Radical MP for Sheffield, to discuss the scheme of arbitration he had initiated in the hosiery trade.[104] Yet these proposals went nowhere, because employers, secure in their control over most operatives in the worsted trade, refused to enter into equal bargaining with their workers.[105] In 1891 a Council of Conciliation was formed, consisting of six employers and six trade unionists, including Fred Jowett, the future Labour MP, but it remained dormant in its early years.[106]

Attacks on trade unions did not go unchallenged by trade unions and their supporters. The newly formed Bradford Trades Council called a meeting on July 20, 1867 to defend trade unions. At it, James

Hardaker, a mason, invoked the masculine defense of liberty against the tyranny of employers to justify trade unions,

> They were told that the union did not improve the conditions of the working man or raise his wages. If the upper classes believed this, why did they make so much bother about them? . . . Because they wanted to think and speak as men, they were accused of dictation to their masters . . . He urged the Trade Unions to act manly, and God defend the right.[107]

For men like Hardaker, trade unions were the only legitimate method of self-defense available to working men. Unionists in Bradford rejected the Liberal orthodoxy that the worker and employer entered into an equal bargain. Although William Forster, the owner of Black Dyke Mills called relations between employee and employer a partnership, one writer termed it a 'Hobson's choice' between the master's terms or starvation.[108] Even the Inspector of Factories, Robert Baker, questioned the old chestnut of an equal bargain between worker and employer.[109] In such circumstances, only collective organizations such as unions gave the workers the ability to stand up to their employers in the bargaining process.[110] Hardaker's call for manly behavior on the part of union members chided employers who wished to avoid such a confrontation for being unmanly.

To defend unions, working men stood the question of coercion and dictation on its head and argued that they represented the struggle for freedom against tyrannical employers. Hardaker reminded his audience,

> They would remember reading about the ancient times when the rich kept their vassals and serfs. 'Masters were masters then', and it was on those 'good' times of old . . . that the masters of the present time would like to see return.

Such language crops up throughout the period. The iron workers union titled the pamphlet defending their strike in 1864 *Slavery or Freedom*, while the spinners and weavers of Idle invoked the Bible in their call for an end to 'Manufacturing feudalism'.[111]

Defenders of unions argued that their position as fathers and husbands depended on the ability of trade unions to raise their wages and prevent the dilution of their trades. They pointed to the differences between organized and unorganized trades as proof of their contentions.[112] George Hillary, a local worker, made this distinction a central feature of his defense of trade unions. For Hillary, the working class was divided into two groups. The larger group, overworked, underpaid and poorly educated, could not raise itself up from poverty. Another, smaller group, better-off than the masses, led the march toward improvement. This latter group needed the rules and restrictions provided by trade unions to check the greed of employers and keep themselves above the mass of poor.[113] For his part, Hardaker believed that 'Trade Unions had done much for the social regeneration of the working classes.' In this way, trade unions were linked to the central values of family and social progress.

Although unions were weak in the worsted trade, other trades proved more capable of organizing. The construction trades were highly unionized, especially the masons, all 1,400 of whom belonged to the union, as did 750 mason's laborers. Heavy industrial workers also tended to be more highly unionized. A coal miners union existed by the early 1860s at the latest and the Ironfounders Union (1859) participated in a bitter strike in 1864 over the right to form a union.[114] By 1868 the ASE had three branches in Bradford, with over 700 members.[115] The Ironfounders, despite a prolonged strike in 1864 and the slow decline of the fine iron trade, increased their strength from 161 members to a steady 250 to 270 members by the late 1860s.[116]

The prosperity of the mid-1860s and early 1870s produced a surge in trade union activity, as workers sought to capitalize on their relatively strong position in the labor market. In addition to the expansion of worsted unions noted in Chapter 2, many skilled unions grew in this period. The construction trades in particular benefited from the economic upturn and all the major unions enjoyed an increase in wages and a reduction in hours.[117] The Operative Stone Masons grew from 75 members in 1859 to 1195 in 1874. In the same period, the Society of Engineers went from two branches with 361 members to three branches with 781 members. By 1874, about 15 per cent of Bradford's adult male labor force belonged to unions.[118]

The legal disabilities of trade unions became the focus of the debate over trade unions in the early 1870s. The use of the conspiracy statute against unions, the passage of the Master and Servant Act raised serious questions of equality before the law. Workers suffered disproportionately from the enforcement of these laws and they alone faced criminal penalties for breach of contract. The failure of the Criminal Law Amendment Act of 1871 to remedy this situation led to a national agitation for legislative relief for trade unions.[119] The particular circumstances of Bradford heightened such concerns. The reliance of local manufacturers on the Worsted Committee and the

Master and Servant Act made legal questions a practical rather than an abstract problem. The skewed composition of the Bradford magistracy, staffed by textile magnates and men of substantial property, raised serious issues of fairness in the application of the law.[120] Bradford magistrates issued the ruling which invalidated legal protection for union funds in the case of *Horby v. Close* in 1867 on the basis that unions constituted illegal conspiracies in restraint of trade. Yet they refused to intervene in cases of acknowledged blacklisting on the grounds that conspiracy laws did not apply to employers.[121] The perception of unfairness led to a movement for a paid magistracy in order to broaden its social composition.[122]

The ambiguous legal status of trade unions galvanized the labor movement in Bradford in the late 1860s. In 1868, an angry group of trade unionists confronted William Forster, the Bradford MP, at an electoral meeting and demanded to know if he would support laws to regularize the position of trade unions.[123] The Trades Council of Bradford, revived after a brief hiatus, led the fight against these laws and sponsored demonstrations against them in the early 1870s.[124] A protest rally in August of 1873, drew a crowd of 4,000 workers despite a steady downpour. The dyers' union was one of several textile unions involved in the formation of the new Trades Council that emerged in the late 1860s and their participation in the repeal campaign strengthened the links between textile and non-textile unions that proved so crucial in the 1890s.

Even after after the reforms of 1875 legalized trade unions and peaceful strike activities, concerns about the fairness of local officials remained. Union leaders testifying before the Royal Commission on Labour in 1891 complained of the lack of enforcement of the Factory Acts by inspectors and unfairness on the part of magistrates. E. A. Forster, a local manufacturer, in his testimony before the Commission denied any bias on the magistrates, but noted that he and four other manufacturers sat on the bench. He also could not recall any specific instances of employers prosecuted for violating the Factory Acts, but mentioned a number of cases being brought against workmen. Despite the legalization of picketing, Bradford magistrates still prosecuted men for intimidation in the 1890s.[125]

Those who defended the independence of trade unions also rejected the more extreme versions of laissez faire. The attack upon unrestricted rights for employers began in the mills with the agitation for the Factory Acts, but the ideas of the reformers spread outside the worsted trade.[126] The head of the Bowling Miners Union attacked unregulated mines, saying, 'Was political economy to be kept up amongst miners by lads being made to work 11–12 hours a day, was it to be protected at the expense of these poor lads lives and limbs?'[127] The known benefits of the factory laws led to widespread support for state intervention to aid the working class, from factory regulation to free education. Opposition to public provision of education on sectarian grounds generated complaints from working men who wished to see free, nonsectarian education.[128]

Many in the working class questioned the pace of political reform and social improvement. Although many Radicals reminded working men of their support for the Ten Hours Act, the consistent opposition of Bradford manufacturers to any extension of the Factory Acts brought into question the unanimity of the party on legislative amelioration for the textile operatives. The resistance to any extension of the Factory Acts by Bradford manufacturers in the mid-1870s further strained the Radical alliance with working men.[129] Similar sentiments arose over the Nine Hours Movement in the early 1870s. The refusal of owners to support a further reduction of hours led many working men to denounce them bitterly. Citing the profits made by manufacturers in the previous years, one letter writer remarked, 'We shall feel obliged if "A Worsted Spinner" [an earlier letter writer hostile to Nine Hours] could tell us when the time will arrive for his class to grant any concession.'[130]

One fruit of these disagreements was the nomination of James Hardaker, the leader of the stone masons, to run for Parliament in 1874. His candidacy showed the strength and weaknesses of the radicalism of Bradford working men in this era. Far from leading a fighting campaign, Hardaker seemed bent on maintaining a calm, low-key image and he failed to mobilize support on issues such as the nine hour day. Hardaker's lack of financial support led him to accept a deal with the Radical wing of the Liberals. In any event, he finished a distant fourth, garnering about 8,000 votes.[131]

The Liberal caucus emerged from the election of 1874 secure in its dominance over Bradford politics. Ironically, the first challenge to the caucus came from women voters within the party. In the early 1880s, women began to demand representation within the party and a place on the slate of candidates for the School Board and the Guardians' elections. The ability of women to vote in local elections made these claims more difficult to resist. A series of demonstrations helped create greater participation by women. A meeting in favor of the repeal of the Contagious Disease Acts, a favorite staple of Radicalism, drew a large audience in early 1882.[132] In November of that year, Lydia Becker, the suffrage activist, headed a large meeting in favor of extending the suffrage to women. A broad spectrum of middle-class women and their husbands, as well as an audience of 2500 women and 500 men attended the meeting.[133] The response of the Liberal establishment can be seen in the *Observer*'s suggestion that the participant's time would be better spent on civic projects or philanthrophy. Undaunted Mrs William Byles, daughter-in-law of the *Observer*'s publisher, Mrs Alfred Priestman and Mrs S.C. Kell, wives of prominent manufacturers, pushed on with their efforts. They defeated the caucus by electing Edith Lupton to the School Board. Mrs William Byles replaced her in 1888, followed by Mary Gregory.[134]

The feminist challenge to the caucus preceded the rise of the Independent Labour Party in the 1890s. A number of social and political changes undermined Radicalism in Bradford and helped expand the potential for independent labor politics. The Third Reform Bill in 1884, in addition to expanding the suffrage in rural areas, created a third parliamentary seat for Bradford, located in the working-class district of East Bradford.[135] However, the continued disenfranchisement of a substantial proportion of working-class men and the restrictions placed on their votes by the use of registration procedures limited the immediate impact of these reforms.[136] Working-class organizations lacked the financial resources to mobilize these voters. The expense of campaigns and supporting labor Members of Parliament often exceeded the ability of working men to pay.[137] One reason for Hardaker's deal with the Liberals in 1874 was his realization that he lacked the funds to campaign and to pay election expenses, and efforts to run labor men in the early 1880s collapsed for the same reason.

In the end, it was the impact of the depression in the worsted trade rather than franchise reform that provided the spark for independent labor politics. The attempt by employers to roll back wages and hours and to attack the Factory Acts embittered relations between Liberals and working men. The increased unemployment in the staple trade and in allied fields like construction and engineering undermined the skilled trades that supplied the backbone of popular Liberalism.[138] The restructuring of the worsted trade threatened the positions of formerly secure trades like sorting and led to the increased casualization of others like dyeing and combing. Many felt that this restructuring preserved the interests of manufacturers at the expense of others in the community, symbolized by the opposition of Bradford industrialists to the Factory Act of 1874, which made the fifty-six-and-one-half-hour week the legal limit for women and children.[139] The *Textile Manufacturer* argued it passed without due consideration of its impact and would have to be altered.[140] Samuel Lister labeled it a tax that cost him £40,000 per year.[141] The Bradford Chamber of Commerce fought the measure in Parliament and then attempted to have its implementation delayed.[142]

The depression in the worsted trade exacerbated existing tensions between capital and labor. Samuel Lister received a great deal of criticism for his conduct. At a meeting on the issue of fair trade, Michael Hardaker, a trade unionist, asked Lister if he wished to extend such protection to trade unions and work people. Furthermore, Hardaker wanted to know why Lister insisted that his workpeople increase their work week to sixty hours. Lister's attempt to dodge the question created an uproar at the meeting.[143] The next day a letter from 'Bottom the Weaver' in the *Observer* sarcastically requested that the public take up a collection for Lister to help him employ his workers.[144] Another letter followed which accused Lister of underpaying his workers.[145] Local discontent with Lister peaked with a mass strike of weavers and other female employees of his mill in August of 1882. After a bitter three week stoppage, the workers returned, but not before abusing Lister as a bad employer. One weaver claimed that her wages had been lowered three times prior to the reduction that sparked the walk out. Others argued that Lister would have to deal with them 'because he got too much brass from their work'.[146] Even paternalistic employers faced worker discontent over wage reductions and speed-ups. In July of 1876, 1200 workers at Saltaire, the mill constructed by Titus Salt, went out on strike. Salt, who had constructed a model village for his workers, was widely considered to be the apotheosis of enlightened capitalism.[147] In response the *Textile Manufacturer* remarked, 'But if anyone wants to pet the working man successfully, he must go beyond this it seems'.[148]

One product of these tensions was a wave of union organizing in Bradford and the West Riding among unskilled and semi-skilled workers, especially textile operatives. For the first time, trade unionists gave support to these efforts in an attempt to shore up skilled unions in the region. These efforts called forth a new generation of labor leaders and politicians, who sought to counter the weakness of unions in the region through greater political activity. The defining moment of this effort came in 1890–1 with the Manningham Mills Strike, which electrified the city and the country and led to the formation of the Independent Labour Party in 1893.[149]

One factor that turned trade union activity in a political direction was the response of local authorities to these developments. The issue of poverty reemerged in the 1880s, to the astonishment of many who thought it banished by the mid-Victorian boom.[150] The stinginess of local relief efforts became more charged as increasing numbers of adult men entered the system. The spread of the household means test, which lacked legal authorization, raised the barrier to adequate relief higher, while undermining many workers' belief in the fair play of the system. The continued high unemployment of the 1890s magnified this concern; one estimate in 1893 put the number of people affected directly or indirectly by unemployment at over 58,000, or 27 per cent of the borough's population.[151]

Equally important was the role of local government and the police in support of employers. The Town Hall Square Riot in April of 1891 during the Manningham strike convinced Fred Jowett and W. H. Drew that an independent labor party was necessary to regain control of local government.[152] They built their party on two pegs. The first was an attack upon the power of the factory lords. The second was the 'defence of the bottom dog': speaking up for the poor and battling for increased services from the local authorities.[153]

It is not surprising that local government issues played a role in the splintering of the old Radical coalition. As Euginio Biagini has argued, the sense of shared community played a vital role in linking middle-class and working-class Radicals.[154] The increasing bitterness of labor-capital relations inevitably eroded this sense of community, a community that was already in many ways a fiction. The growing social and cultural differences between the classes produced two separate ways of life in the borough that undermined the older Radical culture. This erosion opened the way for the socialists of the Independent Labour Party, who in the mid-1880s began to emerge in Bradford out of old Chartist groups, the Land and Labor League and the Positivists. The most significant of these groups proved to be the Bradford branch of the Socialist League, founded in 1886, which enrolled a number of socialist leaders, including Fred Jowett, a future Labour MP. The men who began the Independent Labour Party did not markedly differ in background from the generation that preceded them, for they came from the same milieu of temperance and self-education.[155] Many of them possessed long standing ties with Radicalism, either personally or through their families. Fred Jowett's father was a lifelong Radical and cooperator and a follower of the Chartist Ernest Jones. If these men differed in any significant way, it was in their rejection of Nonconformity.[156]

The overlap between the ILP and Radicalism was considerable. The Radicals' Sunday Society gave them a public forum. The significant middle-class element in the early leadership of the party harked back to earlier radical movements such as Chartism, and many prominent Radicals, such as William Byles, publisher of the *Observer* and Alfred Priestman, a wealthy manufacturer, joined the cause. The ILP's work in local government built on the earlier work of women like Mrs W. P. Byles on the School Board. The highly moral tone of their rhetoric and the incorporation of the Labour Church and Socialist Sunday Schools into the movement mimicked the pattern of popular Liberalism, with its association with Nonconformity.

Even in the themes of the ILP, one can distinguish the echoes of Radicalism. Like many working-class Radicals, the members of the ILP sought a solution to the problems of the day through an expansion of democracy.[157] As Fred Jowett put it,

> I had in me the feeling that the common people should not be driven, and the more Carlyle crowned and canonized a ruling class, the more I felt I was on the side of the common people. I was at heart a democrat.[158]

The experiences of the 1880s, however, undermined their belief that this expansion of democracy could occur within the confines of the Liberal Party. Whatever new winds blew through the party at the national level, in Bradford the old-school Radicals remained in charge.[159] They refused to share power with working men or to support their efforts to organize the worsted trade. In the words of one observer, 'Illingworthism was a gospel without sympathy, comradeship, or hope for the Bradford worker.'[160] This failure allowed the ILP to grab the Progressive mantle.

Some historians see the resultant break with the Liberal Party as a largely symbolic act, devoid of practical consequences prior to 1914. In this view, the cooperation of the Labour Party and the Liberals in national elections and the rise of progressive Liberalism blunted Labour's challenge.[161] But this tells only one side of the story. The ILP broke with Radicalism because the practical consequences of Liberal concessions on the issue of political representation and unionization would have been potentially great, tilting power in the city and the worsted industry toward working men. In such circumstances, separation represented the only available alternative.

But it was more than simply pragmatism or pride that influenced the first generation of English socialists. The squalor and grinding poverty of cities like Bradford led them to reject the older world view of Liberalism with its belief in the inevitability of progress. The influence of Ruskin, Morris, Blatchford and other ethical socialists shaped a critique of the inequalities that surrounded them, a critique which rejected the competitive ideal and the superiority of industry. While this generation came of age in a maturing industrial economy and an expanding working-class culture, they envisioned themselves as regenerators of that life.[162] They sought to elevate working-class taste and to restore the dignity of labor. Fully aware of the many divisions within the working class they wished to unite its various fractions. Toward this end they welcomed women members and women's suffrage and thus took the first tentative steps away from the wholly masculine politics of Radicalism. The ILP also embraced the unskilled and the poor, breaking with Radicalism's disdain for these groups. This created a more inclusive sense of democracy and a wider definition of citizenship.

This vision of citizenship grew out of the experience of life in an industrial city, which differed dramatically from that of the middle class and an older generation of working-class radicals. It combined utopian optimism about the possibilities of life with a keen awareness of the real hardships involved in daily living. It sought to build an alternative community to that offered by Victorian Radicalism. To understand this world view and how it differed from that of the middle class, we need to examine its roots in working-class life.

4 High and Low Culture in Victorian Bradford

The development of Bradford produced two distinctive ways of life in the nineteenth century – one working class and located in the central part of the city and the other middle class and safely tucked away in the surrounding hillsides. As a Bradford man noted in 1856:

> Fifty or even thirty years ago the connection between the employer and employed was quite different. It was then a matter of everyday occurrence for the master to mix socially with his workpeople, to enter into their pastimes with a healthy zest . . . But now employers not only live apart from their operatives but are as socially separated as the Europeans at the Cape are from the Hottentots.[1]

Concerned about this development, socially conscious members of Bradford's middle class hoped to build bonds of mutual sympathy between themselves and the working class in order to restore community. Men and women of property believed that through mutual association in voluntary, private organizations, most notably churches, the classes could achieve a better understanding of one another and thus overcome the distance imposed by differences in material circumstances. As the Reverend John Thompson argued,

> they would never succeed in their object unless the drinking system was destroyed, and the upper and middle classes convinced the working men by their domiciliary visits, by home missionaries, and other modes of contact and influence, that they desired to elevate and improve their condition in society.[2]

The operation of market forces in housing, leisure and work all ran counter to the desire to lessen the gap between classes through personal contact. The physical distance between the classes increased in this era; the result of an increasing spatial segregation of classes within the city. Working-class areas of Bradford became unexplored territory, which required the professional intermediary, the clergyman or 'missionary', to penetrate.[3] The increasing scale of economic activity, particularly the growth in firm size, limited the contact between employer and employee that made paternalism a potential answer to the anomie of the industrial city. The cash nexus, for better or worse, became the link between owner and employee. For most of the middle class, therefore, contact with the working class became a carefully controlled event, either at a works gathering orchestrated by subordinates or in special institutions such as the Mechanics' Institute, where the proper values could be lauded without the nasty possibility of contradiction.

This geographical and social distance also encompassed a growing cultural distance. As the Victorian era progressed, the middle-class retreated to the privatized spheres of the home, the club and the firm.[4] All of these grew more rigidly separated from the public sphere of the street and the city, where working-class culture increasingly found its expression. Both income and personal preference kept the classes apart and led to the development of two distinct cultures within the same borough. These cultures formed their own characteristic institutions. Although both embraced voluntary association, they did so in different ways. Middle-class men sought to confirm their status and to enhance their individual prospects through social networks, while working-class men banded together to anchor the individual and the family in an insecure world. This made working-class culture inward looking and defensive. The friendly society and the trade union, like political action, were longer range and often inadequate solutions to the problems that challenged working-class families.

THE MAKING OF AN INDUSTRIAL CITY

The steady expansion of the worsted industry after 1815 triggered rapid population growth in Bradford. Workers flooded in from the surrounding countryside, the West country and Ireland in response to the increased demand for labor, both in the mills and in the domestic industries of weaving and combing. By 1820, immigration replaced natural increase as the primary source of population growth. The years 1831 to 1851 marked the peak period of expansion in Bradford, as the population increased from 43,000 to 103,000, making Bradford the sixth largest city in Great Britain.[5]

By the 1840s, industry dominated the area. The city, located on the Bradford Beck in a series of valleys ringed by hills, possessed limited room for expansion. Mills crowded the inner city, particularly along the Beck, which supplied water and a waste dump, making it in

Friedrich Engels's words, a 'pitch-black, stinking river'.[6] In the early nineteenth century the open areas in the city disappeared to make way for more mills and housing, as did common lands, previously enclosed in the eighteenth century. The pollution of the Beck and Canal and the dross heaps at the southern end of the city from iron and coal production also cut off sites for potential expansion.[7]

The rapid expansion of the city brought with it unprecedented difficulties. The poor environmental condition of Bradford represented the most visible problem. Visitors and government officials frequently commented on the wretched state of the borough. A severe shortage of clean water aggravated the lack of proper drainage. Dense clouds of smoke from factories and homes filled the air in the hills that enclosed Bradford. The workers of Bradford clustered in inner-city neighborhoods, for they had to live close to the factories and shops that provided employment. An acute shortage of housing in the inner city led to serious overcrowding. In the Irish slums of Goit Side, population density reached 800 persons per acre in the 1840s, and in Nelson Court it was 509 persons per acre. These houses often had more than forty persons per privy even in the 1860s.[8] As Engels described it,

> The older parts of the town are built upon steep hillsides where the streets are narrow and irregular. Heaps of dirt and refuse disfigure the lanes, alleys and courts . . . In general the workers houses at the bottom of the valley are packed between high factory buildings and are among the worst and filthiest in the whole city.[9]

As the inner city grew more congested, the homes of the manufacturers and merchants, no longer used as places of business, migrated up the hillsides in order to escape the filth, disease and noise of the city, establishing hillside suburbs such as Manningham. For the extremely wealthy, there were estates in the countryside. Worsted manufacturer S. C. Lister built his own country home and sold his land to the city as a park. For the less-well to do, or those still engaged in daily business in the city, new suburban developments provided accommodation.[10]

The mid-Victorian era saw the completion of this process of expansion. Although speculative building continued, the insistence of the borough on sanitary improvements and drainage slowed its pace. The completion of the new Exchange building in 1867 and the Town Hall in 1873 provided Bradford with its distinctive landmarks. The choice of Neo-Gothic for these buildings stood in contrast to the Italinate warehouses of Little Germany that sprang up to the east and south of the city.[11] New housing developments in Great Horton and Leeds Road provided space for the better-off workers and the lower middle class that could now afford to leave the city proper.

VOLUNTARISM AND URBAN SOCIETY

Just as the physical expansion of the city and the worsted trade erased the old Bradford, so the growing differentiation of wealth created a new class of merchants and manufacturers who dominated the economic and social life of the city. In the 1830s and 1840s, these men replaced the older Tory gentry and gentlemen entrepreneurs who had controlled Bradford. The ascension of a Liberal middle class to power created a particular type of society. The core of this society was a network of voluntary organizations that connected this new class. Churches, political parties, cultural groups and reform agencies all intermingled in this era and created a unique form of civic life. These organizations embodied the values of self-help, sobriety and Christianity which formed the touchstones of middle-class existence.[12] Bradfordians believed that these values and the model of voluntary association were universal and thus applicable to all social groups.

The rise of voluntarism reflected the predominance of the new manufacturing and mercantile elite. The Liberal party with its laissez-faire economic policies and its belief in unfettered individualism won the loyalty of most of these new men. The churches, especially the Nonconformist chapels, remained the fulcrum between political and civic life. Religious affiliation linked the worsted trade and the Liberal party into the broader professional and social elite of Bradford. The most prominent church, the Horton Lane Congregational Chapel, provided a number of political and social leaders for the borough.[13] Literary clubs, debating societies and scientific institutes supplemented these activities and added a social and intellectual side to complement religious and charitable endeavors.[14]

The middle class believed that voluntarism could counter the centrifugal effects of competitive individualism upon the social order. To succeed in this task, the elite had to seek out contact with those below them in the social ladder. Many felt that only if the lower classes understood the motives and goodwill of those above them could destructive social conflict be avoided. The result was a proliferation of voluntary organizations designed to enlist members of the working class in efforts at self-help and moral reform. Evangelical missions such as the Town Mission, educational societies like the Ragged School and the Mechanics' Institute and charities all flourished in this era, showing the vigor and commitment of middle-class Bradfordians to the ideals of voluntarism and social harmony.[15]

Despite the impressive activism of voluntary groups, they remained curiously ineffective. The hope for a single community tied together by common values and organizations remained unrealized. Although they wished to avoid the heavy-handed paternalism of the Tory gentry, it proved difficult in practice for the middle class to avoid condescension and control. Groups like the Mechanics Institute were top-heavy with wealthy patrons, who insisted on their fitness to lead those below them. This created an artificial community, one based on patronage and influence rather than free association.[16] Although many members of the working class participated in activities sponsored by middle-class organizations, they constituted a small minority of the town's population.

Far more important, in terms of size and impact, were the voluntary organizations of the working class – friendly societies, building clubs and trade unions – that remained outside the web of self-help and social reform. This network of organizations formed the heart of a distinctive working-class culture that came into being in the mid-Victorian era. While this culture expressed itself in a language of self-help and social uplift similar to that of the middle class, it was collective and communal, rather than individualistic. Dominated by adult men in the skilled trades, it emphasized independence, self-help, mutuality and 'manliness' as core values. This emphasis on respectability conflicted with the roughness of street life and pub culture that formed the backdrop within which voluntary associations functioned. Drink, sport and brawling all went along with the friendly society and the trade union.

The belief in solidarity within these organizations belied the many divisions within the working class, divisions that can be seen in the exclusiveness of the voluntary associations that were the epitome of this culture. Yet this culture also reflected the shared hardships of life that few in the working class could escape. Collective action, either in self-help, unions or politics sought to alleviate the harshness of the environment and assert a sense of dignity and purpose for those on the bottom of the social order. This assertion of collective interest helped separate working-class life from the culture of the bourgeoisie that defined the era.

RELIGION IN MID-VICTORIAN BRADFORD

The moral and social values of the Protestant faith constituted the heart of mid-Victorian life. Yet, like all institutions in Bradford, churches found it difficult to meet the challenges of rapid growth. Partly, this reflected the poor response of the Church of England to changing times. The Church failed to provide accommodation for the poor, and in 1859 it offered only 200 free sittings in Bradford township. It also faced a population that contained large numbers of Nonconformists and Irish Catholics. Henry Heap, the Vicar of Bradford from 1820 to 1844, sought cooperation with the Nonconformists, in a quiet acceptance of their predominance. His more authoritarian successor, William Scoresby, chose confrontation and forced the issues of church rates and the condition of the factory population. Neither, however, reversed the Church's decline and by 1851 the Church of England had become a minority church in Bradford.[17]

Nonconformists enjoyed a period of rapid expansion in the early nineteenth century. The evangelical fire burned through the West Riding of Yorkshire in the first three decades of the nineteenth century, catching up many Bradfordians in the ecstasies of conversion. However, this wave of religious feeling became a fractious one, leading to a proliferation of sects, from the Primitive Methodists to the Southcottians.[18] The Methodists, despite their success in attracting converts, encountered considerable difficulty in controlling their members, resulting in a number of splits. The last, in 1848, seriously shook the church in Bradford.[19]

The years of Chartist upheaval, with its Owenite and atheist rumblings, disturbed both the Church of England and the Nonconformists, who recognized the limits to their influence over the working class.[20] The results of the Religious Census of 1851, which showed that the large majority of Bradford's population (about 70 per cent) did not attend church or chapel, confirmed this view. Along with the Established Church, the Old Dissenters failed to keep pace with change, while the newer Nonconformist sects, the Baptists and the Methodists, enjoyed the greatest growth prior to 1851. Working-class adherents tended to belong to smaller chapels, which had a more egalitarian flavor, such as the Tetley Street Baptists or Primitive Methodists, rather than the large chapels dominated by the middle class such as the Horton Lane Congregational Chapel.[21]

The elite tried to remedy this failure to attract working-class converts by focusing on expansion of facilities and evangelical outreach. All denominations agreed on the need to remedy the lack of accommodation. Only 32,000 sittings were available in 1851 to serve a population of 103,000. By 1881, this more than doubled to 73,000. The Catholics increased their places almost tenfold in thirty years, while the Wesleyans more than doubled theirs, as did the Baptists and the Congregationalists. The Church of England undertook a massive campaign of expansion in the inner city in this period, building ten churches from 1860 to 1872. Relying upon the funds of wealthy Anglicans like the iron master John Rand, they sought to become the 'poor man's church' by providing churches and schools to the inner city population. Unfortunately, this plan backfired, for many of the churches were in solidly Irish sections of town and remained under-utilized.[22]

The Town Mission, which grew out of the Mayor's Committee on the Moral Condition of the Town in 1849, became the city's largest evangelical organization and received the support of Nonconformist chapels. It hoped to spread religious feeling through a program of visitation among the poor. Such home visits were 'the great indispensable' in the effort of the Town Mission to fuse social and moral reform.[23] The Mission employed seventeen missionaries, who covered their districts, visiting homes and institutions. By offering aid to the sick and some poor relief, the Mission found greater acceptance in working class homes, particularly in the depression years 1878 and 1879.[24]

From the beginning, Town Mission agents encountered considerable apathy and hostility, particularly among Catholics. Although they found that infidelity was not as prevalent as feared, it did have 'a considerable existence'. One agent reported, 'The amount of Sabbath desecration in this district is almost incredible: *men seem to care nothing whatever about it.*' (Italics in original.)[25] Agents found beerhouses and brothels open for business on Sunday and worshippers on their way to services passed by several of the latter, which were frequented by 'respectable' working men.

To the missionaries, such disdain for religion reflected a tendency for workers to 'think and act for themselves'. This independence of thought came out in comments addressed to the missionaries. One reported that

A considerable number of men find great fault with wealthy professors of religion for not exercising their influence in aiding them in their struggles for political freedom. They sneeringly remark, that if the influential classes were sincere in their anxiety for them in spiritual matters that they would take a deeper interest in their temporal welfare.[26]

Still other workers were

> very free with their remarks about manufacturers, especially those who attend a place of worship, being oppressors. They sometimes tell us we ought to visit the men who are robbing the hireling of his wages, and reprove them for their sins.[27]

As one minister noted, 'nothing is so likely to injure attendance as the hypocrisy of regular worshipers.'[28]

In 1856 J. H. Marshall, the Superintendent of the Mission, introduced the keeping of records of visits, for he felt that both business and religion needed a system for successful operation.[29] The reports of the Mission became a series of victories won against great odds and a mass of statistics about visits. The new spirit was reflected in the observation that,

> It is certain that for this amount of labour our town must be, both socially, morally, and spiritually better. It is impossible to throw so much Gospel leaven into society without it having its due effect.[30]

Despite this optimism, the Mission conceded 'that a large number of our townspeople pay no attention whatever to religion or its ordinances' and that few people actually joined churches as a result of their efforts.[31]

A new Census of Religion conducted by the *Bradford Observer* in December of 1881 confirmed the impressionistic accounts of the Town Mission. The census showed that church attendance as a proportion of the population actually declined to around 20 per cent despite the massive increase in church accommodation. The results were even more unsettling to the Nonconformists who dominated Bradford. The newer Nonconformist sects stagnated, the Church of England enjoyed a modest expansion and the older Dissenting sects entered a period of decline. A number of new, more marginal sects appeared, many appealing to the working class. The most important of these, the Salvation Army, had 6 per cent of the worshippers at services.[32]

Particularly disturbing to the Protestants of Bradford was the continued strength of the Catholic Church, thirty years after the end of wholesale Irish migration to Bradford. In 1851, about 40 per cent of the Catholic population attended mass. The Church created a range of activities to attract worshippers, modeled on those offered by the Protestant churches, from friendly societies to temperance groups.[33] The Protestant churches tried to evangelize Catholics and refused to cooperate with them in temperance and other activities.[34]

The statistics of the 1881 Census of Religion demonstrated convincingly the failure of the Town Mission and other agencies to evangelize Bradford's working class. While some blamed the rainy weather or the popular ignorance for this poor attendance, others saw it as a symptom of a larger problem. Despite unprecedented expenditures and the expansion of a range of social institutions, most people remained indifferent to formal religion. Contemporary observers advanced a number of reasons for this indifference. The Reverend J. Hollywood cited

> The existence of a large number of foreigners among us with their Sabbath-profaning habits; the increased intercourse with the Continent, and the adoption of Continental ways; Sunday excursions, late Saturday nights, intense industry with the consequent prostration or animal indulgence; the prevalence of practical infidelity, the divisions among professing Christians, the craving for excitement in religion, and the distaste for it if it be not exciting – these are among the causes which contribute to the neglect of public worship.[35]

Working-class atheism dated back to the Chartist era and even earlier. Early religious missionaries cited woolcombers in particular as free thinkers. A Secularist society existed from at least the 1860s, though its membership remains uncertain.[36] It arranged meetings and lectures by free-thinking luminaries like Charles Bradlaugh, who spoke on his refusal to take the Parliamentary oath.[37] More common than atheism was the type of hostility or indifference encountered by the Town Missionaries. One letter writer who called himself 'Atheist' attributed the extent of irreligion to the worldliness of the people and their lack of interest in theology. Another letter in response by 'A Unitarian' may have been more accurate in its assertion that neither atheism nor Christianity represented the masses, who were 'for the most part diligently occupied in keeping a whole skin and filling it'.[38]

The question of why organized religion failed to attract more working-class followers remains a puzzle. Whether or not a secular mindset, hostile to religion, emerged along with industry is difficult to document and it is not necessarily the case that secularism and religious belief contradict one another.[39] The popularity of working-class chapels, the emergence of new sects like the Salvation Army and the

Labour Church and the continued survival of religious instruction in schools all point to a role for religious belief among the working class. What is more uncertain, however, is the importance of religious organizations to the social life of workers. The array of mutual aid and voluntary organizations among the working poor lessened the need for the types of activities offered by churches to attract adherents. The chapel was only one of many pursuits available in the mid-Victorian city. As one minister admitted, despite its strenuous efforts to reach the lower classes, 'the pulpit lags behind the age, and makes no attempt to lead it.'[40]

This is not to suggest that the image of the chapel-going, respectable working man, a teetotaler and Liberal, did not have some basis in fact in the mid-Victorian period. But it is important to keep in mind the extent to which this represented a minority among the working class. Even when attending church, workers often sought out their own congregations such as the Primitive Methodists and thus remained somewhat removed from the heavy paternalist messages of middle-class churches. Furthermore, in an age in which appearances counted for so much, the mere fact of church attendance helped to satisfy public demands for 'respectability' without necessarily inferring acceptance of the intent and message of religion.[41] In the final analysis, religion played a limited role in working-class life and that role diminished rather than expanded in this period.

EDUCATION IN BRADFORD

In the minds of most of Bradford's middle class, education stood next to religion as a means of moral and social improvement. Bradford's elite expressed great faith in the ability of education to elevate the nature of working-class life. They saw two main purposes for education: to moralize the working class and to offer them a chance at self-improvement and upward mobility. As was the case with so many other areas of public life, existing facilities proved inadequate to meet the ambitions of the reformers. The rapid growth of the city created a serious shortfall in the provision of schools. Many in Bradford felt that the neglect of education in the boom years damaged both the moral and social order. According to one writer,

Amongst the most striking effects of the popular ignorance . . . and which are the most prominently displayed in the social character of the labouring population of this borough, we may safely mention intemperance, improvidence, profanation of the Sabbath, neglect of public worship, a distaste for lectures, books, or institutions of a purely literary character, habits of uncleanness and filth, and a feverish propensity for excitement, either in the shape of pugilistic encounters, the noise and obscenity of a beershop, or insurrectionary politics, to which even the wildest tenets of chartism form no limit.[42]

The levels of both male and female illiteracy reflected the weakness of the educational system. In 1856, 49 per cent of those marrying used marks, as opposed to 39 per cent for all of England and Wales. Female literacy lagged even farther behind; 63 per cent of females marrying in Bradford signed with a mark, compared to 46 per cent in the nation as a whole.[43]

Prior to 1850, Sunday schools provided the bulk of schooling, due to the severe shortage of day schools in Bradford. Edward Baines estimated the number of Sunday scholars in 1842 at 19,000, about the same number given by the Newcastle Commission in 1859.[44] These schools suffered from a number of drawbacks, including a low standard of teaching and poor attendance (usually less than two-thirds of the registered students attended), yet they provided the only form of schooling for many workers. Along with the Mechanics' Institute and private and church-affiliated night schools, Sunday schools compensated for the lack of educational facilities, particularly for adults, and gave many the opportunity to acquire elementary knowledge, if not advanced skills.[45] They continued to expand in the mid-Victorian era, though they shifted their focus away from elementary education after 1870 and toward more religiously-oriented teaching. By 1880, over 47,000 students attended Nonconformist and Church of England Sunday schools.[46] The provision of day schools lagged much farther behind the Sunday schools. The Quakers established the first day school in 1816 and by 1850 there were 9,500 students in schools run by the various Protestant sects, the Church of England and the Catholic Church.[47]

The 'monster evil', public ignorance, could not be addressed without a dramatic increase in the facilities for education, yet attempts to create a system of public education in Bradford encountered a number of roadblocks. Religious conflicts, lack of resources and an ambivalence about the purposes of education for the masses all handicapped these efforts. The result was the emergence of two separate systems of education in Bradford, one private and serving those who could afford to attend, primarily the middle class, and the other public, serving the working class.

For most of the mid-Victorian era, sectarian conflict dogged the provision of education. The churches of Bradford saw education as part of a larger system of belief, subordinate to religion. Religious leaders conceived of school as a way of teaching the skills necessary to understand religion and to reinforce the moral training imparted by the church. Such moral education could only be accomplished through the auspices of churches and other religious bodies. The Vicar of Bradford, Dr Burnett, felt that without religious control over the content of instruction, education itself could be dangerous.[48]

For the churches of Bradford, education proved to be another battleground. Both the Anglicans and the Nonconformists used school provision as a way of serving the faithful and attracting new converts. This was especially the case in the schooling of the working class, which could not afford to attend private schools and lacked other means of instruction as home learning and apprenticeship declined.[49] Nonconformists resisted efforts to create state-supported schools because they feared that such efforts bolstered the Church of England. This meant that before the 1870s, voluntary efforts dominated education, resulting in an inadequate, fragmented system.

The number of schools expanded prior to passage of the Education Act of 1870. In 1859, H. S. Winder, the Assistant Commissioner for the Newcastle Commission, reported 11,500 full-time students in public and private schools. Of the public school students (about 60 per cent of the total) 4,061 went to Church of England Schools, 1,014 to Wesleyan schools, and the rest to various other types, including 426 in nondenominational schools. Winder concluded that although an adequate supply of places existed, they were poorly distributed through the town and often were unsuitable for full-time schools.[50]

By 1871, over 18,000 places existed in Bradford day schools to serve an estimated 30,000 children of school age. Yet the number of places in 'efficient' schools numbered only slightly more than 13,000. Between 1859 and 1871, the Nonconformist commitment to education slackened, allowing the Anglicans and Catholics to take the lead in the education of the poor and the working class. This reflected the continuing movement of chapels outside the central city, while the Church of England and the Catholics both expanded their religious and educational facilities in these areas.[51]

Alongside the sectarian schools were a large number of private schools. Winder's survey of 1859 found 147 private schools, of which half were 'dame' schools, private schools taught by women, often in their own homes. Only two-thirds of dame schools taught writing and those that did usually taught only the bare essentials, leading Winder to label them 'mere nurseries'.[52] Of the remaining private schools, some appealed to the better-off workers and the lower middle class and offered a slightly higher level of instruction, while the rest essentially duplicated state-supported schools, although for a higher fee. These latter schools competed with the state-supported schools, often opening in areas not served by state schools. This competition made the life of private schools short, and of the 147 schools in 1859, 101 had opened since 1851. Winder reported the private sector was holding its own, but that it provided an inferior education.[53]

The passage of the Factory Acts and the provision of government grants for schools after 1839 provided much of the impetus for the building of schools in the area. One product of the educational provisions of the Factory Acts was the creation of the half-time system. The Factory Acts regulated children and women's labor and allowed children as young as nine (later raised to eleven) to begin work, if they also attended school for half of their time. To ensure their attendance and to measure their progress, the government created a system of inspection and examination. Bradford manufacturers, unlike those in other cities, failed to establish schools for their operatives. In 1859, only five factory schools existed in Bradford, as opposed to thirty-four in Rochdale, a cotton textile town in Lancashire. Bradford manufacturers preferred to rely on private masters or public schools to provide instruction for their workers, which made the education of factory children a cottage industry in Bradford, known as 'farming the pence'.[54]

Half-time students attended school regularly while in work, but suffered from a number of handicaps. They usually began school at a later age and moved between schools quite often. Most millowners required them to attend a specific school, which meant that they shifted schools during their frequent changes of work. During periods of unemployment, half-timers often stopped attending school altogether.[55] Half-timers received no special attention to compensate for these handicaps, they simply fitted into the schedule of the full-time students. Because of the disruptive nature of such arrangements, better schools often banned these students.[56] With little input from the factory owners or inspectors, the system functioned to provide a minimal education, far below that offered to day scholars.[57] In 1873, W. Bailey, a school inspector, argued that the half-time system tended to drag the performance of all students down, saying, 'Nothing is more striking in these half-time schools than the low level of education in them.'[58]

The system of half-time labor persisted until the First World War, despite repeated attempts to limit it. In 1859, Winder reported 1,505 half-timers in Bradford's schools. The half-time system survived the transition to Board schools and the number of half-timers actually increased from 5,700 total in 1870 to 9,732 in public schools alone by 1875, and stood at over 9,000 in 1893.[59] The dependence of the Bradford schools upon the factories and the half-time system remained a stumbling block to efforts to improve the quality of education. Despite statements about the importance of education for the young, Bradford's manufacturers preferred the half-time system, despite its well-documented flaws, for it helped ensure a supply of juvenile labor.

Many have seen the Education Act of 1870 as a crucial milestone in the educational history of England, but what is most striking about Bradford's experience is the continuity between the two eras. The School Board expanded the number of places in state-supported schools and by 1881, it was the largest provider of education in the borough, with 17,355 students, compared to 16,689 students in other state-assisted, private and Catholic schools. By 1896, the Board educated over 26,000 students, with a further 12,000 enrolled in voluntary schools.[60] However, the nature of education, under both the voluntary and the Board system, reflected a belief in economy and the impact of religious disputes.[61] The actions of the Board embodied the attitudes of the Nonconformist Liberals who dominated it. Originally opposed to the Education Act of 1870 for sectarian reasons, they chose to use the Board to provide a minimal education, while using its power to undermine Catholic and Church of England schools. The Nonconformists began to abandon their educational efforts, turning their schools over to the Board.[62]

Bradford's middle class showed little commitment to funding education for the poor. No endowed schools existed in Bradford and, before 1870, no provision for the children of the non-pauper poor existed outside the Ragged School, which many parents refused to allow their children to attend. The manufacturers of Bradford sought to avoid the costs of providing education for the new population that worked in the mills. While some manufacturers like Titus Salt and William Walker provided schools for factory children, most relied upon the efforts of private schools and churches to fill the gap prior to the establishment of the School Board.[63] They complained loudly of the unfairness of paying the costs of supervising schools and evaded regulations concerning half-timers.[64]

The new School Board continued this policy. It provided education to the working class at the lowest possible cost. The fees of school children provided half the funding of the schools, an indication of the low level of funding.[65] The continued importance of school fees demonstrated the lack of commitment on the part of the elite of Bradford to the education of the working class. For these fees, students got the type of schooling their meager resources could provide, while the provision of a place for each student satisfied the legal requirements imposed upon the manufacturers and the borough.[66] The elite avoided the consequences of the underfunding of education by sending their children to private schools. Board schools continued to serve a working-class population, while private schools attracted the better-off students, leading to what Bailey termed a 'great gulf' between middle-class private schools and working-class Board schools.[67] Only one school in the entire borough, in Bailey's opinion, offered 'a thoroughly good education', the Borough West School, run by the Horton Lane Independent Chapel, a church frequented by Bradford's manufacturing and professional elite.[68]

Elementary schools in Bradford provided a minimal education at best. In 1859, Winder reported that, despite variations between schools, the level of attainment in general was low. In his words:

> In a tolerable power of reading, very indifferent writing, and an imperfect acquaintance with the first four rules of arithmetic, is summed up the average equipment of secular knowledge with which the great majority of children enter upon working life.[69]

Winder attributed this to a number of causes. One was the poor quality of instruction, particularly the reliance upon rote memorization and pupil teachers. Another was the inconsistent nature of attendance. Although Winder put the level of attendance at over 80 per cent, he noted that only one-third of the students actually attended the 176 days required to receive the capitation grant. Finally, there was the impact of late starting and half-time attendance. Virtually all students left school by age thirteen and many began to leave school at nine to work, despite what Winder described as 'exceedingly common' late admissions.[70] Often students failed to begin school before eight or nine years of age (when forced to attend school if they worked in textile mills) and often left for periods of time to help at home or work for wages.

Inspectors noted little improvement from 1859 to 1870. In 1870, Reverend Wilden, the Inspector of Church of England schools in the Bradford District, found the level of reading and mathematics poor and the writing level only fair. He reported a great increase in the number of children in school, but noted that over 50 per cent of the students were half-timers.[71] The establishment of the School Board failed to raise the quality of instruction offered to students. W. Bailey, the Inspector for the public schools in the Bradford District, found similar conditions in 1873. The use of pupil teachers, large class size and the half-time system continued unabated under the Board's supervision. Attendance remained poor, with rates of attendance as low as 58 per cent in the 1870s, before leveling off at around 75 per cent in the early 1880s.[72] Large numbers of students were presented at low level exams or held back until old enough to work full time. Bradford school children performed below average on examinations, so much so that Bradford teachers memorialized the Board to complain about the exceptionally high rates of failures.[73]

The difficulties of teaching can be glimpsed in the log books of schools in this period.[74] Teachers complained of the continued absence and slowness of half-timers, as well as interference with schooling by the foremen. In times of bad trade, students left school to seek work in other mills or other cities.[75] Recurrent outbreaks of scarlet fever and other communicable diseases, which spread through the schools and factories quite rapidly, also gave concern. Given the poor conditions in schools, an emphasis on discipline and order took precedence in the teacher's work. The use of monitors and pupil teachers aggravated the problem, as many were poorly educated and inflicted harsh punishments on the children.

The School Attendance Subcommittee found it difficult to enforce attendance and exam standards and it delayed the implementation of higher standards for allowing half-time exemption, which it claimed were too high. While the Committee of Council on Education suggested the Fourth Standard for exemption for half-time work, the Board adopted the Second Standard for exemption, claiming that less than half the students currently at work would pass at the higher standard. Even after the passage of this bye-law, enforcement remained uncertain. The Attendance Subcommittee resisted attempts to force them to apply the laws on illegal employment, instead trying to place the responsibility on the Factory Inspectors. For his part, William Beaumont, the Factory Inspector for the district, said that 'he had no power to carry out an arrangement for preventing children being taken into employment in future who had not passed the Standard for half-time exemption.'[76] Once the Board began to prosecute offenders, it pursued parents and children rather than employers. In March of 1879, the Board reported 604 prosecutions under the bye-laws, none of which involved employers.[77]

The limits of public education reflected not only a desire to save money, but also an ambivalence about the nature and purpose of education itself. For all their rhetoric about the need to educate and uplift the masses, the elite of Bradford retained a certain anxiety about the content of education and the use to which it would be put. Local commentators warned the Board and educational reformers about the dangers of educating workers above their station and damaging their usefulness for factory labor.[78] One writer believed education lacked real substance and could harm workers, leaving them 'sadly uninformed even though crammed – unable through want of real mental discipline to grapple with the ordinary duties of life'.[79] What many wished was to impress upon the young certain values and lessons that would make them not better scholars, but 'better workers'. As the Reverend Wilden argued, 'do not try to turn out good work from your school, but good workers.'[80] This meant an emphasis on order, discipline and respect for authority as represented by the school master. The anti-militarist Board of Education added drill to the curriculum in 1875 in order to enhance such learning.[81]

However, the nature of schooling, with its crowded and chaotic conditions, limited its effectiveness as a tool of social control.[82] Students spent perhaps five to seven years in school, during which they learned only rudimentary skills. Schools offered only the most perfunctory historical and religious lessons, and many students failed to take even these subjects due to the vagaries of the half-time system and grant allocations.[83] Discipline, the watchword of Victorian schooling, was a tenuous affair in mid-Victorian Bradford, if school logbooks are to be believed. Students persistently misbehaved, despite the frequent use of corporal punishment. The ability of students to find a new school if they wished lessened the hold of both school and teacher.

EDUCATION AND SOCIAL MOBILITY

As a result of both private and public efforts, most of Bradford's children gained access to elementary education by the 1880s at the latest. The results of the expansion of educational provision can be glimpsed in the improved levels of attendance and literacy. By 1871, only 29 per cent of the brides and grooms in Bradford signed with a mark, a decline of some 20 per cent in fifteen years.[84] Levels of attendance among nine to fourteen year olds among all classes increased steadily throughout the period 1851 to 1881.[85]

The undoubted success of attempts to increase school provision needs to be considered in light of an equally important issue – the role of education in fostering social mobility for the working class and the extent to which it displaced existing family-based systems of job finding. Recent work on education suggests that working-class pupils derived some benefits from increasing levels of education in the form of greater social mobility than previous generations.[86] Such figures are tempered by the fact that for the overwhelming majority, including most women, education offered limited rewards. In David Vincent's view, over 90 per cent of the sons of working-men remained working-men and many of those who experienced occupational mobility failed to leave behind working-class status.[87]

The limited impact of increased literacy upon working-class life grew out of the nature of job recruitment and employment in the Victorian economy. Despite the rise of new white-collar occupations in the second half of the nineteenth century, access to work still relied upon local networks and family connections, especially in the initial job search. Employers preferred such recruitment tactics because they helped cement workplace loyalty. Thus, literacy served as only one qualification among many in the process of finding work. Working-class families valued literacy, but its value could not be measured in purely economic or occupational terms.[88]

These processes were at work in mid-Victorian Bradford. More children were at school at the end of the period than at the beginning. Many working-class parents took a keen interest in their children's education and would move them from school to school seeking a better education.[89] Parents were not above intervening (and even threatening the teacher) if they felt that teachers punished their children unnecessarily.[90] More generally, workers supported a national system of non-sectarian, free education for all. Winder found this to be true in 1859 and it was one of the points stressed by the Positivists in their campaign for a labor party.[91]

The desire for greater literacy among the working-class confronted the straitened circumstances of working-class family life. Many families balanced the desire for an education against the costs of school, whether in the form of fees and lost wages or the loss of domestic aid. This could lead to 'the refusal, for the sake of schooling, to forego the wages which the child can earn, or the assistance which it can give in household affairs'.[92]

School remained a limited phase in the life of working-class children, during which they acquired certain useful skills, particularly reading. Education began earlier in 1881 than in 1851, but for all intents and purposes, it ended by age thirteen, as the children entered into their true destiny, full-time labor. The end result of education seems to have remained the same, one teacher noting,

> the almost daily occurrence of my best boys and girls going full time. During the present quarter no less than ten in the first and second classes have gone full time. No sooner than they begin to make headway than away they go work.[93]

The limits to educational mobility can be seen more clearly in the system of further education developed in the mid-Victorian era. Prior to the development of higher grade school by the school board in 1876, only private, fee-paying schools offered a secondary education. Working-class students relied upon scholarships or benefactors to attend secondary schools. The situation actually worsened in the late 1860s after the consolidation of Bradford High School and Bradford Grammar School in response to government criticism. The new school now charged fees and offered only a limited number of scholarships, not limited to the poor or needy. As a consequence, the school became dominated by the manufacturing and commercial elite.[94]

The higher grade schools sought to close the gap somewhat by offering advanced education in mathematics, languages and science. By 1895, the five higher grade schools enrolled about 2,000 pupils.[95] Often considered secondary schools for the working class, they suffered from a number of drawbacks. They served primarily elementary students, with only a limited number of more advanced students. Of the 802 boys in the schools, 605 were under thirteen and only 62 above fourteen. While these students could compete for scholarships to the Grammar School or Technical College, only thirteen were available to the Grammar School and about forty to the College. Classes were large and the schools lacked libraries and other facilities.[96] According to one observer, the schools were 'rather middle class', filled with the children of 'tradesmen and shopkeepers' seeking a better education.[97] Ironically, the passage of the 1902 Education Act eliminated them in favor of more traditional secondary schools favored by the upper middle class.[98]

Even after the formation of technical colleges and higher grade schools, the cost of schooling remained an obstacle to advanced education for working-class students. In addition to the fees, which were about 9d. per week for higher grade schools, there was the cost of forgone wages, which for a young skilled worker could be considerable. If a working-class child persevered, the rewards for further education were mixed. Most work available required 'manual dexterity' and not intellectual attainment or technical knowledge. The importance of local and family connections for finding work, especially in the skilled worsted trades, limited the ability of outsiders to break into the narrow hierarchy of the mill or the trade. The insistence of local unions such as the overlookers and woolsorters on maintenance of control over the admission of learners and the right to admit their sons to the trade kept these trades in the hands of the few.[99]

For those seeking social advancement, the era after the 1870s presented difficult choices. The older avenues of individual effort in shopkeeping and small-scale worsted entrepreneurship suffered as a result of the slowdown in the worsted trade that affected the regional economy.[100] On the other hand, the growth in service and white-collar jobs offered new opportunities for educated working-class men. The position of pupil teacher also offered a way out of the mills. J.B. Priestley's father started his ascent from the working class as a teacher, as did many others.[101]

Those seeking to better themselves encountered a number of obstacles. They faced competition from the children of the lower middle classes who sought to hold onto their status in a society where the stigma of class origin carried considerable weight. In the words of one observer, 'There are plenty and more to spare among the middle classes to fill up all rising situations.'[102] Higher grade school students found it difficult to compete with those from private schools of a better quality and reputation such as the Bradford Grammar School.[103]

Even for those who found new employment, the rewards could be less than anticipated.[104] As Winder noted in 1859,

Suppose a working man to be willing to make sacrifices in order to give his child a good start in life, and place him on a higher level than that on which he was born. He sends him to school steadily and continuously, till he is 13 or 14, and till the boy has gone through the whole of the national school curriculum. At the close what has his superior instruction opened to him? Possibly, by no means probably, an introduction to a warehouse or office. A man is little, if at all, better off as clerk than an artisan.[105]

Those who could afford to attend school full-time after age thirteen constituted only a small minority of the working class, even in 1881.[106] The need to work forced those interested in further education to attend night schools. The most important of these adult educational institutes, the Mechanics' Institute, drew on the older autodidact traditions of working men. The first Mechanics' Institute, set up in 1824, failed financially because the elite perceived it as too independent. The second, set up in 1832, remained under middle-class tutelage throughout this period. Its middle-class and Nonconformist sponsors saw the Mechanics' Institute as a means for self-improvement and social mobility for the intelligent working class. Reverend Ackworth welcomed the Institute as 'a substitute for many of those species of recreation and amusement which are rising up in town, and which threaten[ed] to diffuse vice and its baneful consequences'.[107] John Godwin, a local manufacturer, claimed,

> Those who have watched the Bradford Mechanics' Institute are able to state that they have seen, year after year, an unbroken stream of youths, sons of working men, rising to positions of responsibility, which in all probability they never would have filled without its aid, and in many cases entering upon and pursuing a successful middle class career by the habits, knowledge, and the connections acquired in this Institute.[108]

Despite such statements, working men, who constituted two-thirds of the members, made a more utilitarian use of the Institute. Workers saw the Institute as a means for basic instruction and cheap diversion. Only basic reading and writing courses enjoyed full enrollment (although they suffered from poor attendance), while advanced classes went begging for students. Courses such as the one on political economy offered by James Hanson, Radical editor of the *Bradford Review*, found virtually no audience. The Institute's lectures, while better attended than those of other educational societies, could only draw crowds for literary and amusing lectures, while scientific lectures failed to attract attention. The library, which offered any number of 'dull and heavy books', found most of its trade in current journals and fiction, despite attempts to discourage such reading.[109]

The value of the Mechanics' Institute as a place for self-education in the mid-Victorian period is unquestionable.[110] At its peak in 1872, the

Mechanics' Institute had almost 2,000 members, with perhaps half as many in classes. Men like Fred Jowett, the future Labour MP, used the library and night courses in order to better themselves. Once alternative means of instruction appeared, however, its usefulness for working men diminished. The Mechanics' Institute experienced a rapid decline after the passage of the Education Act of 1870 and the opening of the Free Library in 1872.[111] Increasingly, the Institute found itself involved in the projects for the creation of a technical college and thus moving away from its ideal of a working-class institution of self-study.

The process through which the Mechanics' Institute became supplanted by the Technical College reveals a great deal about the possibilities and limits of further education for working men. It reflected a shift in the thinking about the purpose of advanced education for working men. Instead of offering opportunities for advancement toward middle-class status through self-education (the Institute as 'People's College'), the emphasis was increasingly placed on technical education, controlled by the teachers and trustees and offering at best limited advancement within the working class.[112] To this end the Institute set up courses in drawing, design, chemistry and building for the aspiring student. The directors added a scientific department to the Mechanics' Institute in 1868 and supplemented this with a weaving school in 1878. This arrangement expanded into a school for all textile departments, which formed the basis of the future Technical College.[113]

The hostility of skilled unions to the Technical College demonstrated the continuing importance of family and trade-based training, even after the establishment of both elementary and secondary education.[114] Even if overlookers and other skilled workers had demonstrated more interest in technical education, their own financial circumstances prevented their sons, the presumed beneficiaries, from attending school. As Henry Ripley recognized, an overlooker who made less than £100 per year could not afford to allow his son to attend school beyond the age of thirteen or fourteen.[115] The Technical School required nine terms of instruction, lasting three years, beginning at age fourteen or fifteen at the youngest. Students paid between 45s. to 50s. per term for day classes or 13s. to 15s. for the night classes.

Not surprisingly, the early years of the Technical College failed to fulfill the expectations of its backers.[116] The *Observer* noted that, 'Judging from previous experiences, the greatest difficulty will be, not in obtaining sufficient support from employers, but in gathering pupils.'[117] Workers who could earn assistant overlookers' wages were reluctant to give up their wages for a chance, a slim one at best, to parlay a day school education into a lower middle-class job. In 1882, four years after its founding, only one hundred students enrolled in the school, which had places for a thousand.[118] The sons of manufacturers and merchants, seeking to broaden their knowledge before joining their family's business, filled the day school.[119] Even the employers' support for the project faded, and the school relied upon state funding before being municipalized in 1899.[120]

By the late nineteenth century, Bradford possessed two separate and unequal systems that laid the basis for the future development of education. Out of these parallel systems arose two different ideas about the value and usefulness of education. For the middle class, education provided the knowledge required to fill one's station in life and a path for upward mobility. For the working class, education gave the individual a set of rudimentary skills, but no real headstart in life. Ordinary men and women sought to obtain the necessary education for functioning in life, particularly reading, but saw little purpose in continued education or advanced learning. Workers valued education, but they lived in a society that failed to reward learning by working people in a consistent fashion. The great majority of the working class ended the period better educated, but still firmly fixed in older patterns of employment.

TEMPERANCE AND THE QUESTION OF LEISURE

The emphasis on self-help and improvement also colored the patterns of leisure that emerged in this era. With the rise of the factory and the growth of urban centers such as Bradford, new forms of public life came into existence. By the 1850s the mill and its division of the week increasingly influenced the people of Bradford.[121] At the beginning of the mid-Victorian period, both factory operatives and artisans worked an average of sixty hours a week. The Ten Hours Bill of 1847 regularized the length of the working day and subjected it to minimal supervision. The gradual acceptance by employers of the Saturday half-holiday, under the pressure of Short-Time Committees, factory laws and trade unions reinforced this pattern. By the mid-1870s, the work week shrank to around fifty-four to fifty-six hours for many workers, with workers in the building and engineering trades enjoying weeks as short as fifty to fifty-two hours.[122]

√ The shrinking work week provoked concern over how the members of the working class spent their time outside of work. The seriousness of middle-class culture and its emphasis on self-improvement shaped these anxieties. Religious activities remained the most important area of social life for most members of the middle class and Sunday was usually given over to worship and church-going. Secular leisure concentrated on improving one's mind and moral worth. This led to a proliferation of philosophical and literary societies. As Bradford society matured, it began to support other cultural pursuits, including art exhibits, lectures, a choral society and a symphony orchestra, a process greatly assisted by the German immigrant community.[123]

Although religion and religious affiliations provided the core of middle-class life, a number of secular associations provided social outlets. Middle-class men enjoyed a greater range of leisure activities, many of them connected to business and politics. The Bradford Club, the Schillerverein, the Union Club and the Liberal Club provided opportunities for socializing. In addition, there were quasi-political or business organizations, like the Bradford Chamber of Commerce or the Association of Manufacturers. On a more informal level, the Bradford Exchange and other business venues were popular meeting spots. All of these activities mingled dinners, drinking and political discussion in a socially exclusive, all-male environment.[124]

For all the importance of formal activities, the home remained the site of most leisure. The centrality of family and home for the middle-class led to the expansion of the household and its activities. The greater size and comfort of middle class homes made it possible for families to entertain guests and to lead private lives sheltered from the outside world. Music, reading, horse riding and family trips filled the time.[125]

As leisure time increased in this period, many argued that it had gone too far and in combination with higher wages provided too many opportunities for working men to drink or pursue other undesirable pleasures.[126] In 1849, the Mayor's Committee on the Moral Condition of the Town identified the debased nature of popular recreations, particularly the role of the pub, as a source of social unrest.[127] Ministers frequently decried the increased time available for leisure and recognized only certain recreations as legitimate. They suggested serious reading and study and condemned light entertainment such as novels and theater, not to mention the pub or music hall.[128]

This unease about the nature of popular leisure combined with a desire to use recreation to aid the improvement of the individual and society. Schools, by raising the level of mass literacy and taste, played a part, but the middle class also designed specific institutions to assist this effort. Often this meant directing preexisting activities into the proper mold, as with works teams in cricket or the educational and religious lectures offered to working men. Churches and mills sponsored choral music clubs to attract workers away from music halls and singing saloons.[129] Other efforts, more ambitious in scope, sought to fundamentally alter working-class leisure. The most significant of these efforts was the temperance movement.[130]

Although its middle-class proponents saw temperance as a way to assist the lower classes, in its early years it possessed a strong working-class thrust. Bradford was an early center for temperance activity, and the first temperance society in England was established in Bradford in 1830. Many local clergymen shunned the first societies because of their association with Chartism and Owenite socialism.[131] With the decline of radical political activity, however, the temperance movement took on a new significance in middle-class eyes. Reformers promoted it as a primary solution for poverty and misery among the working poor.[132] Many regarded drinking as 'the chief obstacle to religious and moral progress and social improvement'.[133] As one letter writer put it:

On all occasions when plans are entertained for social improvement, the desideratum is to 'keep men away from the house'. Social improvement, therefore, requires that drinking houses in general, as they are at present conducted – being evil in their influence on those who frequent them – should be thoroughly reformed and their number considerably reduced.[134]

Temperance societies became an integral part of middle-class reform efforts. In the words of the *Bradford Telegraph*, describing similar efforts in Ireland, 'As is natural, the movement ... finds most influential support from the upper and middle classes, from judges and magistrates, corporate authorities, and clergymen.'[135] Three distinct strands existed in the societies. One sought to convince working men not to drink by appealing to medical science, political economy and morality and by offering alternatives. Another sought to limit the sale of drink, either through outright prohibition or by changing licensing laws and hours. Finally, the Band of Hope movement sought to reach the children of the working class by combining education, entertainment and temperance.

Of these efforts only the last prospered after 1850. The Band of Hope in Bradford grew to 105 chapters with over 20,000 members by 1881.[136]

The others found only limited acceptance. The teetotal movement faced a slowdown in the 1850s and 1860s and repeated financial difficulties forced several differing groups to combine their operations. In spite of efforts to reach the 'respectable and intelligent class of operatives' through open air meetings and tracts, the Bradford United Temperance Society conceded 'the progressive increase of the drink system'.[137] Such judgments seemed to be substantiated by the 1867 election of M. W. Thompson, a brewer, during a campaign marked by a strong stance by the Liberation Society's candidate, Edward Miall, on the issue of licensing.[138]

Despite its limited success, the movement contained elements of working-class self-help, an echo of the older spirit of Chartist self-respect, as indicated by the existence of purely working-men's societies such as the Working Man's Long Pledged Society.[139] For such men, the establishment of the coffee taverns allowed for the type of sociability provided in the pub, without its temptations.[140] The very real problems of drink within working-class culture gave such temperance societies a base of support among both men and women. The Rechabites, a temperance friendly society, flourished in this period.[141]

The same could not be said of the movements for prohibition or changes in licensing laws. These efforts appeared to be much more hostile to popular culture and many in Bradford harshly criticized such efforts. One pamphlet accused the prohibitionists of 'arrogating to themselves the right of deciding on a matter which essentially and entirely belongs to the working class'.[142] At a meeting for the Prohibition of the Liquor Traffic on Sunday, a local councillor and several others attacked the meeting as an imposition upon the working man, who only had Sunday for recreation and who could only afford the beerhouse, unlike the middle class who could afford to drink at home.[143] The U.K. Alliance and the Sunday Closing Association fought a losing battle to close pubs and beershops. Lacking public support for their efforts and faced with the indifference of the police toward drinking, they employed spies to observe pubs and then sought to bring complaints to the magistrates.[144] Such efforts failed to bring a response from the authorities and the temperance societies despaired of their efforts. Reformers acknowledged that 'the young have been largely educated in drinking shops and a generation has arisen in taste neglecting all self-improvement – insubordinate to parents and employers and to authority.'[145]

For reformers who saw drink and degradation as linked, such a failure proved particularly disheartening and some questioned the efficacy of any reform as long as drink remained plentiful. Yet their records demonstrate their exaggerated sense of the problem. The Sunday Closing Association admitted that Sunday drinking was not as prevalent as was thought. Several of its spies contradicted the stereotyped claims of the temperance societies about pubs and music halls.[146] One observer stated that he found very little in his nights of watching. Although there were a few drunks and women of 'loose habits', many in the pubs were respectable persons, out with their spouses. He even encountered acquaintances, including a Sunday School teacher in his church.[147]

These reports highlight the exaggerated notions of 'respectability' that many reformers possessed and the gap between their view and that of the working class. Working men saw social drinking as part of a way of life that included the friendly society and trade union, rather than as a mark of dishonor or non-respectable behavior.[148] At the same time, such organizations distinguished between social drinking and drunkenness and they routinely excluded heavy drinkers. The dilemmas faced by temperance organizations grew out of a misunderstanding about the nature of working-class life and leisure. Working men preferred the pub because it belonged to them and was not under the control of the upper classes, as were other institutions such as the Mechanics Institute.[149] In the words of one observer, 'there are always free sittings at the pub.'[150] The pub, cheap and easily accessible, provided a center for working-class life. In an era when homes were overcrowded and poorly constructed, the pub's attractions were obvious.

What was true about the pub was true about working-class recreation in general. Working-class families lacked the income, time and private space to enjoy the leisure activities of the middle class. This meant that leisure focused on what was affordable and nearby. It also meant that many activities took place in public, outside the home. Until the later nineteenth century, recreation was confined to the streets and waste areas within the city, or in private spaces such as the theater or pub. No open public grounds existed in Bradford and the first public park would not open until the 1860s, with the creation of Peel and Manningham Parks.[151]

A worker's free time was concentrated on the weekend, from Saturday afternoon through Sunday and the use of this leisure time began to take on a familiar pattern as early as the 1850s.[152] Saturday became the primary shopping day of the working class. Reformers tried to get shops to close earlier on Saturdays, both to allow their workers a respite and to remove people from the street. They hoped that by reducing the amount of traffic, they could lessen the attraction of the city streets, especially for the young. Such hopes proved futile, for on the chief night out, Saturday, literally thousands of Bradfordians clogged the inner city streets, going to pubs, beershops and music halls seeking amusement. One local temperance advocate estimated that at least 19,000 people (or one in seven of the entire population) drank on a typical Saturday night.[153]

The professionalization of entertainment grew out of the combination of the new patterns of leisure and consumption among the working-class public.[154] In addition to pubs and other drinking establishments, the tradition of pub singing gave rise to the large music halls, the first of which was the Bermondsey Singing Saloon in the 1840s. This was succeeded by a number of halls, including the Star Theater and Pullans, which seated over 3,000 people.[155] The halls were lively places which served food and drink and where men and women of all ages mingled.[156] In addition to the music halls, several theaters in Bradford offered both stage plays and variety entertainment.[157] Finally, various groups arranged lecture series, lantern shows and other events at the public halls in the city, such as the Oddfellows' Hall, the Temperance Hall and St George's Hall.

While generally peaceful, this culture possessed a rougher side. The increased presence of the police after 1847 served to limit overt violence, but they generally took a hands-off attitude. This tolerance reflected not only an acceptance of drinking, but also a fear of confrontation. Bradford papers carried numerous reports of policemen who suffered beatings at the hands of outraged drinkers and their friends.[158] Lower middle-class or middle-class men might mingle among the crowd or visit brothels, but this too was a risky experience. On Derby Day in 1872, four revelers returning from the race hit the wife of a railway porter with flour. In response an outraged crowd pulled them from their cab, rolled them in the mud and covered them with flour.[159] Such violence could even intrude into middle class areas, as when New Year's Eve mummers went in search of money and drink.[160]

The other side of Saturday night was the emergence of the English Sunday. On Sunday, the great day of leisure, people engaged in a variety of activities. For a minority, this meant the round of church and Sunday school, while the majority combined domestic duties, rest and recreation. As one agent of the Town Mission reported,

In the course of visitation this afternoon I found strong men in bed, others reading the papers, females baking, old Sunday School scholars polishing furniture and scrubbing floors.[161]

Letter writers to local papers complained of 'indecent recreations' on Sunday, including pitch and toss, nude racing, and dog running, which the police allowed to take place.[162] Sunday was the principal day for wakes and funerals, and their commotion disturbed middle-class observers already upset at the general level of activity on Sunday.[163]

The presence of such activities constituted another distinctive aspect of leisure patterns among the working class. While the middle class moved away from older public pastimes, they remained important among the working class even after the rise of newer consumer pursuits. Each township retained its own fairs and tidings, which drew the ire of temperance advocates for their sales of alcohol.[164] Teachers reported considerable declines in attendance during these fairs and the advocates of thrift decried the expense and extravagance that working-class families incurred to enjoy them.[165] In addition race meets, Whitsuntide galas, as well as special celebrations like the Sunday School and Band of Hope gatherings punctuated the year. Factory outings and those of clubs and societies provided another form of diversion for working men and women. By the end of this period, the round of galas and holidays took their modern form, with the advent of Bank Holidays and seasonal festivities such as Whitsuntide and Christmas.

Much leisure remained informal and spontaneous, relying on makeshift equipment and grounds. Cricket, racing, swimming, walking and wrestling were popular. One teacher noted that for schoolboys in the summer, 'Cricket seems to absorb the leisure of their evening.'[166] The lack of open ground made it difficult to play, and cricket teams searched for new venues as fields disappeared. Working-class children, lacking the facilities for skating except on mill ponds, constructed snow slides, which the police destroyed when they found them.[167] Swimmers bathed in what pond or hole could be found, sometimes to the displeasure (or amusement) of bystanders.[168] Gambling and the sports associated with it, dog racing and boxing, survived despite attempts by the police to suppress them.[169] Often gambling took place within the pub, as shown by the arrest of beerhouse keeper Christopher Simians for gaming in 1855.[170] Boxing, despite its reputation among the middle class as a degenerate pleasure of the aristocracy, flourished underground, with fights being held on the moors, until it reemerged as a club sport in the 1890s.[171]

As was the case with pubs and music halls, increased leisure time led to the creation of new forms of professional sport geared to the working-class audience in the 1870s. Professional cricket grew out of the local love of the game and works and neighborhood teams preceded the professional leagues. With the addition of a few professionals for each side and the erection of the Park Avenue grounds in 1880, the structure of the modern sport was in place. In football, semi-professional city and area teams, whose exploits were well covered by the local papers, appeared in the 1860s. Bradford's first rugby club was organized in 1866, and a match in 1880 against Huddersfield drew over 10,000 spectators.[172]

A distinctive pattern of working-class leisure emerged in the mid-Victorian era that differed from both earlier working-class patterns and those of the middle class. The new division of time by work, the creation of the weekend and the influence of the new urban environment created this distinctive pattern of recreation and it endured until the advent of new forms of mass entertainment in the twentieth century. Echoes of it still survive today in the Saturday shopping and football matches that punctuate the week in northern towns.

VOLUNTARY ORGANIZATIONS

Nowhere were the differences between working class and middle class life more pronounced than in the area of voluntary organizations. Middle-class supporters of voluntarism emphasized the benefits of self-improvement that voluntary organizations offered to the working class. At the same time, commentators recognized that the relative social fluidity of the early nineteenth century no longer existed. As Reverend John Deduces noted, the attainments of an earlier group of self-made men such as Arkwright would most likely not be recreated.[173] With the slump of the 1870s, it became evident that self-help alone would not lift up the majority of the working class nor even supply them with the means to weather periodic economic downturns.[174] As the limits to self-help appeared, the elite began to redefine its value to the working class. Self-help had an increasingly individualistic, moral definition for its middle-class proponents. The Reverend Eddowes suggested, if instead of ambitiously longing for an eminence which we are never likely to attain, we content ourselves with the diligent cultivation of such powers as we have, the reward of our diligence will be sure to follow.[175]

Another minister noted that diligence did not always bring material riches, 'Competence, and contentment, reliance on God, and resignation to his will, these are true riches, and within the reach of all.'[176]

This individualistic and moral view of the aims of voluntary association and self-help deemphasized the collective solidarity prized by working-class organizations. Middle-class institutions were less committed to the idea of the group.[177] In the words of the president of the Halifax United YMCA,

> Self-reliance is only another word for self-activity . . . Organizations can do little or nothing for any of us, unless there be a personal conviction of the importance of mental and moral progress, combined with individual energy, self-denial, and perseverance in the several tasks to which we address ourselves . . . Organizations cannot supply the real strength needful for work; they may supply a little stimulant or a little sympathy, and these we admit are not without their value.[178]

The focus of the middle class upon a moral definition of self-help conflicted with that held by working-class voluntary organizations. From the beginning working-class organizations had a different motivation and purpose than that promoted by the elite. Working-class institutions – friendly societies, building societies and trade unions – combined leisure with the more practical goal of self-help. The desire to protect the worker from the effects of the New Poor Law and its treatment of the indigent provided the impetus for the expansion of the societies.[179] The harsh nature of Poor Relief and the use of Test-Work made workers reluctant to apply to the Guardians, even in cases of real destitution.[180] The increased insistence from the 1860s upon indoor relief in the workhouse as opposed to outdoor relief only reinforced this reluctance.[181]

In addition, the disciplinary nature of tests to distinguish the 'deserving' from 'undeserving' poor began to drift from the Poor Law Guardians to private charity. Many saw charity as harmful to the poor and sought to eliminate vagrancy and beggary through the use of the police.[182] Charities felt the pressure to identify and aid only the deserving poor. These fears led to the establishment of the Charity

Organization Society in London in 1869 in order to tighten the administration of charity.[183] A Bradford branch of the COS began in 1880 to oversee the distribution of charity in the city and to prevent 'it from being abused by impostors or incorrigible idlers'.[184] Using the criteria of 'deserving poor', the society denied relief to 3,643 out of 7,164 applicants, distributing only £410 in 1881. The BCOS defended itself against charges of inadequate charity by arguing its true purpose was to end the abuse of charity rampant in Bradford. In contrast, the Bradford Tradesmen's Benevolent Institution, set up to help fallen middle-class men and women by supplying money and housing, gave out £881 to forty-two pensioners in 1877, part of more than £12,000 spent on such pensions from 1857 to 1877.[185]

Such disparities led some to accuse the wealthy of self-interest and hypocrisy in their charitable efforts. James Firth noted that the charitable Quakers were quick to hound a man for debt.[186] The Wool Combers Aid Society, set up in spring of 1854, existed to encourage the emigration of destitute wool combers and thus lessen applications for relief in a period of depression. It continued despite the fact that many of its intended beneficiaries encountered unemployment and harsh treatment in their new homes.[187] The medical charities of Bradford also received their share of criticism. While they treated the sick and injured members of the working class, they also provided a necessary service for the millowners. Factory owners no longer retained their own surgeon or doctor, but simply paid a small subscription to the Bradford Infirmary to receive the right to admit patients. One-third of the cases treated and half the deaths in the Infirmary were the result of injuries.[188] The concern of the elite did not extend to illness outside the workplace; the wealthy shunned the Bradford Homeopathic Dispensary, which catered to working-class patients. The Dispensary, flooded with cases, shut down because it could not survive on the small payments such patients made.[189] The poor remained critically short of health care services and the Poor Law Guardians failed to fill this gap in medical services. In 1871 each of Bradford's seven medical districts had over 20,000 inhabitants per medical officer.[190]

The combination of limited financial benefits and condescending treatment limited private charity's impact upon Bradford's working class. The largest voluntary organizations in the working-class community – the friendly societies – reflected the harsh realities of the Poor Law and the inadequacy of private charity that forced working men to combine to aid themselves in times of sickness or death. This defensive mindset, with its more pragmatic and collective goals, was very different from that of the middle class and gave voluntary organizations among the working class their special character.[191] Unlike middle-class organizations, these groups retained a more collective spirit after 1850.

Working people felt more comfortable turning to their own resources in this era. Bradford possessed a well-established system of working-class self-help. In 1874, C.L. Stanley, the Assistant Commissioner for the Committee on Friendly Societies, reported that there were over 10,000 members of friendly societies in Bradford and 3,800 trade union members, who received more than £13,000 a year in benefits.[192] The societies varied in size and type from the large affiliated orders such as the Oddfellows and Foresters to more specialized groups such as the Rechabites (temperance) and the Orangemen. The friendly societies also provided adult men with another source of entertainment, for they often met in pubs, with a portion of the proceeds going for liquor.[193]

The largest of the friendly societies was the Manchester Unity Independent Order of Oddfellows. The first chapter in Bradford, established in 1829, had 3,382 members by 1874. The society offered both sickness and death benefits through a network of lodges in the city. In addition, it created a Medical Aid Association, which for the payment of a 3s. fee, gave the member and his family access to a doctor on retainer to the Association.[194] Despite the general prosperity of the period, the Oddfellows' membership stagnated at about 3,500 after the initial period of growth in the 1840s. A key problem was the cost of membership, for most workers could not afford a subscriptions of 2s. to 3s. per month. Bradford's societies remained the preserve of the upper working classes; the members of trade unions and friendly societies constituted only one-third of the adult male population.

In addition to the friendly societies, there were also several cooperatives, a savings bank, and two building societies. All these institutions provided working men with an opportunity to save and invest, but it must be questioned to what extent they embraced a majority of the working class or whether they provided the means for the escape from the problems of poverty and insecurity.[195] Cooperatives in Bradford dated back to the 1830s and two societies that started in 1860 with 200 members had over 6,000 members by the end of 1881.[196] Employers such as Jacob Behrens saw them as tools of practical political economy and a way to smooth the relations between labor and capital. Working-class supporters emphasized the possibility of creating a new type of economic order and even more the pragmatic goal of securing cheap and good food.[197] Despite their success, cooperatives failed to cover more than a fraction of the working class and their refusal to allow the use of credit (as well as their policy of charging full price for goods) prevented many members of the working class from using their facilities.[198]

The building societies present an even more ambiguous picture. Originally, building societies started as a means of allowing working men and others to acquire freehold property, partly to obtain the vote and partly to get decent housing. The first societies were terminating societies, set up by a small group of individuals in order to build homes for them to occupy or lease. These suffered from a lack of capital and were often associated with speculative building.[199] In the 1850s, permanent societies appeared in Bradford. The Second (1851) and Third (1854) Equitable Building Societies sought to create a more stable environment for house construction and to allow working men to own homes. J. A. Binns, president of the Third Equitable Building Society, portrayed the societies as a form of self-help, praising the 'homey wisdom of Yorkshire' found in them and lauding their beneficial 'effect . . . not only in the financial prosperity, but in the moral character, of a large portion of the people.'[200]

Despite such rhetoric, the goal of aiding working men quickly became a secondary concern. Although both societies grew rapidly, they came under criticism for serving the interest of middle-class borrowers and ignoring the needs of primarily working-class depositors. By 1880, the Second Equitable possessed over £2,000,000 in assets and enrolled 7,000 members, of whom over 440 were depositors, 1,500 were investors and 1,100 borrowers.[201] Unlike the Third Equitable, the Second Equitable allowed borrowers a say in the running of the society. One member charged that the borrowers controlled the board and acted in their own self-interest. Even the official historian of the society admitted, 'Some advances were made to owners of single houses, but many more were made to builders and property investors, as well as to manufacturers and tradesmen.'[202] The Third Society tended to loan more to small borrowers, generally of the upper ranges of the operative class, 'overlookers, warehousemen, and clerks'.[203] This group made up 80 per cent of the investors and perhaps 50 per cent of the borrowers, the rest being, in the words of Joseph Binns, society president, 'middle class'. This contradicted the original purpose of the society, as Binns admitted.

Observers lauded building societies as institutions of self-help that allowed working men to achieve independence, both through accumulating capital and by participating in the management of the society. They contrasted them to the Yorkshire Penny Bank, which mobilized the savings of the working class by allowing one shilling deposits. Such savings banks, paternalistic institutions utilized mainly by women and children, were run by a group of the elite, with the express purpose of teaching proper habits of thrift.[204] Yet, in practice, there appears to have been little difference in the operation of the two institutions. The working class participated in building societies primarily as depositors and investors, while the middle class directed the building societies and borrowed the majority of funds. Businessmen in Bradford used the building societies as an alternative source of capital, outside the control of merchants or banking houses.[205] By mobilizing the capital of the lower middle class and artisans under the wing of Friendly Societies legislation, they obtained much more favorable conditions of operation than commercial banks.[206]

Even in their primary task of providing housing, the building societies had a poor record. Their requirements for payment limited the pool of borrowers to those with 20–25 per cent of the capital up front, in addition to a well-paying, steady job that allowed them to take on a mortgage of up to twenty-four years.[207] The societies aided speculative building, either by building clubs or land societies, and helped foster the growth of the notorious back-to-back house favored by these groups. This involvement in speculative building created severe difficulties for the societies in the late 1850s and 1870s as the collapse of the housing market produced a wave of failures by borrowers.[208] In the end, the societies may have made the provision of housing worse for the working poor excluded from using their services.[209]

The trade unions of Bradford produced the sharpest conflict over the purposes of collective action and association. These organizations proved to be a constant thorn in the side of the Bradford elite, who undertook a vigorous campaign to persuade the working class not to belong. By the mid-1870s, C. L. Stanley estimated the membership in sixteen of the largest unions at over 3,800. This excluded a number of large unions, such as the bricklayers, dyers and miners, which meant that 10 to 15 per cent of the adult male workforce belonged to unions. This figure also excluded more ephemeral organizations of unskilled and skilled workers that sprang up in response to particular grievances. Trade unions offered many of the same benefits as the friendly societies, with two important additions – many offered both strike and unemployment pay to their members. They sought to enforce work rules, control hiring, and bargain for higher wages.

DEMOCRACY AND VOLUNTARY ASSOCIATION

Working-class voluntary organizations attempted to realize a more collective and democratic vision of the social order.[210] This spirit found its expression in the mode of operation of friendly societies. Despite their ceremonial regalia and elaborate procedures, the societies were internally democratic.[211] All members voted in elections using secret ballots and conflicts were settled by agreed upon rules and arbitration by ones's peers. Such practices allowed men to realize democratic principles denied them by the electoral and judicial structures of mid-Victorian England. The societies can partly be seen as the training ground of working men for politics. The procedures of these societies, along with their drinking and sociability, differed from the notion of 'respectable' self-help promoted by the elite for working men. They were also very different from the methods of governance chosen by middle-class clubs, like the Bradford Union Club, which retained the blackball.[212]

While respectability, along with independence, remains a term with a multiplicity of meanings, it clearly animated much of the activity of the voluntary associations.[213] The societies' rituals provided a public verification of respectability that demonstrated the worthiness of their members. Participation in parades and other public events gave members greater visibility in the eyes of their community. This hard-won status rested on their ability to maintain themselves above the mass of other workers and to protect their independence in times of unemployment or sickness.

Voluntary organizations, for all their emphasis on solidarity and collective self-help, served to mark the lines of division and conflict within the working-class community. By their very nature, they tended to exclude large portions of the community. The poor and transient were kept out by their lack of resources, which mirrored their marginality within the working class. Unable to join, they fell back upon informal clubs and societies, as well as relief.[214] Friendly societies, trade unions, cooperatives and building societies all appealed to more prosperous workers, who possessed the extra resources required to subscribe to their funds. The exclusiveness of self-help contradicted the claims of working men that they represented the working class as a whole.

Voluntary organizations marginalized women, for they were entirely male and their activities, centered in the pub, gave few opportunities for women to participate in even an auxiliary capacity. The societies, along with trade unions and the rites of passage associated with work, became a part of the reconstruction of manhood in the mid-century. Acceptance into these groups marked the entrance into respectable adult life for young men.[215] Voluntary societies built upon an assumed division of male and female spheres and the separation of public and private action that characterized Victorian ideals of gender.

The assumption of female dependence and a lack of resources inhibited independent action by most women in this era. Formal organizations among women were limited to middle-class women involved in charity or moral reform. Women staffed and supported groups like the Society for the Care of Friendless Girls, but these organizations remained dependent upon constant infusions of money to stay afloat. The same was true of friendly societies for working-class women attached to such organizations. Only in the 1890s, with the rise of the ILP, new unions and suffrage societies did opportunities for independent action come into existence. Even then, the dominance of men at the top of both political and trade union groups limited women to a secondary role. Julia Varley, daughter of a weaver and radical unionist and feminist, remained the exception rather than the rule.

The societies also reflected the ethnic divisions within the community. Excluded by income and background from many voluntary associations, the Irish founded their own social and political groups. The Catholic Church served as a focus of communal life. Despite the image of a monolithic Catholicism held by contemporaries, the Catholic Church in Bradford faced many of the same problems as other churches. Priests tried to attract a poor, working-class population to services in competition with the many alternatives offered by city life by using friendly societies and other social organizations.[216] Many of the Irish of Bradford retained a strong sense of national identification and lectures and discussions of Irish life held by the Mechanics' Institute attracted large crowds.[217] This nationalist identity also found expression in movements for Irish liberation, which built on earlier Irish political activism in the 1840s. Nationalist organizations found ready support among the local Irish population. A branch of the Irish National League was formed in 1864 and the Fenian society had its adherents in a later era.[218] In 1880, the arrest of John Tobin, a construction worker, for the possession of weapons revealed the existence of a Fenian network. Police claimed Tobin had over a hundred associates in Bradford and more in the surrounding area.[219]

The presence of the Irish proved to be a sore point for many in the city. They depicted the Irish as drunken, coarse creatures, incapable of reformation. In the 1840s and 1850s, the Poor Law Union deported many back to Ireland on dubious legal grounds.[220] The anti-Irish animus found its clearest expression in a voluntary society, the Orangemen.[221] Headed by Squire Auty, a Tory compositor and editor of the *Orange Banner*, the Orangemen engaged in a series of conflicts with the Irish, culminating in a pitched street fight in 1863 after a notorious anti-Catholic speaker lectured in the city. Fearing disturbances, the Borough Council called on the army in March of 1867 in order to keep order with the approach of St Patrick's Day and swore in special constables before canceling Christmas Mass in the same year.[222] This anti-Irish feeling began to fade in the late nineteenth century as migration slowed, but the Irish maintained their distinctiveness into the twentieth century.[223]

The entire range of working-class activities demonstrates the tendencies toward fragmentation within working-class culture in this era. Divided by occupation, gender and ethnicity, the public culture of the working class provides only a partial version of the experiences of workers in mid-Victorian England. Women lived much of their lives in the domestic sphere, out of view. Similarly, the poor and Irish, by virtue of their exclusion from 'respectable' society, left little permanent record. What survives is the experience of adult male skilled workers and the world they built upon shared sensibilities and opportunities. The societies and their counterparts, the trade unions, increasingly put themselves forward as the spokesmen of their class, reserving to themselves the voice of protest and accommodation. The agenda they pursued was set by their position as adult male, skilled workers and consequently, their struggles with the Liberal elite of Bradford revolved around their concerns.

To what extent did this culture express the needs of the entire working class and not simply this narrow stratum? The formal organizations of the working class, trade unions and friendly societies, expressed the aspirations of the most well-to-do members of that class to be an association of equals. They also built upon the inescapable reality of economic insecurity, which forced them to seek shelter in mutual aid. As a result, the skilled and the unskilled shared a common outlook and mentality, one of caution and thrift. Both groups, in their attitudes toward education and mutual aid, recognized that they were unlikely to escape their status through individual effort alone. Only through collective action, either in trade unions or in political agitation, could they hope to raise their lot in life. Common patterns of residence and leisure created a bond between differing members of the working-class community and reinforced their separation from middle-class culture.

This separation created divergent visions of social and domestic order. These differences informed questions like family size and family relations. For the middle class, the stages of home, school, work and marriage came in easy succession, while for the working class, both home and education were subordinate to the necessity of earning a living. Family limitation came out of the limited horizons and resources that lay at the heart of working-class life in this era. The use of birth control, like emigration, offered immediate rewards and thus could be integrated within this culture without fundamentally altering it.

9780333604793

5 Gender and Family Life in Mid-Victorian Bradford

In a letter to the *Bradford Observer* on January 7, 1864, a 'Voice from the Back Slums' raised the issue he termed the 'most important question of modern times' – the homes of the working class. The writer noted that their significance went beyond their obvious importance as shelter, 'homes being, as has been truly said, the manufactories of men'. The idea of the home as a manufactory represents the antithesis of Victorian ideals that pictured the home as a separate sphere removed from the marketplace. On several levels, however, it addresses the reality of family life for many in nineteenth-century England. The rise of industry and the spread of urban life transformed the home and family life. The decline of the home as a place of work and its isolation as a place of consumption and reproduction failed to shield its inhabitants from the public sphere of the marketplace. Family members entered the market as workers, under the control and influence of others. Inevitably this shift changed the relationships within the family and brought the market, in the form of wage labor, into the home. Such a rearrangement of the family and the home served the needs of industry, making the family an adjunct of the mill.

The discourse of family life in Victorian England centered on the consequences of this change. The belief in the separateness of the home and market denied the reality of the shift in working-class family life, while offering a solution to the disruption of the family. This solution called on men and women to embrace domesticity and a specific set of gender roles and moral precepts to guide the family. The idealized image of the family dominated the discourse of the era, but it repeatedly collided with the realities of family and gender, opening the way for alternative explanations of the problems of family life and new solutions for these problems.

Throughout the second half of the century, the family, especially the working-class family, remained the subject of an intense debate. By

141

tracing this debate and the anxieties it generated, we can reconstruct how Victorians of all classes felt about a range of issues tied to the family – child care, birth control, relations within the family and gender roles. This debate did not solve the problems of family life, rather it laid bare its central contradictions. Conflicts between work and home, between the needs of children and the limits of parents and between men and women over resources and sexual power all existed in the Victorian family. These issues appear only tangentially in the discourse on the family, for the dominant ideology of separate spheres displaced these concerns and reduced them to adjuncts of the larger question of the moral fitness of parents and children. Yet these issues were crucial to working-class families as they struggled to meet the needs of home and work. They also lay at at the heart of family limitation in the late nineteenth century.

THE DEBATE OVER THE FAMILY

The Victorian middle class saw the family through its own vision of domesticity. In this vision, the home constituted a refuge from the larger world, a private haven from the pressures of the public marketplace. In turn, the division of the world in separate spheres, public and private, was premised on the belief in the differing characters and abilities of men and women. Men entered the public world of business and politics, where their rationality, aggressiveness and intellectual power allowed them to succeed. Women remained at home in order to cultivate their moral and nurturing characters, which they used to guide their children and husbands.[1] While this model reflected the experience of middle-class families, Victorians considered it a universal one to which all should aspire. Middle-class Bradfordians shared this idea of domesticity. For most, it was axiomatic that the family should be the primary focus of life. One local magazine referred to domestic life as 'the prime charm of life'.[2] Another described the home as 'the crystal of society; it is the school of civilization; it is the centre around which the moral and social world revolves'.[3]

The ability of the home to serve as a 'moral regulator' depended on its ability to counter the effects of the marketplace and the world upon the members of the family. Without the strict separation of public and private worlds, it would be difficult to prevent the outside world from corrupting the family. The belief in the purity of the home coexisted uneasily with the reality that middle-class incomes often relied upon the labor of working-class women and children and that this labor shaped the working-class home. The need to address the seeming contradiction between the needs of industry and the idealization of domestic life constituted a primary task for the middle class, particularly in textile areas of the north like Bradford.

Victorian commentators on family life in Bradford acknowledged the impact of industry upon the working-class family. Bradford, an early site of industrialization, completed the shift from domestic labor to factory employment by the 1850s.[4] Both critics and defenders of the industrial system pointed to the ways in which the the triumph of the factory system affected family relationships within the working-class. J. H. Marshall, head of the Town Mission, felt that the factory, while a social good because it provided wealth, was not yet a moral blessing because of its 'corrupting influence'. Robert Baker, Inspector of Factories for the Bradford District, argued that the employment of women and children inverted the moral order, but he also recognized that this benefited the employer 'by affording him a more docile set of workpeople and by enabling him, by a lower rate of wages, to compete more successfully in all markets'.[5]

The factory separated family members and removed women and children in the worsted trade from the direct supervision of fathers and husbands.[6] The decline of home work also created a greater division between the domestic and work worlds, a trend reinforced by the tendency for children to work and go to school. Observers believed that the ample opportunities for work for women and children in the worsted trade undermined the normal patterns of authority within the working-class family by allowing women and children to earn an independent income.[7] To many, such earning power, in conjunction with the decline of older skilled trades, implied a lessening of paternal authority.

The political conflicts of the 1830s and 1840s mobilized these concerns about changes within the family. The attack upon the emerging industrial order by the anti-Poor Law movement, Chartism and the Factory Agitation raised more than issues of political empowerment and economic justice. Working-class leaders and those sympathetic to their plight used issues of family and gender to attack their enemies and to bolster their claims of moral superiority.[8] Critics of the New Poor Law attacked its provisions for the separation of the family in the workhouse, which they viewed as an attack upon the integrity of the working-class family. Women in particular criticized the lack of concern for single mothers, who could not receive outdoor relief and who could not pursue the father for payment. Supporters of factory legislation also invoked the negative impact of industry upon the working-class family to gather support for a Ten-Hours Bill.[9] For Richard Oastler, a leader of the Factory Agitation, the unregulated factory system destroyed 'the home of the working man; for he had no wife there, no child there: it was to him no longer [home]!'[10]

These claims called into question the morality of industrial capitalism. Chartists and others in Bradford depicted the employment of women and children as a moral failing on the part of factory owners, an indictment of their greed and their inability to live up to the ideal of a good employer.[11] While mill owners accepted that they should attend to the 'vast numbers of persons whom the system of mill labour place under their control', they sought to resolve these problems outside the realm of the factory, by focusing on moral and social reform rather than restrictive legislation.[12] Thus, in 1849 the Mayor's Committee on the Moral Condition of the Town dismissed an attempt by Reverend W. F. Black to bring up the issue of shift work by women and children because it lay outside the competence of that body.[13]

Women played an ambiguous role in these campaigns. Their participation in _____ activities gave greater credence to criticisms of the _____ of women, part of a crowd protestin _____ Board, attacked the Guardians. Th _____ rmed in 1839, organized marches _____ back up their call for political reform _____ processions and street battles that ch _____ up until its demise in 1848.[14] This p _____ their position within the working _____ s, particularly in the Owenite socialist camp, believed that _____ deserved an equal role with men and the possession of the vote, this remained a minority viewpoint.[15] The hope for equality between men and women within the working class did not survive the 1840s. As men increasingly formalized and controlled the institutions of the movement, women's roles greatly diminished.[16]

The role of women within working-class radical movements reflected the larger construction of their place within the working-class community. Women participated as an outgrowth of their role as wives and mothers, which gave them greater moral authority, rather than an equal voice. This in turn reflected the consolidation of conceptions of gender and family within Chartism and the working-class as a whole. The ideal of a universal definition of the working-class public that included men and women as equals gave way to an ideology that relegated women to a secondary role.[17] Working-class men, seeking to counter claims of moral and social inferiority on the part of middle-class critics, argued that in a better world women would be confined to the home, leaving work and the public sphere to men.[18] The language of Chartism and other working-class movements became a double-edged sword, which asserted masculine privilege in public, even as it attacked the privileges of capital and landowners within England.

The assertion of masculine privilege was hardly new or unique, for it built on older traditions of male crafts and political groups.[19] Yet, in the context of industrialization, this rhetoric rang hollow. In new cities like Bradford, artisan traditions held little sway. Part of the reason for the location of the worsted industry in the West Riding of Yorkshire lay in the weakness of artisan guilds that could have blocked innovations by manufacturers. No golden age of domestic labor characterized the worsted trade, for it had been built on the labor of the family under the dominance of the merchants who controlled the industry. By the 1840s, the surviving pockets of domestic labor in weaving and combing suffered from low wages, poor conditions and extreme self-exploitation.[20]

Given the centrality of the factory in the worsted trade from the 1850s on, men did not simply struggle to preserve their crafts and their homes from the depredations of greedy masters, they also sought to secure advantages for themselves within the factory's hierarchy of labor at the expense of other workers. In practice this meant that skilled labor became a male monopoly, while women and children remained marginalized as semi-skilled workers. The new skilled trades of the worsted factory, trades that did not exist before the 1820s or 1830s, relied upon this exclusion and its acceptance by mill owners to flourish.[21]

The rhetoric of Chartism could be assimilated by men in the worsted trade, for it elevated their struggle for position into a struggle for empowerment for the class as a whole. Even after the collapse of Chartism and the passage of the Ten Hours Bill, men invoked domestic rhetoric in their efforts to improve their position. During the mid-Victorian era, male unionists in Bradford and elsewhere campaigned for shorter hours and restrictive legislation, both of which ultimately benefited them, by citing the need to educate and shelter women and children.[22] In a letter to the *Bradford Observer* in 1871, 'Blandini' called for the adoption of the nine-hour day for men and a six-hour day for women and children. He justified this limitation by arguing that, wives and daughters shall be restricted to six hours per day, to give them a chance to learn domestic duties, for why should females be employed outside the domestic hearth. The domestic hearth is the only sphere in which they can shine in all their brilliance. What business have they outside of it?[23]

As the sole voices of their class and their families, working-class men felt obliged to defend women and children. This obligation could be seen as one of the duties of manhood and an assertion of masculinity. In the contest between workers and employers, both sides questioned the manliness of the other. During the controversy over the Nine Hour Day in the 1870s, a leader of the movement derided owners for failing the take a 'manly' stance in opposition.[24] For their part, employers accused skilled workers, especially overlookers, of hiding behind women. As one put it,

In conclusion, it is my opinion that it is not at all a question with the women and children. They are satisfied, and it remains for the overlookers who have the matter in hand to prove their work calls forth such physical exertion as to demand the concession.[25]

Such arguments asserted a new notion of domestic order and masculinity among working-class males. Increasingly, calls for regulation of the work place, union recognition and higher wages built upon the notion of the head of the household as sole provider, entitled to a 'family wage' and protection from the worst forms of competition in order to preserve the family.[26] Unions and political organizations formed part of an increasingly masculine public sphere among the working-class.[27] The self-identity of men as respectable providers informed these organizations and their efforts to buttress the position of the male wage earner.

This attitude among unionists prevailed up until the First World War. Even progressives like William Drew of the General Union of Textile Workers, who supported women's rights, opposed the employment of women. In testimony before the Royal Commission on Labour, he argued that women's and children's labor competed with that of men and should be prohibited.

I expect that by taking these people [half-timers and women] out of the mills, there would be a greater scarcity of labour than there is now; that there would be a lessened competition of operatives, and a greater demand for them, and I am sure we would get more for our labour.[28]

He supported this demand by arguing that women's natural sphere lay within the home. Drew's testimony anticipated the arguments of unionists and others within the Independent Labour Party in the 1890s, who pushed for protective legislation and the restriction of women's work.[29]

The ILP, despite its support for women's suffrage, remained ambivalent about the role of women within society and the socialist movement. Women in the rank and file sometimes found themselves relegated to 'womanly' duties such as organizing teas and fund-raising bazaars. Female leaders like Margaret McMillan, acknowledged as effective writers and speakers, found themselves involved in what the ILP considered their sphere of activity – child welfare, family issues and education. While this reflected the interests of some female activists, it also revealed the limits of progressive working-class men when it came to women's place in society. The ILP and union members in the West Riding and elsewhere tended to subsume these campaigns by women to the achievement of the family wage, as in the drive for fair contracts at union wages from borough councils.[30]

In the later nineteenth century, working-class men located the causes of familial and social ills in the excesses of the competitive system, which failed to offer an adequate wage to men and which forced women and children into the workplace. While this conception allowed them to criticize the middle class and argue for a better position for themselves, it also made them vulnerable to middle-class attacks on the personal character of working-class men and women. The lack of an alternative vision of family life made it difficult for working-class men and women to defend their actual family arrangements, which often differed from the Victorian ideal.

THE WORKING-CLASS CHILD

Middle-class observers often seized upon the differences in working-class families to criticize them. In their view, the problems of working-class life could be traced to the moral failings of individuals and an inadequate home life. The inability of working-class men and women to conform to their expected roles and the resultant disorder in working-class homes lay at the heart of the poverty and misery of the age and only a return to proper domestic values could ensure progress. The role of children within the family constituted one key area of difference between the middle class and the working class. The eighteenth century saw a change in English views of childhood, at least among the middle class. Children came to be viewed as innocent and childhood became a unique period in which the young should be nurtured and shaped by their parents.[31] The Victorian middle-class, which emphasized the bonds of family, placed the care of children at the center of domestic life.[32]

The belief that children should be nurtured in the home contrasted starkly with the reality of children's labor. The widespread use of children in industry, especially textiles, struck many as a violation of the innocence of children. While many commented on the ill-effects of such labor upon the child, most in the middle class proved reluctant to condemn child labor. The centrality of such labor for the worsted trade led many to point to its beneficial qualities and the opportunities for education and training it offered.[33]

However, middle-class critics could and did criticize the erosion of parental authority by factory employment. The ability of children to earn money outside the home opened up the possibility for greater freedom, especially for those over thirteen who could work full-time. Once a full-time worker, a young person could move out of the family home and into the network of lodging homes. Most young workers stayed within the family household, but with a different relationship to their parents.[34] According to Robert Baker, a Leeds physician and the Factory Inspector for Bradford in the 1850s, parents grew increasingly dependent on their children's wages as they aged. Yet these children became more independent as they grew older, a situation he blamed upon a lack of education and high wages.[35] Forty years later, Margaret McMillan painted a similar picture,

> As for the half-timer, he is still more revolutionary. The claims of the human being, irrespective of age, sex, and conditions, are urged loudly today. Who has stirred up all the clamour, if it be not this eleven year old urchin with clogs, or the like of him? It dawns on him, on the day following his eleventh birthday, that he is in a new relationship to his parents – the relationship of a person who pays part of the rent, the nature of this new relationship becomes very clear. Parental control can obtain only where children are dependent on their parents. With manhood and womanhood the leading strings are loosed, and the half-timer is, economically at least, an adult.[36]

Some in Bradford linked child labor to a loss of communal and parental control over children and adolescents. The city provided ample opportunities for the young to enjoy greater freedom and to spend their incomes.[37] Young people crowded the streets of the inner borough, especially on Saturday night. The church steps, the Free Library and the Art Gallery all offered arenas for meeting the opposite sex away from the watchful eyes of parents and neighbors, while local pubs and music halls appealed to older adolescents.[38] Clergymen spoke with disapproval of the swarms of young people on the streets on weekend evenings, who strayed into music halls or worse and thereby sank into corruption and vice. According to one pamphlet.

> All who are accustomed to manufacturing towns must have been painfully impressed by the sight of hundreds of operatives of both sexes, wandering listlessly, or standing idly at street corners, ready for any mischief and wearied of inaction.[39]

To many it seemed as if an entire generation had grown up outside the control of both their parents and the moralizing agencies of the town fathers.

THE QUESTION OF GENDER IN VICTORIAN BRADFORD

The decline of parental authority proved especially significant when it came to young women. As both Joan Scott and Robert Gray have noted, questions of child labor also overlapped with ideas of gender through concerns about the moral and physical health of young women.[40] In the eyes of middle-class social reformers, the problems of working-class family life began with the immorality and inadequate domestic training of women. The women of Bradford, 'unsexed' by their labor in the mills and their experiences prior to marriage, lacked the capacity to perform the domestic duties that ensured the well-being of their families.

As was the case with children's labor, few in Bradford advocated the abolition of women's work. Young single women flocked to Bradford from outlying areas of Yorkshire, and from as far away as Ireland, seeking employment. They made up over a quarter of the worsted textile labor force, primarily in spinning and weaving.[41] The existence of this 'floating population' seemed to flaunt the principles of domestic order and their presence generated considerable unease among Bradford's middle class.

This state of affairs provoked a number of proposals for controlling these women. In 1846, the Reverend William Scoresby, the Vicar of Bradford, called for the establishment of regulated lodging houses along the lines of those in American textile cities such as Lowell. These would provide women with religious and moral guidance, rational amusements, opportunities for improvement and domestic training.[42] Robert Baker echoed this attitude when he supported the regulation and control of this population; while J. H. Marshall, head of the Town Mission, called for more reformatories and prisons to eradicate the problem.[43] Such concerns led to the licensing of common lodging houses and the appointment of a lodging officer to inspect them in the mid-1850s.[44]

Local activists also relied on less drastic measures to guide the female population. Special charities and institutes sprang up to assist young women. The Female Refuge for 'fallen women' set up a home in May of 1861 to reform prostitutes. The Church of England tried to create the proper environment for single women with its Girls' Friendly Society, which mixed friendly society functions with religious and domestic training.[45] The Bradford Ladies Association for the Care of Friendless Girls joined these efforts in 1881. It provided lodgings, instruction, a clothing club and a registry for domestic employment.

Despite good intentions, these projects failed to make an impression upon most young women. Robert Baker argued that efforts to create 'respectable' lodging houses failed because they infringed upon the freedom of their inhabitants. The reports of the Bradford Ladies Association for the Care of Friendless Girls showed some of the difficulties encountered by would-be benefactors. The Association existed to aid young women, either newly arrived in town or unemployed, who faced difficult circumstances. Often it sought to find them positions as servants with the wealthy women who ran the Association. The girls brought into the club, however, failed to live up to expectations. They disliked formal lessons and 'if left alone to their own conversation for any length of time, they usually violently abuse somebody, probably their employer or overlooker, or else they quarrel.'[46] In its 1884 report the Association complained,

It is a familiar fact that, in spite of many drawbacks, and to the loss of many advantages, a vast number of girls prefer working in the mills to domestic service because of the freedom which the former leaves to them in the evenings . . . How and where then do they spend their evenings? Sunday Schools and Band of Hope meetings, and various entertainments keep many in safety, but beyond and below those thus cared for are a large number of girls who spend their evenings in the streets, drifting towards low theaters, dancing saloons, music halls, public houses, and other dens of iniquity and vice.[47]

In a large city like Bradford, attempts to create a web of paternalistic institutions linked to the mills or charities failed to achieve significant success.[48] Young women in Bradford evaded control and supervision away from the job. No single employer in the town dominated employment and thus no one mill owner could impose conditions of employment on young women without losing workers to his rivals. Manufacturers preferred to leave the costs and difficulties of social control to others and instead to concentrate on the control of labor within the mill, while denying that mill labor necessarily corrupted women.[49]

The issue of living arrangements proved crucial for young women. For those living with family or friends, work could bring a release from domestic labor and some spending money.[50] For those who lacked friends or kin to live with or who preferred to live outside the home, alternatives existed. Young single women made up half of the lodging population, living in commercial houses located in the city center or with families. It was not uncommon for young women to pool their wages to establish a household and unmarried women headed five per cent of all households in mid-Victorian Bradford. Robert Baker reported that many young women banded together to rent lodgings or houses and traveled home to their villages on Saturdays, returning on Sunday for the work week.[51] Lodging with widows, who headed over 10 per cent of all households, offered another niche for the independent woman.[52]

Many single women in mid-Victorian Bradford 'voted with their feet' and chose to live independently. This freedom, however, carried a price. Lacking access to trade unions and the independent friendly societies available to men, these women depended entirely on their wages for survival. Given the low level of their wages relative to men and the frequent interruptions of work in the worsted industry, life could be precarious for single women. Yet it was their moral well-being, rather than their economic vulnerability, that concerned the middle class.

Most commentators focused on the ability of young women with their own incomes to pursue an independent life. Women could and did go out in public. They participated in the mainly masculine pub culture, drinking and mingling with men. The numbers of 'loose' women out on a Saturday night, many still wearing mill clothing,

appalled temperance advocates.[53] Incidents in which women were
arrested for drunkenness or assaulting a police officer only added to
the dismay of reformers.[54] J. P. Chown, a local minister, spoke of the
sorrow of parents separated from their daughters by migration. Fearful
of the consequences, he sought to persuade young women to return to
their parents by depicting the dangers that awaited them in Bradford,

> I know many of you are situated so that your time is your own after
> your labour, so that you can go out where and when you please, I
> know many are in receipt of earnings that enable them to do more
> than their sisters in many parts of the country, and when I think of
> this and remember how many there are – a disgrace to our humanity,
> and for whom I know of scarcely any indignation and contempt too
> strong or punishment too severe – who are always lying in wait to
> draw aside and ruin those whom they may inveigle into their power,
> and when I know in addition, what traps and snares unmentionable
> and abominable surround our young women, I feel that nothing that
> could ever be done in reason for their guidance and preservation
> could be too much.[55]

The sexual terrors faced by unattached women obsessed Bradford's
social reformers, who feared that these young women would be drawn
into illicit activities. Although the level of illegitimate births remained
fairly constant, many believed that illegitimacy would rise as a result of
greater freedom for women.[56] The middle class considered mill girls
particularly vulnerable because of their allegedly lax upbringing and
their early contact with men and boys in the factory.[57] In the words of
J. H. Marshall,

> The promiscuous assemblage of so many youth of both sexes –
> especially where there is, as is generally more or less the case in the
> factory, the absence of proper and adequate superintendence and
> government – had the inevitable tendency to viciousness of habits.

The master of the Wibsey Wesleyan School agreed, arguing, 'The
moral atmosphere of the mill and the street is unsalutary in its
influences'.[58]

Reformers linked prostitution and factory labor, arguing that most
prostitutes began life as factory women. The oft-repeated tale of the
factory girl seduced and abandoned served to remind working women
of the lack of alternatives to the traditional family.[59] The operation of
over fifty brothels and the presence in the borough of hundreds of
known prostitutes seemed to confirm the worst fears of the middle

class.[60] Equally troubling was the free choice available to ordinary women. Temperance advocates felt the mere presence of women drinking, dancing and mixing freely with men implied degradation. J. H. Marshall referred to 'gratuitous prostitution, a sort which neither expects nor receives any rewards save the evening's pleasure and enjoyment'.[61]

This view of the sexuality of single women highlights what Lyn Pykett describes as a dual or contrary discourse about women's sexuality in the 1850s and 1860s. In this discourse, the prostitute stood as the antithesis of the proper female, who was married, healthy and asexual. The existence of the prostitute, however, called into question the stability of the middle class marriage and the asexual nature of the wife could be seen as a cause of prostitution.[62] The single woman, by virtue of her free choice, represented a threat to the solidity of marriage, and by extension society, and must be controlled.

Many in the working class resented the implication of sexual license on the part of mill workers and sought to repudiate such claims. At the National Association for the Promotion of Social Science Meeting held in Bradford in 1859, assertions about the immorality of factory women brought a denial from a working man at an evening meeting.[63] In the 1880s, a local poet addressed the issue in verse,

> I know a sweet young maiden
>   And Annie is her name
> She works down at the factory
>   She minds a winding frame
> I've fallen in love with Annie
>   Though she's a 'factory lass'
> She's lovelier than many
>   Among the 'better class'.[64]

Despite such protests, complaints about sexual license struck a chord with working-class men and women. Numerous workers complained about the immorality of the mills and the sexual aggressiveness of foremen and others.[65] Workers looked down upon mill labor by women, even if these same workers often had female relatives in the mills. Many considered mill women rough because of their allegedly crude behavior and frank language. As late as the early twentieth century, this stigma remained. J. B. Priestley, the Bradford-born writer and son and grandson of mill workers, distinguished between the 'solid, steady' family of his father and the 'raffish kind' of family his mother grew up in, 'the clogs and shawls back o't mill' working class.[66] The

definition of rough and respectable in sexual terms linked status within
the community to the appearance and behavior of women.[67] The
working woman, especially if a wife and mother, had to tread carefully
to avoid the stain of mill work and the degradation it implied.

DOMESTIC LIFE AND THE WORKING-CLASS MOTHER

This dichotomous view of feminine nature carried over into assess-
ments of working-class women as wives and mothers. To many in the
middle class, the early lives of factory women rendered them suspect.
Their familiarity with men, their lack of domestic skills and their desire
for independence made them ill-suited to fulfill the role set aside for
them. Middle-class reformers defended the status quo from 'those
prejudiced against our social and industrial life' by focusing attention
on the failings of working-class families rather than the environment in
which they lived and worked.[68] Since Victorians delegated chief
responsibility for the moral and social well-being of the family to the
mother, the use of domestic ideology shifted a considerable portion of
the blame for the problems of domestic life to women. While
occasionally the blame could be shared by the husband too weak or
improvident to do without his wife's labor, the true onus lay upon the
woman who failed to perform her duties.

Behind such concerns also lay a fear of the independence women
might gain from the ability to earn a wage on their own. According to
Margaret McMillan, the specter of the 'new woman' haunted
Bradford.

> For who should be a New Woman, if not the Factory Woman? Was
> there ever another like her? Who can earn as good a wage as her
> husband, who can bring up children, who does a man's work and a
> woman's, and yet has no vote?[69]

Commentators subjected the 'Factory Woman' to numerous critical
appraisals. Her poor cooking, inadequate cleaning and thriftlessness
slowed the improvement of conditions for her family. In the words of
one journal, 'The cookery of the poorer classes of England is generally
of the most wretched kind, and much of the suffering, and many of the
diseases, which afflict the poor, arise, in a great measure, from this
cause.'[70] Observers attacked working-class wives for their extravagant
desires, nagging and their inability to create a warm and comfortable
home, which drove men out of the house and into the pub. Mothers

who worked ignored their children, who then became 'idlers and criminals'. A temperance newspaper made the connection clear in a piece titled 'Mother Stay at Home':

> A mother's place is at home, not at the mill. For your health, stay at home. Mill work in the day, house work at night, will wear out most women before forty. For your husband's sake, stay at home. If you wish him to be sober and keep at home – give him a clean hearth, a warm fireside, a warm welcome and a warm supper ready when he comes home. For your children's sake stay at home. How can you teach them to love God and obey you and father when you are at the mill?[71]

Middle-class reformers argued that neglect and improvidence lay at the root of the problems of the working-class family. Poor household management, rather than poverty, forced married women to work outside the home. The Reverend A. McKechnie put it this way:

> Whether a family will daily possess such wealth (a little to spare above real wants) or not does not depend upon the amount of wages, but on how the wages are spent.[72]

These commentaries on working-class life reflected the same mentality that blamed the poor for their problems and offered a solution on an individual basis. By shifting the emphasis to the role of mothers, the blame for social ills could be moralized, personalized and transferred from the public sphere of politics and the market to the private sphere of the family.

This focus on domesticity obscured the greatest problem of working-class families – their lack of resources. This lack of resources led both women and children to engage in difficult, low-wage labor in order to supplement the inadequate wages of fathers and husbands. The ease with which they found work revealed the clash between domestic ideals and the crucial role of cheap women's and children's labor for the worsted trade. For working-class women, the distinction between public and private spheres so central to the middle class held little meaning. The dual labor of 'mill and house' shaped these women's lives and dictated their household arrangements. The domestic ideal remained a luxury out of reach for many in the working-class throughout this era. Given the opportunities for semi-skilled labor in textiles or in home consumer trades, women moved in and out of the labor force quite easily. A permeable barrier, rather than a fixed wall, separated the home and the outside world. When necessary, women engaged in whatever work could be found. From this perspective, factory work represented a relatively well-paying alternative.

Working-class men also played a role in this dilemma for women. Their attempts to advance a claim to higher wages and legislative protection ignored the reality of women's and children's labor. The exclusion of women from skilled labor and their marginal status within the worsted mill failed to create greater security for adult men or to establish the family wage. The acceptance of domestic ideology and the attempt to use it to attack the competitive system left them vulnerable to charges that their personal behavior, rather than their material circumstances, produced the misery so apparent in mid-Victorian Bradford. Given their frequent dependence upon the labor of women and children, working-class men found themselves on the defensive when discussing the family.

INFANT MORTALITY, ABORTION, INFANTICIDE AND THE WORKING-CLASS FAMILY

While the alleged shortcomings of the working-class family could deflect criticism of the worsted trade, these short-comings also served as a general explanation for social ills in Bradford. The consolidation of the system of birth and death registration and the statistical work of William Farr of the Registrar-General's office, made the death rate, especially among the young, a tangible sign of social problems.[73] In Bradford, which suffered from one of the highest infant mortality rates in England, concern over the excessive death rate of children persisted throughout the nineteenth century.[74] Until the early twentieth century, however, commentators focused not on the environmental causes of this wastage of life, but rather on the pathology of the working-class family.

The association of infant mortality with problems of family life grew out of the debate over public health in the later nineteenth century. In Bradford, as elsewhere in England, earlier concern with sanitary reform and public health drew its impetus from fears of the epidemic diseases that ravaged nineteenth-century cities, such as the cholera outbreaks of the 1830s and 1840s.[75] This concern led to the passage of laws allowing cities to provide sewers, water and other sanitary improvements. Bradford, like other cities, acted rapidly to establish a sanitary authority and to undertake public works in the 1850s, which included the purchase of the privately-held waterworks and the construction of a drainage system.[76]

The persistence of high death rates, especially among children, reflected the limited nature of sanitary improvements and the massive scale of the problem. Bradford's sanitary improvements failed to solve the problem of water contamination and the borough suffered shortages of water into the 1890s. Attempts at expansion met the resistance of local ratepayers, especially small property owners hurt by the rapid increase in rates in the mid-Victorian era. It proved difficult to force local property owners to conform even to existing sanitary codes. Owners balked at the cost of connecting to city drains, of installing water closets and providing better ventilation. As was the case with the attempt to eliminate back-to-back houses in the borough, the shortage of housing gave owners little incentive to improve housing in order to attract tenants, while the low incomes of workers made it difficult for owners to pass along the costs of better facilities. Bradford's local government found itself in the unenviable position of lacking the resources to further sanitary improvements and being unable to force private owners to undertake necessary changes on their own.

Local officials faced criticism for the poor state of the borough and its high death rates. Studies of local conditions began to appear in the 1860s and they sharply attacked the inactivity of the borough government in matters of health.[77] One observer in the 1870s argued that 'the sanitary organization and administration of the borough are defective, and the sanitary measures devised fail of their object.'[78] Officials attempted to counter these criticisms by calling attention to personal behavior and physical constitution as the key to death rates. In the case of infant mortality, they cited 'home influences', particularly the impact of working mothers.

Physicians played a key role in the construction of infant mortality as a problem of familial and maternal concern. Participation in issues of public health, especially those relating to the health of women and children, enhanced the claims of doctors to professional status and social importance. Physicians gained access to the poor and their families through local infirmaries, charity medical work, factory inspection and Poor Law Dispensaries. They drew upon this experience to give weight to their discussion of high death rates in urban areas.[79]

The increasingly statistical bent in medicine allowed physicians to trace the spread of disease, while the work of Pasteur and others gave them a new understanding of their origins. Despite the growing influence of laboratory science in medicine, physicians struggled to understand the causes of many illnesses. Miasmatic and zymotic theories of disease emphasized the influence of environment, focusing on the build-up of decaying matter in poorly ventilated areas.[80] The belief that 'sewer gases' transmitted disease lay behind much of the sanitary movement, with its emphasis on drainage and ventilation. Before the acceptance of germ theory in the later nineteenth century, the exact causes of infant death remained obscure.[81]

Doctors shared the values and attitudes of their middle-class contemporaries, mixing humanitarian concern about the poor with judgments about their moral worthiness. Physicians strongly believed in the influence of individual behavior and constitution on health and sickness. In seeking to explain the high infant mortality of urban areas they focused on the standard of parental care and the debilitated constitutions of the working class.[82] This medical definition overlapped with those in common usage among the middle class, who argued for many of the same beliefs from a lay perspective.

The process of professionalization and the shifting basis of medical knowledge affected the understanding of infant mortality in Bradford. The Medico-Chirurgical Society, a local organization founded in 1863 and affiliated with the British Medical Association, provided a forum for the growing interest in scientific medicine. Among the participants were Dr Rabagliati, House Surgeon to the Bradford Infirmary, Harris Butterfield, the Medical Officer of Health (MOH) for the Borough and J. H. Bridges, a medical officer for the Local Government Board.[83] Local physicians and surgeons combined discussions of public health with presentations on obstetrics, gynecology and other specialties.

Obstetrics and gynecology proved to be of particular importance in the discussion of infant mortality. In the nineteenth century gynecology provided a scientific basis for the understanding of femininity and sexuality. Doctors gave new weight to the belief that women inhabited a separate sphere by creating a 'science of women' that saw women as a group uniquely defined by their sexuality and reproductive capacities. Women's nurturing of children represented a natural extension of their biological role as mothers.[84] Medical debate revolved around the reasons why women failed as mothers. The inability of women to fulfill their maternal role through ignorance or absence from the home constituted the heart of the problem. Doctors condemned the practice of married women, especially those with young children, working outside the home, which they believed led to the neglect of children.[85]

Even education for women was suspect. A physician presenting the case of a young woman with amenorrhea argued that the overdevelopment of a woman's intellectual powers through education 'unsexed' her, making her unfit for marriage by removing her from her proper sphere.[86]

The role of the mother in child care provided the connection between women's roles and infant mortality. Mothers who worked or who could not adequately care for children were responsible for the excessive death rate of young children. In 1873 J. Nettien Radcliffe linked infant mortality to the poor care given children by working mothers.[87] J. H. Bridges and T. Holmes echoed this argument in their report on factory conditions in the same year, in which they noted the large number of married women in the weaving mills and claimed that these women worked late into their pregnancies and returned shortly after giving birth.[88] Harris Butterfield came to the same conclusion in a series of reports in the late 1870s.[89]

Doctors agreed with other middle-class observers who believed that the use of improper food, contaminated milk and child care practices such as baby binding led to the high death rate.[90] The Medical Officer of Health (MOH) and other doctors blamed the poor feeding habits of uneducated mothers for much of the problem. The MOH argued that

> the major part of the diseases to which they [children] are liable are due to carelessness and ignorance on the part of parents . . . A very small proportion of infants in Bradford are entirely nourished by the food which nature has provided for them . . . Considering the treatment . . . to which infants are subjected, it is rather to be marveled at that so many survive than that so many die.[91]

Ironically some observers claimed that since working-class women did not rely upon wet-nurses or nannies their infants should be healthier than those of the upper classes. As one put it,

> If the parents of the working classes understood Physiology and Hygiene, their children would have a much better chance of being strong and healthy than those of the wealthy classes, for in the former case, the mother's care is directly brought to bear upon the children.[92]

Physicians also focused on the use of midwives by working-class families. Doctors questioned the care given by midwives, blaming them for the high rates of prematurity and post-natal mortality of both mothers and children.[93] Dr Burnie, the medical advisor to the Town

Mission, blasted the 'careless midwifery in the manufacturing district' at a May 1884 meeting. Doctors used such criticisms to advance their right to regulate midwives and thus further control the medical treatment of women.[94]

For their part, working-class families disputed the charge that the use of midwives and other birth practices represented a form of neglect. They argued that they could not afford the fees of physicians and therefore, midwives offered the only alternative for most families.[95] Midwives and their working-class defenders accused doctors of refusing to come unless guaranteed payment.[96] The resentment generated by the attitudes of doctors surfaced during a controversy in the press over the death of a young child. A coroner's jury blamed the death on the refusal of a Dr Clarke to attend to the child. The verdict brought an angry letter from a 'Bradford Surgeon', who argued that parents allowed children, especially if they were illegitimate, to sicken to the point of near-death before the doctor was called, which he labeled a form of child murder. In response, 'A Juror' attacked Dr Clarke, pointing out that in the case in question the parents loved their child and were not guilty of neglect. Another letter writer placed the blame for the delay in calling a doctor on the high cost of medical care for the working class.[97]

Both doctors and ordinary citizens believed that infant mortality represented only one part of a larger problem. Physicians linked infant mortality with family limitation, infanticide and abortion, associating all of them with maternal and parental neglect. The dramatic fall in the birth rate that began in Bradford in the 1870s came to be viewed as a result of the degeneration of the parental instinct.[98] Local doctors called attention to the decline in fertility in the 1880s, when the Medical Officer of Health first noted the phenomenon.[99] Doctors argued that selfishness, rather than material necessity, lay behind family limitation. Married couples sought to evade their duty to bear children in order to enjoy material comfort at the expense of domestic pleasures. As a consequence, Bradford's medical community stood firm in its opposition to birth control and family limitation. Some doctors went so far as to reject abstinence as a form of family limitation, even if necessary to ensure the wife's well-being, fearing that it could lead to immorality.[100]

Behind family limitation lay the specter of infanticide and abortion. Men and women relied upon both to avoid the burden of children. Dr Tibbetts, head of the Bradford Infirmary, remarked that 'Some parents treated their children as if they desired their death, especially those who considered it immoral to have more than three'.[101] Another doctor echoed this belief saying, 'people . . . thought some children should be gotten rid of, and they were neglected on purpose'.[102] Doctors made little distinction between infanticide and abortion, claiming the latter was on the increase, while attacking local authorities for their reluctance to prosecute known cases of the former.[103]

The outcry over the alleged prevalence of infanticide resembled the debate about infant mortality. Claims of thousands of infant murders throughout England went unchallenged and led to attempts to prosecute single women for infanticide. Such prosecutions demonized the single mother, portraying her as driven to murder by her shame and weakness.[104] Although reformers gave considerable attention to the problem of infanticide, juries in this era remained reluctant to convict mothers of infanticide, preferring instead the charge of concealment of birth, which carried a sentence of a few months.[105] Jurors in England balked at the idea of execution or long prison sentences for clearly troubled women found in ambiguous circumstances.[106] This implicit consensus did not extend to those convicted of procuring or performing abortions, who received long sentences of hard labor.[107]

Since they believed that most infant deaths could be prevented if parents knew how to care for their children, doctors endorsed public education on child care to 'correct the inadequate or inaccurate knowledge of domestic matters acquired in the home', as well as the 'prejudices of mothers and grandmothers'.[108] Doctors advocated breast-feeding, but also warned about the dangers of 'prolonged lactation' (a known method of delaying births) and suggested ways of safely preparing cow's milk for infant consumption. To ensure proper care, mothers should be banned from returning to work while nursing and public nurseries should be provided for those forced to work.

By defining the issues of high mortality and low birth rates in terms of science and knowledge, physicians offered a new approach to the problems of the family. The ills of the family resulted from ignorance and that ignorance could be attacked through a program of instruction and consultation. While this formulation of the problem retained the old moral distinction between good and evil, redefined as neglectful or caring, it offered a new method of countering this dichotomy that avoided the necessity of conversion or moral reform as a precondition for improvement. Proper education offered a way for both good and bad mothers to benefit, regardless of their personal morality or religious opinions.

The medical discourse was not one-sided or unanimous in its condemnation of the working-class family. Robert Baker, also a doctor, sided with the working-class mother, blaming infant deaths not on lack of love or care, but rather on poor sanitary conditions, a belief echoed by other sympathetic observers.[109] Such comments reflected the differing experiences and political orientations of medical men. Baker, a Leeds surgeon, supported the Ten Hours Bill as well as other legislative efforts to regulate women's and children's labor. J. H. Bridges, despite his desire to limit women's work, embraced the beliefs of the Positivists and supported a number of Radical causes, including working-class suffrage. Doctors like Bridges blamed the factory system for many of the problems of the working class, arguing that it undermined their constitutions and forced them to live in unsanitary conditions.[110] This alternative view of the causes of public health problems, with its critique of the industrial order, never displaced mainstream views. At the same time, Baker and Bridges accepted the notion that women belonged in the domestic sphere and that working mothers represented a potential problem.[111]

The importance of maternal influences even for doctors sympathetic to the working class obscured the role of environmental factors in infant mortality. The concern of early sanitary reformers with environmental causes of sickness made it impossible to discount such factors. The studies of infant mortality undertaken in Bradford and the rest of England pointed out the class and geographical differences in death rates. One local study of 101 infant deaths from diarrhea (the second largest killer of infants) in 1878 found that ninety of the infants lived in the notorious back-to-back homes that housed the poorer members of the working-class.[112] Consistently, reports on death rates noted that some areas of Bradford, such as the central wards and the Irish slums, had considerably higher rates than the outlying middle-class districts such as Manningham.[113] Yet one physician, reporting on infantile diarrhea in 1883, claimed he could not explain why the disease appeared confined to the artisan class.[114]

The contradictory assertions about the influence of environment could not be resolved in this era. Doctors and other observers saw this influence in more than simply physical terms. The surrounding environment undermined the constitution of the poor and led to moral and social degeneration.[115] This degeneration, not simply bad drainage or ventilation, produced the appalling death rates of the poor and reversing it ranked as high as slum clearance or sanitary improvements in the agenda of local reformers. Ultimately, doctors downplayed environment as a factor in infant mortality in order to concentrate on the role of the mother.

Middle-class commentators on infant mortality invariably exaggerated the problem of the working mother. Despite assertions about the role of women's work and its impact on infant feeding, several studies reported that few mothers with young children worked and that many attempted to breast feed their children. The previously mentioned study of infant deaths reported that only eleven of the 101 mothers worked and forty-four of the infants were at least partially breast-fed, figures confirmed by a larger study in 1908.[116] Fears about working mothers flowed in part from exaggerated claims about the numbers of wives at work. Although married women worked in textile mills, less than one-third of all married women were employed in this period. Participation in the formal labor market declined steadily with age and thus became less important for women, especially those above the age of thirty with children at home. The claims that most women returned to work immediately after delivery is not confirmed by the census. In 1851, only 21.5 per cent of married mothers with at least one child under the age of one worked and only 19.6 per cent of mothers with at least one child below the age of five worked, a situation little changed by 1881.[117] In general, the more children a woman had at home, the less likely she was to be employed.[118] Although the problem of the working mother was a real one, it was not the predominant issue in maternal and child health. Much more relevant were the difficulties of obtaining adequate food and shelter in a family reliant on a male wage earner or the labor of small children.

Poor housing, low wages and inadequate nutrition played a much larger role in infant and child mortality than neglect, yet the elite of Bradford refused to acknowledge the influence of such factors.[119] When forced to note the condition of the city, they tended to blame unscrupulous speculators or the rapid growth of the city. This reduction of the state of the city to the process of urban growth itself ignored the role played by entrepreneurs in the construction of the city and the complicity of local authorities, either through passivity or lack of concern. Bradfordians, who never tired of homilies about the glories of the marketplace, grew curiously silent when confronted with its darker side represented by poverty, urban squalor and women's and children's labor. By displacing these issues into the arena of domesticity and personal behavior. Bradford's elite could address them without calling the larger order of society into question.

In the end, the debate over family life in the nineteenth century focused attention on issues of domesticity rather than on issues of material necessity or the unequal burdens of gender roles. Among the middle class, the deep-seated belief in separate spheres and the moral influence of the family led them to see the social ills of the time as a reflection of the problems of family life among the working class. For their part, working-class males accepted the legitimacy of domestic ideology, but sought to turn that ideology on its head by blaming the competitive system for forcing the working-class family away from its preferred ideal. Neither attempted to reconcile their beliefs with the reality of family life. Left out the picture was the possibility of greater gender equity as a potential solution to the problems of family life. The implications of this understanding of gender and family become clear when we turn to efforts to shape and assist the family in the later Victorian era.

6 From Voluntarism to the Sanitary Gospel: The Family and Social Reform

In 1849, the Mayor's Committee on the Moral Condition of the Town met to map out a program to address the problems of poverty and social disorder in the borough. The Reverend Ryland stated the task of reform in this way:

> Let them then, each in his own sphere, cultivate a proper religious and moral spirit and communicate that influence to those around them in all their relations, in all their occupations, all their concerns, all their institutions.[1]

A central theme in moral reform was the family and its failure to adequately train and educate the young. For middle-class observers, the working-class family and its problems lay at the root of the social dilemmas of the era. Thus, the family became the subject of a number of special agencies and charities, which sought to reach its members to persuade them to adopt new values. A stream of propaganda poured forth to convince women that the solution to any domestic difficulties lay in their adherence to female norms, while charities and home missionaries attempted to persuade women of the need for moral and religious instruction within the family.

In the latter part of the century, state effort increasingly supplemented and then superseded these private agencies. Despite the evolution of social reform in this era, there was considerable continuity. The view of the working-class family as troubled lay at the heart of such efforts, although the language of reform changed its expression. The other striking similarity was the limited impact that such activity had upon the well-being and prospects of the working-class family. Most men and women remained dependent upon their own efforts for survival. As a consequence, the family continued to be plagued by insecurity and short-term crises that charity or social work could do little to relieve.

The transformation of social work in the late Victorian and early Edwardian periods remains a subject of considerable interest among historians. A previous generation of historians saw this change as part of a gradual evolution away from laissez-faire toward collectivism. The late Victorian and Edwardian eras were transitional periods, when the methods and ideas of the modern welfare state were first tested and slowly expanded.[2] Recent work challenges this teleological conception of the rise of the welfare state and focuses on the continuities of this era with earlier ones, particularly in their understanding of class and gender.[3]

One feature of social welfare work in the late nineteenth century was its increasing diversity. A variety of groups sought to shape social reform to fit their own perceptions of disorder and need. Feminists, progressive Liberals, eugenicists, Fabians, trade unionists and others advanced often conflicting arguments in favor of state intervention. The balance of these forces varied depending upon the location and scope of reforms. A distinction must be made between debates at the national level, which are frequently the focus of much of the secondary literature on social welfare, and local or regional discussions, which involved a different array of actors and alliances. The central government only began to allocate significant resources after 1906 and most social welfare work remained locally controlled and funded before 1914. Although the national debate often informed the work of social activists, many of the issues on a national level proved irrelevant to their concerns.

In the case of Bradford, the gap between local and national concerns necessitates an examination of the lingering influence of orthodox Liberal thought about the individual and the proper limits of state aid. A Whiggish view of social welfare gives too little attention to the desires and intentions of these middle-class reformers, who still believed in the vitality of voluntarism and the private sector. The quasi-public agencies of the late nineteenth and early twentieth century did not envision themselves as gateways to greater state intervention, but rather as modernized defenders of older notions of private assistance that would obviate the need for further steps towards collectivism. At the same time, the belief in an essentially personal explanation of poverty and social disorder survived. Despite a new scientific language of poverty, the middle class still viewed the behavior and actions of the poor as the greatest obstacles to social improvement.

THE RISE AND DECLINE OF VOLUNTARISM

In mid-Victorian Bradford, groups concerned with the welfare of the family and children operated within the context of a variety of charities and aid societies. This voluntary effort, or voluntarism, grew out of the larger social milieu of provincial urban life.[4] Voluntarism eschewed state assistance, particularly in cities like Bradford, where Nonconformist churches dominated. Wealthy inhabitants of the town raised the funds for these groups and ministers and prominent citizens headed them. These activities affirmed the vitality of civic culture and its ability to provide for the less fortunate without state interference. Voluntarism meant more than private effort at social reform, it also involved a view of the roots of poverty and social disorder. Middle-class Bradfordians, like their counterparts elsewhere in England, saw poverty through a moral lens. The personal failings of the poor – their improvidence, their drinking and their lack of religious faith – produced the squalor and misery that characterized their lives. Charities and missionary societies attempted to change the values of the poor through moral suasion and good works.

The emergence of voluntarism reflected a new era of stability in Bradford and the recognition that earlier efforts at reform failed to contain the new social problems that accompanied industrialization. Charity in Bradford enjoyed a long history and some endowed charities dated from the eighteenth century. Prior to the early nineteenth century, these charities, in conjunction with poor relief, sought to meet the needs of the poor. However, industrialization overwhelmed the old community basis of relief. The influx of migrants and the cycles of boom and bust in the worsted trade created unprecedented levels of destitution in Bradford. The poverty of the 1830s and 1840s presented far too great a problem to be dealt with by private means and the Poor Law increasingly bore the brunt of poor relief in Bradford.[5] At the peak of the destitution from 1847 to 1849, one in ten of the borough's inhabitants relied upon some form of relief.[6]

The collapse of Chartism and the return of prosperity to the worsted trade in 1848 marked a turning point in Bradford's history. The ascension of a Liberal bourgeoisie possessing the economic and social means of pursuing its vision of the city and the creation of a factory-based industry played central roles in the new stability. While most members of the middle class regarded the factory as the solution to the problems of labor control and discipline that plagued the worsted industry for the first half of the century, they felt less confident about the world which lay outside the factory gates. The example of Chartism remained as a warning of the potential for social conflict that existed. More prosaically, the squalor and disorder of the crowded inner city districts offered an affront to the notions of morality and efficiency held by Bradford's upper class. The stabilization of the Liberal elite effectively limited the threat of working-class politics, but the breeding grounds of disaffection that remained seemed to require a more fundamental effort to understand and reach the working class.

The new elite of Bradford sought to reshape the city in order to ensure social peace and harmony. It was this desire which led to the formation of the Mayor's Committee on the Moral Condition of the Town in 1849. The Committee consisted of clergymen from all the major Protestant denominations in the city, including the vicar of Bradford, but excluding representatives of the Catholic Church. The Committee argued that the rapid growth of the city led to the degradation of the population. Brothels, beerhouses, dance halls and obscene publications overwhelmed the agencies of order and morality and only by expanding the reach of such agencies could the lower classes be approached and reformed. To accomplish this task, the Committee sought to establish new missionary institutions to work among the poor. Rather than the *ad hoc* efforts of earlier years, which sought to relieve physical distress brought by depressions in trade, these new agencies were intended to be permanent agencies of moral reform.[7]

The Mayor's Committee initiated a period of intense effort on the part of Bradford's elite to reach out to the poor and the working class. In the 1850s, charities and religious groups sprang up to meet the challenge set forth by the Committee. The older endowed charities faded in importance and new institutions, such as the Bradford Infirmary, replaced them. In addition to the special charities for young women mentioned in the previous chapter, a number of groups existed that could be defined broadly as family or child-oriented. Support for education was mobilized through the Ragged School and the Sunday School movement. Temperance and missionary groups attempted to change families by attacking the evils of alcohol and disbelief.[8] As the Reverend Jonathan Glyde, a prominent Nonconformist minister, argued in 1853,

> We must have town missionaries. . . . We must have schools. . . . We must have schools of design and literary institutions, museums and music halls; and on all grounds, and by all honest arts and arms, the battle against ignorance, intemperance, and vice.[9]

Churches played a critical role in voluntarism and their efforts formed part of a broader evangelical effort by all denominations. The inadequate accommodations for worship revealed by the Religious Census of 1851 led to a burst of church building, particularly by the Anglicans. In addition to physical expansion, all religious groups increased their evangelical efforts among the working class. Both the Anglicans and the Nonconformists sought to go directly to the working class by visiting their homes and they created urban missions to rival those of colonial areas.[10] They recognized that the older methods of distributing tracts and holding open meetings no longer sufficed. Therefore, they sought to combine social and moral agency by creating new institutions, such as societies for friendless girls, female refuges, and educational institutes.[11]

The desire to cultivate mutual understanding between the classes gave a central role to women. The day-to-day functioning of most aid societies and charities relied on the female members of the churches of the city, who flocked to these groups to assist their fellow women in need. Middle-class women could instruct their sisters in religious belief and in domestic arts. This extension of women's sphere gave a public role to middle-class women in an age in which few existed.[12] Thus, Mrs Charles Garnett, wife of a manufacturer, wrote of her experiences among 'My Friends the Navvies', while other wives of businessmen served as home visitors and sat on the boards of various charities.[13]

Despite its vigor and the commitment of its supporters, by the 1880s voluntarism was in crisis. Throughout England, a wave of concern over the persistence of poverty, stimulated in part by the efforts of investigators like Charles Booth to quantify its existence, produced doubts about the existing methods of social reform.[14] Among the middle class there was a growing acceptance of the reality of poverty and the belief that greater state effort would be necessary to alleviate it. In Bradford, the prolonged slump in the worsted trade that persisted in varying degrees from the 1870s until 1914 provided the specific context for the crisis of voluntarism. The difficulties of Bradford's major industry created peaks of destitution, as in the winter of 1878–79, when the town's prominent citizens organized special relief efforts to reduce the pressure on Poor Law authorities.[15] The periodic nature of these downturns and their persistence despite occasional good years produced doubts among Bradfordians about the future of their city and a search for solutions to the malaise that afflicted commercial society.

The economic slump both highlighted and exacerbated the financial problems of Bradford's voluntary agencies. Every charity reported

considerable difficulties in obtaining sufficient funding to offer services
to the poor. The Town Mission, a prominent evangelical agency, began
to encounter financial problems in the 1870s and cut back on the
number of its missionaries. The Bradford Ladies Charity took in only
£117 in 1870–1 and visited 196 homes in the course of the year, while
the Female Refuge supported thirteen inmates in 1861 and only eight in
1871. Even the Bradford Infirmary, the best supported of local
charities, found itself living from hand to mouth.[16] The insufficiency
of charity placed a greater burden on the Poor Law authorities. Unlike
London, private charity played a secondary role to public assistance.[17]
The total amount spent by charities in the prosperous years from 1860
to 1870 reached £12,000 per year, compared to a yearly expenditure in
the mid-1860s of £21,000 by the Poor Law authorities.[18] In a city of
150,000, such efforts barely scratched the surface of the problems of
working-class life.

The duplication of services and a lack of cooperation on common
problems by Bradford's churches aggravated this shortage of resources. Different Protestant sects competed for status and members
through their charities and societies, creating their own organizations.
In response to the Mechanics Institute, set up by Nonconformists, the
Church of England set up the Church Institute. The two separate
Sunday School organizations could not even agree to hold a common
celebration of the anniversary of the movement.[19] The temperance and
evangelical movements also divided along sectarian lines. The desire by
each religious group to serve only its own community hampered reform
in a city as religiously diverse as Bradford, which had a large Catholic
minority as well as an abundance of Protestant denominations.
Furthermore, the political overtones of religious differences, especially
their association with Liberal–Tory disputes, lent social work a
partisan air, which further inhibited a unified approach.[20] This
division only further weakened a movement hampered by meager
resources and limited public interest.

The changing nature of religious affiliation and participation played
a role as well. Some criticized the churches for abandoning the poor in
favor of more comfortable surroundings and activities.[21] The flight of
the wealthy middle class to hillside areas such as Manningham led to
the suburbanization of churches and their parishioners.[22] This meant
that congregations no longer experienced the daily contact with the
poor and the inner city that informed earlier activism.[23] Church of
England supporters contrasted their program of central city church

construction to the abandonment of Nonconformist chapels as the middle classes moved out of the city.[24]

The very success of the Nonconformist elite made it more difficult for them to concentrate their efforts upon missionary outreach among the poor. As one minister noted,

> The sacrifices once made in the interests of religion by the devout are no longer possible. That which was a duty, involving self-denial, and discharged frequently at some cost and inconvenience, yet always with enthusiasm, is now an irksome task often pursued out of regard for respectable appearances rather than from a rational and sincere recognition of the real need of personal religion and public worship.[25]

Another minister argued that temporal concerns took priority for many:

> It [irreligion] has its root in too many instances in the materiality and excitement of the period. Wealth has never been pursued with a more absorbing desire than it is in the present age; the pursuit of it has become a passionate enthusiasm, to which the love of higher things must be subordinated.[26]

The overall decline of church attendance in the mid-Victorian era also undermined voluntarism. A new Census of Religion conducted by the *Bradford Observer* in December of 1881 showed that church attendance as a proportion of the population actually declined to around 20 per cent despite the massive increases in church accommodation. A number of new, more marginal, sects appeared that appealed to the working class, such as the Salvation Army, which further fragmented the religious community.[27]

THE EMERGENCE OF THE SANITARY GOSPEL

By the late 1880s, the sense of crisis among Bradford's middle class produced a growing consensus that older forms of voluntary effort no longer sufficed to handle the perceived expansion of social ills. Nonconformists like H. B. Priestman and J. A. Godwin hoped to update voluntarism by explicitly addressing social problems like housing and malnutrition. This led to organizations such as the Darkest England Society and the Social Reform Union, but these initiatives failed to reestablish the centrality of churches in social reform.[28] One consequence of this failure was an evolution in the ideology, organization and personnel of social service in order to address the problems of urban life.

'The gospel of sanitation', as one local group termed it, emerged piecemeal in the 1880s and 1890s. The ideology of this new movement mixed older views of the poor and 'the social problem' with a new faith in science and education. Issues of sanitary construction and medical practice gained preeminence over strictly moral understandings of poverty. Thus, drains and sources of infection in milk occupied as much time as the fecklessness of mothers and fathers. This focus on science allowed local agencies to formulate more concrete initiatives.

The emphasis on science in the sanitary gospel also appealed to the professionals drawn to the movement and reflected their influence on its direction. The middle-class women so important in the mid-Victorian era began to be replaced by professionally trained and oriented men and women with special qualifications.[29] Although ministers never disappeared from social work, its driving force increasingly came from the doctors, civil engineers and other experts who dominated groups like the Sanitary Association, founded in 1881.[30] These professionals portrayed themselves as an 'enlightened few', an elite advancing a 'science so progressive' in the face of ignorance and hostility from the masses.[31]

This change in personnel diminished the role of women. The many charities and other voluntary agencies that continued to operate in the late nineteenth century offered an outlet for women, although their importance declined. Often these voluntary groups came under the influence or direct control of the new professionals or local government officials. At the same time, the growth of areas of female professional activity like health visiting and factory inspection provided a new niche for women. Women could pursue a career in public service, but as professionals they remained inferior to and subordinate to men.[32]

While some have argued that this process involved the replacement of voluntary, female-dominated charity with compulsory, male social regulation, the net impact on women's role remains unclear.[33] Women's work in charity had always been rife with contradictions. The extension of women's domestic role within voluntary societies allowed them to work for public good, yet it denied them a permanent alternative to domesticity, for they always remained within its limits. Similarly the relationship of middle-class women to their poorer sisters stood somewhere between friendship and patronage, a balance that proved difficult for many women to maintain.[34]

In the later nineteenth century, the emergence of feminism transformed the nature of women's mission. While traditional ideas of service persisted, feminists advanced a variety of justifications for their social work. Some in the feminist movement argued for suffrage as part of a larger effort to produce gender equality, while others used women's special nature to justify votes for women.[35] Such arguments could justify new forms of social activism as well. Feminists who believed in the special character of women argued that women could best formulate and administer welfare programs. These maternalists pushed programs that aided women with protective legislation and state benefits in the name of endowing motherhood. These efforts produced concrete proposals to provide payments to mothers, minimum wages and school feeding.[36]

Differences in class and experience affected this maternalist program. By claiming to speak for all women, middle-class women reserved to themselves the right to decide the nature of women's struggle for better conditions at work and home. The question of whether to extend the suffrage to cover all working-class men and women is only the best known of these dilemmas, but they reappeared throughout the late nineteenth century. Women active in groups like the Women's Protective and Provident League encountered the problem of how to deal with issues of trade unions and strikes. Female trade-union supporters, for their part, had to find ways to justify concern with issues of gender over issues of class. Both struggled over the issue of protective legislation for women and children.[37]

While maternalist rhetoric could be used to justify progressive programs, it also served the interests of those who denied the causal role of poverty in social problems. The emphasis on maternal education as the solution to high rates of infant mortality shows how the energies and arguments of maternalists could be turned to an essentially conservative direction. This channeling of maternalism reflected the domination of political life by men, especially the organs of local government that dominated social welfare work in the early twentieth century.[38]

The growth of a feminist movement in Bradford during the early 1880s affected the development of the sanitary gospel.[39] The fruits of this political activity appeared in the 1880s and 1890s with the elections of Edith Lupton and Mary Gregory to the School Board and Florence Moser to the Board of Guardians. While on these bodies, these women pursued issues of half-time education and the care of children within the Union workhouse. They saw their work as an extension of their philanthropic activities, but also as an assertion of their right to participate fully in public life.[40]

The emergence of the Independent Labour Party and a later generation of feminists like Margaret McMillan and Julia Varley, gave a more political thrust to women's social activism. In particular, their work on the issues of poor relief set them apart from their Liberal predecessors.[41] Yet they fit uncomfortably into the ILP, with its emphasis on the male wage earner. Protective legislation and other attempts to push women back into the domestic sphere potentially undermined the women they represented. Children and education represented the areas open to them, yet, in these areas, like their Liberal counterparts, they remained constrained by larger political realities. While Margaret McMillan sat on the Bradford School Board, she was surrounded by a majority of officials drawn from the ranks of the local Liberal and Conservative establishment.[42]

The transformation of the social welfare movement brought a shift in the relationship between reformers and recipients. Earlier efforts at moral persuasion and charity sought to involve those receiving assistance through the agency of conversion and religious belief. Missionaries wanted to enlist the poor in the struggle for redemption, indeed they felt it essential that a change of heart occur in order for the gift to bear fruit. The sanitary gospel, on the other hand, with its language of education and professional knowledge, limited recipients to a passive, secondary role. The ideal of womanly influence gave way to an emphasis on the special role of the trained visitor, equipped with information and new techniques of record keeping.[43]

The sanitary gospel placed a great emphasis on new methods of social work. Voluntary groups relied upon the tried and true methods of missionary work – revival meetings, door to door visits and random gatherings of the needy. The new agencies of reform, however, used case work and home visitation on a systematic basis. This allowed them to track and type the poor, so as to control and regulate their behavior on the basis of recorded experience and established procedures rather than on an *ad hoc* basis. Greater systemization held out the promise of savings by eliminating fraud and waste. Indeed, one of the most telling arguments in favor of the new agencies was their promise to rid the city of fraudulent claims and to force the poor to actually pay for the care of their children.[44]

The desire for a more efficient and comprehensive approach to social work provided a justification for state intervention. The acceptance of a larger role for government necessitated a shift in attitude on the part of local officials about how to achieve efficiency. Previously, these officials supported voluntarism for reasons of both personal ideology and fiscal expediency, for it allowed local government to avoid providing certain types of social services and relief efforts. Such savings proved welcome in an era of large-scale capital projects by local government in the areas of water services, sewers, roads and slum clearance.[45] The piecemeal expansion of local government and the fragmentation of local authority exacerbated these problems. The financial and legal independence of agencies such as the School Board and the Poor Law Union made it difficult for local officials to coordinate the delivery of services to the poor.

The limits of such an approach became increasingly clear in the late nineteenth century. Government, which stood above sectarian struggles, could better coordinate the multitude of private agencies involved in social welfare. This role resembled the one that the Charity Organization Society claimed, but failed to achieve in Bradford in the 1880s.[46] The desire for greater efficiency reflected the perceived expansion of the problems of poverty, which threatened to overwhelm the modest resources of private agencies. Each group could only hope to reach a fraction of the poor, especially in light of the sanitary gospel's concern with environmental issues such as health and housing. In a period of economic slowdown, only the state possessed the ability to raise sufficient funds to undertake creation of public health agencies and to reconstruct housing. In addition, the changing nature of the social project called for far greater intrusion into the lives and homes of ordinary people. Visiting homes and assessing family circumstances required powers of inspection and compulsion beyond those likely to be granted to a group of private citizens, no matter how respectable. Yet the overheated rhetoric of the time increasingly called for drastic action to solve a set of problems believed to be undermining the nation's vitality.

Public officials proved willing to use their powers, some newly granted by Parliament, to pass laws to enact the core of the sanitary gospel. They provided the framework within which private agencies could operate and stepped in with police and regulatory powers when necessary. The mutual reliance of private and public agencies on each other marked a critical divergence from past attempts at social reform. Yet, the expansion of state power did not displace completely the existing ideological framework. Private persuasion and effort remained the method of choice, and initially at least, the state stood to one side. Furthermore, the goals of these activities were consistent with the individualist and voluntarist mindset still influential among the middle class. The state only intervened when individuals clearly failed to exercise their responsibilities, at least in theory. The state sought to reinforce, not replace, private ideas of morality by forcing people to reform their behavior.

Social workers continued to argue that innocent victims and dependent persons deserved the protection of the state. Whereas many believed adults should suffer the consequences of their own behavior, children deserved the protection of the community until they reached the age of independence. Similar arguments previously sanctioned the limitation and control of women's and children's labor, in a construction that equated women and children as dependants.[47] In this case, however, the new problems called not simply for the regulation of the market, but in the long run, the provision of state services on a greatly expanded scale.

Older ideas of the family and gender survived within the sanitary gospel. Social activists still defined the women's sphere as the home and attempted to persuade her to conform to domestic ideals for the sake of her family. For women this involved accepting their 'true vocation' – the nurturing of children. To assist the work of home visitors and school clinics, the schools would also educate young women in their maternal responsibilities, or what one writer called 'their true part in the future of the state'.[48] The working-class family remained the primary focus of reformers and the sanitary gospel sought to educate and regulate it in order to eliminate social disorder. A series of interlocking agencies, endowed with special judicial powers, intruded upon working-class life, seeking to reform or punish those men and women who had not yet changed their behavior. Although activists acknowledged the importance of wages and housing in the state of the family, they believed that the first step remained the reformation of the family.

In the later nineteenth century, this discussion took on eugenic overtones.[49] Reformers saw the relatively higher fertility of the lower classes and the persistence of high infant mortality in the city as an ominous trend. Many feared that the best members of society would not reproduce themselves if they resorted to family limitation in the face of continued high infant mortality. The Sanitary Association remarked in 1912, 'Yet as the birth rate decreases, the rate of infant mortality amongst the fit, not the unfit, gives no compensation by diminution'.[50] Another local official argued that 'the future generation runs the risk of being chiefly recruited from the slum class'.[51]

Like eugenicists, the local sanitary movement saw the questions of family limitation and infant mortality in the context of a general deterioration of England's population. Sanitary reformers appealed to patriotism to gather support for corrective measures.[52] Eva Jones, the Female Sanitary Inspector for Bradford, explained it this way in 1901:

> the health of a country should be a nation's first consideration, for the *very existence* [italics in original] of the nation is involved, and all true patriots must view this matter from its widest national standpoint.[53]

At the Sanitary Conference held in Bradford in July of 1904, Miss E. M. Evans made explicit the link between the condition of England and national power, noting, 'from such a generation we, as a nation, expect to raise an army and a navy second to none in the world'.[54]

Echoing the members of the Medico-Chirurgical society, sanitary activists linked the question of birth and death rates to issues of selfishness and duty. In the view of Eva Jones,

> in the present day, selfishness results in a wanton disregard of the sacred responsibilities of parentage. People refuse to face duties, and in all classes of life race-suicide is encouraged; this assumes its worst form when abortion is resorted to, which practice, accounts for several of the premature births.[55]

To counter these trends, men and women needed to reject selfishness and materialism and embrace their duties. Increased attention to the joys of parenthood went hand in hand with greater concern for the care of infants and children. In the words of the Sanitary Association,

> Let us eliminate disturbing factors, and it may possibly be found that with parents fairly well to do and comfortably housed, the highest birth-rate is coincident with the lowest infantile death rate.[56]

One fruit of the renewed concern with the family was a burst of organizational activity among the middle class that began in the 1880s and continued until the First World War. The agencies set up in the 1880s concerned themselves with the care of children. The Children's Hospital appeared in 1883, followed by the Nest in 1885 and the Cinderella Club in 1890. Each provided care and food to children on an outrelief basis, and sought to educate both children and parents.

Jacob and Florence Moser founded the Nest in order to improve the condition of the children of Bradford by employing the latest techniques of child care. The Nest provided meals for poor children, day care and domestic training for mothers and young girls. It made the purpose of these services clear in its first report. Speaking of the need for domestic care, it called attention to

> those poor babies . . . exposed to all the evils of ignorance, poverty, or greed, hence this tremendous infant mortality; or what is still sadder, these numbers of crippled sickly children, whose lives are a burden to themselves, their parents, or the ratepayers.[57]

The Nest wished to avoid what it termed the 'needlessly pauperizing effects' of charity, so it charged a fee on a sliding scale up to 2s.6d. for child care. To distinguish between the deserving and undeserving poor, the Nest used the Charity Organization Society (COS). It investigated applicants, giving its recommendations to the agency and prosecuting those it suspected of misrepresentation. So vigilant were its efforts on behalf of the Nest that of 152 families that applied for assistance in the first year, only 65 received approval.[58]

In 1889 local notables, including Alfred Illingworth, a local MP and Henry Mitchell, a prominent merchant, set up a Bradford branch of the National Society for the Prevention of Cruelty to Children. The Society combined educational efforts with social investigation and legal sanctions, using powers granted by Parliament to prosecute persons it believed guilty of cruelty or neglect.[59] In Bradford the Secretary of the Society and a paid official examined thousands of complaints and used the police to aid in investigations and to carry out arrests.[60] In 1896, the Society appointed three inspectors to work full time, but it still relied upon the police for assistance.[61] The Society maintained a close relationship with local officials, working with both the Board of Education and the Poor Law Guardians.

The most sophisticated and comprehensive agency during this era was the Bradford City Guild of Help, founded in 1904. The Guild used volunteers to visit families referred to it by local charities and the authorities. The Guild endeavored to cover the entire city, dividing it into districts. Two volunteers visited each family, keeping diaries which the district supervisor used to determine future action on the case. The Guild provided relief both in kind and in cash and sought to coordinate the activities of various charities. The Guild also referred cases to the Poor Law Guardians and the NSPCC for action.[62] In the years before 1914, the Guild dealt with thousands of cases.[63]

The work of these private agencies supplemented the increased activism of local officials. With the establishment of Board schools in the 1870s, provisions had to be made for the remission of fees from poor children and Poor Law officials investigated the families of applicants.[64] These investigations increased as education became compulsory, and the Board of Education added Enquiry Officers, who reported on the family situations of truant children to the Board. The School Health Department also included a clinic run by the Medical Officer, Dr Kerr.[65]

The Poor Law Guardians also increased their scope of action in the 1880s and 1890s. In addition to investigations for school fees, they made arrangements for the care of indigent children, either within their own nursery and homes or with foster parents. In both cases, the circumstances of the child's family came under scrutiny. The Children's Committee screened requests by parents to have their children returned and sent investigators to determine if the parents had sufficiently reformed to allow the children to go home. The Infant Life Protection Act of 1897 expanded the competence of the Board of Guardians to deal not only with children in the workhouse, but also with cases of neglect outside the workhouse referred to it by the NSPCC and other groups. The power to prosecute parents or other care givers and determine the status of children in their care gave the Poor Law Guardians considerable influence over working-class families.

In 1899, the Board of Education, the Poor Law Guardians, the Cinderella Club and the Health Committee of the Borough Council held a joint meeting to take steps to improve the physical condition of the poorer children of Bradford.[66] The meeting led to the creation of the position of Female Sanitary Inspector, who was empowered to visit all newborns, instruct mothers in the care of children and inspect midwives. In cases of neglect or indigence, she could recommend cases to local charities or the appropriate authorities. The borough government found itself increasingly drawn into the provision of services to the poor. In 1906, school meals for the poor, supported out of the rates, became available. The system of municipal inspection and visitation steadily expanded and by 1915 it included thirteen visitors, five municipal midwives, clinics and a milk depot.[67]

One force behind this expansion of local government was the emergence in the 1880s and 1890s of independent labor and socialist groups. The Independent Labour Party (ILP) became a force in Bradford politics in the 1890s, electing officials to the Board of Guardians, the Borough Council and the Board of Education.[68] A key difference between the ILP and the Liberals who dominated the Council prior to 1914 involved the distinction between charity and entitlement. The ILP rejected the notion of deserving and undeserving poor central to social reformers.[69] Instead, the ILP called for municipal services, publicly funded and available to all the poor. It also called for a greater role in housing by local government, in order to provide decent accommodations for the thousands of working poor unable to escape the slums.[70] As Fred Jowett, Labour MP, put it,

> The Socialist seeks to establish the Socialist City . . . so he must needs work his passage to [it] by means of municipal trading, housing, reform, municipal coal, municipal milk supply, and education.[71]

Margaret McMillan helped define the ILP's stance toward issues of children and family. Her work on the school board in Bradford and later writings on childhood and education advanced a view of the child as the victim of unregulated industry and greed. Her understanding of childhood and the problems of young people in Bradford drew heavily upon the work of Dr James Kerr, the Medical Superintendent of the School Board in the 1890s.[72] Kerr argued that the factory 'exerted the most pernicious influence on family life, and destroyed anything like home influences'.[73] He documented the poor state of Bradford's children through physical examinations and comparison with other children.

Concern with the welfare of children by labor activists led to the establishment of the Cinderella Club in 1890. Modeled after the original club founded by Robert Blatchford, the socialist and editor of the *Clarion*, it was staffed primarily by local ILP members.[74] Initially the Cinderella Club offered 'blowouts' to children, where they gorged themselves, much to the dismay of observers like Margaret McMillan. In time, the Club resembled other child welfare groups in the city. It focused on older children, rather than infants, and provided thousands of meals weekly by the early twentieth century. The Club divided up the city into districts and visited individual homes to determine a family's eligibility. A worker distributed checks for free meals to the children under twelve of an eligible family.[75] No money changed hands and the charity gained access to the home for its educational work. Increasing monetary difficulties led to the creation of a city-wide program known as the Lord Mayor's Fund, prior to the establishment of school feeding.[76] School meals and other municipal services bore the imprint of local socialists like Jowett and McMillan. Despite such successes, the ability of the Liberal and Conservative parties to dominate the borough government prevented more radical reforms and the ILP's vision of the city remained unrealized before 1914. Only with the aid of progressive Liberals on local elective bodies could the ILP carry forward its program.[77]

Did the working-class family benefit materially from these efforts? Contemporary evidence suggests that despite the growth of municipal effort, the problems of poverty and health remained intractable in the years before 1914. The improved mortality of adults and older children could not disguise the continued high rate of infant mortality, which averaged 132 per 1000 from 1906 to 1910.[78] The arrangements made for the care and feeding of children proved inadequate to remedy larger environmental problems. The reports of officials sent to study the borough's poor health in the early twentieth century belied the insistence of Bradford's middle class that education and limited aid could conquer infant mortality. They cited the factors noted by observers since the 1860s – poor sanitation, bad housing and low incomes.[79]

In addition, the quality of services delivered left much to be desired. A Local Government Board report noted that the Milk Depot left its milk open to the air, unrefrigerated, and failed to sterilize it before distribution. Similarly, the Infant Clinic functioned more as an outpatient department than a clinic, for it saw few healthy children, concentrating instead on those already ill.[80] The Poor Law Guardians complained about the poor quality of goods supplied them, citing the greed of private contractors in coal, food and clothing.[81] Similarly officials complained that the doctors attached to the Workhouse failed to attend regularly and paid insufficient attention to the problems of managing the young children in their care.[82]

In the end, the programs of the local government remained limited in coverage and intent. Reformers premised much of their work on the belief that poorly educated and overworked mothers lacked the knowledge needed to care for their children properly. Local and national investigations documenting the relationship between environment and high mortality, especially among infants, proved only partially successful in transforming the debate over the solution to poverty. The Female Sanitary Inspectors concluded that economic conditions played a large role in the infant mortality rate due to the role of low income in poor maternal nutrition, yet they continued to insist that 'lazy, careless, and negligent parents' had to be dealt with in order to address the problem.[83]

The focus on education and regulation defined the limits of government action. Municipal government drew the line at interference in the free markets of housing and employment. Attempts to deal with housing were blocked by the central government and local resistance. Efforts by ILP councillors on the Health Committee to have the borough provide housing for the poor failed. Even less likely to succeed were initiatives aimed at raising the general wage rate in the city, even though one sanitary inspector admitted that higher wages, especially for adult men, represented the best alternative to municipal feeding and regulation.[84]

The most striking feature of the sanitary gospel from the point of view of the working-class family was its irrelevance. As was the case in the mid-Victorian era, the stigma attached to charity or public assistance limited its appeal to most families. Only in times of severe destitution would families with a resident bread-winner rely on these sources of support. Those who did receive aid displayed a far less dependent attitude than the pauperized who constituted the primary focus of the sanitary gospel. During periods of high unemployment, men unaccustomed to the regime of poverty encountered outdoor labor, so-called Test Work, such as road maintenance, as part of the price for receiving assistance. The discontent of men performing Test Work in the early 1880s forced the Poor Law Union to station police with the men while they worked and on at least two occasions riots broke out when they refused to work.[85]

As a consequence, the very poor and the transient formed the bulk of the case load of the new agencies. Many of the men were unskilled and/ or unemployed and they changed jobs frequently and moved in order to find work. Even these families on the edge of subsistence resisted the stigma of poor relief. Aid workers reported that many refused any form of assistance, even medical aid in the workhouse. In the words of one, workers 'prefer[ed] poverty with liberty to comfort in the workhouse'.[86] A Guild of Help visitor reported that when she suggested one unemployed man do Test Work, he replied that 'he would rather steal'.[87]

Female-headed families constituted another category of vulnerable families. The low wages of women made it difficult to support a family on their own, even if their children or other relatives assisted them. Widows, single mothers and separated or deserted women faced an uphill struggle to sustain independence. If these women cohabited with a man, they further risked being labeled as degraded and undeserving by home visitors who disapproved of such arrangements.[88] Disapproval of the informal unions of some working-class couples led the Bradford Guardians to insist that some couples marry before their children would be returned to them.[89]

Women most likely bore the greatest burden in the new system. As several recent studies of charity and the Poor Law have argued, women constituted the primary recipients of assistance and represented the family in its dealings with outside agencies. The use of such assistance, whether in the form of outdoor relief or medical aid, could be one part of a larger strategy to cope with the problems of illness, unemployment and the burdens of dependent elderly or young family members. The increasing scope of concern, improved record keeping and disciplinary power of the new agencies complicated such strategies. Indeed, the inquisitory efforts of home visitors most likely inspired efforts to conceal rather than display poverty in order to be considered eligible to receive assistance.[90]

The reluctance of many families to accept aid reflected the rather severe and arbitrary definitions employed by aid workers. From their reports, it is clear that for many poverty was equivalent to neglect. Their comments on the lack of clothing and furniture in working-class homes and their run-down condition revealed an unfamiliarity with city life and a belief that squalor indicated a lack of fitness and concern. The authorities refused to release the children of one women because 'the house is not in a fit state', despite the fact that the woman repaired her rented home and purchased bedclothes.[91]

For parents who ran afoul of the authorities, it proved quite difficult to retrieve their families and to restore their independence. The Poor Law Guardians repeatedly denied parents access to their children in the Workhouse and sent them to foster homes outside the city. Numerous examples existed of children running away to be reunited with their parents and parents attempting to deceive the authorities in order to remain near their children. The prison sentences served by parents convicted of neglect or cruelty only compounded the problems of family togetherness.[92] Parents imprisoned for neglect often waited considerable periods, with limited visiting rights, for the return of their children.[93] Of course, such cases need to balanced by consideration of others in which abusive or truly neglectful parents abrogated their responsibilities.[94]

The harshness of the system from the point of view of the recipients points out the contradictions of social work in this era. By the late nineteenth century, a number of progressive experiments in family welfare had been implemented in Bradford. Catherine M'Turk and Florence Moser pioneered the use of separate facilities for children and the boarding out of children in the Union workhouse to foster homes. They also labored to improve conditions for the adult inmates of the workhouse, particularly the elderly and the chronically ill.[95] This effort to humanize the treatment of the poor continued when ILP members began to enter local government. Anne Ellis and Margaret McMillan worked with the Liberal women elected to the School Board and the Guardians. Fred Jowett, in his time on the Borough Council, found an ally in E. J. Smith, a stalwart Liberal, who supported municipal services for eugenic reasons.[96]

Despite attempts to build cross-gender and cross-class alliances in social welfare on the basis of a common humanitarian feeling, the system itself continued to rely heavily on punitive sanctions and a belief in the need for economy in expenditure. Typical of this attitude was the decision by the Board of Guardians, before the advent of municipally-supported school feeding, to sue twenty-five families for support after providing meals to their children at school.[97]

Far too often the use of the powers of compulsion and punishment constituted the working-class family's primary experience with the new institutions. This treatment reflected the perception of working-class family life as degraded by middle-class observers. Although one writer called for women 'unconscious of class difference and able to hold intercourse with the poorest classes without condescension', class attitudes pervaded the new system.[98] Typical of such attitudes was the Poor Law visitor who referred to one mother as 'a drunken, dirty woman'.[99] The distinction of deserving versus undeserving poor retained its power despite the new rhetoric of social obligation.

A couple of examples clarify the interplay of these factors. The case of one man, an unemployed joiner, his wife and child came to the attention of the Guild of Help in 1906. Despite help from friends, the family lacked basic necessities and had fallen behind in their rent. The Guild provided assistance, but pressed the man to do Test Work, in this case stone breaking. The relationship between the visitor and the family remained tense. The visitor complained that the family seemed reluctant to share information and did not appear grateful for the Guild's help. Despite the fact that the husband displayed signs of serious depression over his inability to work and his wife's health suffered, the Guild defined the case as one requiring 'moral pressure'.[100]

In another case, an injured, unemployed driver with a wife and four children was referred to the Guild in February 1908. The Guild gave the father crutches, but the case worker worried that he might sell them. The man found irregular work, but he refused to reveal his wages to the Guild. Later the husband developed an ulcerated stomach and the wife resorted to borrowing from relatives and begging in the street. At the this point the Guild terminated the case because it felt the woman was of 'bad character'.[101]

The issues of perception and class differences stood at the core of the problem of poverty in the late Victorian and early Edwardian period. Although the language and methods of social reformers changed after 1880, several important beliefs remained intact. Middle-class observers continued to focus on the individual's responsibility for his or her situation. The reasons for this individual failure shifted from moral or religious grounds to ignorance of the scientific principles of sanitation or child care, but the source of the problem remained the behavior of the individual. In particular, the behavior of women remained the critical issue for many reformers, even those who rejected the harsher versions of laissez faire. Social activists sought to change women, to perfect their domestic abilities, in order to eliminate the problems of poverty.

As long as this mindset continued to dominate conceptions of poverty, the solutions offered would remain limited and punitive, seeking to transform the individual rather than his or her environment or material circumstances. As a result, the quasi-public agencies that emerged after the 1880s failed to come to grips with the dimensions of the problems they faced or to create a more humane environment for the poor and dependent. Improvements in housing and mortality had to wait until the working class achieved a higher standard of living. Ironically, the First World War proved more beneficial than existing welfare schemes by providing full employment at higher wages.[102] If one considers entitlement a key component of the modern welfare state, then the pre-1914 developments in welfare provision did not anticipate the welfare state, for they were premised on the acceptability of the recipient.

Such a conclusion should not prove particularly surprising. Fear of social disorder as well as humanitarian sentiment motivated the expansion of welfare provision after 1880. The definition of poverty as a threat to national survival justified new methods of care and a growth in expenditure on the indigent, but it also led to an expansion of police powers. The machinery of the modern welfare state, if not its ethos, developed in these early agencies. They offered the middle class a way of combating novel social problems, while retaining the social distinctions that informed the definition of such problems in class and gender terms. Social categories could be maintained without fear that egalitarian sentiment might breach the wall of separation between public and private society. Private agencies could step in where the state felt incapable and vice versa, ensuring that control remained in the hands of a relatively self-selective group of civic-minded and wealthy individuals. The sanitary gospel allowed private society to call upon the state for the maintenance of the social order without ceding control of matters like wages and private property. The existence of an alternative vision, in which the municipality delivered all services on the basis of need, advanced by the ILP, forced the Liberal elite of Bradford into a more advanced position than they otherwise might have embraced, but they maintained their own peculiar brand of voluntarism and firm control over the delivery of services. Thus, the new reform movement did not represent a step on the road to the modern welfare state, but rather an alternative path.

The limitations of the sanitary gospel illustrate the domestic consequences of the social and economic structures of mid-Victorian Bradford with remarkable clarity. The working-class family stood at the intersection of all the divergent forces of the age and responded in ways both unforeseen and unprecedented. The working-class family remained reliant upon its own efforts for survival. It was this overarching reality that lay behind the adoption of family limitation before 1914.

7 Family Limitation and Family Economy in Bradford 1851–81

In 1885, a correspondent to the *Cotton Factory Times* calling himself 'A Weaver' wrote in support of family limitation, arguing that

> If the working man wished to raise himself from the position he now occupies, it must be by self-help; and I consider conjugal prudence, combined with cooperation and trades unionism, to be the very essence of self-help.[1]

From the 1870s to 1914, this 'conjugal prudence' spread throughout England. The pace and extent of fertility decline varied by both region and social class. Textile cities in Lancashire and Yorkshire, like Bradford, stood at the forefront of this process for a number of reasons. As early centers of the industrial revolution, their populations possessed a second or even third generation experience of urban industrial life. Other areas and occupations, slower to develop or more isolated from the currents of change, followed these cities in a remarkably short span of time.[2]

Bradford represents an early, but not exceptional, example of this process. In Bradford, the reorganization of the worsted trade in the later nineteenth century, which undermined wages and security of employment, helped trigger the onset of family limitation, but the reasons for this change lay deeply rooted in the social and economic structures of working-class life. Family limitation was the product of the consolidation of working-class life in the mid-Victorian era. This consolidation created within working-class culture structures of gender and family relations, as well as a set of norms and values, amenable to family limitation. Working-class fertility decline came out of the intersection of these values and structures with material necessity. In the last quarter of the nineteenth century, as a national working-class culture spread and as the English economy faced growing competitive challenges, many other areas encountered the same combination of social and economic circumstances experienced by Bradford in the

1870s and 1880s. In space of forty years, working-class families abandoned their hostility to birth control and embraced family limitation as one of the many forms of 'self-help' they employed to face the dilemmas they encountered in everyday life.

THE STANDARD OF LIVING AND THE WORKING-CLASS FAMILY

The question of living standards constitutes one key to understanding the onset of family limitation. Conventional theories emphasize the importance of rising living standards to the decline of fertility. The belief that fertility decline began among the better off and spread down into the working class lends credence to the idea that higher incomes caused lower fertility. Left unexplained is why higher income groups waited so long to limit family size. Population historians also argue that the increased possibilities for social mobility gave families an incentive to concentrate their resources on fewer children to help them obtain a better education and other attributes necessary for success. Finally, workers, in receipt of higher incomes and better educations, sampled the pleasures of consumer life and sought to ensure its enjoyment by reducing their family size. Behind these propositions lies the idea that the working-class family changed in the later nineteenth century, becoming more individualistic, wealthier and more rational in its behavior.[3]

To assess this argument requires an examination not only of the nature of working-class family life, but also the material circumstances of that life. The standard of living debate represents one of the most enduring disputes of English history, as pessimists and optimists wrangle over issues of economic growth and the distribution of wealth and income.[4] In the last fifteen years, the optimists, using new econometric techniques of analysis, have dominated the discussion. They argue that the per capita incomes of ordinary people improved from the late 1820s and perhaps even earlier.[5] Yet, as Joel Mokyr points out in a review of recent work on the industrial revolution, estimates that show lower growth than previously assumed and a worsening of the distribution of wealth, as well as greater capital accumulation before 1850, cannot be easily squared with the assertion that ordinary people experienced an improvement in their standard of living.[6]

While the national outlines of the debate receive the most attention, for the historian of the family and the local community the gaps are significant. Both pessimists and optimists readily admit that some sectors and regions gained in the process of industrialization, while others lost.[7] Furthermore, most of the debate concerns the wages of adult men in formal employment, which excludes women and children as well as many domestic workers.[8] Thus, while one may make a pessimist or optimist case at the national level, at the level of regions, cities and families, much remains unknown.

Bradford and its hinterland underwent dramatic change in the first half of the nineteenth century. The notion of an industrial revolution is pertinent to the experiences of many in the region, but the material impact of this change needs to be considered carefully.[9] The wool combers and hand-loom weavers faced the worst conditions. Forced to live and work in cramped quarters, often located in cellars, these workers suffered greatly from the effects of overcrowding and poverty.[10] The Commission on the Hand-loom weavers in 1838 and a local study of wool combers in 1845 established the poor conditions of life in these trades.[11] For many skilled workers, however, the 1830s and 1840s saw the emergence of new occupations and opportunities for work in the rapidly growing worsted industry.

The cyclical nature of the early industrial economy also contributed to the material impact of industrialization. While life for the majority of the working class did not fall to the level of the combers, the economic slumps of 1837 to 1841 and 1845 to 1848 produced widespread hardship. In the winter of 1847, 5,000 families were on relief as a result of a serious downturn in the worsted trade.[12] Such sharp depressions, combined with the generally poor state of the environment, contributed to the political ferment among Bradford's working class in the 1830s and 1840s.[13]

The rapid pace of development, combined with a lack of regulation and low incomes, created an environmental disaster for the city as a whole.[14] Infant mortality ran over two hundred per thousand and overall mortality peaked in the 1840s at about twenty-seven per thousand. Epidemics of cholera and typhoid reoccurred in this period, and endemic killers such as measles and tuberculosis claimed a heavy toll.[15] James Smith, writing to the Health of Towns Commission in the early 1840s, labeled Bradford 'the most filthy town I visited'. He added,

> The main sewerage of the town has been very defective . . . The chief sewerage, if sewerage it can be called, of the inferior streets and of the courts, is in open channels, and from the rough and unequal surface of the streets, the flow is tardy, and the whole soil is saturated

with sewerage water. The main sewers are discharged either into the brook or into the terminus or basin of a canal which runs into the lower part of town. The water of this basin is often so charged with decaying matter, that in hot weather bubbles of sulphuretted hydrogen are continually rising to the surface; and so much is the atmosphere loaded with the gas, that the watch cases and other materials of silver become black in the pockets of workmen employed near the canal.[16]

While many would acknowledge the difficulties of life in early industrial cities like Bradford, in general such conditions are seen as a temporary problem. Most historians argue that the mid-Victorian boom, followed by the deflation of the last quarter of the nineteenth century, produced a sustained and widespread improvement in the standard of living for the working class. As a result of higher wages, shifts in occupational structure and lower prices, workers' real wages rose as much as 55 per cent from 1870 to 1913.[17] Such figures conceal a number of uncertainties and ambiguities. Since much of the improvement in real wages derived from a lower cost of living, the level of improvement depends in part upon an index of prices. As Charles Feinstein has shown, the inclusion or exclusion of items can affect one's index. Thus, Feinstein argues that A.L. Bowley's index overstated the decline in prices in the 1870s and their subsequent rise in the early twentieth century.[18]

The choice of indices may also affect the measurement of how working-class households benefited from this fall in prices after 1875. Broad measures of house rents or wholesale prices may not accurately represent purchases by working-class consumers, whose markets in food and housing were more constricted. Feinstein's work on the cost of living showed a divergence between rents, with working-class rents rising after 1876, while those of the middle class fell.[19] Working-class families, often dependent on credit offered by neighborhood stores and who purchased smaller quantities, may not have enjoyed all the benefits of falling food prices.[20]

The improvement in real wages also needs to be considered in light of the overall level of consumption enjoyed by the working class at the beginning and end of this period. Even after 40 years of expansion, levels of consumption, as reflected by high expenditures on food and basic necessities and the low level of savings, indicated that much of the population still lived with chronic insecurity and possessed little margin above subsistence in the event of unemployment or illness.[21]

Another critical issue concerns the variability of income over time, place and occupation. The increase in real wages was not uniform after 1850 or 1870, as regions and occupations fared differently and as trade cycles affected both regions and the nation.[22] The upward trend could disguise marked peaks and valleys of wages and unemployment that did not show up in the aggregate statistics.[23] Finally, most observers agree that the deflation-led increase in real wages slowed considerably in the period 1899–1913, as prices began to rise and wages failed to keep up.[24]

These trends affected the working-class standard of living in Bradford in the second half of the nineteenth century. As can be seen in Figure 7.1, the nominal wages of worsted workers increased after 1850, but until the mid-1860s, gains in real wages were modest, as the cost of living moved upward as well. The boom years from the mid-1860s to mid-1870s led to a substantial increase in real wages, as wages outpaced prices.[25] However, the gains of the mid-Victorian era were not evenly distributed. The amount of taxes assessed on profits increased 250 per cent from 1856 to 1867, yet by 1871 only 15 per cent of adult males in the borough earned enough to be assessed for taxes. The disparity in income showed in the tax figures. Out of 38,000 adult males in 1871, 32,000 earned less than £100 per year, 2,000 earned £100–150 and 3,846 earned an average of £406. On the lower end of the scale, over 20 per cent of the adult male work force still relied on casual labor in the mid-Victorian era.[26]

Seasonal and cyclical fluctuations in income restrained the improvement in the standard of living after 1850. Bradford's manufacturers changed over their production lines twice yearly, leading to short-time or temporary unemployment.[27] One observer in the early 1890s estimated that worsted workers lost around 10 per cent of their yearly wages as a result.[28] Other trades, most notably construction, experienced similar seasonal slowdowns related to weather. In addition to yearly fluctuations, cyclical downturns affected the worsted trade from 1854 to 1855, 1856 to 1857 and 1867 to 1868. Such downturns could seriously erode the resources and well-being of working-class families.[29]

Finally, the problem of family wages versus individual earnings complicates any assessment of the standard of living. In the working-class family, the standard of comfort depended on the relationship of total family income to family size. While the husband's wage remained a primary determinant of family income, the role of secondary wage earners and the numbers of dependents must be considered in any

Figure 7.1 Money wages in the worsted industry, 1850–1901 (1901 = 100)

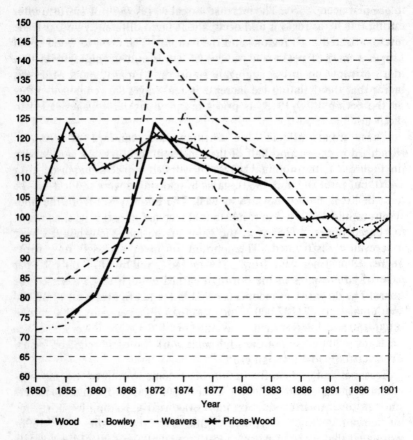

Sources: Wood (1902), Bowley (1909).

assessment of material life.[30] Theodore Koditschek's study of over 800 working-class families in Bradford in 1851 demonstrates the importance of these factors. Families with several young children endured higher levels of poverty and relied on the wages of the father for survival. Such dependence could be problematic given the fluctuations in the economy and the possibilities of death, sickness or injury for the main wage earner.[31] As a result, a majority of families in 1851 lived below the poverty line despite full employment.[32]

These factors taken together may help explain the slow improvement in environmental conditions in the city in the mid-Victorian era.

Housing remained overcrowded and expensive, forcing many to live in primitive conditions. The average size of a household in the borough during this period was a little over five persons, but one survey found nine persons per household in crowded inner-city areas such as the Leys.[33] Less than 10 per cent of all homes in 1872 had water closets and most households relied on outdoor privies, which were emptied infrequently and shared by as many as forty persons.[34] In 1871, over 1000 cellar dwellings in use failed to meet even the minimum standards of the Public Health Act.[35] Not surprisingly, mortality also showed limited improvement. Death rates for infants and children remained high in this period and the adult death rates from some contagious diseases such as tuberculosis increased in the decade after 1861. Diarrhea, a major cause of infant deaths, continued to run rampant and the infant mortality rate hovered around two hundred per thousand throughout the 1870s.[36]

The existing problems of poverty and subsistence became more acute as a result of the depression in the worsted trade that began in the mid-1870s. Depending upon their place in the labor hierarchy, workers experienced different problems.[37] The bottom two tiers of worsted operatives, unskilled laborers and the weaving and spinning personnel, bore the brunt of the depression. Lacking the skills and trade union organizations possessed by other operatives, these workers could not resist the demands of manufacturers for wage reductions. A number of observers reported that wages in the worsted industry fell between 10 - 15 per cent in the late 1870s through 'tacit rather than formal' cooperation between mill owners.[38] General wage levels in the textile trade in the late 1870s and early 1880s failed to recover and remained lower than those of ten years earlier.[39] The real wages of worsted workers declined in the decade after 1873 as wage cuts exceeded the fall in the cost of living, wiping out some of the advances of the previous two decades (Figure 7.1).[40]

The slump in the textile trade resulted in higher unemployment and lower wages not only for semi-skilled factory operatives, but for skilled and supervisory workers in the mills and other trades.[41] The iron industry, machine-making and the construction trades, the principle alternatives to the worsted industry, shared its fate.[42] The collapse of prosperity brought short-time and unemployment, as orders for mills, homes and machinery withered.[43] The weakness of the local economy allowed employers to win back some of the gains of the mid-Victorian era. In the engineering trade, the major employer, Hodgson's, reinstated a fifty-six hour work week in the late 1870s after granting a nine hour day in 1871.[44] In the stone cutting trade, the owners pressed quarrymen for a 10 per cent reduction in wages in January of 1879.[45] Even the top of the labor hierarchy, the mill overlookers, agreed to reductions. The records of the overlookers' societies, as well as the woolsorters, dyers and pattern makers, all show a sharp increase in the benefits paid to unemployed members in the late 1870s.[46] These developments led the *Bradford Observer* to comment,

> It is to be feared that the reduction [of wages] and short time will find many homes unprepared for the strain, especially in those families the majority of whose members are engaged in mills.[47]

The impact of the depression showed up in a number of ways. Arrests for desertion, begging, vagrancy and prostitution increased markedly during the 1870s, reaching their highest level between 1877 and 1879.[48] In correspondence with the Local Government Board, the relieving officer of the Bradford Poor Law Union complained of the large numbers of vagrants and able-bodied men requesting relief, a complaint confirmed by the Union's records.[49] For the half year ending on September 30, 1872, the Poor Law Union relieved a total of 3,342 paupers, both in and out of the workhouse. By contrast, in the half year ending March 25, 1879, the union cared for 10,778 persons. More importantly, the number of able-bodied men given relief due to unemployment jumped from 8 to 1,450.[50] These figures considerably understate the incidence of poverty and unemployment, because many families preferred to undergo considerable hardship rather than submit to the humiliation of applying to the Guardians.[51] For these people, credit from shopowners, the aid of private charities, friendly societies, trade unions, friends and family allowed them to survive.

The peaks of destitution created by the slump passed in the 1880s and wages stabilized, but higher unemployment characterized the worsted trade and the city until the First World War. The passage of restrictive tariffs in the 1890s, especially the McKinnley and Dingley tariffs in the United States, hurt the worsted trade.[52] This produced a growing fragmentation of the trade and increased casualization in combing, dyeing and sorting, as well as continued wage cuts and short-time in spinning and weaving.[53] The town's iron trade began a precipitous decline in the same era for different reasons, which compounded the difficulties of the local economy.[54] In 1893, a survey found 25 per cent of the borough's population either unemployed or dependent upon an unemployed bread winner, while in the winter of 1903–4, another survey found over 10,000 underfed children.[55]

The experience of Bradford in the late nineteenth century needs to be put into a broader perspective. Despite variations in wage levels and greater problems of unemployment, the majority of working-class families ended up materially better-off by 1900. Yet growing real wages failed to eliminate back-to-back houses or dramatically lower the infant mortality rate.[56] In addition, considerable uncertainty accompanied this improvement. The crisis of the 1870s scarred the generation that came of age in late nineteenth century Bradford and left a legacy of unemployment and short-term dislocations. Many working-class families across England shared this uncertain future in the late nineteenth century as the economy adapted to the pressures of world competition across a broad range of industries and older forms of skill and employment came into question.[57] Forty years of overall growth in real wages failed to eliminate the chronic insecurity of working-class life; indeed the growing pace of change could have heightened such insecurity. The fear of poverty and a desire to shelter the family from sudden dislocations formed the background to the family economy throughout this period.

THE FAMILY ECONOMY IN MID-VICTORIAN ENGLAND

John Lee in his *Handy Guide to Bradford*, published in 1873, described a family that earned £10 a week when trade was flourishing:

> The father, a managing overlooker in a worsted mill, had £3 a week; two sons, overlookers, each earned 30s; three daughters, weavers, brought home 20s. each; and the remainder of the family earned 20s. The only thing exceptional in this instance was that the father occupied a rather better position than other men of his class.[58]

Such earning power in an era when 30s. a week could maintain a family supported Lee's belief that 'A large family is a blessing to the Bradford operative'. While this example represents an exaggerated case, the assumption that families worked together for mutual benefit underlies many contemporary and historical accounts of working-class family life. Yet what do we really know about the nature of work and family life in this period? Only a handful of studies exist that look at the family economy of the working class and most cover limited time spans and geographical areas.[59] The complex gender relationships that lay behind this division of labor and the emergence of a separate domestic sphere make any simple description of family economy inadequate.[60] The ability of the working-class family to reproduce itself, both materially and biologically, depended upon its ability to balance the competing claims of members for goods and power within the family, while still accommodating the necessity for maximizing family income.[61]

Most studies of family limitation attempt to explain fertility decline in terms of the changing dynamics of the family economy. Both demographers and economists view the family as a utility maximizing entity, along the lines of a firm. In this model, children can be seen as a form of investment or a durable good. The increasing costs of educating and caring for children and the reduced returns for their labor dictate that the family shift to lower fertility in order to better use its resources.[62]

However, this model, by assuming a single measure of utility for the family, ignores generational and gender differences. Women and children occupied subordinate positions within households to adult men, especially the household head. This inferiority reflected their lower status in the larger world that prevented them from earning sufficient wages to escape dependency in a male-dominated household. The division of labor within the family, far from being a 'natural' by-product of tastes, inclinations and choice, instead grew out of this dual subordination, which relegated women to poorly paid or unwaged labor – women engaged in unpaid domestic labor, as well as part-time employment within and outside the home, which helped maintain the family, but trapped the woman in a dependent relationship within the household.[63]

Although historians disagree with the more abstract components of the new home economics, they have yet to offer a radically different vision of how family economy and fertility interacted in the late nineteenth century.[64] Most studies of fertility decline emphasize the transformation of the family economy as a key factor in the process of family limitation. Historians and demographers argue that the increasing economic role of women and the decreasing economic importance of children gave families new material incentives to control family size. Children, an asset in the domestic economy, initially earned their way through waged labor in factories and workshops. The decline of child labor and the growth of compulsory education made children an economic burden.[65] Population historians have also pointed to the changing nature of women's work as a critical component in the transformation of the family economy. The increased participation of women in the work force and the need for women's wages provided another reason to delay or limit births.[66]

Women's wage labor increased and children's labor decreased over the long term after 1800. What is uncertain, however, is how such trends affected the working-class family in the 1870s and 1880s. The impact of changes in women's and children's labor cannot be demonstrated using aggregate figures of labor force participation at the national level, but only by an examination of the family economy at a micro-level. Even at the macro-level, the discussion of women and children's labor remains confused. Proponents of the family economy thesis conflate the traditional family economy with that of the mid-Victorian era. By 1851, only a minority of children worked for wages in England and women worked in considerable numbers outside the home. This reflected the impact of over fifty years of social and economic change and preceded the decline of working-class fertility by thirty to fifty years.

One could argue that several generations lag could be necessary for this change to affect fertility decisions, but this fails to take into account the inconsistent pace of change. Women's work force participation changed little from 1851 to 1911 and one could argue that their relative position in the labor force declined in the mid-Victorian era as men disproportionately enjoyed the gains in employment opportunities in skilled trades.[67] Children's labor declined slowly after 1851, dropped sharply after 1871, but actually increased from 1881 to 1891.[68]

Paradoxically, in textile areas like Bradford, fertility declined earlier, even though levels of child labor were higher than elsewhere in England and remained so even after the onset of family limitation.[69] Women's labor, although higher than in other industrial regions, remained essentially stable after 1851.[70] These figures suggest that no radical transformation of the family economy occurred directly before the onset of fertility decline and that minimal differences characterized pre- and post-decline families. Fertility control represented an adaptation within an established family economy in the decade of the 1870s as changes in the surrounding environment – most importantly the growing instability within the worsted trade – intensified the problems of family life for older married couples. Such changes took place in the midst of a working-class culture which stressed the importance of self-reliance and thrift and within which the need to survive and to maintain one's independence justified almost any effort. In this context, fertility control can be viewed as one possible response among many. Like family limitation, emigration, political action, friendly society membership and trade-union organization worked toward the same end of enhancing the security of the individual and the family.

THE NATURE OF THE FAMILY ECONOMY IN BRADFORD

Despite the changing nature of family relationships in the nineteenth century, the nuclear family remained the dominant form of residence.[71] Around 80 per cent of all people lived in nuclear families in this period, and a further 10 per cent lived with members of their extended family.[72] For most people, daily life and survival still depended upon the family. In Bradford the working-class family existed in a symbiotic relationship with the worsted trade. In 1851, about 40 per cent of all male household heads found work in the textile trades; over the next thirty years this declined to about 25 per cent, but textiles still provided the single largest source of employment for men who headed households.[73] At the same time, the steady demand for women's and children's labor led to high levels of employment for other family members.[74] As a result, the majority of families remained connected with the worsted industry in this era.[75]

Bradford, a city characterized by high levels of child labor, offers us one of the best examples of the role of children in the family economy. Despite their importance to the worsted industry and their high levels of employment compared to the rest of England, the majority of children below the age of fourteen (the minimum for full-time work under the Factory Acts) did not work for wages in this period. Children below the age of ten possessed only limited opportunities for work; only 5 per cent of eight-year-olds worked in 1851 and only 0.5 per cent in 1881. Even in 1851, children moved into the labor force gradually and only after age eleven did a majority of children work for wages (Table 7.1).

While overall the participation rate of children aged nine to thirteen declined from 49.5 per cent to 20.5 per cent from 1851 to 1881, the reasons for this decline and its impact need to considered. Many historians believe that a connection exists between the Education Act of 1870 and the fall of the birth rate that began in the 1870s.[76] Yet in Bradford, the withdrawal of young children from work started as early as the 1850s despite the continued strong demand for their labor. Factory inspectors in the 1860s noted the persistent shortage of young operatives in Bradford and the subsequent call for easier medical and educational requirements for their entry into work.[77] In 1871 Reverend

Table 7.1   Children's employment (percentages), 1851–1881

	Year			
Age	1851	1861	1871	1881
8 (*n*)	119			200
Home	31.1			3.5
School	63.9			96.0
Work	5.0			0.5
9 (*n*)	145	124	109	187
Home	30.3	24.2	14.7	5.9
School	52.4	66.9	70.6	92.0
Work	17.3	8.9	14.9	2.1
10 (*n*)	179	122	104	185
Home	20.1	9.8	10.6	3.2
School	36.3	63.0	50.0	88.1
Work	43.6	26.2	39.4	8.6
11 (*n*)	141	98	97	165
Home	16.3	15.3	8.2	7.3
School	32.6	48.9	42.3	70.3
Work	51.1	36.7	53.6	22.4
12 (*n*)	146	108	115	177
Home	13.0	14.8	7.0	2.3
School	19.9	38.0	35.7	62.7
Work	67.1	47.2	57.4	35.0
13 (*n*)	165	112	98	172
Home	7.8	8.0	3.1	4.7
School	8.5	14.3	14.3	34.9
Work	84.7	78.7	82.6	60.5
14 (*n*)	188	108	122	185
Home	7.4	6.5	5.7	5.4
School	5.3	10.2	10.7	14.6
Work	87.2	83.3	83.6	80.0
15 (*n*)	186	125	152	166
Home	5.9	4.8	3.9	2.4
School	1.6	8.8	5.3	6.6
Work	92.7	86.4	90.8	91.0
14–19 (*n*)	998			1,078
Home	5.7	4.2		
School	2.1	5.8		
Work	92.2	89.5		

Source: Sample of Bradford 1851, 1861, 1871, 1881.

Wilden, Inspector for the Bradford district Church of England schools, reported, 'There is a great competition for children. In many districts there are not enough and men with large families are even imported from other counties.'[78] Manufacturers continued this policy of recruitment into the 1870s.[79] Participation rates for children nine to thirteen actually rose from 32.4 per cent to 44.2 per cent between 1861 and 1871, reflecting the increased opportunities for work during the boom of the late 1860s and early 1870s.

One unintended outcome of the expansion of education was the withdrawal of children from the home to school. Prior to 1881, the census listed significant numbers of children at home. While some of these children were misenumerated, many performed domestic work to ease the burden on the mother.[80] This category registered a far steeper decline from 1851 to 1881 than that of children at work. Thus, while school eased some of the child care worries of mothers, it may have intensified their domestic labor by removing potential assistants from home to school.[81] The decline of 'dame' schools, which served as de facto day care for many mothers, compounded this problem.[82]

How did these changes in children's work affect the family economy? Children's earnings averaged between 1s.6d. to 4s. per week. Only in families without a male wage earner could their wages contribute a significant amount to family income because of its desperately low level. A study of 504 working-class families (about one-third of whom were from Bradford) undertaken by the Interdepartmental Committee on Partial Exemption from School Attendance in 1909 illustrates this point. Of those families with an employed father (395) children earned 33.9 per cent of family income, while in those with an unemployed or absent father (97), children earned 76.9 per cent. More importantly, in the latter households, half-timers earned 15.2 per cent of family income, while in the former they earned 6.3 per cent of family income.[83]

Far from deriving benefit from children, most parents kept their children from work as long as possible. The decision to send a young child to work was more likely the result of family necessity rather than a central feature of the family economy. A significant decline in child labor occurred prior to 1870 because of parental choice rather than state intervention, as parents chose to allow their children at least the rudiments of an education before they began work. This was done despite the loss of income and extra expense this choice entailed.

Young children were not a paying proposition in Bradford; they needed to be supported for most of their lives and when some began to work, their wages did not add significantly to family income. The removal of some of these children from the work force, while it lengthened their period of dependency and lowered the income of some families, hardly constituted a transformation of the family economy of the working class. Most young children never worked for wages and many withdrew from the labor market before the arrival of compulsory education or family limitation.

However, the importance of young persons' labor may have gone beyond any immediate return in the form of wages. Children could have provided a form of insurance in case of a temporary shortfall in family income, as the family budget study cited above suggests. Thus, the level of child labor in any one census year may not have reflected the true probability of children working throughout their entire childhood or their continuing economic value. Children could also offer insurance for the care of their parents in old age. Recent studies of the care of older adults suggest that despite the expansion of the Poor Law and its disproportionate provision for the elderly, most elderly still could not depend on state assistance for subsistence outside the workhouse.[84] In both cases, the economic value of children cannot be simply measured by the levels of child labor.[85]

The situation of older children differed markedly from that of younger children. There appears to have been an almost universal expectation that older children would contribute to family income. Over 80 per cent of all fourteen-year-olds and 90 per cent of all fifteen-year-olds worked in each of the four censuses. In fact, the percentage at work increased between 1871 and 1881, despite the expansion of educational opportunities. It is this group of younger workers, from fourteen to nineteen, who provided a crucial portion of the family's income as the parents grew older.[86] These workers earned close to adult wages (10s. to 20s. per week) and tended to remain at home at least to the age of twenty, perhaps even after marriage.[87]

What slender evidence we have from the West Riding suggests that young men and women contributed most or all of their earnings to the family and received back a small sum for themselves.[88] Joanna Bornat's work in the Colne Valley woolen district portrays 'tipping up' as common, especially among young women. The practice of paying board to one's parents was another alternative, but Bornat believes it existed primarily among better off workers.[89] Barbara Thompson argues that tipping up occurred in Bradford as well.[90] The high rates of coresidence tends to support the idea of shared resources. In 1851 92 per cent of young people fourteen to nineteen worked and 82 per cent lived with their parents or relatives, while in 1881 91.4 per cent were employed, with 86.6 per cent at home or with relatives.

The relatively few children in school after age thirteen makes it difficult to see how a new pattern of educational mobility emerged that altered the dynamics of the family economy. While rising literacy rates and nearly universal elementary schooling reflected the spread of education, families still dominated the choice of both education and work.[91] For working-class families, survival rather than upward mobility remained the primary goal. As a result, children left school at fourteen to pursue their true role in life – labor.[92]

If we examine the pattern of women's work in Bradford in this era, we see a similar pattern of overall stability. Women worked in large numbers before marriage; once they married, however, their involvement in wage labor began to decline (see Table 7.2). About 30–35 per cent of all married women in this period listed an occupation, but this was not evenly distributed. About 40–45 per cent of married women below age thirty worked, whereas above age thirty, only 25–35 per cent did so. Above the age of fifty, the rates fell even further, reaching about 5 per cent after age sixty.

While this age pattern remained intact, the work-place participation of married women increased from 1851 to 1881. The greatest increase occurred among women thirty-five to forty-nine years old, whose participation rates rose over 10 per cent. Only a small portion of the increase involved jobs such as cleaning or clothing production that could be done part-time or at home; most of these women found employment in the mills. The extent to which this was an attempt to compensate for lower earnings from children or adult males is not clear, but more married women worked at the end of the period than at the beginning. Yet this change was gradual and failed to fundamentally alter the existing pattern of employment for women.[93]

In addition to children and mothers, other groups within the household potentially provided income and domestic aid – kin and lodgers. Kin comprised 5 to 8 per cent of the total population of Bradford between 1851 and 1881, and in 1881 21.1 per cent of all families had at least one relative other than nuclear family members coresiding. Married children with their own children living in the parent's household comprised 50 per cent of coresident kin, the result of the inability of a significant minority of young married couples to set up their own households.[94] Siblings, followed by parents, formed the next most common kin groups. All of these groups could contribute to family income, although the presence of young grandchildren and the

Table 7.2   Married women's employment 1851 and 1881 (percentages)

1851	Age of Mother					
	20–24	*25–29*	*30–34*	*35–39*	*40–44*	*45–49*
n	161	238	204	185	128	115
Home	52.1	55.0	68.6	75.7	80.4	86.1
Employed	47.9	45.0	31.4	24.3	19.6	13.9
Textiles	41.6	31.5	20.1	14.1	10.2	5.2
Combing	3.7	2.9	2.5	2.7	0.8	1.7
Service	0.6	2.9	1.0	2.1	3.9	3.4
Shop	0.0	0.0	1.0	1.1	0.8	1.8

1881	Age of mother					
	20–24	*25–29*	*30–34*	*35–39*	*40–44*	*45–49*
n	109	168	166	152	156	124
At home	42.2	57.1	65.8	66.5	68.0	67.7
Employed	57.8	42.9	34.2	33.5	32.0	32.3
Textiles	46.8	32.1	21.1	23.0	21.8	17.7
Clothing	3.7	2.4	3.6	4.7	2.5	4.8
Service	0.9	1.8	1.2	3.3	5.1	7.3
Shop	0.0	0.6	0.6	0.7	1.2	0.0
Unemployed	3.7	0.6	2.4	0.7	0.6	1.6

Source: Sample of Bradford 1851, 1861, 1871, 1881.

elderly could have added to the strain on family resources.[95] A disproportionate number of kin fell into the fourteen to nineteen age group that supplied many secondary wage earners, and into the over fifty age group who could have provided domestic help for mothers.[96]

Lodgers, who made up 9–11 per cent of the total population in this era, also played an important role in the family economy. They resided in 23 per cent of all households in 1851 and 17.4 per cent in 1881.[97] The households they belonged to differed in several respects from other households in the city. Households with lodgers were more likely to be headed by women.[98] These women were older and overwhelmingly widowed (about 75 per cent in both censuses) and more likely to be employed for wages. Male heads of households with lodgers tended to be in less well-paying occupations. In 1851 woolcombers headed 36 per cent of these households compared with 24 per cent for all households. In 1881, the proportion of general laborers among male heads of lodger households was twice that for all household heads. At the same time, the wives of these household heads had a greater likelihood of being unemployed and their children made less of a contribution to family income.[99]

Finally, over 20 per cent of families with lodgers had Irish fathers or mothers, compared with less than 13 per cent for all families. Irish families generally inhabited the worst and most crowded districts and lodging reflected both the general state of poverty and the overcrowded state of housing in the Irish slums. Lodging appears to have been a method of helping families cope by bringing in extra income to compensate for lower family earnings.[100] To a limited extent, these lodgers also substituted for kin, for households with lodgers present had slightly fewer kin than average and those kin who did live with them were more likely to be unemployed.[101]

Despite these alternative sources of income within the family, the male household head's wage remained central to the family's standard of living. In 1851, 36.9 per cent of working-class families with the husband present had only one wage earner, while a further 33.4 per cent had only two wage earners.[102] In 1881, 43.7 per cent of working-class families had a single wage earner and 31.2 per cent had two wage earners, while 2.0 per cent of working-class households failed to list even one wage earner. The example cited by Lee of a family with at least seven wage earners represented only 0.5 per cent of working-class households in 1881. The idea of a family living in comfort due to the ability of all its members to earn wages in the mills was a myth, although one cherished by middle-class defenders of low wages. In most cases a working-class family lived on the edge of subsistence, for if the primary wage earner lost his or her job or suffered a reduction in wages, the family faced severe hardship. In fact, the desire to shield the family from such occurrences created a more uniform family economy within the working class by 1881.

The families of master artisans, professionals and small property owners, as well as those of more substantial capitalists exhibited a different pattern of family labor. These groups depended far more upon the father's income, with over 57 per cent of all of these families having only one wage earner in both 1851 and 1881. Both lower middle class and bourgeois families had far lower levels of children's and wives' labor throughout the period.[103] No bourgeois children aged ten to thirteen worked from 1851 to 1881, while among lower middle-class families, the percentage of children at work dropped from 28.3 per cent in 1851 to 10.6 per cent in 1881. Among middle-class families in 1851, only 5.4 per cent of wives worked, while in 1881 12.4 per cent worked. The gain in women's employment occurred among lower middle-class families, such as shopkeepers and master artisans, who supplemented family income through women's work. By contrast, 29.7 per cent of working-class wives worked in 1851 and 30.6 per cent in 1881.

All social groups experienced a rise in the number of children aged ten to thirteen in school after 1851, reflecting the general trend away from young persons' employment. While increased schooling narrowed inter-class differentials in education and child labor, a substantial gap remained between workers and the middle class (See Table 7.3). In 1851, 55.8 per cent of middle-class children age ten to thirteen attended school, while only 24.4 per cent of those from working-class families went to school. In 1881, 85.4 per cent of middle-class children in this age group were in school, while for the children of working-class families, 64.9 per cent stayed in school. From 1851 to 1881 the educational gap between the children of skilled and unskilled workers disappeared. In 1851, 36 per cent of the children of skilled fathers were in school from ages ten to thirteen compared to 16.9 per cent for those of unskilled fathers. By 1881, they attended in virtually identical proportion, with 65.2 per cent of the children of unskilled fathers and 63.3 per cent of the children of skilled fathers in school.

A similar shift in mothers' work occurred within the working class. In 1851, 34.7 per cent of the wives of unskilled men worked compared to 22.2 per cent for those of skilled operatives. By 1881, 27.6 per cent of the wives of skilled men and 33 per cent of the wives of unskilled men worked. Interestingly, in both 1851 and 1881, whether the mother worked or not had little relationship to the child's (age 10–13) participation in the labor force, although women at work tended to have more children at work and at home in 1881, while non-working mothers tended to have more children in school (see Table 7.3).

Certain material realities – the low wages of the worsted trade, the opportunities for women and children to work and the overcrowded and expensive state of housing – shaped the family economy of Bradford's working class. Yet it also varied considerably depending upon the age of the husband and wife and when they married. The life cycle of the family and the changing composition of the household it inhabited is the key link between fertility and the family economy. Within the life cycle, stresses upon the family were unevenly distributed. These stresses were determined in large part by the relationship between family size and the number of wage earners.[104]

Table 7.3   Relationship between fathers' occupations and those of children and wives (percentages)

	Father's occupation (skill level)							
	1851				1881			
	1	*2*	*3*	*4*	*1*	*2*	*3*	*4*
Children								
Home								
10–13	18.1	10.6	19.6	16.7	4.0	4.3	4.6	12.5
14–19	5.8	4.5	14.8	16.7	2.4	4.9	4.8	30.0
School								
10–13	16.9	36.0	52.3	83.3	65.2	63.3	84.8	87.5
14–19	0.6	3.5	7.4	0	4.9	6.2	16.9	10.0
Work								
10–13	65.1	53.4	28.3	0	30.8	32.4	10.6	0
14–19	93.6	91.9	77.7	83.3	92.7	87.8	78.3	60.0

	Father's occupation (skill level)							
	1851				1881			
	1	*2*	*3*	*4*	*1*	*2*	*3*	*4*
Wife								
Home	65.3	77.8	94.5	95.2	66.8	72.4	85.5	94.6
Work	34.7	22.2	5.5	4.8	33.2	27.6	14.5	5.6
Total *n*	647	392	109	21	473	380	138	18

Skill level 1 is unskilled.
Skill level 2 is skilled.
Skill level 3 is lower middle/upper working classes – master artisans,
shopkeepers, white-collar workers.
Skill level 4 is capitalist/property-owning.

The family economy of the working class remained stable over this period. Figure 7.2 shows the wage earner ratio (wage earners divided by family members) by the age of the mother from 1851 to 1881. Young married couples faced fewer potential problems due to the lower number of children at home and the greater likelihood of the mother working, resulting in a high ratio between wage earners and

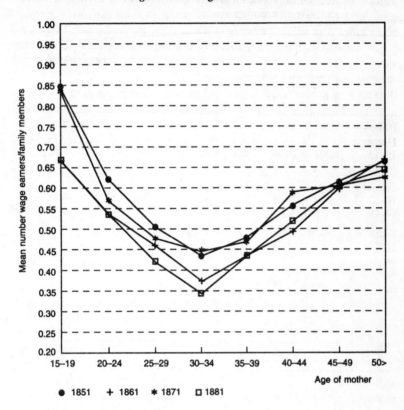

Figure 7.2   Wage earner ratio

Source: Manuscript Census of Bradford.

family members. As mothers grew older, this ratio fell as the number of children increased and fewer wives worked for wages. In general, the families of women from thirty to forty years old grew more dependent upon the husband's wage, as the children remained too young to contribute to family income. This meant that the family could be subject to an income crisis should the husband's wage suddenly cease. The pressure on the family income eased somewhat after the wife reached age forty-five, as children began to play a greater role in family income, although the mother's monetary contribution continued to decline. This family economy contrasted with that shown by middle class and wealthy families. Although they showed a similar pattern, the higher incomes of these men allowed them to forgo the work of women and children. Families in this social group showed far lower levels of child labor and women's work at all ages (Figure 7.3).

On the whole, from 1851 to 1881, the wage earner ratio for families in which the mother was below age forty-five decreased, indicating a lessening of their ability to maintain the family's material position. This decline was greater for women below thirty, despite the fact that the greatest drop-off in the mean number of children working occurred in families where the mother was thirty-five and older. For women thirty-five and above, workplace participation increased, which compensated for lower levels of child labor. Of greater importance, however, was the decline in the mean number of children at home. For women thirty-five

Figure 7.3   Wage earner ratio by social class, 1881

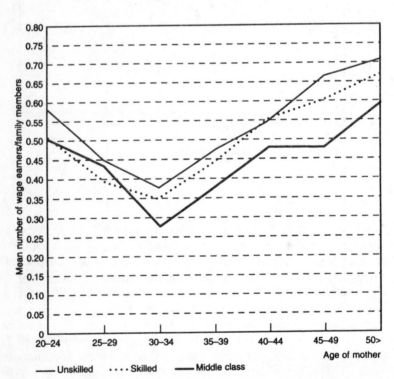

Source: Manuscript Census of Bradford.

and above in 1881, a decline in the mean number of children eased the dependency burden. Yet for women below age thirty-five, the mean number of children actually increased. These women had larger families at an earlier age than the previous generation, thereby heightening the age squeeze for their families and providing an incentive for increased use of family limitation in later decades. This explains, in part, why the pace of fertility decline continued to increase in Bradford up to the First World War (Figure 7.4).[105]

For women in all social groups and all ages, the 10–20 per cent decline in infant mortality over the period would have on its own led to

Figure 7.4   Mean number of children under ten

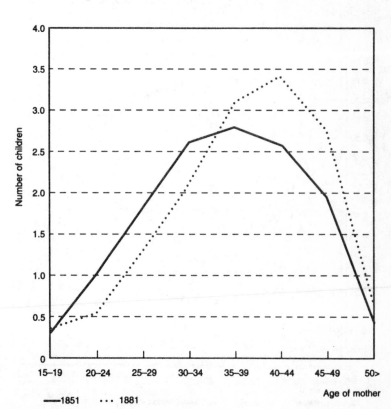

Source: Manuscript Census of Bradford.

larger numbers of surviving children. However, the distribution of this change in terms of individual families and social groups is unknown. Attempts to link changes in infant mortality to those in fertility have shown little relationship at the aggregate level, but some evidence exists that links individual families' lower infant mortality and family limitation.[106] Middle and upper-class mothers had larger numbers of children at home overall and up until age thirty-five (Figure 7.5). This pattern probably resulted from the differences in infant and child

Figure 7.5   Mean number of children by social class, 1881

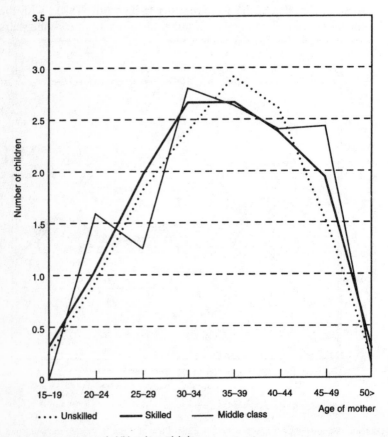

Source: Mean number of children by social class.

mortality among middle-class and working-class families. Some inner city wards of Bradford suffered from infant mortality rates two to three times as high as those on the outskirts of the city inhabited by the middle class, which would produce a larger family size for many middle-class families.[107] As parents aged, class differences in children's propensity to stay in the family household may have also played a role in these differentials.

The decline in the mean number of children at home from 1851 to 1881 reflected the fall in the birth rate. Overall marital fertility declined about 10 per cent between the 1840s and the 1870s (Figure 7.6). Decadal averages of age-specific marital fertility show that fertility for women twenty to twenty-nine exhibited little change in this era, even increasing slightly.[108] Married women thirty to forty-four, however, experienced a decline in fertility from the 1840s to the 1870s, with the decline most pronounced among women thirty-five to thirty-nine years

Figure 7.6   Marital fertility, 1841–80 (three year average)

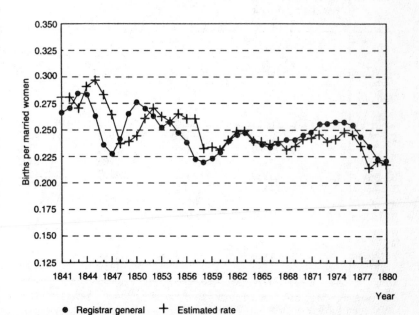

Sources: Manuscript Census of Bradford; Registrar-General of Births, Deaths, and Marriages, Census of Great Britain 1851–81.

INFORMATION RESOURCE SERVICES
UNIVERSITY OF WESTMINSTER
HARROW IRS CENTRE
WATFORD ROAD

of age (Table 7.4 and Figure 7.7). This matches the results of other studies, which have shown a pattern of declining fertility among older women during the onset of family limitation.[109]

We can use Coale and Trussell's *m* and *M* to assess the extent to which this pattern of fertility reflected the deliberate use of fertility control within marriage.[110] The level of *m* increased over the period from −0.1466 to 0.4139 for women 20–44, which is well above the threshold level of 0.2 suggested by Coale and Trussell. The level of *M* also functions in the expected manner, showing an increase in the level of fertility from around 0.762 to 0.910.[111] Changes in marriage patterns produced lower fertility in addition to the drop brought by lower rates of age-specific marital fertility.[112] For the sample population, both the singulate mean age at marriage and the proportions never married increased from 1871 to 1881.[113]

The social composition of this decline needs to be considered as well. Did middle-class families show greater evidence of decline than

Table 7.4   Marital fertility in Bradford 1841–81: mean age specific marital fertility by decade

	Decade			
	1841–51	*1851–61*	*1861–71*	*1871–81*
Age of mother				
15–19	.0853	.5075	.7162	.3472
20–24	.3505	.3685	.3602	.4185
25–29	.3202	.3455	.3193	.3718
30–34	.3318	.3166	.2703	.2821
35–39	.2839	.2574	.2257	.1758
40–44	.1515	.1098	.1035	.0911
45–49	.0227	.0142	.0258	.0155
TMFR at 20	7.303	7.061	6.524	6.774
M	.762	.801	.7830	.91
m (20–44)	−.1466	.1128	.1424	.4139
m (25–44)*	−.1533	.1093	.1319	.4195
s(m)†	.0136	.0266	.0138	.0285

*Weighted for age distribution 25–44.
†Standard error.

Source: Sample of Bradford 1851, 1861, 1871, 1881.

Figure 7.7 Age-specific marital fertility

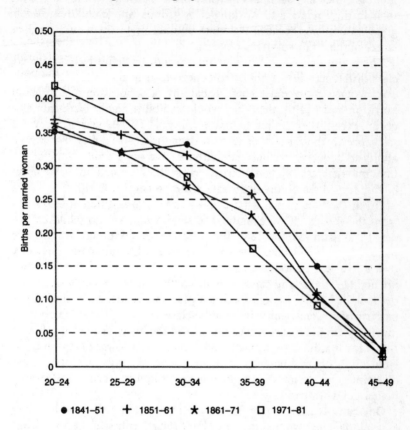

Source: Manuscript Census of Bradford.

working-class families? What about inter-class differentials in marital fertility? One problem that handicaps any attempt at an answer is the unknown impact of differential mortality on mothers and children. If better off mothers enjoyed lower maternal and age-specific death rates, then as a group fewer would have died over a ten year period in relation to a group of poorer women. In other words, two groups of the same size from different classes would not be same size after ten years. Without class specific death rates we cannot measure this difference, but we do know it would tend to produce an overstatement of middle-class fertility. If the children of middle-class mothers survived in greater numbers, then any summary measure of class fertility would exaggerate their fertility relative to working-class groups whose children died in greater numbers, because the same number of births would produce larger numbers of surviving children.

There also exists another issue that cannot be definitively answered, class differences in the ability to conceive, or fecundibility. If middle-class women enjoyed a higher probability of conception due to better nutrition and health, then they would exhibit a higher birth rate as a group, even if they desired to limit fertility.[114] This issue is of particular relevance to the fertility of women over the age of thirty-five, whose ability to conceive declines markedly. At the same time, to the extent that middle-class women married later, they tended to have fewer births, regardless of any deliberate effort to control fertility.

Given these cautions, what can we learn about differential fertility from the census? If we examine the child–woman ratio (children 0–4 per 1,000 women) for 1881 for different occupational groups, the picture is a mixed one. The child–woman ratio summarizes fertility over a five year period, net of infant and child deaths.[115] Overall ratios are higher for working-class women, whether their husbands are skilled or unskilled, but the age-specific ratios fail to demonstrate a clear pattern of lower fertility for middle-class women (Table 7.5). Infant mortality could affect these results, for in the lower age groups, higher ratios for middle-class women could result from lower death rates for children. For middle-class women above the age of forty, class differences in fecundibility may have produced their considerably higher child-woman ratios.

One can plausibly argue from these results that both working class and middle-class women began to limit their fertility in the 1870s, but in very different circumstances. Middle-class women faced the problem that higher survival rates for children led to larger families than previous generations. For some in the middle class, faced with greater competition for educational and business positions, fertility decline could have followed the path mapped out by J.A. Banks, family limitation in order to preserve their families' prospects.[116] For wealthier families, issues of the emotional and physical well being of both mothers and children may have played a greater role.[117]

The changed economic environment of the late nineteenth century affected the timing and pattern of fertility decline for working-class families. The sharp depression in the worsted trade during the 1870s and its continued sluggishness into the 1890s altered the life of Bradford's working class. Unemployment for all workers, particularly

Table 7.5   Child–woman ratios by social class, 1851 and 1881: children 0–4 per thousand married women 20–29 (standardized)

	1851	*1881*
Age		
20–24		
1	967.4	1447.4
2	916.9	1690.5
3/4	377.4	587.8
25–29		
1	848.4	1216.7
2	1064.1	1535.1
3/4	1193.4	954.4
30–34		
1	817.5	855.6
2	1008.9	1187.4
3/4	1273.8	1024.9
35–39		
1	713.7	751.4
2	765.8	604.6
3/4	1106.2	789.5
40–45		
1	454.2	437.3
2	586.0	225.2
3/4	495.7	651.7
45–49		
1	34.7	41.5
2	167.7	31.0
3	94.6	134.5
Overall		
1	690.2	799.0
2	812.0	891.4
3/4	861.1	725.4

1: unskilled working class
2: skilled working class
3/4: middle and upper class

Source: Manuscript censuses of Bradford 1851 and 1881.

for young workers fourteen to nineteen and for male heads of households, increased. Since most families relied on one or two wage earners, this increase represented a crisis of the first order. The fear of unemployment and the far more common problem of short-time affected even those not directly touched by the loss of work. Given the fall in real wages at the same time, the situation of many families in Bradford deteriorated during the 1870s.[118]

The impact of these changes varied according to the life-cycle stage of the family. Women thirty to forty-five faced the greatest potential difficulties providing for their families throughout this era. The gap between family size and the number of wage earners presented a dilemma for these mothers. Should they work or should they try to survive on the wages of the husband alone?[119] Ethel Elderton, in her study of fertility decline in the early twentieth century, clearly saw this dilemma:

> When pressure makes the wage earned by the woman an essential factor in the household economy, a large family not only increases the expenditure but removes for a great or lesser period one source of income, the mother's work.[120]

This issue became more worrisome for working-class families in the 1870s for a number of reasons. The decline in young children's work lengthened their period of dependency, particularly in those crucial mid-thirties years for the mother, reducing somewhat the contribution of children to family income. Second, greater numbers of older married women who worked outside the home faced the difficulty of combining domestic needs, such as child care, with work. The withdrawal of children from home to school who could have provided assistance compounded this problem.[121] Women above the age of thirty-five suffered the greatest hardships because their husband's wages had most likely peaked. Because older women tended to be of higher parity (number of births per mother), they possessed a greater incentive to control their family size than younger women in the same circumstances. Fertility control within marriage offered one way to bridge a crisis in family income caused by unemployment, illness, wage cuts or short-time.

These problems affected the families of skilled and unskilled workers alike, as the position of male wage earners of all skill levels deteriorated in this decade. Unskilled workers faced the most pressing problems, as they were most subject to unemployment and short-time and they had the fewest resources to deal with any crisis in family income. However, even skilled workers had a more difficult time of it. Wage cuts, increased unemployment and pressure on job rights and trade union privileges all affected the skilled worker in the 1870s. Skilled workers possessed a greater margin of security, but they were not immune from economic uncertainty.[122]

THE PROBLEM OF THRIFT IN WORKING-CLASS FAMILIES

The relationship between the larger socioeconomic environment and the family economy of the working class provided the material incentives necessary for the widespread adoption of family limitation, but these incentives would be important only if working-class families accepted the idea of family limitation as a solution. The culture of Bradford's working class in the mid-Victorian era proved amenable to a justification of birth control that built upon familiar notions of working-class life such as thrift, respectability, independence and self-help. This justification derived its main force from its ability to address the primary concern of working-class families not simply with the quality of life, but with subsistence.

These values found expression within the public culture of the working class that developed after 1850. Whether in the formal network of friendly societies and clubs, or the more informal networks of kin and neighborhood, this culture placed a high value on respectability and independence.[123] While the elaborate rituals of voluntary societies sought to order and verify respectable behavior, the judgment of neighbors and friends carried weight as well. In this way, the private concerns of families with their material circumstances mingled with the public culture and daily life of the working class. While similar social expectations may have dogged middle-class families, the lack of privacy in inner-city neighborhoods, the public nature of respectability and the survival of certain communal norms of behavior made working-class families more open to sanctions by their neighbors.[124] Ironically, such surveillance coexisted with middle class views of working-class neighborhoods as nests of immorality and vice.

The desire for respectability extended to issues of sexuality and childbearing.[125] Women were not supposed to acknowledge sexual matters or engage in sexual activity outside marriage. The reticence within working-class culture about sexuality made issues of illegitimacy and sexual misconduct more disgraceful in the later nineteenth century. As David Levine has argued these values could extend to the idea of childbearing, with large families becoming a sign of nonrespectable behavior. 'Respectable reproduction' through family limitation could enhance a family's material and social status.[126]

In order to achieve independence, the working-class family depended upon the efforts of all its members. For the mother, thrift constituted a key tool to balance the household's needs and income. Thrift meant more than simply frugality, it represented a tool for household management under the most trying of circumstances and offered a family the means to achieve the cherished goal of living within one's means. Almanacs and family journals drove home the point that family survival and respectability depended on frugality, especially on the part of the mother.[127] In hard times, self-sacrifice and denial became essential to maintain one's independence.

Not surprisingly, both workers and the middle class paid homage to this central Victorian value. William Forster, Bradford MP, addressing the Oddfellows in 1877, spoke of the 'habits of thrift and self denial they had developed'. Noting the increase in their receipts despite the downturn in trade, Forster praised them, saying, 'it showed that they were determined to submit to considerable sacrifices to keep up their position in society.'[128]

However, workers and the middle class saw thrift in a different light. For the middle class, thrift constituted one tool in the struggle for self-help and advancement. In the eyes of middle-class observers, the working class earned enough to live decently, if they avoided extravagance and drink.[129] According to one minister,

> something less than a sovereign a year places the benefits of societies of this kind [friendly societies] . . . within the reach of every labouring man. They are few indeed who would not well afford that sum, and fewer still who would not be all the better for the slight self-denial it might in some cases involve.[130]

While the middle class saw thrift as a moral issue – the avoidance of improvident behavior – other observers more sympathetic to the plight of poor families argued that the material hardships facing workers made thrift alone inadequate to sustain the family, let alone create social mobility. George Hillary, a skilled worker, argued that a significant portion of the working class was overworked, underpaid and undereducated and therefore incapable of lifting itself up through self-help and thrift.[131] J. H. Bridges, a local physician, put it more starkly when he wrote

> The great bulk of the people consists of unskilled laborers earning low wages, unable to save money, untaught and unable to afford

time for learning and constantly driven by bad times close to the brink of the frightful abyss of pauperism.[132]

In the minds of some, the problems of subsistence and overcrowding demanded a more active response – the use of birth control. Family limitation required many working-class men and women to overcome a deep-rooted hostility to birth control, the legacy of opposition to Malthus and his doctrines, which many felt blamed the poor for their own poverty and attacked working-class marriage.[133] As John Gast, the early nineteenth-century radical, argued,

> Malthus & Co . . . would reduce the whole matter to a question between Mechanics and their sweethearts and wives [rather than] a question between the employed and their employers.[134]

The foundation of the Malthusian League in 1877 failed to alter the conservative nature of Malthusian arguments for population limitation, a bias heightened by the League's focus on economic arguments rather than on birth control.[135] One could, however, reject Malthus and still argue in favor of delayed marriage or even birth control. As early as 1850, one locally available pamphlet urged working-class men to delay marriage as long as possible. The author, George Cooper, claimed not to be a supporter of Malthus but supported delayed marriage as a way to raise the price of labor by reducing its supply. In Cooper's view,

> why bring increasing numbers into the world to toil and suffer, and thereby increase your own suffering! True there are others who consider themselves at liberty to 'increase and multiply', and to live upon your earnings in riotous plenty; but you cannot revenge yourselves upon them by marrying improvidently. This evil system under which we live must be changed by other means. Self-denial must aid your deliverance. The more the toilers under the present system are increased, the lower the price of toil must be depressed . . . But suppose the evils of bad legislation, and of faulty industrial systems are likely to last to the end of the century, all experience will show you that you are likely to gain by avoiding early marriages.[136]

A local advocate of Malthusian doctrines, G. A. Gaskell, echoed such arguments. Gaskell, a photographer by trade and a pioneer socialist, carried on a campaign to encourage family limitation in the 1870s and 1880s.[137] He wrote several pamphlets on the topic, sent letters to the local press, organized visits by such Neo-Malthusian luminaries as Annie Besant and distributed literature door to door.[138]

Gaskell was a complex figure, for he combined praise of Malthus's preventative check with socialist arguments about the origins of poverty, a stance he shared with a number of other advocates of birth control.[139] Gaskell saw family limitation as a possible way out of the trap of impoverishment created by an unfair society, arguing, 'We cannot have marriage increasing and poverty diminishing without families being much smaller than they are.'[140] Gaskell's support of birth control was based on a rejection of thrift, as well as competition and acquisitiveness. In his view, thrift led only to greater misery for the poor:

> My main argument against thrift may be put thus, – the more provident and thrifty the working people are, the more capital there may be in the hands of their employers; while thrift, implying a lowering of the standard of comfort, means ultimately greater general poverty.[141]

For Gaskell, competition and greed produced the war of all against all and overwork, rather than progress:

> I perceive, as all must when they contemplate at all, the many evils which flow from this present state of social high pressure. I do more than recognize this fact; I reason that to lessen this pressure would of course, lessen the evils of which that pressure is the cause. What does this high pressure mean? It means in business that each strives to outdo or outwit his neighbor, for if he does not, he may go to the wall of the poorhouse. Hence cheating, adulteration, etc. In wage-earning, it means work to the death, or semi-starvation when out of employment; it means to so many continual anxiety, and poverty, with all that follows.[142]

Gaskell went further to suggest that a Malthusian framework, rather than the more optimistic views of the mid-Victorian middle class, could best explain this state of affairs. In his words,

> To Malthus is due undying fame of having discovered a simple law of nature which explains the reason of this high pressure.[143]

Such statements irritated local elites, for they attacked the belief in progress and self-help that stood at the heart of Victorian ideology. In response they asserted the need for the working class to work harder and to make further sacrifices. In March of 1880, Benjamin Illingworth, a member of a prominent local family, attacked Gaskell. In a letter to the *Bradford Observer*, he wrote that

> Some of you may recollect that a few days ago there appeared a long letter in the Bradford Observer from a philosophical wiseacre advocating the Malthusian doctrine of restriction of the growth of population as the needful cure for the evils of population. I think . . . that there would be no need of such advocacy if working people, as a rule would become members of building societies, and practice the virtues and habits which those institutions are designed and adapted to foster and promote.[144]

Gaskell was not simply a lone 'wiseacre'. One of his co-workers in the cause was a Leeds physician, H.A. Albutt, who appeared on stage during several Neo-Malthusian meetings in Bradford.[145] Albutt achieved notoriety with the publication in 1885 of a medical self-help book entitled *The Wife's Handbook*, which contained a section on birth control. As a consequence, the British Medical Association expelled Albutt, but his book went on to at least fifty printings in the next forty years and sold as many as 500,000 copies.[146] In fact, Albutt claimed that the BMA expelled him because he wrote an inexpensive sixpenny pamphlet rather than a guinea book.[147]

Albutt justified his work in a number of ways. He claimed that he wished to aid mothers overwhelmed by domestic concerns, and in fact Albutt included advice on pregnancy and child care similar in tone to that available in almanacs and magazines. In addition to the individual happiness that would result from family limitation, he believed that smaller families would also reduce poverty and overcrowding.[148] Albutt argued that he intended the information in his pamphlet only for married adults and that in any case, his suggestions could be found elsewhere, either in medical literature or in 'indecent literature' sold in the streets.[149]

Albutt's pamphlet was only the most notable example of a flourishing local trade in birth control information.[150] Rising literacy coupled with a well-developed local printing industry assisted the trade.[151] Elderton reported that

> Advertisements for the limitation of the family have been in evidence for 25 years; the urinals are decorated with the hand-bills openly advertising preventives and books on prevention.[152]

The nature of towns like Bradford accelerated the diffusion of knowledge by bringing people together and providing a mass audience for information about birth control techniques. Ethel Elderton linked the rise of a mass audience for birth control with urbanization and industrialization:

> In the textile and woolen towns, with the joint industrial occupation of both men and women, the greatest opportunity for the spread of new knowledge and the creation of tradition [exists]. What is true of restriction of the family is equally applicable to the spread of any new habit or fashion, or the adoption of any new food or form of amusement; the factory towns are places where advertisement is the most profitable and where information is most rapidly disseminated. [153]

While the audience for this literature cannot be easily measured, it contributed to a growing debate over family limitation in the 1870s and 1880s. In 1881, the Medical Officer of Health for the Borough alluded to this when he wrote, 'How far the doctrines – advocated by a certain notorious publication – may have influenced the birth-rate is a matter which has been much debated.'[154] Members of the Bradford Medico-Chirurgical Society discussed the decline in the local birth rate at their meetings. One doctor believed that local families thought it 'immoral' to have more than three children and others accused workers of resorting to abortion and infanticide to spare themselves the problem of excess children.[155] While acknowledging the hardships faced by large families, doctors rejected Albutt's advocacy of birth control.[156] Dr A. F. C. Rabagliati, a Bradford physician, in a paper before the BMA on August 7, 1879, conceded the need for smaller families in order to ensure the health and well-being of children, but went on to argue, 'abstinence alone should be advocated to bring about the desired result: no other method could command respect from rightly disposed and high-minded persons.'[157]

Such opposition from respectable society to birth control reflected prevailing views about working-class family life.[158] Middle-class observers believed that immorality and improvidence lay at the root of poverty and social disorder. Accordingly, no real material necessity compelled men and women to resort to family limitation. Selfishness and neglect of parental responsibilities lay behind falling birth rates. Ironically, clear evidence of fertility decline among members of the middle class, who possessed far fewer material incentives for family limitation, began to emerge at about the same time.[159]

GENDER, MARRIAGE AND THE PROBLEMS OF FAMILY LIFE

The public culture of the working class presupposed and gave form to a private, domestic culture, in which women constituted the main actors. If voluntary association was a manly sphere, then the home was meant to be a feminine one. Domestic culture grew out of the exclusion of women from public life and their relegation to a secondary arena of activity. Women, however, through their roles as wage earners and consumers, inevitably intruded upon the public sphere. At the same time, the concerns of public and private life overlapped and supported one another. Thrift in the household dovetailed with mutual aid outside to provide security and a sense of control over the world. The impulse for security animated both public and private action in the mid-Victorian world and makes easy distinctions between spheres difficult to maintain.

The issues of family, gender and domesticity can be viewed in part as a question of generational change. The men and women of the 1840s brought to Bradford the experiences of family life elsewhere, whether the Yorkshire countryside or Ireland.[160] The continuation of domestic labor into the 1840s, the persistence of cultural enclaves like the Irish slums, even the survival of older rural ways such as raising pigs and other animals all eased the transition to urban life for this generation. It may have sheltered older family patterns as well.[161]

The working men and women of the 1870s confronted quite a different environment. Having lived through the transition to a new way of life, they possessed few links to the older world of domestic labor and farming of their parents.[162] For most, the mill and the urban neighborhood constituted the primary experience of their adult lives. Many women lived the life of a single factory operative before marriage and encountered alternatives to both marriage and children. This generation also confronted the problematic nature of family relationships in this era when the ability of women and children to earn wages seemed to undermine patriarchal and familial authority.[163] The problems of domestic life filtered through a different lens for these women, at the same time that the problems of dependency and subsistence remained. Seen from this perspective, it should not surprise us that this generation of women chose to experiment, attempting to gain some measure of control over their lives by limiting their fertility.

The shifts in life and work that accompanied the rise of the factory created often contradictory notions of gender. Men derived a sense of identity from both their role as workers, engaged in physical labor, and as heads of the family. The loss of control over work, symbolized by the factory, undermined the assertion of independence critical to the artisan's sense of masculinity, but the rituals of work often created new signs of maleness that were not related to owning property or running a shop. Independence was redefined as the ability to provide for the family without charity or state assistance. This meant that masculinity was intertwined with domesticity, for the respectable household was anchored by the wife and men remained critically dependent upon the unwaged labor of women for their day-to-day existence.[164]

For women, gender identity also involved contradictory roles. The Victorian definition of women as domestic angels conflicted with the prevalence of women's labor outside the home and the differing sensibilities that this experience created. Women who worked in mills inhabited a largely female work place, where adult men functioned as supervisors or skilled workers in separate parts of the mill. The mill developed its own female culture, with its own rituals and values, which many viewed as degraded and crude. In Bradford, the practice of 'sunning', pulling down the pants of young men on their first day of work and exposing their genitals, persisted until the early twentieth century.[165] On a more pragmatic level, women relied upon each other to find work and often for training in mill jobs such as weaving.[166]

For men and women in the mid-century, a period of extended adolescence developed. Both sexes enjoyed a time of life between childhood and marriage that gave them greater freedom to explore life. Possessed of income (or what remained after tipping in) from jobs that paid nearly adult wages, and having no other expenses if they lived at home, they could indulge in limited social experimentation and frivolous consumption of clothing, food, entertainment and drink. The central part of the city and its parks filled with men and women in their teens and twenties on the evening and weekends, who acted out the rituals of same-sex sociability and courtship.[167] J.B. Priestley described the 'innocent parade . . . of girls wearing their best clothes and usually in arm-linked trios and quartets' during summer music concerts at Lister Park in the early twentieth century.[168]

The realities of family existence constrained this freedom, for most of these young people still lived with their parents or with relatives, and were expected to share their wages or to engage in child minding or other domestic duties. Only for the young migrants to the city, primarily female, could one see true freedom from familial control. Living in lodgings or group homes, these young people stood at the polar end of Victorian ideas of domesticity. Yet even these women kept in touch with family by returning home on weekends or holidays.[169]

For all the changes brought by the rise of industry, the traditional expectation that most men and women would marry survived.[170] Single life constituted only a brief period before the responsibilities of the adult world inevitably arrived. In part due to the imbalance of women and men in the city between the ages of fifteen and thirty, women in Bradford married later than their counterparts in England, but they also tended to marry in greater numbers over the course of their lives (Figure 7.8). The average age of marriage for women in Bradford in 1881 was slightly over 26 years, about three-quarters of a year later than the rest of England, but between the ages of forty-five and fifty-four around 91–95 per cent of all women had married.[171]

The realities of working-class courtship and marriage are still only partly known. Most historians argue that a growing concern with respectability and controlled sexuality led to a decline in premarital sexual experimentation and illegitimacy, as well as a greater emphasis on formal marriage.[172] Anecdotal evidence from Bradford suggests that, at least for some, this concern with respectability failed to overcome older, more informal patterns. For many working men and women, the formalities of legal ceremonies mattered less than the substance of the relationship. J. B. Priestley viewed such arrangements as completely normal, noting that mill women

> were devoted to their own men, generally working in the same mill, and kept on 'courting', though the actual courtship state was over early, for years and years until a baby was due, when they married.[173]

Middle-class observers believed that the informality of working-class unions undermined their legitimacy. Uncontrolled sexuality threatened to undermine the family by creating new types of households, based on free choice rather than legal obligation. The Town Mission, in its survey of working-class neighborhoods in the early 1850s, found that many couples lived together without benefit of marriage as common-law spouses.[174] Forty years later, Poor Law investigators found a similar lack of concern for the legalities of marriage among their charges and they insisted on proof of marriage before allowing the removal of children from the workhouse.[175] Generalizations derived from the lives of poor or from mill workers may not be representative

Figure 7.8   Age structure of Bradford in 1881

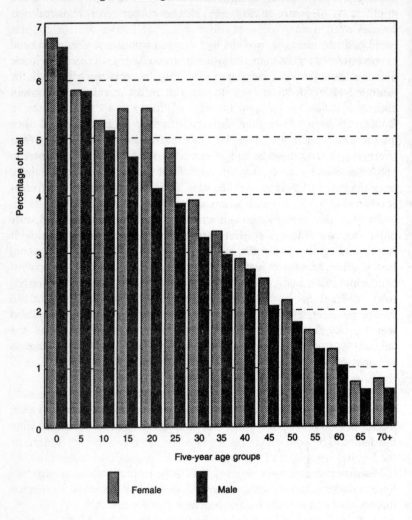

of the skilled working class that saw itself as distinct from the poor and unskilled, and who may have possessed different standards of sexual respectability.[176]

Regardless of the formality of courtship or marriage, the young couple entered into a new world after marriage. Many found it necessary to live with their families or as lodgers in other homes in the initial years of marriage. Between 30 and 40 per cent of all married couples aged twenty to twenty-four and over 20 per cent of couples twenty-five to twenty-nine lived this way. Cramped quarters may have exacerbated domestic tensions, but low incomes and expensive housing dictated such arrangements. The depression of the 1870s extended this period of coresidence well into the thirties for many couples.[177]

Once children arrived, the pattern of life for couples changed once more. The arrival of children did not necessarily transform life overnight. Younger wives tended to continue to work and domestic pressures were less, due to smaller family size and higher family income, if both spouses worked. In 1881, 30.5 per cent of women aged twenty to twenty-nine with children less than a year old worked, while 31.1 per cent of those with children below age five worked. For older married women, the responsibilities of domestic life made it increasingly difficult to balance children and work outside the home. For women thirty to thirty-nine, only 16.1 per cent of those with children below the age of one worked, while 18.7 per cent with children below the age of five did. For these women, the growing size of the family put pressure on the wages of the husband, which led some to seek employment outside the home. In one study of the woolen and worsted districts of Yorkshire in the early twentieth century, over 60 per cent of working wives listed their husbands' inadequate wages as the primary reason for working outside the home.[178]

For working women with children, the routine of work and domestic life could prove daunting. Though men, especially if unemployed, might help out, the working wife and mother bore a considerable burden.[179] The wife remained responsible for the care and feeding of the family, regardless of the degree of involvement by the husband. In the words of one observer, 'the chief care rests with the mother'.[180] Fred Jowett, a Labour MP, described the life of the working mother during his childhood in the late nineteenth century:

Up at six in the morning to start work at six-thirty, contriving if possible to suckle the child and take a hurried breakfast in the half-hour stop at eight, a hurried dinner and child-feeding during the three-quarter hour stop at twelve-thirty, then working in the mill until five-forty-five, after which was housework until bedtime. Extra cleaning, clothes-washing, and bread baking were done at week-ends.[181]

Ironically, for many working mothers the period of confinement represented a rare break in this routine, leading West Riding women to refer to the confinement as 'going to Blackpool'.[182]

Neighbors and kin provided child care for working mothers, though the cost could be considerable. Jowett estimated the cost in the late nineteenth century to a woman weaver earning 10s. to 12s. per week at half a crown (2s.6d.). The Nest, a charity nursery, charged 2s.6d. in the mid-1880s to care for each child, though it later lowered the cost to 1s.[183] William Drew, a leader of the weavers' union, and his wife relied upon a handicapped aunt and they paid a minder 5s. per child to care for their infants.[184] Dame schools, which accepted children under the age of three, provided an alternative form of child care until superseded by the establishment of Board Schools in the 1870s and 1880s.[185] The cost of child care considerably reduced the effective earnings of married women, but as Drew observed, 'If a woman makes 2s. by it she considers she is in pocket by the process, forgetful of all the disadvantages.'[186]

Before the establishment of factory canteens and cheap ready-cooked food in the late nineteenth and early twentieth centuries, mothers still struggled to put a meal on the table. Sandwiches or cold 'ten to one pies' (ten pieces of potato to one piece of meat) constituted the mid-day meal.[187] Some women in working-class neighborhoods supplemented their incomes by supplying pies and other food to mill workers.[188] The survival of home baking in the West Riding added to the difficulties of feeding the family.[189]

For those who stayed at home, life remained quite hard regardless of the wages of the husband. The overcrowded state of Bradford's housing, which remained fairly constant at five and one-half persons per household in this period, but which could reach as high as ten to fifteen per household (in a two up, two down home), aggravated this problem, as did the primitive state of domestic arrangements.[190] Most homes in Bradford shared a privy midden between four to eight households. To clean this privy, night soil men shoveled waste from these pits into the backyard and then into carts. Jowett offers us a vivid picture of what followed:

> Next day there was the swilling to be done, often necessarily after working hours: tired women scrubbing their respective share of the paved yard, with water carried from the house-tap in bucketsful by the husband or grown-up son or daughter or by a neighbor for each other.[191]

The domestic labor of working-class mothers sustained the household, but their role embraced more than just cooking and cleaning. Most accounts of working-class life agree that the mother took charge of the family's money and dominated the daily life of the family.[192] Women usually received household money from their husbands' wages, but often this proved inadequate. In Bradford, the mother also controlled the 'tipping up' of young men and women, who often surrendered the major portion of their wages for the family's use. Women could also call on the local pawnshop for immediate assistance, pawning the 'Sunday respectables' to obtain cash.[193] Mothers also used local connections to provide resources. Credit from shopkeepers, loans from neighbors, child-minding and other part-time work supplemented family income. The large number of mills and millworkers in the city gave married women the opportunity to find part-time replacement work for a day or several weeks.[194] Such situations overlapped with the obligations of women to assist their friends and neighbors in times of need and formed part of the reciprocal networks that working-class women constructed in their communities.[195]

These networks could be mobilized under a variety of circumstances. Strikes and other stoppages of work could force women to call on outside resources to maintain the family, as could illness or injury. They could also be used to avoid the workhouse. Women in working-class neighborhoods would often leave their children with friends or neighbors, as well as relatives, in order to keep them out of workhouse, or try to put them in the workhouse while remaining at large in the homes of friends or family.[196] Poor Law Guardians devoted considerable effort to tracking down such truants and attempting to force them to enter the workhouse or pay for maintenance. The Guardians also enlisted neighbors in efforts to investigate families seeking return of their children from the workhouse.[197]

Within marriage, the central role of the wife and mother lay in uneasy balance with the belief in male power and authority. Men often expected to receive the best food, as well as money for drink, no matter what the circumstances of the family.[198] This struggle for resources could result in secrecy about money on both sides and considerable resentment at lapses in either wage earning or domestic management.[199] Often problems of money, compounded by drink, precipitated domestic violence.[200] James Burnley, in his story of a day in Bradford's courts, mentioned a case where a battered wife accused the husband of drunkenness and not 'having brought in a penny in ten weeks'.[201] The

Bradford newspapers carried numerous accounts of assaults upon wives. In one ten-day period in January 1878, the *Bradford Observer* reported five assaults upon wives sufficiently violent to lead to criminal charges. By the 1870s, twenty to forty men a year were convicted of attacking their wives. This represents a considerable undercount of the actual level of violence, for the police refused to prosecute many assaults.[202] Convictions for assault increased after 1880, when assault charges could be used to obtain a judicial separation order and police proved more willing to file charges.[203] The most sensational case of domestic violence, the murder of Jane Kelly in October 1882 by her husband, occurred after she had been sent back to the home by magistrates who presided over the assault trial of her husband. Lydia Becker, the feminist, raised the issue from the platform of a suffrage demonstration and accused the judges of murder.[204]

These difficult conditions help explain the cautionary note contained in homilies about family life. One such tale, in the form of a dialogue between family members, told the story of a woman burdened with a drunken husband, struggling to keep her family alive with the help of friends and family. Her sister argued that 'it is better to be alone than to be the hag and slave of an idle, selfish, and drunken husband'.[205] Such advice contained a ring of truth for the thousands of married and unmarried women of Bradford, for it addressed the reality that family and home were not always a refuge or joy.

The expectation that children followed naturally from marriage conflicted with the realization that too many children could threaten the family. The danger of improvident marriage for the working class provided a recurrent theme in stories in the press in this period. Many writers associated large families and poverty, despite the contradictory assertion by others that children earned their way. The Reverend Robinson put it this way:

> Nothing, therefore, can excuse a man from providing before-hand against such casualties, except the fact that from his large family and small means, he had been unable to spare even the trifling sum which insured relief from a Benevolent Society.[206]

In a similar vein, the hero of the story, 'The Bachelor's Dream', resisted marriage because of the hardships suffered by his parents as a result of their large family. In the end, a dream of the domestic joys awaiting him persuaded the young man to marry.[207]

The dilemmas of family life help explain why working-class men and women resorted to family limitation. The availability of the necessary information locally made it possible for almost anyone to acquire it. Many women likely learned about birth control through discussions at the mill, and Ethel Elderton argued that 'the question of restriction is openly discussed within the factory gates'.[208] Most women in Bradford worked in the worsted trade or knew kin or neighbors who did, which gave them their own networks of knowledge. The increasing literacy of both sexes may have also helped them obtain information.

The primary methods of birth control in nineteenth-century England appear to have been abstinence, coitus interruptus and abortion.[209] Local evidence suggests that knowledge of these practices existed in the 1870s and 1880s. H. A. Albutt's *The Wife's Handbook* mentioned coitus interruptus, diaphragms, sponges and abstinence as methods of birth control, although Albutt considered the latter harmful. He also noted the widespread belief that prolonged breast-feeding delayed conception.[210] Albutt, like most birth control advocates, rejected abortion as immoral, but it was practiced locally. In 1878, the trial of a local herbalist, Ezekiel Thornton, for performing an abortion, brought the issue to the attention of the public. Thornton, originally tried and acquitted on a murder charge, used both herbal preparations and instruments to induce an abortion on Margaret Allison, who later died. The young woman, previously married, did not wish to marry the father and 'she wanted it stopping'. Margaret, who had already visited an abortionist in Leeds, was aided in her search by her lover, a textile overlooker, who knew of Thornton.[211]

Another trial in 1883 revealed a similar set of circumstances. Elizabeth Hustler, a dressmaker, and Hannah Moulson, a housewife, were charged with procuring an abortion and endangering the life of Elizabeth Edwards. Edwards, who already had three children, 'kept company' with Alfred Costin, brother of Moulson. Moulson and Costin, who wanted to avoid marrying Edwards, pressured Hustler to perform two separate operations on Edwards, who almost died from the effects of poison. Despite a plea for mercy from the jury, the magistrate sentenced Hustler to six years of penal servitude, for he believed that abortionists like her performed their services 'habitually'.[212]

Although infrequent, such trials revealed a network of abortionists and assistants as well as a variety of techniques for inducing abortion. Court records mention abortions performed by both men and women using instruments and chemical preparations. Oil of savin, 'penny royal', ergot of rye and other 'noxious chemicals' were listed, while syringes, male catheters and speculums assisted the abortionist in his or her task.[213] Ethel Elderton believed that

> There is also a great deal of abortion practiced in the district, and for every case which comes to the notice of police, there are hundreds that do not. Many abortions are produced by lead preparations, more by the use of instruments, either by the pregnant themselves or by the women to whom they resort for advice and help.[214]

The evidence suggests that the circumstances through which birth control came to be widely used struck at the heart of the ideas and values of working-class men and women. The work of historians such as Ellen Ross and Elizabeth Roberts on working-class women, which emphasizes the prudishness of the working class, especially women, suggests that efforts to limit family size encountered reticence and ignorance that would severely handicap their effectiveness. Furthermore, the subordination of women within marriage, in combination with their lack of knowledge, makes it difficult to see how they could be active partners in the use of birth control or force their partners to cooperate in family limitation. Some historians argue that the increasing importance of the father's wage to the survival of family gave him the dominant role in such decisions, as well as fewer economic reasons to have children.[215]

Contemporary birth controllers were aware of these problems and argued against such reticence on the part of women. Gaskell condemned celibacy as absurd and argued that 'sexual passion is at the spring of much that is noble in life and is nothing to be ashamed of, but requires only to be regulated.'[216] In the 1890s, H. A. Albutt wrote pamphlets addressing questions of sexuality and sexual disease, which he justified in terms of better conjugal relations and honesty. He explicitly rejected the notion that a woman's modesty prevented such discussion, saying, 'Her naturally frank and inquiring nature has been suppressed.'[217]

However, Albutt's attack on sexual naivete contradicts other reports from Bradford about the sexuality of women, especially those who worked in the mills. The frankness and straightforwardness of these women struck observers, who often felt nonplussed by it. In the 1860s a letter writer to a local paper expressed his outrage at happening upon a boisterous crowd of mill women watching a group of nude men bathing.[218] J.B. Priestly recalled encountering similar crowds in the streets in the early twentieth century whose comments made his cheeks burn. This type of behavior could be construed as promiscuous, but Priestley himself saw it as 'traditional female bawdiness ... far removed from cynical whoring. There was nothing sly, nothing hypocritical about these coarse dames and screaming lasses.'[219] Such bawdiness may have been nothing more than a front, a socially sanctioned form of turning the tables of sexual aggression on men.

On the other hand, accounts of working-class life recalled after the fact may gloss over issues of sexuality, in part to heighten the contrast between the present and past, especially in light of a perceived revolution in sexual behavior in the twentieth century.[220] It is also interesting to note that whatever the sexual attitudes of the generation of the 1870s and 1880s, the next generation wholeheartedly embraced the use of birth control. Diana Gittens, writing about the generation of women from 1900 to 1939, distinguishes between women who worked outside the home, especially in textiles, and those who remained at home. She argues that working wives possessed greater knowledge of sex and birth control and were willing to use it.[221]

Most historians argue that, whatever the state of sexual knowledge or sexual desire on the part of men and women, working-class marriages did not focus on these issues or on the satisfaction of desires for intimacy. A good marriage required an alliance that crossed the gap between genders and in which both partners satisfied the expectations of the other. For men this meant being a good provider and being a decent sort, not harassing one's wife with unnecessary or brutal demands. For women, expectations focused on household management, child rearing and maintaining a respectable appearance.[222]

Birth control both challenged and reinforced these symbiotic ideas of marriage and gender identity. For men, ideas of masculinity tied to reproduction often revolved around having a large family as a sign of virility.[223] Yet, the difficulties of maintaining such a family severely tested another attribute of masculinity, the adequate support of one's dependents. For women, having a family laid their claim to domestic primacy through the bearing and rearing of children. Yet, aside from the enormous hardships and physical dangers involved in reproduction, too many children undermined the ability of women to fulfill their domestic role. As one worker asked,

> Why should a working man be nothing but a machine for grinding out a morsel of food for his famished children, and his wife a machine for multiplying them?[224]

These conflicting demands existed at all levels of the working class and not simply among skilled workers' families, for the relative and shifting nature of respectability could span a wide variety of material circumstances. For both men and women family limitation involved issues of gender identity that could not be easily resolved. It also touched upon expectations of partners. For men, being a good husband could involve not pressing sexual demands, while for women, freedom from childbearing could make them better able to meet the demands of their husbands for greater attention and resources without neglecting themselves or their children. Most likely, choosing family limitation involved a compromise of conflicting values and attitudes on the part of individuals and couples. Such compromises may have been impossible for many to make or even consider, but enough men and women chose family limitation to begin the process within the working-class community, and as time passed, more men and women joined them.[225]

All of these considerations turned, at least in part, on the age of the mother and the number of children in the household. Older women, with more children at home and greater experience of married life, constituted the first group to embrace family limitation. Demographers argue that deliberate family limitation involves a decision to stop bearing children after reaching a desired family size and signals a conscious effort to limit family size, not merely to delay or space births. The key indicator is the changing length of birth intervals and falling age at last birth for the mother, from which it is inferred that families wish to stop bearing children altogether, rather than simply delay the next birth.[226] Demographers believe that as family limitation becomes acceptable, families attempt to reach a target size by stopping child-bearing. In this view, fertility becomes a rational, planned act, rather than a 'natural', uncontrolled behavior. Unfortunately, the use of indirect estimation of fertility rather than direct reconstitution makes it impossible to construct the parity-specific measures needed to resolve this issue in purely quantitative terms. However, a case can be made that the model of family limitation implied by demographers in the parity-specific paradigm distorts the nature of working-class family life in this era. The dualism of planned versus unplanned suggests that only with the achievement of a 'rational' mind-set on the part of workers could fertility fall into the realm of conscious control. Yet, throughout this era, the family economy of the working class functioned as just such a 'rational' device to control the behavior of family members. No sudden burst of rationality need be adduced to explain why working-class families chose to limit their size. Their behavior had always been rational; what changed was the environment within which this rationality operated.

Furthermore, it remains to be seen if the dichotomy between stopping and spacing in the early stages of fertility decline is in fact a real phenomenon or an artifact of demographic method. In Bradford in the 1870s, the distinction between stopping and spacing could be a fine one.[227] The older women involved in family limitation had the greatest number of children at home and therefore may have wished to stop bearing children or simply delay conception. In conditions of increased uncertainty, like those in Bradford in the late nineteenth century, there very well could have been a short-term desire to prevent births on the part of older women already burdened with several young children at home. This short-term desire may have led women to use birth control to assist the family through an income crisis. Older women who used birth control already had a lower probability of conceiving and the decision to delay pregnancy may have combined with their lower fecundibility to end their childbearing, whatever their intentions at the time.[228]

A model of family limitation that recognizes the importance of short-term influences on fertility in the initial stages of decline fits the nature of family life among working-class Bradfordians, which did not encourage long-term planning, but rather adaptation to short-term pressures.[229] The most likely methods of birth control – coitus interruptus and abstinence – would only be effective in preventing conception over the short-term due to their high failure rate.[230] Abortion can be seen both as the most sure (although dangerous) method of controlling fertility and as a final recourse in case other methods failed. In a short-term model, final family size emerges from both parity and spacing.

Once fertility control became widespread, a target family size may have emerged, and younger women planned on a certain number of children soon after marriage and then attempted to stop at that figure. This pattern characterizes contemporary England, where expectations of children accompany marriage, but in which ideal family size is two or three children.[231] The adoption of such a target size would have occurred in very different circumstances than that of the 1870s. The possibility of birth control would have been much more widely known in the next generation and infant mortality had declined to levels that would have allowed a greater degree of certainty about a child's survival.

This model of fertility control differs considerably from that proposed by conventional theories. Fertility decline in Bradford resulted not from a generalized prosperity and the transformation of the family's economic role but rather the continuation of an older pattern of family economy in new circumstances. Working-class families in Bradford sought to stabilize themselves in an insecure world which gave them little power over their immediate environment. Social stability, not upward mobility, remained the aim of these men and women. Such a goal is consistent with the working-class culture that developed in Bradford after 1850, with its mutualistic ethos and its resignation to hard times. One need not look for the trickle down of social ideas to explain the motivation of working-class people. In a class-based society like nineteenth-century England, the social distance between classes and the tremendous gap in their material circumstances created a gulf between the working class and the rest of English society. It was for their own reasons that working men and women embraced the limitation of fertility, and continued to do so despite the disapproval of those in positions of authority. In this they merely followed their own inclinations and needs, as always.

Conclusion

The difficulty in writing a work that draws upon both social history and population history is that each has its own special needs and concerns. Yet both potentially offer a great deal to each other. The concern with context promoted by social history can only aid population studies, which constantly seeks to explain the quantities it uncovers. The desire on the part of demographic historians to uncover the larger structures and realities that shape population dynamics provides a wider focus to the more particularistic world of social history. The key lies in finding a fruitful common ground.

The decline of fertility offers such a common ground for cooperation. The evidence of fertility control confronts us with an event that needs to be explained, one that can be measured, graphed and dissected, but ultimately one that must be brought into perspective by human experience. Despite forty years of research we still remain in the dark as to why working-class people chose to limit their family size. Transition theory, the paradigm that has guided this research, has given us a great deal. We now have a sense, however imperfect, of the broad movements of population in the West since the eighteenth century. We do not unfortunately, know much of what lies beneath. The smaller world of the late Victorian working-class lies undiscovered under such a theory and no attempt to stretch a universal explanatory framework to cover the working class will do. The concept of a working-class culture unique to time and place is essential to reconstructing the family lives of workers and their motivation for controlling fertility. Such an attempt would be impossible without the social history of the last twenty years, which has begun at last to uncover the world of the mass of people 'invisible' to history. If we do not apply the lessons of both demography and social history to specific case studies, we can only speculate as to the forces acting upon these men and women.

The decline of fertility in Bradford, West Yorkshire is one such case study. This study of Bradford has been based on a simple fact – the working-class population of Bradford began to control their fertility in the decade of the 1870s. The key questions are why was this so and in what ways was this alike and different from the rest of the English population? My argument is that fertility control in Bradford began as a response to a shift within the larger political economy of the worsted industry that brought increasing pressures to bear on the working-class family in the 1870s. These pressures existed within the context of a way of life that had very little surplus above subsistence and consequently placed a high value on thrift and security. The preservation of the family in the face of change brought a response – fertility control – that could be justified within the framework of this culture.

There were of course a variety of other possible responses. Labor politics and trade unionism were two responses that assumed increasing importance as the century drew to a close. Another, less militant answer was emigration. The simple phrase, 'Left for the USA', in the membership roles of trade unions testifies to the popularity of this option. The worsted industry of American cities like Lawrence relied not only on British technology, but frequently on British labor as well. All these responses signaled a loss of confidence in the ability of the worsted trade to solve the problems of poverty and inequality by lifting everyone to a higher level. In the 1870s, the rhetoric of the mid-Victorian era collided fatally with reality. In the wake of this collision, a new outlook on life emerged.

It is this reorientation of life that links the experience of Bradford to larger trends in English life. In the thirty-five years before the First World War, a new working-class life came into existence in England. Gareth Stedman Jones has described this process as a 'remaking' of the English working class. This new life revolved around home, family and a type of consumerism that is now considered traditional – football, fish and chips shops and seaside holidays. It was at once both more homogeneous within itself, softening regional differences, and more distinct from the life of the middle class.[1] It was accompanied by a disruption of equipoise within the workplace as British industry faced up to the limits of the first phase of industrialization and sought to reestablish itself as a dynamic force in world markets. The growth of new industries and the reorganization of older ones brought both new opportunities and the loss of old skills and privileges. British manufacturers sought to control and intensify labor so as to adapt to new market realities in a variety of industries.[2] If the English working class ended up materially better off by 1914, the transition was by no means a smooth or steady one, nor was the end readily apparent to those in its midst. The persistence of large pockets of poverty and the limited nature of state intervention prior to 1914 ensured that survival and security still ranked as primary concerns in working-class life in a time of change.[3]

It is this combination of a home-centered culture seeking new horizons while still fearing the worst that provided the precondition for fertility control in late Victorian England. As this culture expanded and became nationalized prior to World War I, it carried with it the mindset and incentive structures that underlay family limitation. In a sense fertility control may have underwritten this new culture by allowing a shift in family resources away from child-rearing toward the consumption of the new goods and services that came into existence prior to 1914.[4] Bradford led in this trend because it was precocious; it was an early industrial center dependent on a single industry for continued prosperity. This made it particularly vulnerable to the pressures of deflation and world competition that affected the worsted trade so severely after 1873. Other cities and other industries followed in the footsteps of this reluctant pioneer.

The key to fertility control lies in the disintegration of mid-Victorian stability and the rise of a working-class life in the late nineteenth century that fit the new realities. While the transition between the two eras is real, it is also important to keep in mind that the calm of the mid-century was built upon shifting sands. One of the major reasons for this is the gap between the expectations of mid-Victorian life and its achievements. The existence of poverty and inequality stood as incontrovertible evidence of the failure of mid-Victorian society. Conflicts over political equality and work took on a more subterranean existence, but they remained below the surface of the calm, waiting the opportunity to reemerge. In a sense, this is what demography offers to social history, for the seismic indicators of change first appeared in the family and its structures. In a very direct way, the personal was political, because the problems that first hit home would later radiate outward into work and politics as fertility control alone proved insufficient to stabilize life.

Appendix: Collection and Analysis of the Data

The central problem in historical population studies is finding reliable data and correcting it for known inaccuracies. Once this is accomplished, the proper measures have to be derived from the data in order to study the particular demographic characteristic in question – fertility, mortality, migration or household structure. In this study, the need for certain types of data and data analysis guided the collection and reworking of the data. From the beginning, the focus was upon the level of marital fertility in Bradford during the initial stages of fertility decline. The traditional methods – family reconstitution or aggregate analysis – were not appropriate for this project. Aggregate analysis does not allow for the pin-pointing of controlling groups within the population by age or other characteristics and its also fails to provide adequate household level data to aid in the interpretation of fertility measures. Family reconstitution requires an enormous concentration of effort in order to create a data base and seems difficult if not impossible given the mobility and size of mid-nineteenth century populations. More importantly, the vital events registers are closed to the historian, so that the key elements in reconstructing a family, the records of marriages, births and deaths, are not available.

These problems dictated another approach. Instead of direct reconstruction by tracing vital events, a form of indirect reconstruction was used relying upon the manuscript census for Bradford and published birth and death figures for the registration district of Bradford. This indirect reconstruction is known as the own-child method, a technique pioneered by demographers who wished to study fertility using census materials.[1] This is essentially an estimation of the fertility experience of women aged 15–49 in the census population based on the recognition that the population obtained through a census sample is a surviving population. It is necessary to inflate the number of women and children for deaths and absence from the home in order to arrive at reasonable figures for actual fertility.

In the case of Bradford, the need to use this technique dictated the sampling strategy used. The sample had to be large enough to allow the use of the own-child method. Specifically, there had to be enough married women in each five-year age group to permit its inflation for deaths and to produce a large enough group of children for study. Therefore, a minimum sample size of 1200 households for each census was chosen. These four samples were taken from three areas within the borough of Bradford. The districts were chosen because they were within the central area of Bradford and because they were not reshaped by urban redevelopment and thus they remained essentially intact for the period 1851–81. The districts were chosen using maps from this era and by consulting the manuscript census to see which enumeration districts were needed for the study. The households in these districts were counted and then a random sample was taken for the entire area for each census. The samples, which represented approximately one-tenth of the households from these three districts, and between five and six per cent of the population of the borough of Bradford in each of the four censuses, became the data base for my study.[2]

The own-child method has been used for the study of British fertility by Michael Haines and by R. Woods and C. W. Smith. In both cases, the base populations were children aged 0–4 and their mothers aged 15–49, which were then inflated using life tables and assumptions about absence from the home.[3] In this study, an attempt was made to study fertility on a year by year basis, inflating the number of children for each age of child from 0–9. In order to begin this study, women and children were linked using a FORTRAN program developed by Steve Ruggles and Miriam King that compared characteristics of children aged 0–18 and women above fifteen, matching them on the basis of conventions about age differences, minimum age of child-bearing and most importantly, relationship to household head. The numbers of linked children and mothers were corrected for deaths in the interval between the census and birth of the child using life tables derived from the mortality figures for the registration district of Bradford, which included the borough and the surrounding area. A different life table was used for each five year period 1841–81 in order to account for variations in infant mortality within decades. The absence of children was estimated by calculating the total percentage of children aged 0–4 and 5–9 enumerated as being home with their families and then dividing the total population of children in each year by the appropriate figure.[4] Finally, the numbers of children aged 0–4 were further inflated to account for underenumeration in each census 1851–81. The inflation factor used was based on Glass's estimation of underenumeration in his study of birth underregistration.[5] This technique, which can be used for both total and illegitimate fertility was limited to marital fertility for the purpose of this study. Using the corrected figures for women aged 15–49 and children aged 0–9, age-specific and general marital fertility rates were calculated for each year 1842–81.

In any reconstruction, a series of choices have to be made which affect the accuracy of the results. In my study, several components could be potential sources of error. The inclusion of children aged 5–9 goes beyond most studies, but I felt that the advantage of creating a continuous series of general and age-specific fertility measures outweighed the difficulties of using this age group. The main problem is how to account for their absence from the home, for it is assumed that older children are more likely not to be home. In order to deal with this problem, I simply used a base-line figure for children at home aged 5–9 by calculating the proportion of these children enumerated as the child of the household head or a boarder. Given the fact that for most of this period Bradford was a site of in-migration, especially of women aged 15–24, it seems likely that the outflow of children was limited and that we can use this estimate as an adequate measure of absent children.

The use of published mortality data also involves potential sources of error. The underregistration of births and deaths would tend to distort the mortality rates, especially for infants. However, we have only estimates of under-registration of births for this period, which makes it difficult to correct infant mortality. Therefore, no accounting for underregistration was made in the life tables. A second and potentially greater source of inaccuracy is the difference between mortality measured for the Bradford district as a whole and the borough of Bradford, especially the central townships of Great Horton, Bowling and Bradford used in the samples. The registration district of Bradford included rural areas outside the urbanized borough which most likely had far lower levels of infant and child mortality. Some sense of this difference can be obtained by comparing the infant mortality rate for the district with that of the borough. These figures are available only after 1860, but they show a difference of about 5 per cent for the period 1862–76 and parity for 1877–81. Therefore, each five-year life table prior to 1876 was based on an infant mortality rate inflated five per cent to account for this difference. It is quite likely that this underestimates the level of infant and childhood mortality, for differences in mortality were profound even within the borough. The outlying areas, which were wealthier and less crowded, had infant mortality rates half those of the inner city districts as late as the early twentieth century.[6] Unfortunately, no systematic way of measuring and applying those differences exists, so the method used has to remain as a best estimate of mortality.

For adult women, two sources of potential error exist. No accounting for age misstatement among adult women was made because of the difficulty in estimating the number of women who should be in each five-year age group 15–49.[7] In all the age bearing years 15–49, the disproportionate in-migration of women makes the normal method of estimating such differences problematic.[8] The other source of error is the fact that the mortality for women aged 15–49 is not broken down beyond the categories given in the registrar-general's data. Thus it is assumed, for example, that all women aged 25–34 have the same probability of dying within a single year. While this is not true, given the low level of adult women's mortality, it is unlikely that this assumption introduced unacceptable error into the calculations.

Given these reservations about the quality of the estimates obtained using these methods, the results are encouraging. Looking at Figure 7.6, the fit between the three year running averages of the general marital fertility rate derived from the Registrar General's data for the borough of Bradford and the general marital fertility based on the sample population is quite good. Not only are the absolute totals fairly close, the two curves also follow the same general trends during the period 1842–81. Given the relatively small population involved (by demographic standards), this closeness of fit is reassuring in light of the potentially large random variations in fertility.

Notes

Introduction

1. George Weerth, *Collected Works,* vol. 3, p. 164.
2. Bradford Borough Medical Officer of Health, *Annual Report,* 1881, Bradford Central Library (BCL) p. 7.
3. Susan Watkins and Ansley Coale, eds, *The Decline of Fertility in Europe* (Princeton, 1986).
4. The classic statement of the theory remains Frank Notestein, 'Population: the long view', in T. W. Schultz, ed., *Food for the World* (Chicago, 1945) pp. 36–57.
5. For a review of the literature and issues see Etienne Van de Walle and John Knodel, 'Demographic Transition and Fertility Decline: The European Case', *International Union for the Scientific Study of Population,* Contributed Papers (Sydney, 1967) pp. 47–55; John Caldwell, *Theory of Fertility Decline* (London, 1977); Ron Lesthaeghe and Chris Wilson, 'Modes of Production, Secularization and the Pace of Fertility Decline in Western Europe, 1870–1930', in Watkins and Coale, *Decline of Fertility,* pp. 293–313; Susan Watkins, *From Provinces into Nations,* (Princeton, 1991).
6. David Levine, *Reproducing Families: the political economy of English population history* (Cambridge, 1987); Mark Stern, *Society and Family Strategy, Erie County, New York* (Albany, 1987); Knodel, 1988; Elinor Accampo, *Industrialization, Family Life and Class Relations: Saint Chamond 1815–1914* (Berkeley, 1989); David Kertzer and Dennis Hogan, *Family, Political Economy and Demographic Change, The Transformation of Life in Casalecchio, Italy, 1861–1921* (Madison, 1989); Eilidh Garret, 'The Trials of Labour: Motherhood Versus Employment in a Nineteenth Century Textile Centre', *Continuity and Change,* vol. 5, 1 (May 1990) pp. 121–54; Wally Seccombe, 'Starting to Stop: Working Class Fertility Decline in Britain', *Past and Present,* 126 (Summer 1990) pp. 151–88.
7. The two main methods are the own-child method and family reconstitution. See Lee Jay Cho, Robert Retherford and Minja Kim Choe, *The Own-Child Method of Fertility Estimation* (Honolulu, 1986) for the own-child method. For family reconstitution see Neil Tranter, *Population and Society 1750–1940* (London, 1985) pp. 20–6.
8. Patrick Joyce, *Visions of the People: Industrial England and the question of class 1848–1914* (Cambridge, 1991) p. 20.
9. The most exhaustive study remains John Innes, *Class Fertility Trends in England* (Princeton, 1938). See also Michael Haines, *Fertility and Occupation: Population Patterns in Industrialization* (New York, 1979); Michael Teitelbaum, *The British Fertility Decline* (Princeton, 1984);

George Boyer and Jeffery Williamson, 'A Quantitative Assessment of the Fertility Transition in England 1851–1911', *Research in Economic History*, vol. 12 (1989), pp. 193–217.

10. Daniel Kelves, *In the Name of Eugenics* (New York, 1985); Richard Soloway. *Demography and Degeneration: Eugenics and the Declining Birthrate in Twentieth-Century Britain*, (Chapel Hill, 1990).

11. Ethel Elderton, *Report on the English Birthrate* (London, 1914) p. 43.

12. For a discussion of the debate over birth control see Richard Soloway, *Birth Control and the Population Question in England, 1877–1930* (Chapel Hill, 1982)

13. Royal Commission on Population, *Report* (London, 1949) p. 43.
    For a discussion of the growing homogeneity of demographic behavior in the twentieth century, see Michael Anderson, 'The social implications of demographic change', in F. M. L. Thompson, ed., *The Cambridge Social History of Britain 1750–1950, Volume 2 People and Their Environment* (Cambridge, 1990), pp. 1–70.

14. There are a number of problems with efforts to explain differential fertility. Since social classes lived side by side, regional or even city-wide data will not distinguish between the behavior of different groups. In addition, the use of occupational categories fails to separate social classes adequately, for occupational groups often included both working-class and middle-class employees. As national categories, occupational groups encompassed the same regional or religious variations encountered in other national studies. R. I. Woods, 'Approaches to the Fertility Transition in Victorian England', *Population Studies*, vol. 41 (1987) pp. 283–311. As Teitelbaum admits, the indices could not explain the differential onset of decline, nor its relatively rapid spread to all areas of Britain. Teitelbaum, *British Fertility*, p. 192. For an attempt to use sub districts within London to study class differences in fertility see R.I. Woods, 'Social Class Variations in the Decline of Marital Fertility on Late Nineteenth-Century London', *Geografiska Annaler*, vol. 66B (1984) pp. 29–38 R. I. Woods and C. W. Smith, 'The Decline of Marital Fertility in the Late Nineteenth Century: the Case of England and Wales', *Population Studies*, vol. 37 (1983) pp. 210–14.

15. In Bolton, Oldham, Blackburn, Preston and Bradford the employment rate for all workers under twenty exceeded 30% as late as 1911, compared with a national rate of 22%. When children ten to fourteen are examined, the differences are more striking. The rate for England in 1911 was 4.6%, while in the cities listed above it ranged from 13.6 to 16.8%. Despite this, general marital fertility ranged from 68–98% of the English national mean from 1906 to 1910. Census of England and Wales, 1911, *Ages, Occupations and Civil Condition of the People*; Registrar General, *Annual Summary of Births, Deaths and Marriages in the Great Towns*, 1906–10; Registrar General, *Annual Report of Births, Deaths and Marriages*, 1906–10.

16. Roger Davidson, *Whitehall and the Labour Problem in Late Victorian and Edwardian England* (London, 1985).

17. Gareth Stedman Jones, 'Working-class Politics in London, 1870–1900; Notes in the Remaking of a Working Class', *Journal of Social History*,

vol. 7, 4 (Summer 1974) pp. 459–508; Eric Hobsbawm, 'The Making of the Working Class 1870–1914', in *Worlds of Labour, Further Studies in the History of Labour* (London, 1986) pp. 194–213.

18 Levine, *Reproducing Families*, pp. 174–176.

19. For more on birth control see Angus McLaren, *Birth Control in Nineteenth-Century England* (London, 1978).

1 The Worsted Trade and the Development of Bradford

1. Daniel Defoe, *A Tour through the Whole Island of Great Britain*, vol. 2 (London, revised edition, 1962) pp. 193–201.

2. John James, *History of the Worsted Manufacture in England* (reprint of 1857 edition, London, 1968) p. 612.

3. Edward Collinson, *Collinson's West Riding Worsted Directory* (Bradford, 1857) p. 187.

4. James, *History*, p. 612.

5. Ibid., 545.

6. Adrian Randall, *Before the Luddites: Custom, Community and Machinery in the English Woolen Industry, 1776–1809* (Cambridge, 1991) Randall, 'Work, Culture and Resistance to Machinery in the West of England Woolen Industry', in Pat Hudson, ed., *Regions and Industries: A Perspective on the Industrial Revolution in Britain* (Cambridge, 1989) pp. 175–98.

7. D. T. Jenkins, *The West Riding Wool Textile Industry 1770–1835: A Study of Fixed Capital Formation* (Edington, 1975) pp. 38–45; S. D. Chapman, 'The Pioneers of Worsted Spinning by Power', *Business History*, vol. vii (1965), pp 97–116.

8. Jenkins, *West Riding*, pp. 1–9; Pat Hudson, 'Protoindustrialization: the Case of the West Riding Wool Textile Industry in the 18th and Early 19th Centuries', *History Workshop Journal*, no. 12, (Autumn 1981) pp. 38–40.

9. Jenkins, *West Riding*, pp. 191–204; Pat Hudson, *The Genesis of Industrial Capital: A Study of the West Riding Wool Textile Industry c. 1750–1850* (Cambridge, 1986) pp. 57–104, 211–255.

10. Adrian Randall, 'Peculiar Perquisites and Pernicious Practices: Embezzlement In The West of England Woolen Industry, c. 1750–1840', *International Review of Social History*, vol. XXXV, no. 2, (1990) pp. 193–219.

11. Jack Reynolds, *The Great Paternalist: Titus Salt and the Growth of Nineteenth-Century Bradford* (London, 1983) pp. 12–13; John Rule, *The Experience of Labor in English Eighteenth Century Industry* (New York, 1981).

12. Sigsworth, *Black Dyke Mills*, (Liverpool, 1958) pp. 44–51, 65; James, *History*, pp. 471–9; Reynolds, *Great Paternalist*, pp. 68–9.

13. Reynolds, *Great Paternalist* pp. 28–33; Jonathan Smith, 'The Strike of 1825', in D. G. Wright and J. A. Jowitt, eds, *Victorian Bradford* (Bradford, 1981) pp. 63–80.

14. Sigsworth, *Black Dyke Mills*, pp. 44–51, 65; James, *History*, pp. 471–9; Reynolds, *Great Paternalist*, pp. 68–9.

15. E. P. Thompson, *The Making of the English Working Class* (New York, 1966) pp. 269–313; Reynolds, *Great Paternalist*, pp. 54–5.

16. Thompson, *Making*, pp. 282–3, 425–6; George Taylor, 'Bradford and the Worsted Manufacture', *Practical Magazine*, (October 1873) p. 427.

17. Henry Forbes, *The Rise, Progress and Present State of the Worsted, Alpaca, and Mohair Manufacturers*, pamphlet (Bradford, 1852) Bradford Central Library (BCL).

18. Sigsworth, *Black Dyke Mills*, pp. 34–6; William Cudworth, *A Sketch History of the Town and Trade of Bradford*, pamphlet (Bradford, 1888) BCL, pp. 46–57.

19. Sigsworth, *Black Dyke Mills*, p. 32.

20. James, *History*, pp. 607–9.

21. D. T. Jenkins and K. G. Ponting, *The British Wool Textile Industry 1770–1914* (London 1982), pp. 125–139.

22. Reynolds, *Great Paternalist*, pp. 132–3.

23. Sigsworth, *Black Dyke Mills*, p. 74.

24. Great Britain, Inland Revenue, 2nd Report, P.P. 1855–6 and 12th Report, P.P. 1866–7.

25. Jenkins and Ponting, *British Wool*, pp. 139–65; Sigsworth, *Black Dyke Mills*, pp. 45–74.

26. Archibald Neill, *The Building Trades of Bradford*, pamphlet (Bradford, 1873) BCL.

27. J. W. Banks, 'Progress of Engineering in Bradford', *Journal of the Bradford Engineering Society*, 27th Session, (1925–6), pp. 3–14; George Hodgsons, *Makers of Power Looms for Weaving, Origin and Growth of the Firm*, pamphlet (Bradford, 1898), BCL, pp. 5–11.

28. In 1882, Low Moor used 4000 men and boys to work forty-nine coal and ironstone pits and eight blast furnaces, while the Bowling Iron Works employed over 2000 colliers in 1877. Joseph Willcock, *History, Progress and Description of the Bowling Iron Works*, pamphlet (Bradford, 1873) BCL, pp. 221–2; *Bradford Observer*, January 5, 1882.

29. C. Richardson, *A Geography of Bradford* (Bradford, 1976) pp. 71–3.

30. Reynolds, *Great Paternalist*, pp. 57–60.

31. Adrian Elliott, 'Social Structure in the Mid-Nineteenth Century', in D. G. Wright and J. A. Jowitt, eds, *Victorian Bradford* (Bradford, 1981) pp. 101–13.

32. Based on my sample of the manuscript censuses for 1851–81.

33. Elliott, 'Social Structure', p. 107. By 1881, 8.8 per cent of adult women worked as servants.

34. Theodore Koditschek, *Class Formation and Urban Industrial Society: Bradford 1750–1850* (Cambridge, 1990) pp. 135–227.

35. Based on a sample of the manuscript census for 1851–81.

36. J. B. Priestley described his time as a clerk for a top maker in *Margin Released* (New York, 1962) pp. 14–27.

37. Census of Great Britain, 1861, County of York, pp. 722–8.

38. A. L. Bowley, 'Wages in the Worsted and Woollen Manufactures of the West Riding of Yorkshire', *Journal of the Royal Statistical Society*, Series A, vol. 65, (March, 1902) pp. 103–126. For work practices of the overlookers see William Forster's testimony before the Committee on

Masters and Operatives, pp. 1856, pp. 110–11, and Power Loom Overlookers Society Branch no. 2, Rules 1866, Bradford Archives (BA).

39. These three sectors employed 31.2 per cent of adult male workers in 1871 and 29.7 per cent in 1881.

40. Neill, *Building Trade*.

41. Results from my sample of the 1881 manuscript census; see Gareth Stedman-Jones, *Outcast London* (London, 1971) for a discussion of casual labor markets in the nineteenth century.

42. C. Richardson, 'Irish Settlement in Mid-Nineteenth Century Bradford', *Yorkshire Bulletin of Social and Economic Research*, vol. 20, no. 1, (May 1968), pp. 40–57.

43. Elizabeth Roberts, *A Woman's Place* (Oxford, 1985), pp. 135–48; Edward Higgs, 'Women, Occupations and Work in the Nineteenth-Century Censuses', *History Workshop Journal*, no. 23 (Spring 1987), pp. 59–80.

44. Ivy Pinchbeck, *Women Workers and the Industrial Revolution* (1981 edition, London); E. H. Hunt, *British Labour History 1815–1914* (Atlantic Highlands, 1981) pp. 17–25.

45. Elliott, 'Social Structure', pp. 104–8.

46. D. A. Farnie, *The English Cotton Industry and the World Market* (Oxford, 1979) pp. 81–134.

47. For a discussion of the shift to mixed goods production see Hudson, 'Protoindustrialization', pp. 38–55; Jenkins, *West Riding*, pp. 1–46, 149–90.

48. In 1866, the worsted trade found 70 per cent of its overseas market (by value) in the United States and Europe. By contrast, as early as 1850, only 43 per cent of cotton exports went to the same markets and this share fell by half by 1896. Jenkins and Ponting, *British Wool*, p. 263; Farnie, *English Cotton Industry*, p. 91.

49. Eric Sigsworth, 'The Woolen Textile Industry', in Roy Church ed., *The Dynamics of Victorian Business* (Boston, 1980) pp. 185–7.

50. The absolute price increased up until 1864.

51. Sigsworth, 'Woolen Industry', pp. 188–9. By contrast, the cotton trade enjoyed a fall in cotton prices throughout the nineteenth century. Farnie, *English Cotton Industry*, pp. 82–3.

52. Woolen manufacturers on the other hand could and did lower raw material costs through the increasing use of reprocessed wool ('shoddy' or 'mungo') in the late nineteenth century. D. T. Jenkins and J. C. Malin, 'European Competition in Woolen Cloth, 1870–1914: The Role of Shoddy', in Mary B. Rose, ed., *International Competition and Strategic Response in the Textile Industries since 1870*, (London, 1991) pp. 66–86.

53. For example, the spinning firm of James Tankard tied up about 80 per cent of its capital in stock in the period 1876–82. Records of J. Tankard Ltd, 1876–82, West Yorkshire Archives (WYA). This figure was high, but not not unheard of. The Board of Trade reported that materials represented 61 per cent of costs, wages only 22 per cent. Board of Trade, Report on the Relation of Wages in Certain Industries to Cost of Production. P.P. 1890–1, p. 1079. See also K. Pankhurst, 'Investment in the West Riding Wool Textile Industry in the Nineteenth Century',

Yorkshire Bulletin of Economic and Social Research, vol. 7, no. 2 (September, 1958) pp. 93–116.

54. Lazonick makes a similar point in reference to the cotton trade in Lancashire. William Lazonick, *Competitive Advantage on the Shopfloor* (Cambridge, MA., 1991) pp. 122–3.

55. Bradford Chamber of Commerce, Annual Report, 1859, BCL.

56. *Bradford Observer*, October 13, 1877; Records of J. Tankard Ltd., Spinners 1876–82. Wages totaled about £15 000 per year, or only 20 per cent of materials costs.

57. Sigsworth, *Black Dyke Mills*, p. 60.

58. Taylor, 'Worsted Manufacture', p. 428.

59. *Bradford Observer*, March 20, 1872 and June 13, 1872.

60. Henry Ripley, *Speech on Technical Progress*, pamphlet (Bradford, 1861) BCL.

61. According to the Factory Inspectors Returns, there were 27 855 worsted workers in Bradford in 1871, an increase of only 8 per cent since 1851.

62. E.M. Sigsworth and J.M. Blackman, 'The Woolen and Worsted Industries', in Derek Aldcroft, ed., *British Industry and Foreign Competition, 1875–1914*, pp. 129–31; Reports of the Factory Inspectors, October 1846, P.P. 1847, p. 779.

63. Sigsworth, *Black Dyke Mills*, p. 128

64. Select Committee on Bleaching and Dyeing Works, answers of manufacturers, P.P. 1854–5, pp. 92–3.

65. Commission on the Best Means to Prevent the Pollution of Rivers (Rivers Pollution Commission) 3rd Report P.P. 1873, pp. 125–6..

66. Select Committee on the Bleaching and Dyeing Establishments, 2nd Report, P.P. 1857–8, Testimony of Henry Ripley, pp. 69–72.

67. Deirdre Busfield, 'Skill and the Sexual Division of Labour in the West Riding Textile Industry, 1850–1914', in J.A. Jowitt and A.J. McIvor, eds, *Employers and Labour in the English Textile Industries 1850–1939* (New York, 1988) pp. 155–6.

68. Sigsworth, *Black Dyke Mills*, pp. 129–31.

69. Sigsworth, *Black Dyke Mills*, pp. 120–4; Farnie, *English Cotton Industry*, pp. 277–323.

70. Farnie, *English Cotton Industry*, 277–308.

71. Ibid., pp. 209–76.

72. Sigsworth and Blackman, 'Woolen and Worsted', pp. 131, 151–2.

73. *Textile Manufacturer*, October 1875; Taylor, 'Worsted Manufacture', p. 434.

74. Rivers Pollution Commission, 3rd Report, pp. 119–33, Sigsworth, 'Woolen Industry', p. 191. This compares favorably with cotton industry's average of 110 employees in spinning, 123 in weaving and 413 in combined firms in 1870. Farnie, English *Cotton Industry*, p. 215, 286, 316.

75. *Yorkshire Textile Directory 1909–1910* (Oldham, 1910) pp. 64–95.

76. The Rivers Pollution Commission listed the firm of Philip Haas and Sons, Damask Manufacturers, who employed 12 hands and rented both power and space from Holme Top Mills. Rivers Pollution Commission, 3rd Report.

77. For example in February 1875, the *Textile Manufacturer* reported that Jonathan Cullen, a manager, resigned his position to set up his own business.

78. While it is difficult to quantify such incidents, they did receive coverage in the local press. *Bradford Weekly Telegraph*, January 1, 1879; January 29, 1870.

79. J. B. Priestley, *Margin Released*, pp. 14–5.

80. Hudson, *Genesis*, pp. 168–81.

81. Sigsworth, *Black Dyke Mills*, pp. 65–6.

82. Ibid., pp. 124–29.

83. Hudson, *Genesis*, 168–81. Businessmen, who started firms as long as they could receive credit, moved in and out of the trade. Records of Robert Jowett & Sons, Book no. 63 1881, Ledger Book 1872–81, University of Leeds Archives (ULA).

84. Bradford Chamber of Commerce, Minutebook, January–July 1864, BCL.

85. Sigsworth, *Black Dyke Mills*, p. 126.

86. *Textile Manufacturer*, August 1876 and June 1881.

87. *Textile Manufacturer*, September, 1877 and July 1879.

88. Ibid., June 1877 and January 1879.

89. Select Committee on Scientific Instruction, P.P. 1867–8, testimony of Henry Ripley, pp. 219–20; Royal Commission on Technical Instruction, P.P. 1884, testimony of Henry Mitchell, pp. 254.

90. James, *History*, p. 602.

91. Ripley, Scientific Instruction, p. 219.

92. Oates–Ingham Letter Book, December 4, 1864, University of Leeds Archives (ULA).

93. Thomas Illingworth, *A Sixty Year Retrospective of the Bradford Trade*, pamphlet (Bradford, 1883) pp. 54–5.

94. *Textile Manufacturer*, July 1876.

95. Ripley, Scientific Instruction, p. 260.

96. James, *History*, p. 602.

97. J. H. Lewis, *The Safety of Doing Right*, pamphlet (Bradford, 1878) BCL.

98. US Consul to Bradford, letter 4 1866, BCL; Bradford Chamber of Commerce, minute book, December 22, 1871 BA.

99. Ibid., letter 11, 1866.

100. *Textile Manufacturer*, December 1875; *Bradford Observer*, September 14, 1864.

101. Bradford Chamber of Commerce, minutebook, January 1864.

102. Rivers Pollution Commission, P.P. 1867 testimony of Charles Gott, W. T. McGowan, J. Ingham, pp. 269–81.

103. Bradford Chamber of Commerce, minutebook, July 15, 1872, June 16, 1875, July 24 1877. Bradford manufacturers pioneered the recovery of products and the use of by-products. A local firm, Teal, Simpson & Co. operated a grease recovery works that purchased the liquid waste of local firms. Local warehouses sold dust from sorted wool for manure and the wool bags from bales of wool as floor coverings. Local Government Board, Annual Report, 1880–1, P.P. 1881, J. Spear, 'On Woolsorters' Disease', Appendix A, no. 8, p. 805; Rivers Pollution Commission, P.P.

1867, Testimony of Frederick Anderton, p. 315; Medical Officers to the Local Government Board, P.P. 1877–8, Report of Dr. Ballard, 'On Effluvium Nuisances', pp. 131–3.

104. Oates–Ingham Letter Book, July 1, 1867.

105. Bradford Chamber of Commerce, Annual Report, 1855; Bradford Chamber of Commerce, Minutebook, May 30, 1878.

106. For a general discussion of such efforts see Andrew Yarmie, 'Employers' Organizations in Mid-Victorian England', *International Review of Social History*, vol. XXV, pt. 2, (1980), pp. 209–35.

107. Bradford Chamber of Commerce, minutebook, April–June 1864; Ripley, Committee on Bleaching and Dyeing Establishments, pp. 68–76.

108. Bradford Chamber of Commerce, minutebook May 16, 1872; Yarmie, 'Employers' Organizations', pp. 222–5.

109. James, *History*, p. 612.

110. Herbert Heaton, *The Yorkshire Woolen and Worsted Industries* (2nd edition, Oxford, 1965) p. 273.

111. Claire Delius, *Memories of My Brother* (London, 1935) pp. 32–3.

112. Priestley, *Margin* pp. 12–3.

113. Selected Extracts from the Writings of George Weerth, translated by A. Farrer, typescript, BCL, p. 4.

114. For an interesting discussion of Ruskin see Malcolm Hardman, *Ruskin and Bradford: An Experiment in Victorian Cultural History* (Manchester, 1986).

115. J. A. Jowitt, 'The Retardation of Trade Unionism in the Yorkshire Worsted Textile Industry', in Jowitt and McIvor, *Employers and labour* pp. 96–7.

116. Jenkins and Ponting, *Wool Textile* p. 229. The nature of the trade, with its multitude of specialized firms, makes an accurate assessment of the slump difficult. Further complicating the situation is the poor quality of trade statistics by which to judge total output. Only estimates of the amount of material produced for the home market exist, and the export figures lump woolen and worsted materials together until 1882. Even then, the width of pieces is not noted, despite their increasing size.

117. Letter Book of Robert Jowitt, no. 28, 1876–7, University of Leeds Archives.

118. *Textile Manufacturer* November 15, 1880.

119. *Textile Manufacturer* May 1881.

120. Report of the Royal Commission on Depression of Trade and Industry, P.P. 1886, Testimony of Sir Jacob Behrens, pp. 254–6. This statement ignores the tremendous increase in output from 1865–1873. Those levels of output were not retained in the late 1870s or early 1880s.

121. Depression of Trade and Industry, Testimony of Henry Mitchell, pp. 124–6.

122. Jenkins and Ponting, *British Wool* p. 274; *Textile Manufacturer* 1879. The number of bankruptcies by year were 1875: 42, 1876: 24, 1877: 31, 1878: 34 (source *Bradford Observer* December 28, 1878), 1879: 67, 1880: 23, 1881: 37, 1882: 28.

123. *Textile Manufacturer* June 1877, January 1879.

124. Statement of Income Taxes for the Borough of Bradford April 5, 1880, Inland Revenue Service, BCL.
125. *Textile Manufacturer*, November 1880.
126. Andrew Byles, *Reciprocity and Free Trade*, pamphlet (Bradford, 1879), BCL, p. 11.
127. *Textile Manufacturer*, September 1880.
128. Ibid., December 1875 and July 1879.
129. For more on this see Chapter 3.
130. *Bradford Observer*, February 17, 1879.
131. W.F. Ecroyd, *The Policy of Self Help, Two Letters to the Bradford Observer*, pamphlet, 1879, Letter 2, February 28, 1879, BCL.
132. *Textile Manufacturer*, December 1875.
133. Byles, *Reciprocity*, p. 10.
134. US Consul, Letter of February 13, 1879, June 14, 1878.
135. James Ford, *The Present Position of the Country, A Sermon*, pamphlet (Bradford, 1879) BCL, p. 12. An editorial in the *Bradford Observer* on October 28, 1878 blamed the extravagance of life in Bradford for the depression.
136. Joseph Wrigley and Charles Bousfield, *Report on the Woolen Manufactures of France, Association of the Chambers of Commerce of the United Kingdom*, pamphlet (Bradford, 1877) BCL.
137. Keith Laybourn and Jack Reynolds, *Liberalism and the Rise of Labour 1890–1918* (London, 1984) p. 23.
138. *Textile Manufacturer*, September 1879.
139. Bradford Chamber of Commerce, minutebook, July 29, 1879.
140. *Bradford Observer*, March 22, 1872.
141. F.W. Fison, *Report on the International Congress of Commerce and Industry Brussels, Sept 1880*, pamphlet, (Bradford) 1880, BCL, p. 24.
142. *Textile Manufacturer*, December 1877.
143. James Donnelly, 'The Development of Technical Education in Bradford 1825–1900', MEd Thesis, University of Leeds, 1984, pp. 99–133.
144. Royal Commission on Technical Instruction, P.P. 1884, Testimony of Henry Mitchell, pp. 247–8.
145. *Textile Manufacturer*, April 1877.
146. For a discussion of the changing notions of technical education see J.F. Donnelly, 'Science, technology and industrial work in Britain, 1860–1930: towards a new synthesis', *Social History*, vol. 16, no. 2 (May 1991) pp. 191–201.
147. Alfred Harris, *Technical Education A Lecture on Industry and Art*, pamphlet (Bradford, 1883) BCL.
148. *Bradford Review*, December 14, 1867. In part, this also reflected a division among the middle class on the issue of how best to educate the sons of the elite. Some like Ripley supported a practical education, while others continued to defend the classical pattern popular in the great public schools.
149. Donnelly, 'Development', pp. 95–9.
150. *Bradford Review*, September 14, 1867; Neill, *Building Trade*.
151. Letter from WH, *Bradford Observer*, October 9, 1868.

152. Swire Smith, *Technical Education and Foreign competition*, pamphlet (Bradford, 1887), BCL; C. L. Stanley, *Technical Education Necessary for England's Future Welfare*, pamphlet (Bradford, 1887) BCL.
153. Mitchell, Technical Instruction, p. 250.
154. *Bradford Observer*, October 18, 1877.
155. Ibid., October 16, 1878.
156. Timothy Tappitnose (pseud.), *Technicomania and its Cure*, pamphlet (Bradford, 1878) BCL, p. 5.
157. Bradford Trade Council, Minutes, April 1882, BA.
158. Tappitnose, *Technicomania*, p. 5.
159. He had been a member of the delegation to the Paris Exhibition of 1867 and had reported on worsted fabrics. Bradford Chamber of Commerce, Paris Exhibition, 1867, Bradford Reports of Workmen, pp. 20–2, BA.
160. Thomas Illingworth, *Distributional Reform*, pamphlet (Bradford, 1885) BCL, p. 120.
161. Illingworth, *Retrospective*, p. 49.
162. Ibid., pp. 12–49.
163. Letter from A.P. in the *Bradford Observer*, February 27, 1882.
164. Letter from B.T., *Bradford Observer*, January 10, 1882.
165. William Forster, *Report on the Movement for the Advancement of the British Wool Industry*, pamphlet (Bradford, 1881) BCL.
166. *Textile Manufacturer*, August 1881.
167. Ibid., November 1881.
168. Henry Mitchell, *Trade and Fashion*, pamphlet (Bradford, 1881) BCL, p. 6. Mitchell also noted that the fear of changing tastes inhibited investment in mule spinning.
169. *Bradford Observer*, February 20, 1882. Such public debates often degenerated into accusations of self-interest. One letter writer accused Waugh of advocating reequipping because of his ties to a particular machine maker. February 25, 1882.
170. *Bradford Observer*, December 19, 1881.
171. US Consul in Bradford, Letter, February 21, 1882, BCL.
172. *Bradford Observer*, February 20, 1882.
173. Ibid., February 6, 1879, Letter from A.Z.
174. S. C. Lister, *Free Trade in Corn and Protection to Labour*, pamphlet (Bradford, 1880), BCL, p. 30.

2 Work and Its Discontents

1. For a sense of the emerging body of work on this topic see Patrick Joyce, ed., *The Historical Meanings of Work* (Cambridge, 1987); Gary Cross, *A Quest for Time: The Reduction of Work in Britain and France, 1840–1940* (Berkeley, 1989); James Jaffe, *The Struggle for Market Power: Industrial relations in the British Coal Industry, 1800–1840* (Cambridge, 1991); Adrian Randall, *Before the Luddites* (Cambridge, 1991).
2. Part of the impetus for this reexamination comes from the debate over language initiated by Gareth Stedman Jones in his book, *Languages of*

Class (Cambridge, 1983) especially his article, 'Rethinking Chartism', pp. 90–178. See also Robert Gray, 'The Deconstructing of the English Working Class', *Social History*, v. 11, no. 3, (October 1986), pp. 363–373; Joan Scott, 'On Language, Gender, and Working-Class History', in Joan Scott, *Gender and the Politics of History* (New York, 1988) pp. 53–67. See also Patrick Joyce, *Visions of the People* (Cambridge, 1991).

3. Rev. Charles Robinson, *Christian Diligence*, pamphlet (Bradford, n.d.) p. 8, BCL.
4. Joyce, *Visions*, p. 56.
5. Jonathan Glyde, *Plea for a Park*, pamphlet (Bradford, 1853) BCL.
6. See Chapter 5.
7. *Bradford Observer*, May 30, 1872.
8. Letter from W. H., *Bradford Observer*, October 9, 1868.
9. E. P. Thompson, *The Making of the English Working Class* (New York, 1966) pp. 234–68; John Rule, 'The Property of Skill in the Period of Manufacture', in Joyce, *Historical Meanings*, pp. 99–118.
10. The debate between Patrick Joyce and Richard Price in *Social History* covered many of these issues. Richard Price, 'The Labour Process and Labour History', *Social History*, vol. 8, no. 1 (January 1983) pp. 57–75; Patrick Joyce, 'Labour, Capital and Compromise: a Response to Richard Price', *Social History*, vol. 9, no. 1 (January 1984) pp. 67–76 as well as their replies in *Social History*, vol. 9, no. 2 (May 1984) pp. 217–31.
11. Richard Price, *Labour in British Society* (London, 1986) pp. 71–83, 93–104.
12. For a discussion of these developments see Edward Thompson, 'Homage to Tom Maguire', in Asa Briggs and John Saville, eds, *Essays in Labour History* (New York, 1960) pp. 276–316 and Keith Laybourn and Jack Reynolds, *Liberalism and the Rise of Labour 1890–1918* (New York, 1984).
13. The work on the labor aristocracy is long, but a number of essential works exist. Eric Hobsbawm, 'The Labour Aristocracy in in Nineteenth Century Britain', in Hobsbawm, *Labouring Men* (London, 1964) pp. 272–315; Robert Gray, *The Labour Aristocracy in Victorian Edinburgh* (Oxford, 1976); Geoffrey Crossick, *An Artisan Elite in Victorian Society: Kentish London 1840–1880* (London, 1978); Eric Hobsbawm, 'The Aristocracy of Labour Reconsidered', in Hobsbawm, *Worlds of Labour*, (London, 1984), pp. 227–51.
14. John Foster, *Class Struggle and the Industrial Revolution* (London, 1974).
15. The literature critical of the theory is also extensive. Henry Pelling, 'The Concept of the Labour Aristocracy', in Pelling, *Popular Politics and Society in Late Victorian Britain* (London, 1968) pp. 37–61; A.E. Musson, 'Class Struggle and the Labour Aristocracy.' *Social History*, vol. 1, no. 3, (October 1976) pp. 335–56; H. F. Moorhouse, 'The Marxist Theory of the Labour Aristocracy', *Social history*, vol. 3, no. 1 (January 1978) pp. 61–82; Alistair Reid, 'Intelligent Artisans and Aristocrats of Labour: the Essays of Thomas Wright', in Jay Winter, ed., *The Working Class in Modern British History* (Cambridge, 1983), pp. 171–86.

16. Patrick Joyce, *Work, Society and Politics: The culture of the factory in later Victorian England* (New Brunswick, 1984).

17. Joyce followed the lead of Gareth Stedman Jones in making this distinction. See Gareth Stedman Jones, 'Class Struggle and the Industrial Revolution', in *Languages*, pp. 66–9 and Richard Price, 'Structures of Subordination in Nineteenth-Century British Industry', in Pat Thane, Geoffrey Crossick and Roderick Floud, eds, *The Power of the Past: Essays for Eric Hobsbawm* (Cambridge, 1984) pp. 119–42.

18. Joyce, *Work*, pp. 90–157.

19. Ibid., 50–89.

20. Ibid., pp. 158–168.

21. William Lazonick, *Competitive Advantage on the Shopfloor* (Cambridge, MA., 1991) pp. 115–37.

22. They could also substitute inferior cotton in order to further lower the costs of production. Ibid, pp. 122–24.

23. Ibid., pp. 103–5, 138–78.

24. D. A. Farnie, *The English Cotton Industry and the World Market 1815–1896* (Oxford, 1979) p. 296–7. For the gender divisions within weaving unions see Sonya Rose, *Limited Livelihoods: Gender and Class in Nineteenth-Century England* (Berkeley, 1992) pp. 154–84.

25. Joyce also failed to cite Sigsworth's work on the worsted trade.

26. Hand weaving survived in the woolen trade until the 1870s. D. T. Jenkins and K. G. Ponting, *The British Wool Textile Industry 1770–1914* (London, 1982) pp. 102–19.

27. Ironically, worsted manufactures relied upon the ring spinning that many historians argue should have been adopted by the Lancashire cotton industry.

28. The lag in powerloom weaving was slight between the industries and both used handloom weavers into the 1830s. Farnie, *English Cotton Industry*, pp. 277–84.

29. *Voice of the People and Labour Advocate*, December 12, 1857. In part such sentiments represented an appeal to a mythical golden age of employer–worker relations located in the pre-factory past. For a discussion of such rhetoric and its social and political uses see Joyce, *Visions*, pp. 87–113.

30. Joyce also rules out several areas within Lancashire as exceptions, which allows him to avoid discussions of industrial conflict. See Neville Kirk, *The Growth of Working-Class Reformism in Mid-Victorian England* (Urbana, 1985) pp. 22–4.

31. Joyce, *Visions*, p. 132.

32. A look at the sponsors of his book *Phases of Bradford Life* (Bradford, 1875) makes clear the intended audience of his work.

33. E. M. Sigsworth, *Black Dyke Mills: A History* (Liverpool 1958) pp. 1–68; Thomas Illingworth, *A Sixty Year Retrospective of Bradford Trade*, pamphlet (Bradford, 1883) BCL, p. 30; Select Committee on Scientific Instruction, P.P. 1867–8, Testimony of Henry Ripley, p. 220.

34. For discussion of investment and technical education see Chapter 1.

35. By 1914, the woolen trade had surpassed the worsted trade in importance. D. T. Jenkins and J. C. Malin, 'European Competition in

Woollen Cloth, 1870–1914: The Role of Shoddy', in Mary B. Rose, ed., *International Competition and Strategic Response in the Textile Industries since 1870* (London, 1991) p. 70.

36. See Robert Gray, 'Medical Men and Industrial Labour and the State in Britain, 1830–1850', *Social History*, vol. 16, no. 1 (January 1991) pp. 19–43.

37. For a discussion of paternalism in these terms see Rose, *Limited Livelihoods*, pp. 33–47.

38. Judith Lown, *Women and Industrialization: Gender at Work in Nineteenth-Century England* (Minneapolis, 1990).

39. Joyce, *Work*, pp. 103–23; 134–57. For a critique of Joyce's selectivity about his examples see Kirk, *Reformism*, pp. 22–4, 32–78.

40. J.A. Jowitt, ed., *Model Industrial Communities in Mid-Nineteenth Century Yorkshire* (Bradford, 1986).

41. See Chapter 5.

42. According to the Factory Inspectors Returns, there were 27,855 worsted workers in Bradford in 1871, an increase of only 8 per cent since 1851.

43. Royal Commission on the Hand Loom Weavers, P.P.1838, Report of H.S. Chapman, Assistant Commissioner, p. 587.

44. Henry Forbes, *The Rise Progress and Present State of the Worsted, Alpaca and Mohair Manufactures*, Pamphlet (Bradford, 1852) BCL.

45. Lazonick, *Competitive Advantage*, pp. 88–95.

46. Ibid., pp. 78–88.

47. Ibid., pp. 88–93. Rose, *Limited Livelihoods*, pp. 138–43. For a discussion of skill and technical knowledge see James Donnelly, 'Science, Technology and Industrial Work in Britain, 1860–1930: Towards a New Synthesis', *Social History*, vol. 16, no. 2 (May 1991) pp. 191–201.

48. This is the central point of Sonya Rose's work. For other studies see Deirdre Busfield, 'Skill and the Sexual Division of Labour in the West Riding Textile Industry, 1850–1914', in J.A. Jowitt and A.J. McIvor, *Employers and labour in the English Textile industries 1850–1939* (London, 1988) pp. 153–70. For an additional discussion of the role of gender in cotton textiles see Carol Morgan, 'Women, Work and Consciousness in the Mid-Nineteenth Century English Cotton Industry', *Social History*, vol. 17, no. 1 (January 1992) pp. 23–41 and Mary Freifeld, 'Technological Change and the Self-Acting Mule: A Study of Skill and the Division of Labour', *Social History*, vol. 11, no. 3 (October 1986) pp. 319–43.

49. A lack of size failed to prevent Fred Jowett, a socialist and future MP from becoming a warp beamer. Fenner Brockway, *Socialism Over Sixty Years* (London, 1946) pp. 20–1.

50. Busfield, 'Skill', pp. 162–63 ,

51. Scott, 'Language', pp. 64–5.

52. Royal Commission on Labour, Group C, Textiles, vol. 1, P.P. 1892, Testimony of William Drew, p. 229.

53. J.A. Jowitt, 'The Retardation of Trade Unionism in the Yorkshire Worsted Textile Industry', in Jowitt and McIvor, *Employers and labour*, pp. 89–91.

54. See Chapter 1.

55. The advantage of the cap frame lay in its greater speed; it turned at 5,600 to 7,000 r.p.m., about two to three times as fast as the fly frame. William Cudworth, *Worstedopolis*, pamphlet (Bradford, 1881) BCL, p. 50.

56. Walter McLaren, *Spinning Woolen and Worsted*, pamphlet (Bradford, 1884) BCL, p. 178. Lazonick emphasizes the importance of this arrangement in cotton textiles and the inability of British manufacturers to use mules without using adult males. Lazonick, *Competitive Advantage*, pp. 88–100.

57. Royal Commission on Technical Instruction, P.P. 1884, Report on Foreign Industry, pp. 368–9.

58. Lazonick, *Competitive Advantage*, p. 105.

59. G. H. Wood, Notes on Wages, Huddersfield Polytechnic Archives.

60. *Bradford Observer*, May 20, 1873.

61. The arrangements in the preliminary stages of the spinning process, drawing and doubling, were similar. Local Government Board (P.P. 1873) J. H. Bridges and T. Holmes, 'Report on Proposed changes in Hours and Ages of Employment in Textile Factories', p. 32; Select Committee on Masters and Operatives, P.P.1856, Testimony of William Forster, p. 112; Cudworth, *Worstedopolis*, p. 50.

62. Taylor, 'Bradford and the Worsted Manufacture', p. 429.

63. Ibid., p. 429; Forster, Masters and Operatives, p. 112; Holmes and Bridges, 'Changes in Hours', p. 33.

64. A. L. Bowley, 'Statistics of Wages in the United Kingdom During the Last Hundred Years. Part IX Wages in the Worsted and Woolen Manufacturers of the West Riding of Yorkshire', *Journal of the Royal Statistical Society*, Series A, vol. 65 (March 1902) pp. 102–11.

65. E. A. Forster, testifying to the Royal Commission on Labour estimated the loss to be 8–10 per cent per year due to short-time. Royal Commission on Labour, Group C, vol. 2, Textiles, P.P. 1892, p. 2.

66. *Bradford Observer*, August 31, 1882. It should also be noted that 1871 through to 1874 represented the high point for wages and that they declined some 20% (in nominal terms) by 1883.

67. Jack Reynolds, *The Great Paternalist: Titus Salt and the Growth of Nineteenth-Century Bradford* (London, 1983) pp. 316, 338–9.

68. Forster, Labour Commission, p. 3.

69. This was the opinion of members of the Royal Commission to Inquire into the Depression of Trade and Industry, Second Report, P.P. 1886, p. 258.

70. He even added a note of technological necessity when he pointed out that only children could fit in the narrow space between frames. Report of the Royal Commission on the Working of the Factory Acts, P.P. 1876, testimony of Charles Stead, pp. 615–6.

71. *Textile Manufacturer*, April 1875.

72. E.A. Forster in his testimony before the Royal Commission on Labour estimated that only 16 per cent of operatives were married women in the Bradford district. Forster, Labour Commission, p. 4.

73. Royal Commission on Labour, Group C, 'Textiles', vol. 2 (P.P. 1892) Testimony of Richard Wilson and Alwin Pinder, p. 10. Half of all textile workers were below the age of twenty-five in 1881.

74. Lazonick, *Competitive Advantage*, pp. 106–12.
75. Wesleyan Day School, Logbook, 1874–81; Horton Bank Top Board School, Logbook, 1874–81; Otley Road School, Logbook, 1872–84; Wibsey Wesleyan School, Logbook, 1871–81, BA.
76. Worsted Committee Records, April 1870, BA.
77. Local Government Board, Annual Report, 1880–1, P.P. 1881 Supplement, Appendix A, no. 8, J. Spear, 'On Woolsorters' Disease', pp. 803–5.
78. Bowley, 'Wages', pp. 107–8.
79. Woolsorters Association, Rules, 1840, BA.
80. Friendly Societies Commission P.P. 1874 Report of E. L. Stanley, p. 206; Royal Commission on the Organization and Rules of Trade Unions, Eleventh Report, P.P.1868–9, Appendix J.
81. Cudworth, *Worstedopolis*, p. 46. Cudworth estimated that the new machines increased productivity enormously after 1850, reducing the costs of combing by 75 per cent.
82. Royal Commission on Labour, Group C, vol. 1 'Textiles', P.P. 1892, Testimony of Samuel Shaftoe, pp. 240–52.
83. Holden-Illingworth Letters, December 1865, pp. 390–91, BCL; Forbes, *Rise* pp. 181–2; *Bradford Observer*, May 8, 1872; McLaren, *Spinning*, p. 65; Edward Baines, *Yorkshire Past and Present*, vol. 1, pt. 2 (London, 1874) pp. 341.
84. Select Committee on the Bleaching and Dyeing Works, 2nd Report, P.P. 1878, Testimony of Henry Ripley, pp. 66, 73–6.
85. Commission on the Best Means to Prevent the Pollution of Rivers, (Rivers Pollution Commission) pt. 1, P.P. 1867, pp. xxii–iii; John James, *The History of the Worsted Manufacture in England* (reprint of 1857 edition, London, 1968) pp. 582–3.
86. Ripley, Scientific Instruction, pp. 255–64.
87. Bowley, 'Wages', p. 107–8; G. H. Wood, Wages Statistics. Huddersfield Polytechnic Archives.
88. William Bateson, *The Way We Came* (Bradford, 1928) pp. 8–9, 12–3; Research Notes on the History of the National Union of Dyers, Bleachers and Textile Workers, Bulletin no. 2 (November 1979) pp. 1–3, BCL.
89. *Bradford Observer*, May 20, 1864.
90. John Roberts, 'The Bradford Textile Warehouse 1770–1914', Ph.D dissertation, University of Bradford, 1976, p. 110.
91. *Bradford Observer*, March 23, 1872.
92. Ibid., May 12, 14, 20, June 30, 1864; Roberts, 'Warehouse', pp. 110–15.
93. Here of course is the central issue raised by William Lazonick in his study of the cotton industry – the importance of sharing the rewards of increased productivity with workers in order to both create cooperation and to ensure adequate work effort to fully reap the benefits of technological improvement.
94. Robert Baker, the Inspector of Factories for the Bradford District, reported that the principle grievance of mill hands was the increased number of spindles that each operative tended. Robert Baker, Inspector of Factories, Bradford District, Report, October 31, 1873.
95. Royal Commission on Depression of Trade and Industry, Second Report, P.P. 1886, Testimony of Henry Mitchell, p. 129.

96. Cudworth, *Worstedopolis*, p. 50.
97. Bridges and Holmes, 'Changes in Hours', p. 32.
98. *Bradford Observer*, May 30, 1872.
99. Ibid., June 13, 1872.
100. Ibid., March 20, 1872.
101. Ibid., May 13, 1877.
102. *Textile Manufacturer*, June 1876; Mitchell, *Depression of Trade*, p. 129. Both writers meant a certain level of acquired knowledge and expertise in a task.
103. Taylor, 'Bradford and Worsted Manufacture', p. 429; Cudworth, *Worstedopolis*, p. 57.
104. Royal Commission on Technical Instruction, P.P. 1884, Testimony of Henry Mitchell, p. 242.
105. *Bradford Observer*, May 9, 1872.
106. *Textile Manufacturer*, October, 1881.
107. *Bradford Observer*, June 26, 1877.
108. R. Wilson and A. Pinder, Labour Commission, pp. 15–16.
109. Royal Commission on Labour, Group C, Textiles, vol. 1, P.P. 1892, Testimony of John Downing and Allen Gee, pp. 199–216, and William Drew, p. 223.
110. Drew, Labour Commission, pp. 224–6, Brockway, *Socialism*, pp. 16–7.
111. Medical Officer of Health for the Borough of Bradford, *Ten Year Retrospective*, 1884, pp. 53, 95–6. Observers spoke of the dusty expectorant of worsted mill operatives.
112. J. B. Thompson, 'On the Influence of Woolen Manufactures on Health', *Edinburgh Medical Journal*, vol. iii, pt. 1 (1858) p. 1085.
113. Bradford Medical Officer of Health, Annual Report, 1884.
114. Royal Commission on the Working of the Factory and Workshops Acts, P.P. 1876, Testimony of Matthew Balme, p. 632; Royal Commission on Labour, Group C, Textiles, vol. 1 P.P. 1892, Testimony of William Beaumont, p. 383.
115. For a discussion of these issues in an earlier period see Gray, 'Medical Men', pp. 22–6.
116. The Bradford Infirmary, as well as the Eye and Ear Hospital and the Children's Hospital were funded by local manufacturers. For a discussion of this issue see Ian Inkster, 'Marginal Men: Aspects of the Social Role of the Medical Community in Sheffield 1790–1850', in John Woodward and David Richards, eds, *Health Care and Popular Medicine in Nineteenth Century England* (New York, 1977) pp. 128–63 and John Pickstone, *Medicine and Industrial Society* (Manchester, 1985) pp. 138–55.
117. Medical officers to the Local Government Board, Annual Report, 1880–1, P.P. 1881, John Spears, 'Report on Anthrax in Bradford', pp. 790–5.
118. William Ellis, *A Few Observations on So-Called Sorters' Disease*, pamphlet (Bradford, 1874) BCL.
119. In fact, the Medico-Chirurgical Society voted to communicate with the employers and not the woolsorters' society. Bradford Medico-Chirurgical Society, *Report of the Commission on Woolsorters' Disease*, pamphlet (Bradford, 1882) BCL; Bradford Medico-Chirurgical Society, Minutes, February 3, 1880, BA.

120. Bradford Medico-Chirurgical Society, Minutes, June 14, 1881, BA.
121. The Royal Commission on Labour, Group C, 'Textiles', vol. 1, P.P. 1892, Testimony of Edward Hatton, pp. 254–60
122. *Textile Manufacturer*, April, 1876.
123. Royal Commission on Labour, Group C, 'Textiles', vol. 1, P.P. 1892, Testimony of H. Robinson and J.W. Burgoyne, pp. 397–99.
124. *Textile Manufacturer*, March 1876, p. 64.
125. R. Wilson, A. Pinder, Labour Commission, pp. 4–5.
126. *Bradford Review*, January 5, 1867.
127. *Collinson's Directory of Bradford* (Bradford, 1857) p. 92 BCL; H. Robinson and J.W. Burgoyne, Labour Commission, p. 399.
128. R. Wilson, A. Pinder, Labour Commission, pp. 5–6.
129. *Bradford Observer*, February 9, 1860, February 16, 1880; *Bradford Review*, November 9, 1867; Drew, Labour Commission, p. 223. In fact, the Bradford Royal Infirmary, set up in 1825, existed primarily to treat the victims of industrial accidents; see Chapter 4.
130. W. Fison, *Report on the International Congress of Commerce and Industry, Brussels September 1880*, pamphlet (Bradford, 1880) BCL, p. 42.
131. *Voice of the People and Labour Advocate*, December 12, 1857. For a discussion of this image in popular culture see A. Clark, 'The Politics of Seduction in English Popular Culture, 1748–1848', in J. Radford, ed., *The Progress of Romance: The Politics of Popular Fiction* (New York, 1986), pp. 47–70
132. Robert Gray, 'Medical Men', , pp. 37–40.
133. J. H. Marshall, *The Social Evil In Bradford*, pamphlet (Bradford, 1859) BCL, p. 6.
134. *Bradford Observer*, January 11, 1879. See Jan Lambetz, 'Sexual Harassment in the Nineteenth Century English Cotton Industry', *History Workshop Journal*, no. 19 (Spring 1985) pp. 29–61.
135. Priestley, *Margin Released*, p. 63.
136. Craven and Craven's Waterloo Mills employed thirteen overlookers and 450 workers. Royal Commission on Labour, Group C, Textiles, vol. 1, P.P. 1892, Testimony of John Watson and Greenwood Sutcliffe, p. 428.
137. In Forster's Queensbury Mill, six overlookers supervised 300 weavers.
138. Forster, Masters and Operatives, pp. 113–4. This practice resembled that of the US cotton industry, rather than the British cotton industry, where miners enjoyed greater autonomy in work and hiring. Lazonick, *Competitive Advantage*, pp. 115–37.
139. In the 1881 census sample, all overlookers were men.
140. Power Loom Overlookers Society Branch no. 2, Rules 1866, BCL.
141. Forster, Masters and Operatives, p. 111; Bowley, 'Wages', p. 106.
142. *Bradford Observer*, March 26, 1857, January 7, 1864.
143. *Textile Manufacturer*, December, 1875, p. 522.
144. Forster, Masters and Operatives, p. 110.
145. Ibid., 110–11; *Voice of the People and Labour Advocate*, December 12, 1857.
146. The rules of the Managers and Overlookers's Society urged the overlooker to treat the concern of his employer as if it were his own. Rules of Managers and Overlookers Society, 1873, BCL.
147. Brockway, *Socialism*, p. 21.

148. Ripley, Scientific Instruction, p. 264.
149. See Chapter 4.
150. Fiftieth Anniversary of the Amalgamation of the Managers and Over-lookers Society, pamphlet (Bradford,1927) BCL.
151. Stanley, Friendly Societies, p. 206.
152. Centenary Celebration of Bradford Power Loom Overlookers Society, pamphlet (Bradford, 1944) BCL.
153. Fiftieth Anniversary, p. 72.
154. Power Loom Overlookers, Branch no. 2, Rules 1866, BCL.
155. Power Loom Overlookers, Branch no. 2, Records and Minutes 1862–1881, BA.
156. Fiftieth Anniversary, p. 11.
157. *Bradford Observer*, January 13, 1872 and June 22, 1871. One has the example of an overlooker invoking the Chartist past in a suffrage demonstration, *Bradford Review*, April 20, 1867.
158. Fiftieth Anniversary, p. 11; Royal Commission on Labour, Group C, Textiles, vol. 1, P.P. 1892, Statement of Stuff Makers-up Society.
159. The Power Loom Overlookers became a trade union by 1887, the Managers and Overlookers remained uncommitted before 1912.
160. For more on the Worsted Committee in the late eighteenth and early nineteenth century see John Styles, 'Embezzlement, Industry and the Law in England, 1500–1800', in Maxine Berg, *et al.*, eds, *Manufacture in Town and Country Before the Factory* (Cambridge, 1983) pp. 173–205 and Richard Soderlund, 'Crime, Law and Labor: The Policing of Worsted Work in the West Riding of Yorkshire, 1815–1845', Paper presented at the Social Science History Association Meeting, October 1990.
161. Worsted Committee, Minutes, April 1852, BA.
162. Ibid., June 1858; Stella Macleod, 'The Changing Face of the Bradford Borough Bench 1848–1980', BA Thesis, University of Bradford, 1980, p. 72; Reynolds, *Great Paternalist*, pp. 162–3.
163. Worsted Committee, Record of Convictions, 1851–81, BA.
164. Ibid., June 1875.
165. Adrian Randall, 'Peculiar Perquisites and Pernicious Practices: Embezzlement in the West of England Woolen Industry, 1750–1840', *International Review of Social History*, vol. XXXV, pt. 2 (1990) pp. 193–220.
166. Worsted Committee, Record of Convictions, October 1873.
167. Committee on Council on Education, pp. 1871, 'Report of Rev. R. Wilden, Inspector of Church of England Schools, Bradford District', pp. 246–7.
168. Worsted Committee, Minute book, September 1862.
169. Ibid., June 1870.
170. Ibid., March 1880. The waste dealers, warehouses and brothels of Bradford were the frequent target of searches.
171. Ibid., June 1850.
172. *Bradford Observer*, March 13, 1860.
173. W. Hamish Fraser, *Trade Unions and Society* (Totowa, 1974) pp. 185–207; Jonathan Spain, 'Trade Unionists, Gladstonian Liberals, and the Labour Law Reforms of 1875', in Eugenio Biagini and Alastair Reid, eds, *Currents of Radicalism: Popular Radicalism, organized labour and party politics in Britain, 1850–1914* (Cambridge, 1991) pp. 109–33.

174. *Bradford Observer*, June 15, 1867. The magistrates allowed the black-listing of a journeyman tailor by master tailors.
175. In September 1869, an inspector noted his problems in dealing with numerous 'idle and unprincipled warp dressers and wool sorters' in the previous quarter. Worsted Committee Records, BA.
176. Jowitt, 'Retardation', pp. 84–106.
177. *Bradford Observer*, September 12, 1867, January 21, 1871, December 7, 1871, May 8, 1872; *Bradford Weekly Telegraph*, January 1, 1870.
178. Records of G. H. Wood, Notes on Strikes, Huddersfield Polytechnic Archives.
179. *Bradford Observer*, September 6–13, 1866 and January 1, 1870.
180. Ibid., September, 12, 1871.
181. Bateson, *Way We Came*, pp. 18–27; *Bradford Observer*, February 3–March 9, 1880.
182. Bateson, *Way We Came*, pp. 14–5; History of the Dyers, pp. 4–5.
183. Robinson and Burgoyne, Labour Commission, pp. 396–402.
184. National Union of Woolsorters Cashbook, 1863–81, BA.
185. Hatton, Labour Commission, pp. 252–60.
186. *Textile Manufacturer*, July 1876.
187. *Bradford Observer*, August 14–September 5, 1882.
188. Sonya Rose, 'Gender Antagonism and Class Conflict: Exclusionary Strategies of Male Trade Unionists in Nineteenth-Century Britain', *Social History*, vol. 13, no. 2 (May 1988) pp. 191–208.
189. Certainly this was the case during wildcat actions such as the Manningham Mills strike in 1882.
190. Joanna Bornat, 'Lost Leaders: Women, Trade Unionism and the Case of the General Union of Textile Workers', in Angela John, *Unequal Opportunities: Women's Employment in England 1800–1918* (Oxford, 1986) p. 212. For the Manningham strike see Cyrill Pearce, *The Manningham Mills Strike, Bradford December 1890–April 1891*, University of Hull Occasional Papers in Economic and Social History (1975).
191. Laybourn and Reynolds, *Liberalism*; E. P. Thompson, 'Tom Maguire', pp. 276–316.
192. Report on Trade Unions, 1908–10, P.P. 1912–3, pp. 35–41.
193. Jowitt, 'Retardation', pp. 191–3.
194. Bornat, 'Lost Leaders', pp. 218–27.
195. Wally Seccombe, 'Patriarchy Stabilized: the Construction of the Male Breadwinner Wage Norm in Nineteenth Century Britain', *Social History*, vol. 11, no. 1 (January 1986) pp. 53–76.
196. This trend began to affect other trades as well in the 1880s. See Joseph Melling, '"Non-Commissioned Officers": British Employers and Their Supervisory Workers, 1880–1920', *Social History*, vol. 5, no. 2 (May 1980) pp. 183–220.

3 Politics in Bradford 1850–1900

1. Jonathan Glyde, *Plea for a Park*, pamphlet (Bradford, 1853) BCL.
2. Alfred Illingworth, *Fifty Years of Politics*, pamphlet (Bradford, 1905) BCL p. 15.

3. Patrick Joyce, *Visions of the People* (Cambridge, 1991) pp. 56–84; Euginio Biagini, *Liberty, Retrenchment and Reform: Popular Liberalism in the Age of Gladstone, 1860–1880* (Cambridge, 1992).

4. Biagini argues that this level offers the true test of popular Liberalism in this era. Biagini, *Liberty*, pp. 319–28.

5. See Neville Kirk, *The Growth of Working Class Reformism in Mid-Victorian England* (Urbana, 1985) pp. 174–240.

6. Joyce, *Visions*, 56–84.

7. Theodore Koditschek, *Class Formation and urban-industrial society: Bradford, 1750–1850* (Cambridge, 1990) pp. 135–61; Jack Reynolds, *The Great Paternalist: Titus Salt an the Growth of Nineteenth-Century Bradford* (London, 1983) pp. 5–18; A. Elliott, 'The Incorporation of Bradford', *Northern History*, vol. 15 (1979) pp. 157–63; D. G. Wright, 'A Radical Borough: Parliamentary Politics in Bradford', *Northern History*, vol. 4 (1969) pp. 132–6.

8. Elliott, 'Incorporation', pp. 157–8; Koditschek, *Class Formation*, pp. 320–57.

9. Koditschek, *Class Formation*, pp. 228–51. For an interesting summary of these views see Illingworth, *Fifty Years*.

10. Wright, 'Radical Borough', pp. 163–5. Such charges focused on the practice of treating and the undue influence of employers upon their dependents.

11. Ibid., p. 145.

12. Koditschek, *Class Formation*, pp. 414–44; Cecil Driver, *Tory Radical: The Life of Richard Oastler* (New York, 1946); Robert Gray, 'The Languages of Factory Reform in Britain, c. 1830–1860',, in Patrick Joyce, *Historical Meanings of Work* (Cambridge, 1987) pp. 157–67.

13. Koditschek, *Class Formation*, pp. 342–44; Reynolds, *Great Paternalist* pp. 103–6.

14. David Ashworth, 'The Treatment of Poverty', in D. G. Wright and J. A. Jowitt, eds, *Victorian Bradford* (Bradford, 1981) pp. 87–8.

15. Elliott, 'Municipal Government', pp. 129.

16. Ibid., pp. 140–1.

17. D. G. Wright, 'Politics and Opinion in Nineteenth Century Bradford', PhD dissertation, University of Leeds, 1966, pp. 149–58.

18. Reynolds, *Great Paternalist*, pp. 329–30. For a view of the Bradford caucus see M. Ostrogorski, *Democracy and the Organization of Political Parties* (London, 1902) pp. 194–203. For discussion of Liberal party development see H.J. Hanham, *Elections and Party Management* (London, 1959) and John Vincent, *Formation of the Liberal Party 1857–1868* (London, 1966).

19. Bradford Chamber of Commerce, minutebook and Yearbook, 1851–71, BA.

20. The Chamber sponsored a speech by A. P. Mundella, a stocking manufacturer and MP on ways of arbitrating labor disputes in 1868. A. J. Mundella, *Arbitration as a Means of Preventing Strikes*, pamphlet (Bradford, 1868) BCL.

21. Elliott, 'Municipal Government', pp. 140–1.

22. David James, 'William Byles and the *Bradford Observer*', in Wright and Jowitt, *Victorian Bradford*, pp. 115–36.
23. For example the *Textile Manufacturer* and the *Nonconformist* appealed to the local elite.
24. See Vincent, *Formation*, pp. 1–138.
25. Wright, 'Politics', pp. 424–65.
26. D. G. Wright, 'Mid-Victorian Bradford: 1850–1880', *Bradford Antiquary* (1982) p. 77; Patrick Joyce, *Work, Society and Politics* (New Brunswick, 1984) pp. 240–67.
27. Biagini, *Liberty*, pp. 193–253.
28. E.P. Thompson, *The Making of the English Working Class* (London, 1966) pp. 401–17. E. P. Thompson, 'On History, Sociology and Historical Relevance', *British Journal of Sociology*, vol. 27, no. 3 (September 1976) pp. 387–402.
29. Wright, 'Mid-Victorian', pp. 35–47; Elliott, 'Municipal Government', pp. 166–9.
30. Dissenters Defence League, *Report of Meeting, December 12, 1861*, pamphlet (Bradford, 1861) BCL.
31. George Edward Lyon, *Church of England – The Church of the People*, pamphlet (Bradford, 1874) BCL; Dr. Clarke, *Political Considerations for Working Men-A Lecture*, pamphlet (Bradford, 1870) BCL.
32. Bradford Church Defence Association, Proceedings, November 21, 1861, BCL; John Edward Dibb, *The Fallacies of the Liberation Society*, pamphlet (Bradford, 1874) BCL, pp. 10–7.
33. Lyon, *Church of England*, p. 14.
34. Henry Leach, *The Irish Church*, pamphlet (Bradford, n.d. (1860s?)) p. 13.
35. Bradford Church Defence Association Proceedings, November 21, 1861, p. 12.
36. For a discussion of these issues, see Michael Hurst, 'Liberal Versus Liberal: The General Election of 1874 in Bradford and Sheffield', *The Historical Journal*, vol. xv, no. 4 (1972) pp. 669–713; David Wright','Liberal Versus Liberal, 1874: Some Comments', *The Historical Journal*, vol. xvi, no. 4 (1973) pp. 597–603; Michael Hurst, 'Liberal Versus Liberal, 1874: A Rebuttal', *The Historical Journal*, vol. xvii, no. 1 (1974) pp. 162–4.
37. *Bradford Observer*, November 25, 1881; US Consul in Bradford, Letter August 4, 1881, BCL.
38. Andrew Byles, *Reciprocity and Free Trade*, pamphlet (Bradford, 1879) BCL, p. 12.
39. See Bernard Semmel, *Imperialism and Social Reform: English Social Imperial Thought 1895–1914* (London, 1960).
40. W. F. Ecroyd, *The Policy of Self Help, Two Letters to the Bradford Observer*, pamphlet (Bradford, 1879) BCL, Letters 1 and 2.
41. W. F. Ecroyd, *A Speech in Reply to the Attack Upon the Policy and Advocates of the Fair Trade by W.E. Gladstone*, pamphlet (Bradford, 1881) BCL.
42. S. C. Lister, *Mr Forster and Free Trade, Letter to the Times, February 6, 1879*, pamphlet (Bradford, 1879) BCL.

43. S. C. Lister, *Free Trade in Corn and Protection to Labour*, pamphlet (Bradford, 1880) BCL.

44. Ibid., p. 6.

45. Henry Mitchell, *The French Treaty, 2 letters to the Bradford Morning Chronicle*, pamphlet (Bradford, 1877) BCL.

46. Byles, *Reciprocity*, pp. 6–7.

47. *Bradford Observer*, December 6, 1881.

48. Keith Laybourn, 'Yorkshire Trade Unions and the Great Depression.' PhD dissertation, University of Manchester, 1976, p. 91.

49. For a discussion of these issues see Jon Lawrence, 'Popular Politics and the Limitations of Party: Wolverhampton, 1867–1900', in Eugenio Biagini and Alastair Reid, eds, *Currents of Radicalism* (Cambridge, 1991) pp. 65–85.

50. Keith Laybourn and Jack Reynolds, *Liberalism and the Rise of Labour 1890–1918* (New York, 1984) pp. 76–8.

51. *Bradford Observer*, November 25, 1881.

52. Eric Sigsworth, *Black Dyke Mills: A History* (Livepool, 1958) p. 105–7.

53. John James, *The History of the Worsted Manufacture in England* (reprint of 1857 edition, London, 1968) pp. 168–9; J.T. Ward, *Chartism* (London, 1973) pp. 89–90.

54. Reynolds, *Great Paternalist*, pp. 28–33; Jonathan Smith, 'The Strike of 1825', in Wright and Jowitt, *Victorian Bradford*, pp. 63–80.

55. J. T. Ward, *The Factory Movement 1830–1855* (New York, 1962) pp. 182–3.

56. A. Peacock, 'Bradford Chartism 1838–40', Borthwick Papers no. 36, 1969, pp. 9–28; Koditschek, *Class Formation*, pp. 484–516.

57. Reynolds, *Great Paternalist*, p. 105.

58. Peacock, 'Bradford Chartism', pp. 38–40; Wright, 'Politics', pp. 144–7; Koditschek, *Class Formation*, pp. 484–516.

59. Gareth Stedman Jones, *Languages of Class* (Cambridge, 1983) pp. 90–178; 53–67.

60. Reynolds, *Great Paternalist*, pp. 34–5, 110–11.

61. Ibid., pp. 146–7; Koditschek, *Class Formation*, pp. 517–65.

62. Elliot, 'Municipal Government', p. 116.

63. Reynolds, *Great Paternalist*, pp. 117–9.

64. Ibid., pp. 103–6. The records of the Bradford Reform Union, 1842–50, BA, show that a number of skilled working men, particularly in the worsted trade, had joined with progressive manufacturers and merchants in calling for an expanded suffrage, but not the Charter.

65. Ibid., pp. 130–31; Koditschek, *Class Formation*, pp. 521–23.

66. Joan Scott, 'On Language, Gender, and Working-Class History',, in Joan Scott, *Gender and the Politics of History* (New York, 1988) pp. 53–67; Robert Gray, 'Factory Legislation and the Gendering of Jobs in the North of England, 1830–1860', *Gender and History*, vol. 5, no. 1 (Spring 1991) pp. 56–80.

67. Reynolds, *Great Paternalist*, pp. 194–5, 204–5; Elliot, 'Municipal Government', pp. 148–50.

68. *Bradford Review*, September 14, 1867.

69. Laybourne and Reynolds, *Liberalism*, p. 17.
70. Bradford Workingman's Conservative Association Records, 1870–80, BA.
71. *Bradford Observer*, December 5, 1880. It merged with the Conservative Club, a more elite-controlled group.
72. Captain Lepper, *Right Road to a Bull's Eye*, pamphlet (Bradford,1863) BCL; Records of Bradford Volunteers, BA. For a discussion of the Volunteer Corps, see Hugh Cunningham, *The Volunteer Force* (London, 1975).
73. *Dissenters Defense League Meeting; The Suffrage, A Series of Articles from the Nonconformist*, pamphlet (Bradford, n.d. (1860s?)) BCL.
74. Malcolm Hardman, *Ruskin and Bradford: An Experiment in Victorian Cultural History* (Manchester, 1986) pp. 224–31.
75. Kenneth Brown, 'Nonconformity and trade unionism: the Sheffield outrages of 1866', in Biagini and Reid, *Radicalism*, p. 90.
76. Biagini admits this limitation of Radicalism, but fails to develop this point systematically. Biagini, *Liberty*, pp. 306–9.
77. S. Heynemann, *Review of the Speech of Alfred Illingworth at the Bradford Debating Society*, pamphlet (London, 1880) BCL.
78. Letters and Papers of the Reform Union, 1850–1860s, BA.
79. *Bradford Observer*, November 25, 1871.
80. Dibb, *Fallacies*, pp. 5, 9.
81. James Campbell, *Lessons in Social Science*, pamphlet (Bradford, 1859) BCL.
82. Reynolds, *Great Paternalist*, pp. 117–33; Elliott, 'Municipal Government', pp. 130–48.
83. Medical Officers of the Privy Council, Fourteenth Report, J. Nettien Radcliffe, 'Defects in the Sanitary Administration of Bradford', P.P. 1873, pp. 9–10.
84. Commission on the Best Means to Prevent the Pollution of Rivers (Rivers Pollution Commission) P.P. 1867, Minutes of Evidence, pp. xxii–iii.
85. Michael Mortimore, 'Urban Growth in Bradford and Its Environs, 1800–1960', MA Thesis, University of Leeds, 1963, pp. 102–3.
86. Elliott, 'Municipal Government', pp. 130–1. This faction continued to exist throughout this period. In a pamphlet published in 1881 entitled *A Circular to the Ratepayers and Property Owners of Bradford*, this group attacked the city council for its spending and inspections.
87. See Eugenio Biagini, 'Popular Liberals, Gladstonian Finance, and the Debate on Taxation, 1860–1874', in Biagini and Reid, *Radicalism*, pp. 134–62.
88. In the same time period, the population increased about 80 per cent. Bradford Corporation Report Book, 1847, BCL; Bradford Borough Police Report, 1882, BCL.
89. Police pay was comparable to that of the upper working class, but without the disadvantage of lost time or layoffs. Most made 15s. to 18s. a week in 1847, with the rate for officers and sergeants higher.
90. David Jones, *Crime, Protest, Community and Police in Nineteenth Century Britain* (London, 1982); Robert Storch, 'The Plague of Blue

Locusts: Police Reform and Popular Resistance in Northern England, 1840–1857', *International Review of Social History*, vol. XX, pt.1 (1975) pp. 61–90; For reform of the borough police see Elliott, 'Municipal government', pp. 131–3. Although the threat of revolution receded after 1848, the Bradford town fathers, all good pacifist Liberals and anti-militarists, acquiesced to the presence of the army in Bowling.

91. One candidate defended himself against charges that he used his borough offices to support his private interests by charging his opponent with using Corporation funds to improve an estate he owned. Charles Gott, *Election Manifesto, 1875 Municipal Election-Manningham Ward*, pamphlet (Bradford, 1875) BCL.

92. Bob West, 'Water and Worstedopolis', Unpublished paper, 1982, BCL. Attempts to expand the water supply in the 1860s brought demands for compensation by affected landowners, many of whom benefited from the increased supply as mill owners, Bradford Waterworks and Improvement Bill, P.P. 1868, Minutes of Evidence.

93. Reynolds, *Great Paternalist*, pp. 330–1; Ben Hardacre, *Lord H.W. Ripley*, pamphlet (Bradford, 1874) BCL; Anonymous, *A Lay of the Bradford Election, October 1867*, pamphlet (Bradford, 1867) BCL; Anonymous, *Bradford Borough Election 1874–Replies to Mr Forster*, pamphlet (Bradford, 1874) BCL.

94. *Bradford Observer*, August 4, 1873.

95. D.G. Wright, 'The Second Reform Agitation 1857–67', in Wright and Jowitt, *Victorian Bradford*, pp. 189–90. For more on the Positivists and a prominent local supporter, J.H. Bridges, see Royden Harrison, *Before the Socialists* (London, 1965) pp. 251–342.

96. Letter of W. Sharman, trade union leader, *Bradford Review*, September 7, 1867.

97. Reynolds, *Great Paternalist*, pp. 326–39.

98. Euginio Biagini, 'British Trade Unions and Popular Political Economy, 1860–1880', *Historical Journal*, vol. 30, no. 4 (1987) pp. 811–40.

99. For this see *The Law of Wages – Four Essays by Working Men of Bradford*, pamphlet (Bradford, 1859) BCL.

100. *Bradford Observer*, April 28, 1864.

101. *Bradford Review*, June 15, 1867.

102. Ibid., June 22, 1867.

103. Malcolm Ross, *An Address to Trades Unionists on the Question of Strikes*, pamphlet (Bradford, n.d. (1860s?)) BCL.

104. The meeting with Mundella was filled with accusations of bad faith because of the refusal of employers to allow arbitration. Mundella, *Arbitration*, pp. 21–2. Henry Ripley, the dyer, at one point supported arbitration, but rejected it when it was proposed during the dyers' strike in 1880. *Bradford Observer*, February 3–12, 1880.

105. For a discussion of arbitration see Biagini, 'Trade Unions', pp. 832–38.

106. Royal Commission on Labour, Group C, 'Textiles', vol. 1 P.P. 1892, testimony of E.A. Forster, p. 263; 'The Yorkshire Worsted Manufacture', *Bulletin of the National Association of Wool Manufacturers* (1895) pp. 388–9.

107. *Bradford Review*, July 20, 1867.

108. Select Committtee on Masters and Operatives, P.P. 1856, Testimony of William Forster, p. 110; Anonymous, *The Age of the Long Chimneys or the Rule of the Factory Lords*, pamphlet (Bradford, n.d.) BCL.

109. Robert Baker, *Condition of the Working Class of Bradford,* pamphlet (Bradford, 1851) BCL.

110. Jonathan Spain, 'Trade Unionists, Gladstonian Liberals and the Labour Law Reforms of 1875', in Biagini and Reid, *Radicalism*, p. 117.

111. Anonymous, *The Dispute in the Iron Trade: Freedom and Slavery in the Balance, Which is to Go Down?*, pamphlet (Bradford, 1864); Anonymous, *An Appeal to Ministers of Religion and the Religious Public Generally*, pamphlet (Bradford, 1850).

112. *Bradford Observer*, December 27, 1871. Keith McClelland, 'Time to Work, Time to Live: Some Aspects of Work and the Reformation of Class in Britain, 1850–1880', in Joyce, *Historical Meanings*, pp. 190–200.

113. *Bradford Review*, December 28, 1867.

114. *The Dispute in the Iron Trade*; *Bradford Observer*, April–September 1864.

115. Eleventh and Final Report of the Royal Commissioners Appointed to Inquire into the Organization and Rules of Trades Unions and other Associations, P.P. 1868–9, Appendix J, p. 284.

116. Ibid., pp. 284, 306, 309.

117. G.H. Wood, Wage Notes, Huddersfield Polytechnic Archives.

118. Royal Commission on Friendly Societies and Benefit Societies, Report of Assistant Commissioner, E. L. Stanley, P.P. 1874, p. 206.

119. For more on this struggle see Henry Pelling, 'Trade Unions, Workers and the Law'; in Henry Pelling, *Popular Politics and Society in Late Victorian Britain* (London, 1968) pp. 62–81; Spain, 'Trade unionists', pp. 109–33; W. Hamish Fraser, *Trade Unions and Society* (Totowa, 1974) pp. 185–207.

120. Stella Macleod, 'The Changing Face of the Bradford Borough Bench 1848–1980', B.A. Thesis, University of Bradford, 1980, p. 72.

121. For example the magistrates allowed the blacklisting of a journeyman tailor by local employers, *Bradford Observer*, June 15, 1867.

122. Reynolds, *The Great Paternalist*, pp. 162–163.

123. *Bradford Observer*, October 12, 1868.

124. Bradford Trade Council, Minutes, June 10, 1873, BA.

125. Royal Commission on Labour, Group C, 'Textiles', vol. 1, pp. 1892, Testimony of Willam Drew and Ben Turner, p. 226; Testimony of E.A. Forster, pp. 267–8.

126. Gray, 'Languages of Factory Reform', pp. 143–79; For an earlier period see Noel Thompson, *The People's Science: The Popular Political Economy of Exploitation and Crisis 1816–1834* (Cambridge, 1984).

127. *Bradford Observer*, February 6, 1866.

128. Wright, 'Politics', pp. 855–61.

129. Reynolds, *Great Paternalist*, pp. 149, 157. The Bradford Chamber of Commerce in 1874 helped organize a campaign against the extension of the Factory Act. Bradford Chamber of Commerce, Yearbook, 1874, BA.

130. Letter from 'One of the Unwashed', *Bradford Observer*, March 22, 1872. This was one of a number on the issue.

131. Reynolds, *Great Paternalist*, pp. 337–45.
132. *Bradford Observer.*, January 27, 1882.
133. Ibid., November 24, 1882.
134. Patricia Hollis, *Ladies Elect: Women in English Local Government 1865–1914* (Oxford, 1987) pp. 178–85.
135. Laybourn and Reynolds, *Liberalism*, pp. 16–39.
136. H.F. Moorhouse, 'The Incorporation of the Working Class', *British Journal of Sociology*, vol. VII, no. 3 (September, 1973) pp. 341–59.
137. Ibid., pp. 349–52.
138. See Chapter 2.
139. Thomas Illingworth, *Distributional Reform*, pamphlet (Bradford, 1885) BCL.
140. *Textile Manufacturer*, September 1879.
141. Lister, 'Forster and Free Trade'.
142. Bradford Chamber of Commerce, minutebook, June 5, 1874.
143. *Bradford Observer*, February 3, 1880.
144. Ibid., February. 4, 1880.
145. Ibid., February 5, 1880.
146. Ibid., September 2, 1882.
147. Jack Reynolds, 'Reflections on Saltaire', in J.A. Jowitt, ed., *Model Industrial Communities* (Bradford, 1986) p. 57.
148. *Textile Manufacturer*, July 1876.
149. Cyrill Pearce, *The Manningham Mills Strike, Bradford December 1890–April 1891*, University of Hull Occasional Papers in Economic and Social History (1975).
150. E.P. Thompson, 'Homage to Tom Maguire', in Asa Briggs and John Saville, *Essays in Labour History* (New York, 1960) pp. 279–86.
151. Keith Laybourn, 'The Defence of the Bottom Dog, The ILP in Local Politics', in Wright and Jowitt, *Victorian Bradford*, p. 231.
152. Fenner Brockway, *Socialism Over Sixty Years* (London, 1946) pp. 37–8.
153. Thompson, 'Tom Maguire', 1960, pp. 279–316; Keith Laybourn, 'Defence', pp. 223–44; Jack Reynolds and Keith Laybourn, 'The Emergence of the ILP in Bradford', *International Review of Social History*, vol. XX, pt.3 (1975) pp. 313–46; Laybourn and Reynolds, *Liberalism*, passim.
154. Biagini, *Liberty*, p. 12.
155. Jowett later recalled long hours of reading and discussion of works by Carlyle, Ruskin and Morris in the early years of the Socialist League. Brockway, *Socialism* pp. 29–31. For more on ethical socialism see David Howell, *British Workers and the Independent Labour Party 1888–1906* (Manchester, 1983) pp. 352–62.
156. Brockway, *Socialism*, p. 31.
157. Biagini, *Liberty*, p. 257–312.
158. Fred Jowett, 'What Made Me A Socialist', cited in Brockway, *Socialism*, p. 28.
159. Laybourn and Reynolds, *Liberalism*, pp. 4–7.
160. Cited in Laybourn, 'Defence',, p. 225.
161. Joyce, *Visions*, pp. 77–84; P.F. Clark, *Lancashire and the New Liberalism* (Cambridge, 1971).

162. For a discussion of the ambivalent relationship between such men and the culture of the working class see Chris Waters, *British Socialists and the Politics of Popular Culture, 1884–1914* (Stanford, 1984).

4 High and Low Culture in Victorian Bradford

1. *Leeds Times*, July 26, 1856. Cited in Robert Storch, 'Introduction: Persistence and Change in Nineteenth-Century Popular Culture', in Robert Storch, ed., *Popular Culture and Custom in Nineteenth-Century England* (London, 1982) p. 2.
2. The Mayor's Committee on the Moral Condition of the Town, Photocopy of the original report printed in the *Bradford Observer*, March 7, 1850.
3. For the notion of the darkest inner city see Gareth Stedman-Jones, *Outcast London* (London, 1971) pp. 241–61.
4. Leonore Davidoff and Catherine Hall, *Family Fortunes: Men and Women of the English middle class, 1780–1850* (Chicago, 1987) pp. 357–96.
5. In 1851 only half of Bradford's inhabitants were native born. Jack Reynolds, *The Great Paternalist: Titus Salt and the Growth of Nineteenth Century Bradford* (London, 1983) pp. 23–24; C. Richardson, *A Geography of Bradford* (Bradford, 1976) pp. 91–102.
6. Friedrich Engels, *The Condition of the Working Class in England in 1844* (Stanford, 1968) p. 49.
7. Richardson, *Geography*, pp. 74–5.
8. Ibid., pp. 97–8, 107–20; C. Richardson, 'Irish Settlement in Mid-Nineteenth Century Bradford', *Yorkshire Bulletin of Social and Economic Research*, vol. 20, no. 1 (May 1968) pp. 40–57.
9. Engels, *Condition*, p. 49.
10. Richardson, *Geography*, 105–8. The creation of commuter rail services and other forms of public transportation from the 1870s on facilitated this process. See Richard Dennis, *English Industrial Cities of the Nineteenth Century* (Cambridge, 1984).
11. Igor Webb, 'The Bradford Wool Exchange: Industrial Capitalism and the Popularity of Gothic', *Victorian Studies*, vol. 20, no. 1 (Autumn 1976) pp. 45–68.
12. Theodore Koditschek, *Class Formation and Urban Industrial Society: Bradford 1750–1850* (Cambridge, 1990) pp. 395–413; R.J. Morris, *Class, Sect and Party: the Making of the British Middle Classes, Leeds 1820–1850* (Manchester, 1990) 161–227.
13. J.A. Jowitt, 'The Pattern Of Religion in Victorian Bradford', in D.G. Wright and J.A. Jowitt, eds, *Victorian Bradford* (Bradford, 1981) pp. 45–6; Koditschek, *Class Formation*, pp. 252–92.
14. See also Robert Morris, *Class*, pp. 161–203, and Davidoff and Hall, *Family Fortunes*, pp. 416–49.
15. Koditschek, *Class Formation*, pp. 293–319. Both the Town Mission and the Mechanics' Institute saw themselves as a means of exerting influence upon the working class. Bradford Town Mission, Annual Report, 1850–1851; Bradford Mechanics' Institute, Annual Reports, 1851–81, both BCL.

16. Koditschek makes this point. Koditschek, *Class Formation*, p. 315.
17. Jowitt, 'Pattern Of Religion', in Wright and Jowitt, eds, *Victorian Bradford*, pp. 39–43.
18. In fact the leader of the Southcottians after the death of Joanna Southcott was a Bradfordian. E.P. Thompson, *The Making of the English Working Class* (New York, 1966) pp. 350–402.
19. William Cudworth, *Methodism in Bradford*, pamphlet (Bradford 1878) BCL.
20. For a discussion of middle-class religious patterns in Bradford see Koditschek, *Class Formation*, pp. 252–92.
21. Jowitt, 'Pattern of Religion', p. 44.
22. Ibid., pp. 46–7.
23. J.H. Marshall, *Our Great Work and How to Do It*, pamphlet (Bradford, 1859) BCL.
24. Town Mission Report, 1850–1, 1851–2, 1866–7, 1874–5, 1878–9, BCL.
25. Ibid., 1850–1.
26. Ibid.
27. Ibid., 1851–2.
28. Ibid.
29. Marshall, *Great Work*, p. 19.
30. Town Mission Report, 1866–7.
31. Ibid., 1874–5, 1878–9.
32. Jowitt, 'Pattern of Religion', pp 48–52; *Census of Public Worship*, pamphlet (Bradford, 1882) BCL.
33. Colin Garnett, 'Irish Immigration and the Roman Catholic Church in Bradford 1835–1880', PhD dissertation, University of Bradford, 1984, pp. 142–201.
34. Select Committee on Friendly Societies, P.P. 1854–5, Testimony of Squire Auty, pp. 106–7;. Rev. Henry Leach, *The Irish Church*, pamphlet (Bradford, 1868) BCL.
35. *Public Worship*, p. 42.
36. Some material still survives, such as a pamphlet attacking a minister for his views on the Sabbath, A Working Man, *Reply to the Rev. Brewin Grant's Half-Penny Letter*, pamphlet (Bradford, 1853) BCL.
37. Reynolds, *Great Paternalist*, pp. 186–8; *Bradford Observer*, March 28, 1882.
38. *Bradford Observer*, November 22 and 25, 1881.
39. This is one key part of Cox's argument about the nature of religious belief in late Victorian Britain. Jeffery Cox, *The English Churches in a Secular Society: Lambeth, 1870–1930* (Oxford, 1982) pp. 3–20
40. *Public Worship*, p. 47.
41. Victor Bailey, 'Will the Real Bill Bailey Stand Up? Towards a Role Analysis of Mid-Victorian Working-Class Respectability', *Journal of Social History*, vol. 12, no. 1 (Fall 1979) pp. 336–53.
42. Swire Smith, *Educational Comparisons: Remarks on Industrial Schools*, pamphlet (Bradford, 1873) BCL, p. 193.
43. W.B Stephens, *Education, Literacy and Society, 1830–1870: the geography of diversity in provincial England* (Manchester, 1987) p. 94. David Mitch also notes this initial lag in literacy in textile areas: David Mitch,

The Rise of Popular Literacy in Victorian England: The Influence of Private Choice and Public Policy (Philadelphia, 1992) p. 188.

44. Geoffrey Fenn, 'The Development of Education in An Industrial Town During the Nineteenth Century', University of Leeds, Institute of Educational Researches and Studies (1952–3) pp. 29–30.

45. Commissioners Appointed to Inquire into the State of Popular Education In England (Newcastle Commission) P.P. 1861, 'Report of H. S. Winder on Bradford (Yorks) and Rochdale (Lancs)' pp. 234–6. For a general discussion of the Sunday School movement see, Thomas Laqueur, *Religion and Respectability: Sunday Schools and Working-Class Culture 1780–1850* (New Haven, 1976).

46. Norman Brian Roper, 'The Contribution of Non-Conformists to the Development of Education in Bradford in the Nineteenth Century', MEd Thesis, University of Leeds, 1976, pp. 65–97; The Nonconformist Bradford Sunday School Union reported 24,636 scholars in 1878. Bradford Sunday School Union, Report, 1878, BCL.

47. Fenn, 'Development of Education', pp. 33–37.

48. Mayor's Committee on the Moral Condition of the Town.

49. For the issue of apprenticeship see Keith McClelland, 'Time to Work, Time to Live: Some Aspects of Work and the Reformation of Class in Britain, 1850–1880,: in Patrick Joyce, ed., *Historical Meanings of Work* (Cambridge, 1987) pp. 190–5; Charles More, *Skill and the English Working Class 1870–1914* (London, 1980).

50. Winder, 'Popular Education', pp. 178–9, 186–7.

51. Roper, 'Contribution of Nonconformists', pp. 113–53; Fenn, Development of Education', pp. 37–9, Part II, pp. 7–9.

52. Winder, 'Popular Education', p. 183.

53. Ibid., pp. 182–3.

54. Ibid., pp. 184, 201–2, 211–12, 216–18. The phrase is from the Committee of Council on Education, P.P. 1871, Rev. Wilden, 'Report on the Church of England Schools, Bradford District', p. 241.

55. Wilden, 'Church of England Schools', p. 239.

56. The Otley Road directors banned them. Otley Road School Logbook, November 5, 1875.

57. Winder, 'Popular Education', pp. 228–234.

58. Committee of Council on Education, P.P. 1871, W. Bailey, 'Report on Bradford District Schools', p. 47.

59. Report of the Departmental Committee Appointed to Inquire into the Condition of School Attendance and Child Labour, P.P. 1893–4, pp. 21–3.

60. Education Department, Return of Detailed Statistics of Inspected Schools 1896–97, P.P. 1898, p. 515.

61. Anonymous, *A Peep Behind the Scenes*, pamphlet (Bradford, n.d. (1870s?)) BCL; W. Claradge, *Conditions of Educational Progress*, pamphlet (Bradford, 1885) BCL; Fudge or the Bradford Oracle *A School Board Discussion*, pamphlet (Bradford, n.d. (1870s)) BCL. All attacked the Board for its sectarianism.

62. Fenn, 'Development of Education', pp. 9–10; Roper, 'Contribution of Nonconformists', pp. 218, 314.

63. Stephens, *Education*, p. 90.

64. This reluctance remained throughout this period. Robert Saunders, 'Report Upon the Establishment of Schools in the Factory Districts', P.P. 1843, pp. 3–4; Both Winder and Bailey complained of the low level of charitable support for education. Bailey put the figure for private contributions at one-eighth the cost of running the schools. For evasion, see the Attendance Subcommittee Minutes, October 17 and November 7, 1876, BCL.
65. Wilden, 'Church of England Schools', p. 241.
66. Even this resource could fail and in the late 1870s, the Board had to remit the fees of hundreds of students who could no longer afford to pay as a result of the trade depression. Yet this was done grudgingly, for the Board required parents to apply to the Guardians first. Subcommittee on Attendance Minutes, May 1877.
67. Bailey, 'Bradford District Schools', p. 52
68. Ibid., p. 51.
69. Winder, 'Popular Education', p. 239.
70. Ibid., p. 192.
71. Wilden, 'Church of England Schools', p. 239. Unlike other observers he argued that half-timers did not fall that far behind other students.
72. Bradford School Board, Report, 1885, BCL. Bailey put the attendance at around 50 per cent in 1873. Given the disparity between the figures presented by the Board and those of Winder in 1859, it is likely that Winder both underestimated the extent of the half-time system and overestimated the level of attendance. Part of the gap may be explained by the bringing into the system of children formerly not at school for economic reasons, whose attendance may have been more irregular.
73. Memorial of the Bradford and District Teachers Association, pamphlet (Bradford, 1880) BCL.
74. Wibsey Wesleyan School Logbook, 1871–81; Wesleyan Day School, Logbook 1874–81; Horton Bank Top Board School Logbook, 1874–1881, Otley Road School Logbook, 1872–84, all BA.
75. Otley Road School, Logbook, April 26, 1878, March 29, 1880, May 25, 1883; Wibsey Day School, Logbook, September 22, 1871, April 2, 1874; Wesleyan Day School, Logbook, March 22, 1878.
76. Bradford School Board, Attendance Subcommittee Minutes, November 9, 1880.
77. Attendance Subcommittee, Minutes, March 1879. As testimony to the Labour Commission revealed, the practice continued into the 1890s. Royal Commission on Labour, Group C, Textiles, vol. 1, p. 1892, Testimony of Henry Robinson and J.W. Burgoyne, pp. 397–9, Testimony of William Drew, p. 223.
78. US Consul to Bradford, Letter June 14, 1878.
79. Fudge, *School Board Discussion*.
80. Wilden, 'Church of England Schools', p. 245.
81. Report of Board of Education, 1879, BCL; For a discussion of the role of drill in schooling, see J. S. Hurt, 'Drill, Discipline, and the Elementary School Ethos', in Phillip McCann, ed., *Popular Education and Socialization in the Nineteenth Century* (London, 1977) pp. 167–92.
82. See Richard Johnson, 'Educating the Educators: "Experts" and the State 1833–39', in A. P. Donajgrodzki, *Social Control in Nineteenth-Century Britain* (London, 1977) pp. 77–107 and Simon Firth, 'Socializa-

tion and Rational Schooling: Elementary Education in Leeds Before 1870', in McCann, *Popular Education*, pp. 67–92, for a discussion of the social control aspects of popular education.

83. The most common extra subject according to Wilden was geography. Winder reported the teaching of topics outside reading and writing as 'nominal'. Bailey blamed the lack of incentives for instructors to teach special subjects.

84. Stephens, *Education*, p. 94.

85. See Chapter 7, Table 7–1, p. 199. David Mitch argues this case for England as a whole during the period. Mitch, *Rise* pp. 157–99.

86. Mitch, *Rise*, pp. 11–42; David Vincent, *Literacy and Popular Culture in England 1750–1914* (Cambridge, 1989) pp. 95–134.

87. Vincent, *Literacy*, p. 130.

88. Ibid., pp. 104–28. Mitch speaks of an oversupply of literate workers, reflected in a fall in the wage premium for literacy in the later nineteenth century. Mitch, *Rise*, p. 38.

89. In 1878, the master of the Otley Road School reported several parents withdrawing children because they felt their children were not learning enough. Otley Road School Logbook, February 1, 1878.

90. Otley Road School Logbook, July 3, 1873; December 1, 1875; August 4, 1876; April 8, 1878; December 5, 1879; February 23, 1883 BA.

91. Royden Harrison, *Before the Socialists* (London, 1965).

92. Winder, 'Popular Education', p. 203.

93. Wibsey Wesleyan School Logbook, January 16, 1874.

94. Reynolds, *Great Paternalist*, pp. 346–8.

95. Fenn, 'Development of Education', Part II, pp. 19–21.

96. These figures must be considered in light of a total student population of over 35,000 for the borough. Secondary Education Commission, Yorkshire, P.P. 1895, pp. 183–7.

97. Royal Commission on Technical Instruction, P.P. 1884, Testimony of Henry Mitchell, p. 245.

98. Carolyn Steedman, *Childhood, Culture and Class in Britain: Margaret McMillan 1860–1931* (New Brunswick, 1990) pp. 49–50.

99. See Chapter 2, pp. 68–71.

100. See Chapter 1.

101. J. B. Priestley, *Margin Released* (New York, 1962) pp. 10–12.

102. Anonymous, *Remarks on Popular Education*, pamphlet, (Bradford, 1861) BCL.

103. This attitude was clear from the reports of the Secondary Education Commission, which lauded the university-trained masters of the Grammar School and drew attention to the low level of literary and classical learning in the higher grade schools.

104. Vincent, *Literacy*, pp. 125–6

105. Winder, 'Popular Education', p. 204.

106. In 1881 4.9 per cent of unskilled workers' children 14–19 attended school, while 6.2 per cent of skilled workers' children did. 6.6 per cent of all children aged 15 were in school.

107. Mechanics' Institute, Report, 1852, BCL.

108. John Godwin, *The Bradford Mechanics' Institute*, pamphlet (Bradford, 1859) BCL, p. 3.

109. Mechanics' Institute Reports, 1851–82, BCL. See Mabel Tylecote, *The Mechanics' Institutes of Lancashire and Yorkshire Before 1851* (Manchester, 1957) pp. 224–40, 272. For more on working-class reading see Vincent, *Literacy*, pp. 196–227.

110. Neville Kirk, *Working-Class Reformism in Mid-Victorian England* (Urbana, 1985) pp. 189–98.

111. Bradford Mechanics' Institute, Report, 1881, BCL.

112. Rather than an elected board, the new technical school had a council heavily weighted with wealthy businessmen. Mitchell, Technical Instruction, p. 250.

113. James Donnelly, 'The Development of Technical Education in Bradford 1825–1900', MEd Thesis, University of Leeds, 1984, pp. 99–103, 127–9.

114. See Chapter 1, pp. 32–5, for more on this issue. For a discussion of technical education see Vincent, *Literacy*, pp. 113–19.

115. Select Committee on Scientific Instruction, P.P. 1867–8, Testimony of Henry Ripley, p. 215.

116. Students of the Bradford Technical School, *Report on the Weaving Schools of Germany*, pamphlet (Bradford, 1879) BCL.

117. *Bradford Observer*, October 18, 1877.

118. Mitchell, Technical Instruction, p. 249.

119. Ibid., pp. 246–7.

120. Donnelly, 'Development of Technical Education', pp. 169–74.

121. For an early view of this issue see E. P. Thompson, 'Time, Work-Discipline and Industrial Capitalism', *Past and Present*, no. 38 (February 1968) pp. 57–97. For later discussions see Gary Cross, ed., *Worktime and Industrialization* (Philadelphia, 1988) and Gary Cross, *A Quest for Time: The Reduction of Work in Britain and France, 1840–1940* (Berkeley, 1989).

122. G. H. Wood Collection, Notes on Hours and Wages, Huddersfield Polytechnic Archives; J. Banks, 'The Progress of Engineering In Bradford', *Journal of the Bradford Engineering Society*, 27th Session (1925–6); *George Hodgsons, Maker of Power Looms, Origins and Growth of the Firm*, pamphlet (Bradford, 1898) BCL.

123. Koditschek, *Class Formation*, pp. 293–8; Reynolds, *Great Paternalist*, pp. 149–52.

124. Koditschek, *Class Formation*, pp. 147–53.

125. For a sense of this from the perspective of a middle-class child growing up in Bradford see Clare Delius, *Memories of My Brother* (London, 1935) and William Rothernstein, *Men and Memories* (London, 1931) pp. 1–15.

126. Rev. J. Morgan, Meeting of Sunday Closing Association, May 5, 1874, BCL; US Consul at Bradford, Letter of February 13, 1879, BCL.

127. Mayor's Committee on the Moral Condition of the Town.

128. J. Eddowes, *Leisure Hours*, pamphlet (Bradford,1855) BCL.

129. David Russell, 'The Popular Musical Societies of Bradford', PhD dissertation, University of York, 1979.

130. The classic account of the movement remains Brian Harrison, *Drink and the Victorians* (Pittsburgh, 1971).

131. Malcolm Collins, 'Drink, Temperance and Prostitution in Victorian Bradford', MA Thesis, University of Leeds, pp. 33–34; George Field, *An*

Historical Survey of the Bradford Temperance Society, pamphlet (Bradford, 1897) BCL, pp. 15–16; Koditschek, *Class Formation*, pp. 298–308.

132. *Facts and Figures for the Consideration of Working Men*, pamphlet (Bradford, n.d. (post-1840s?)) BCL.

133. Meeting of Bradford United Temperance Society, November 11, 1875.

134. *Bradford Observer*, December 14, 1871.

135. *Bradford Telegraph*, February 1, 1876.

136. Band of Hope Union Reports, 1868–82, BCL. For a discussion of the movement see Lilian Lewis Shiman, 'The Band of Hope Movement: Respectable Recreation for Working-Class Children', *Victorian Studies*, vol. XVIII, no. 1 (September 1973) pp. 49–74. For a contemporary (and more cynical) view of the Band of Hope see Robert Roberts, *The Classic Slum* (Manchester, 1971) pp. 120–1.

137. Bradford Temperance Society, Report, 1872–3, BA. The number of pubs and beer shops per capita continued to increase until the late 1870s. In 1879 there were over 1,200 licenses of all kinds in the borough.

138. Collins, 'Drink, Temperance', pp. 82–4. The conduct of the election itself became a temperance issue, for there were widespread allegations of treating and drunkenness.

139. Ibid., pp. 32–41; this group had over 276 members in 1870.

140. For example, the Coffee Tavern Movement and the British Association both opened temperance pubs in Bradford. *Opening of the Old Mechanics' Institute Branch Number 18 of the Bradford Coffee Tavern Ltd, October 29, 1881* pamphlet (Bradford 1881) BCL.

141. The Rechabites noted the heavy drinking of other societies in their reports and attributed their lower death rate to abstinence. Z. Catlow, *Friendly Societies with Special Reference to the Independent Order of Rechabites*, pamphlet (Bradford, 1875) BCL.

142. Anonymous, *A Few Thoughts on the Sabbath Question*, pamphlet (Bradford, 1856) BCL.

143. *Bradford Observer*, February 15, 1855; also see Reynolds, *Great Paternalist*, p. 184.

144. Letters, Reports on Sunday Closing and Temperance, 1860s and 1870s, BA; Letters and Accounts of Temperance Societies, BA.

145. Letter in Collection of Temperance Societies, 1870s.

146. Sunday Closing Association, Report on Music Halls, April 21, 1875, BA. The Association found little drunkenness or riotous behavior.

147. Ibid., Report of James Scurrah, Spring 1875.

148. For example, the Overlookers Society met in the Shoulder of Mutton.

149. *Popular Amusements – Four Essays by Working Men*, pamphlet (Bradford, 1858) BCL. In this collection of essays assembled by the *Bradford Review* to support rational recreation, even moderate working men attacked temperance advocates for dictating to working men. For a discussion of these issues in a broader framework see Michael Smith, 'Social Usages of the Public Drinking House: Changing Aspects of Class and Leisure', *British Journal of Sociology*, vol. XXXIV, no. 3 (September 1983) pp. 367–85.

150. Anon *Sabbath Question*, p. 7.

151. Reynolds, *Great Paternalist*, pp. 174–7; Select Committee on Public Walks, P.P. 1833, Testimony of E. C. Lister, pp. 52–4; C. Richardson, *Geography*, pp. 115–16.
152. See Peter Bailey, *Leisure and Class in Victorian England* (London, 1978); Hugh Cunningham, *Leisure in the Industrial Revolution* (New York, 1980); James Walvin, *Leisure and Society 1832–1950* (London, 1978).
153. Sunday Closing Association, Report on Pubs, 1876, BA.
154. Bailey, *Leisure and Class*, pp. 147–68.
155. David Russell, 'The Pursuit of Leisure', in Wright and Jowitt, *Victorian Bradford*, pp. 199–221.
156. Sunday Closing Association, Reports on Music Halls, 1875, BA.
157. Geoff Mellor, 'Theaters of Bradford' (n.d.) BCL.
158. A letter in the papers of Sunday Closing Association described a riot caused when two police tried to arrest a drunk. Memorial to Watch Committee, 1875, BA.
159. *Bradford Observer*, May 31, 1872.
160. Cited in Robert Storch, 'Persistence', pp. 1–2.
161. Town Mission, Report, 1850–1, pamphlet, BCL.
162. *Bradford Review*, September 13, 1867.
163. Ibid., August 29, September 14, 1867.
164. Sunday Closing Association, Records, April 27, 1874, BA. See John K. Walton and Robert Poole, 'The Lancashire Wakes in the Nineteenth Century', in Storch, *Popular Culture*, pp. 100–24.
165. Anonymous, *Questions Addressed to Parents and Masters on Their Conduct at the Times of Fairs and Feasts*, pamphlet (Bradford, n.d.) BCL.
166. Wibsey Wesleyan School, Northfield, Logbook, July 15, 1881, BA.
167. *Bradford Observer*, January 12, 1880.
168. *Cricket Journal*, May 9, 1874, BCL. A letter writer, X, complained of a group of male bathers attracting an audience of mill girls, *Bradford Review*, May 11, 1867.
169. Bailey, *Leisure and Class*, pp. 8–34; Cunningham, Leisure, pp. 15–75; Russell, 'Pursuit of Leisure', pp. 204–5; Reynolds, *Great Paternalist*, pp. 173–4; Ross McKibbin, 'Working-Class Gambling in Britain, 1880–1939', *Past and Present*, no. 82 (February 1979) pp. 147–9. For a discussion of survivals see Richard Holt, *Sport and the British* (Oxford, 1989) pp. 57–73.
170. *Bradford Observer*, February 15, 1855.
171. Ibid., April 26, 1860; Ronald Wharton, *History of Boxing in Bradford* (Bradford, 1980).
172. Anonymous, *History of Bradford Northern* (n.d.) BCL; Russell, 'Pursuit of Leisure', p. 214. For a discussion of the development of spectator sports see Holt, *Sport*, pp. 148–79.
173. Eddowes, *Leisure*.
174. For a discussion of this issue see Paul Johnson, *Saving and Spending: the Working Class Economy in Britain 1870–1939* (Oxford, 1985).
175. Eddowes, *Leisure*.
176. Rev. Charles Best Robinson, *Christian Diligence – A Sermon to St Peters Lodge of the Independent Order of Oddfellows*, pamphlet (Bradford, n.d. (1860s?)) BCL.

177. For this in an earlier period see Koditschek, *Class Formation*, pp. 293–319.
178. President of the Halifax YMCA, *Practical Hints for Young Men on Social, Intellectual and Moral Progress*, pamphlet (Bradford, 1866) BCL.
179. P.H.J.H. Gosden, *Self-Help* (New York, 1974) p. 69; Trygve R. Tholfsen, *Working-Class Radicalism in Mid-Victorian England* (New York, 1977) pp. 288–305.
180. David Ashworth, 'The Treatment of Poverty', in Wright and Jowitt, *Victorian Bradford*, p. 96; Select Committee on Poor Removal, P.P. 1854–5, Testimony of John Darlington, pp. 335–43. The death of an inmate who was forced to work while sick only highlighted the inhumanity of the system of relief, *Bradford Weekly Telegraph*, January 1, 1870.
181. Mary MacKinnon, 'English Poor Law Policy and the Crusade Against Outrelief', *Journal of Economic History*, vol. 47, no. 3 (September. 1987) pp. 603–25.
182. One temperance tract argued that 'many a fraud was palmed upon the well-to-do population, by those pretending to be objects of charity.' James Hanson, *Tales from Everyday Life*, pamphlet (Bradford, n.d. (1860s)) BCL.
183. For discussions of the COS see Stedman-Jones, *Outcast London*, pp. 271–314 and Alan Kidd, 'Charity organization and the unemployed in Manchester c. 1870–1914',, *Social History*, vol. IX (1984) pp. 45–66.
184. Bradford Charity Organization, Report, 1881, BCL, p. 4.
185. Bradford Tradesmens' Benevolent Institution, Report, 1877, BCL.
186. James Firth, *One of the Principle Causes of Vice Ruling Predominant*, pamphlet (Bradford, 1865) BCL.
187. Woolcombers Aid Association, Accounts and Letters, 1854–7, BA.
188. Letter From Honesty, in Dr Bell's Collection, BA; Medical Officer of Health, Sixth Report to the Privy Council, P.P. 1864, Appendix no. 15, Dr Bristowe and Mr Holmes, 'Report on Bradford Infirmary', pp. 623–4.
189. Bradford Homeopathic Dispensary, Records, 1859–81, BA.
190. Ashworth, 'Treatment', pp. 92–3. Although a Workhouse Infirmary existed, the sick poor were reluctant to make use of it according to the relief officers.
191. This point has been made for the concept of respectability itself in Bailey, 'Bill Banks', pp. 336–53.
192. Friendly Societies Commission, P.P. 1874, report of E. L. Stanley, pp. 204–5. This amount exceeded that spent by the private charities. It does not include less formal or unrecognized societies.
193. See Kirk, *Working-Class Reformism* pp. 174–82 on this issue. Several members of the Bradford Volunteers were reprimanded for drunkenness while on parade, while the respectable members of the Orangemen engaged in street fighting with Catholics during this era.
194. *Progress of Oddfellowship In Yorkshire*, pamphlet (Bradford, 1866) BCL; Bradford District Oddfellows, Report, 1874, BCL; Rules of the Bradford District Oddfellows, pamphlet (Bradford, 1872) BCL. The Medical Aid Association enrolled over 1,800 members of the Order in 1874.
195. For a discussion of this issue see Johnson, *Saving and Spending*.
196. Joseph Bennett and John Baldwin, *City of Bradford Cooperative Society Ltd Jubilee History 1860–1910* (Bradford, 1911) pp. 4–131.

197. The initial meetings of the Bradford Cooperative society were marked by conflict between members on political issues related to cooperation. J. Hallen, *Cooperation, A Poem Addressed to Working Men*, pamphlet (Bradford, 1855) BCL; John Holmes, *The Advantages of Cooperation Substantiated, A Letter Addressed to the Rev. Norman MacLeod*, pamphlet (Bradford, 1860) BCL; Jacob Behrens, *Cooperation in Germany*, pamphlet (Bradford, 1867) BCL. For a discussion of these issues and how coops were transformed see Sidney Pollard, 'Nineteenth-Century Co-operation: From Community Building to Shopkeeping', in Asa Briggs and John Saville, eds, *Essays in Labour History* (London, 1960) pp. 74–112.

198. There were also charges of nepotism on the part of the directors and difficulties finding workers for the shops. Bennett and Baldwin, *Jubilee History*, pp. 146–7.

199. Michael J. Mortimore, 'Urban Growth in Bradford and Environs 1800–1960', MA Thesis, University of Leeds, 1963, pp. 75–81; Ash Grove Building Society, Rules of Agreement, December 1860, BCL; W. Wightman, *How I Joined A Building Club*, pamphlet (Bradford, 1880) BCL.

200. J. A. Binns, President of the Third Equitable Building Society, *Notes on Yorkshire Building Societies* (Bradford, 1898) p. 6.

201. The Third Equitable by this time had assets in excess of £7,000,000. Francis Lumb, *Second Thoughts – A History of the Bradford Second Equitable Benefit Building Society* (Bradford, 1951) p. 11.

202. Ibid., pp. 19–21.

203. Friendly Societies Commission, Report on Building Societies, P.P. 1871, Testimony of J. A. Binns, p. 175. In 1871, the Third Equitable had 4,512 investors, and 1,503 borrowers and received more in loan or deposit funds per year than from shareholders.

204. Edward Ackroyd, *The Yorkshire Penny Bank – A Narrative*, pamphlet (Bradford, 1872) BCL.

205. For a discussion of the problems of obtaining credit, see Chapter 1, pp. 24–5. Cooperatives in Lancashire played a similar role. D.A. Farnie, *The English Cotton Industry and the World Market 1815–1896* (Oxford, 1979) pp. 255–6.

206. A proposal was even floated to pay for municipal improvements by creating a municipal savings bank to attract funds from the working class to cover the shortfall of rates and loans for sanitary improvements. Joseph Rayner, *Municipal Savings Banks for Working Men*, pamphlet (Bradford, 1865) BCL.

207. Mortimore, 'Urban Growth', p. 78.

208. Binns, *Notes*, pp. 13–14.

209. Mortimore, 'Urban Growth', pp. 132–3.

210. For a comparative assessment see Ira Katzenstein, 'Working-Class Formation and the State: Nineteenth-Century England in American Perspective', in Peter Evans, Dietrich Rueschemeyer, Theda Skocpol, eds, *Bringing the State Back In* (Cambridge, 1985) pp. 257–84.

211. Tholfsen, *Working-Class Radicalism*, pp. 303–5.

212. Rules of the Bradford Union Club, pamphlet (Bradford, n.d.) BCL; Bradford Choral Musical Society, pamphlet (Bradford, n.d.) BCL. For more on the structure of these societies see Morris, *Class*, pp. 184–203.
213. See Kirk, *Working-Class Reformism*, pp. 174–240. For the rather fluid nature of respectability see Ellen Ross, "Not the Sort that Would Sit on the Doorstep': Respectability in Pre-World War I London Neighborhoods', *International Labor and Working-Class History*, no. 27 (Spring 1985) pp. 39–59.
214. Reynolds, *Great Paternalist*, pp. 185, 192.
215. For a discussion of adolescence see John Springhall, *Coming of Age: Adolescence in Britain 1860–1960* (Dublin, 1986).
216. Garnett, 'Irish Immigration', pp. 142–201.
217. *Bradford Review*, December 14, 1867. Among the topics were the Irish Church, St Patrick and Irish warriors.
218. *Bradford Observer*, October 6, 1864.
219. Ibid., December 7, 1881.
220. Darlington, Poor Removal, p. 105.
221. See Frank Neal, *Sectarian Violence: the Liverpool Experience, 1819–1914* (Manchester, 1988) for more on the Orangemen.
222. *Bradford Review*, March 7 and December 28, 1867.
223. Keith Laybourn and Jack Reynolds, *Liberalism and the Rise of Labour 1890–1918* (London, 1984) p. 8.

5 Gender and Family Life in Mid-Victorian Bradford

1. For a discussion of separate spheres, particularly in regard to the dynamics of households, see Leonore Davidoff and Catherine Hall, *Family Fortunes: Men and Women of the English Middle Class, 1780–1850* (Chicago, 1987) pp. 149–92, 321–415.
2. *Waddington's Pictorial Magazine*, Bradford, August 1858.
3. *Lancashire and Yorkshire Penny Almanack*, Bradford, September 1860.
4. In the 1851 census, over 20 per cent of adult men worked in hand combing, though they disappeared (sometimes literally through emigration) by 1861. Despite the survival of significant sectors of domestic labor in small shops and consumer trades, the 1850s marked a turning point – the disappearance of domestic industry on a large scale. These consumer trades employed 10.7 per cent of all men over fifteen in 1881.
5. Robert Baker, *The Present Condition of the Working Classes Generally Considered*, pamphlet (Bradford, 1851) BCL, p. 5.
6. Despite frequent assertions to the contrary, little evidence exists that family members continued to work together in the mills, perhaps because men, women and children occupied separate spheres within the work place. The belief that men supervised family members in early factories rests on an extremely thin evidentiary base. Neil Smelser, *Social Change in the Industrial Revolution* (Chicago, 1959) puts forth the most forceful case. Also see Patrick Joyce, *Work, Society and Politics* (New Brunswick, 1984) pp. 53–5, 110–12. For a critique of Smelser see Michael Anderson,

'Sociological history and the working-class family: Smelser revisited', *Social History*, vol. 1, no. 3 (October 1976) pp. 317–35.

7. For an overview of this process see Louise Tilly and Joan Scott, *Women, Work and the Family* (New York, 1978) pp. 104–45.

8. Sonya Rose, *Limited Livelihoods: Gender and Class in Nineteenth-Century England* (Berkeley, 1992) pp. 50–9; Anna Clark, 'The Rhetoric of Chartist Domesticity: Gender, Language, and Class in the 1830s and 1840s', *Journal of British Studies*, 31 (January 1992) pp. 62–88.

9. For the role of physicians in this process see Robert Gray, 'Medical Men, Industrial Labor and the State in Britain 1830–1850', *Social History*, vol. 16, no. 1 (January 1991) pp. 19–43.

10. Richard Oastler, 'The Working-Men Are Thinking', Address, February, 1850, clipping from *Bell's Weekly Messenger*, March 4, 1850, BA.

11. Robert Gray, 'The Languages of Factory Reform in Britain, *c.* 1830–1860', in Patrick Joyce (ed.) *The Historical Meanings of Work* (Cambridge, 1987) pp. 150–2; Marianna Valverde, 'Giving the Female a Domestic Turn': The Social, Legal and Moral Regulation of Women's Work in British Cotton Mills, 1820–1850', *Journal of Social History*, vol. 21, no. 4 (Summer 1988) pp. 619–34; Per Bolin-Hart, *Work, Family and the State: Child Labour and the Organization of Production in the British Cotton Industry, 1780–1920* (Lund, 1989) pp. 59–66.

12. 'The Mayor's Committee on the Moral Condition of the Town', Photocopy of the original report printed in the *Bradford Observer*, March 7, 1850, statement by Rev. Ryland.

13. Ibid., Second Meeting.

14. Dorothy Thompson, *The Chartists: Popular Politics in the Industrial Revolution* (New York, 1984) pp. 34–6, 134–6; Jack Reynolds, *The Great Paternalist: Titus Salt and the Growth of Nineteenth-Century Bradford* (London, 1984) pp. 96–7.

15. Barbara Taylor, *Eve and the New Jerusalem* (New York, 1983).

16. Thompson, *Chartists*, pp. 120–36; Schwarzkopf, Jutta, *Women in the Chartist Movement* (New York, 1991) pp. 89–122; Catherine Hall, 'The Tale of Samuel and Jemima: Gender and Working-Class Culture in Nineteenth-Century England', in Harvey Kaye and Keith McClelland, eds, *E.P. Thompson: Critical Perspectives* (Philadelphia, 1990) pp. 90–4.

17. Joan Scott, 'On Language, Gender, and Working-Class History', in Scott, *Gender and the Politics of History* (New York, 1988) pp. 61–65.

18. In addition to Anna Clark a number of feminist scholars have examined the nature of Chartist arguments about gender. See Sonya Rose, '"Gender at Work": Sex, Class and Industrial Capitalism', *History Workshop Journal*, no. 21 (Spring 1988) 122–8; Sally Alexander, 'Women, Class and Sexual Difference in the 1830s and 1840s: Some Reflections on the Writing of a Feminist History', *History Workshop Journal*, no. 17 (Spring 1984) pp. 135–46.

19. Hall, 'Samuel and Jemima', pp. 83–4. John Rule, 'The Property of Skill in the Period of Manufacture', in Joyce, *Historical Meanings of Work*, pp. 99–118. For a discussion of the impact of artisan traditions in France see Joan Scott, 'Men and Women in the Parisian Garment Trades: Discussions of Family and Work in the 1830s and 1840s', in Pat Thane,

Geoffrey Crossick and Roderick Floud, eds, *The Power of the Past: Essays for Eric Hobsbawm* (Cambridge, 1984) pp. 67–93.

20. Theodore Koditschek, *Class Formation and Urban Industrial Society: Bradford 1750–1850* (Cambridge, 1990) pp. 29–52; Pat Hudson, 'From Manor to Mill: the West Riding in Transition', in Maxine Berg, Pat Hudson, and Michael Sonenscher, eds, *Manufacture in Town and Country Before the Factory* (Cambridge, 1983) pp. 124–144.

21. Sonya Rose draws on William Lazonick's work on the spinning industry of Lancashire to support her argument about the social determination of skill and access to technology, Rose, *Limited Livelihoods*, pp. 22–49, 102–25. See also Gareth Stedman Jones, 'Class Struggle and the Industrial Revolution', in Jones, *Languages of Class: Studies in English Working Class History 1832–1982* (Cambridge, 1983) pp. 67–75.

22. Rosemary Feurer's discussion of post-1848 labor legislation examines the ambiguities involved in debates over protective legislation for women in the feminist community in the late nineteenth century. Rosemary Feurer, 'The Meaning of "Sisterhood": the British Women's Movement and Protective Legislation, 1870–1900', *Victorian Studies*, vol. 31, no. 2 (Winter 1988) pp. 233–60.

23. *Bradford Observer*, December 27, 1871.

24. Ibid., March 22, May 25, 1872.

25. Ibid., May 29, 1872.

26. Wally Seccombe, 'Patriarchy Stabilized: the Construction of the Male Breadwinner Wage Norm in Nineteenth-Century Britain', *Social History*, vol. 11, no. 1 (January 1986) pp. 53–76; Rose, *Limited Livelihoods*, pp. 126–53. For a response see Jane Mark-Lawson and Anne Witz, 'From "Family Labour" to "Family Wage"? The Case of Women's Labour in Nineteenth-Century Coalmining', *Social History*, vol. 13, no. 2 (May 1988) pp. 151–74.

27. For a discussion of this masculine culture within fraternal societies, see Mary Ann Clawson, *Constructing Brotherhood: Class, Gender and Fraternalism* (Princeton, 1989).

28. Royal Commission on Labour, Group C, 'Textiles', vol. 1, P.P. 1892, Testimony of William Drew, p. 237.

29. Joanna Bornat, 'Lost Leaders: Women, Trade Unionism and the Case of the General Union of Textile Workers, 1875–1914', in Angela John, ed., *Unequal Opportunities: Women's Employment in England 1800–1919* (Oxford, 1986) pp. 220–9.

30. For discussions of the role of women within the ILP see June Hannam, '"In the Comradeship of the Sexes Lies the Hope of Progress and Social Regeneration": Women in the West Riding ILP, c.1890–1914', in Jane Rendall, *Equal or Different: Women's Politics 1800–1914* (Oxford, 1987) pp. 214–38; Carolyn Steedman, *Childhood, Culture and Class in Britain: Margaret McMillan* (New Brunswick, 1990) pp. 131–40.

31. J. H. Plumb, 'The New World of Children in 18th Century England', in N. McKendrick, J. Brewer and J. H. Plumb, eds, *The Birth of a Consumer Society: the Commercialization of the 18th Century England* (Bloomington, 1982) pp. 286–315.

32. Davidoff and Hall, *Family Fortunes*, pp. 343–8.

33. Bolin-Hart, *Work*, pp. 62–8.
34. Over 80 per cent of fourteen to nineteen year olds were still at home from 1851 to 1881.
35. Baker, *Present Condition*, pp. 28, 45.
36. Margaret McMillan, *Child Labour and the Half-Time System*, pamphlet (Clarion Newspaper, 1896) p. 11.
37. For more on these issues see John Gillis, *For Better For Worse, English Marriages, 1600 to the Present* (Oxford, 1985) pp. 260–84.
38. For one account see *Bradford, a Review of Social Affairs*, April 4th, 1896.
39. Rev. Robert Young, *The Church and the Children*, pamphlet (Bradford 1860) BCL.
40. Gray, 'Languages of Factory Reform', pp. 150–1.
41. Women 15–24 made up 28.9 per cent of the textile labor force and were overwhelmingly single, over 80 per cent being unmarried.
42. William Scoresby, *Report on Town Meeting On Female Operatives*, pamphlet (Bradford, 1846) BCL. His survey put the number of single women in the textile trade living in lodgings at 1200, or about 10 per cent of the total.
43. Baker, *Present Condition*, p. 48.
44. Bradford Corporation Report Book, Sanitary Committee, 1855, BA.
45. Hannah Lambert, *Friendly Letter to the Members of the Bradford Branch of the Girls' Friendly Society*, pamphlet (Bradford, 1886) BCL.
46. Bradford Ladies Association for the Care of Friendless Girls, Annual Report, 1884, BCL.
47. Ibid.
48. Joyce, *Work, Society*, pp. 103–23; 134–57. For a discussion of how paternalism sought to address issues of gender raised by the factory see Rose, *Limited Livelihoods*, pp. 33–47 and Judith Lown, *Women and Industrialization: Gender at Work in Nineteenth-Century England* (Minneapolis, 1990).
49. John James, *History of the Worsted Manufacture in England* (reprint of 1857 edition, London, 1969) pp. 555–6.
50. Rev. J. P. Chown, *The Excelling Daughter – A Sermon to Young Women*, pamphlet (Bradford, 1861) BCL, p. 7.
51. Baker, *Present Condition*, p. 47.
52. Sample of the manuscript census of Bradford, 1851, 1861, 1871, 1881.
53. Report on Pubs by the SCA, Report of James Scurrah, Spring 1875, BCL.
54. *Bradford Observer*, January 3, 1878.
55. Chown, *Excelling Daughter*, p. 6.
56. Illegitimacy averaged from 5.5 to 8.3 per cent of all births from 1845–81. Registrar-General, *Annual Report of Births, Deaths and Marriages*, 1845–81.
57. See National Association for the Promotion of Social Science, Meeting, 1859, Bradford, for several examples of this literature. J. H. Marshall, *The Social Evil in Bradford*, pamphlet (Bradford, 1859) BCL.
58. Wibsey Wesleyan School, Logbook, November 27, 1874.

59. For example the locally circulated pamphlet, *Some Account of the Life of Elizabeth Kenning*, pamphlet (Liverpool, n.d.) BCL, told the story of a young women drawn into a life of prostitution because she left a supervised life and instead sought a life of pleasure.

60. Bradford Borough Police Report, 1882. These were only the acknowledged and well known ones. For a discussion of this see Judith Walkowitz, *Prostitution in Victorian Society* (Cambridge, 1980) pp. 13–47.

61. J. H. Marshall, *Social Evil*, p. 4.

62. Lyn Pykett, *The Improper Feminine* (London, 1992) pp. 62–6.

63. Barbara Thompson, 'Infant Mortality in Nineteenth-Century Bradford', in Robert Woods and John Woodward, eds, *Urban Disease and Mortality in Nineteenth Century England* (London, 1984) p. 128.

64. J. W Clay, 'Annie', in Dr Forshaw, ed., *Local Poets Past and Present* (Bradford, 1888) BCL, p. 9.

65. See Gray, 'Medical Men', for these fears in the 1830s, while Drew in his testimony before the Royal Commission on Labour expressed similar fears 60 years later. Drew, Labour Commission, p. 227.

66. J. B. Priestley, *Margin Released* (New York, 1962) p. 12.

67. Ellen Ross, '"Not the Sort that Would Sit on the Doorstep": Respectability in Pre-World-War I London Neighborhoods', *International Labor and Working-Class History*, no. 27 (Spring 1985) pp. 49–51.

68. Rev. J. P. Chown, *Excelling Daughter*. See also James Campbell, *Lessons in Social Science from the Blessed Savior*, pamphlet (Bradford, 1859) BCL, in which he blamed the loosening of family bonds not on children working in factories, but the neglect of parents.

69. McMillan, *Child Labour*, p. 11.

70. *Lancashire and Yorkshire Penny Almanack*, Bradford, July 1860.

71. *Temperance Advocate and Advertiser*, October 2, 1866.

72. Rev. A. McKechnie, *Sugar Candy for Spoiled Husbands*, pamphlet (Bradford, n.d.) BCL, p. 7.

73. John Eyler, *Victorian Social Medicine: The Ideas and Methods of William Farr* (Baltimore, 1979).

74. The borough as a whole had an infant mortality rate that remained close to 200 per 1000 into the twentieth century. In fact the rate was higher than that in some areas as late as the early twentieth century. Barbara Thompson, 'Infant Mortality', pp. 120–47.

75. Anthony Wohl, *Endangered Lives: Public Health in Victorian Britain* (Cambridge, MA., 1983).

76. Adrian Elliott, 'Municipal Government in Bradford in the Mid-Nineteenth Century', in Derek Fraser, ed., *Municipal Reform and the Industrial City* (New York, 1982) pp. 118–31.

77. Eighth Report of the Medical Officers to the Privy Council, P.P. 1866, Dr Hunter, 'On the Housing of the Poor in Towns' Fourteenth Report of the Medical Officers to the Privy Council, P.P. 1873, J. Nettien Radcliffe, 'Defects in the Sanitary Administration of Bradford'.

78. Radcliffe, 'Defects', p. 9

79. Ann Higgenbotham, '"Sin of the Age": Infanticide and Illegitimacy in Victorian London', *Victorian Studies*, vol. 32, no. 3 (Spring, 1989) p.

324; Jeanne Petersen, *The Medical Profession in Mid-Victorian London* (Berkeley, 1978) pp. 110–14.

80. For an overview of the development of disease theory see Eyler, *Social Medicine*, pp. 97–122.

81. Deborah Dwork, *War is Good for Babies and Other Young Children* (London, 1987) pp. 22–51.

82. Carol Dyhouse, 'Working-Class Mothers and Infant Mortality in England, 1895–1914', *Journal of Social History*, vol. 12, no. 2 (Winter, 1978) pp. 248–62.

83. David Goyer, *History of the First Twenty-Five Years of the Bradford Medico-Chirurgical Society from May 1863 to June 1888*, pamphlet (Bradford, 1888) BCL.

84. Ornella Moscucci, *The Science of Women: Gynecology and Gender in England 1800–1929* (Cambridge, 1990).

85. Bradford Medico-Chirurgical Society, Minutes, BA.

86. Ibid., January, 1887. Also see Moscucci, *Science*, pp. 39–40.

87. Radcliffe, 'Defects', p. 5.

88. Local Government Board, P.P. 1873, J.H. Bridges and T. Holmes, 'Report on Proposed Changes in Hours and Ages of Employment in Textile Factories', p. 33.

89. Bradford Medical Officer of Health, Annual Report, 1876 and 1880, BCL.

90. For the role of milk see Dwork, *War*, pp. 52–90.

91. Bradford Medical Officer of Health, Annual Report, 1876, p. 9.

92. Catherine Buckton, *Two Winters' Experience Giving Lectures to My Fellow Townswomen (Leeds) of the the Working Classes on Physiology and Hygiene*, pamphlet (Leeds 1873) BCL.

93. For a similar view by London physicians see Ellen Ross, 'Labour and Love: Rediscovering London's Working-Class Mothers, 1870–1918', in Jane Lewis, ed., *Labour and Love: Women's Experience of Home and Family, 1850–1940* (Oxford, 1986) p. 83.

94. Jean Donnison, *Midwives and Medical Men* (London, 1977).

95. With fees of 1s. midwives existed in a far different realm than doctors. Female Sanitary Inspectors, Report, June 1907, pp. 9–10; Return for the Medical Department of the Local Government Board, 'The Prevention of Infant and Child Mortality', November 21, 29, 1913, PRO, Kew, MH 48/196.

96. Female Sanitary Inspectors, Report, June 1907, pp. 9–10, BCL.

97. *Bradford Observer*, January 26 and January 30, 1878.

98. Karl Ittmann, 'Family Limitation and Family Economy in Bradford, West Yorkshire, 1851–1881', *Journal of Social History*, vol. 25, no. 3 (Spring 1992) pp. 547–73.

99. Bradford Medical Officer of Health, Annual Report, 1881, p. 7, BCL.

100. Bradford Medico-Chirurgical Society, Minutes, March 1889, BA.

101. Ibid., February 1884.

102. Ibid., February 1882.

103. Dr Rabagliati made this accusation at the February 1882 meeting of the Bradford Medico-Chirurgical Society.

104. Higgenbotham, 'Sin', pp. 319–39.

105. This argument is based on an analysis of the Leeds Assize Records for the years 1859–1889. PRO, Chancery Lane, Northeastern Circuit, Assize 41/21–31.

106. For a similar pattern in France, see James Donovan, 'Infanticide and the Juries in France, 1825–1913', *Journal of Family History*, vol. 16, no. 2 (1991) pp. 157–76.

107. Hezekiah Thornton received a ten year sentence for performing an abortion on a women who later died. *Bradford Observer*, February 7, 1879. Another women who performed an abortion received a six year sentence. *Bradford Observer*, August 7, 1885. For more on abortion see Patricia Knight, 'Women and Abortion in Victorian and Edwardian England', *History Workshop Journal*, no. 4 (Autumn 1977) pp. 52–70; R. Sauer, 'Infanticide and Abortion in Nineteenth-Century England', *Population Studies*, vol. 32 (1978) pp. 81–93.

108. Bradford Medico-Chirurgical Society, Minutes, February 1882, October 1882, March 1883, February 1884.

109. Baker, *Present Condition*, p. 41.

110. J. H. Bridges, *Health – A Lecture*, pamphlet (Bradford, 1862) BCL, p. 7.

111. For Robert Baker's career see Gray, 'Medical Men', p. 24. For Bridges see Royden Harrison, *Before the Socialists* (London, 1965) pp. 255–6, 311.

112. Bradford Medical Officer of Health, Annual Report, 1878, pp. 32–3.

113. Bridges, *Health*, p. 27.

114. Bradford Medico-Chirurgical Society, Minutes, March 1883, BA.

115. James Hanson, *Why Houses Are So Scarce and Rents So High*, pamphlet (Bradford, 1865) BCL, p. 11.

116. A 1908 report by the Female Sanitary Inspectors showed that of 2,085 children visited, only 200 had working mothers. Furthermore, the great majority, 1,464, were breast-fed, with a further 250 at least partially breast-fed. Female Sanitary Inspectors, Report, March 1909, BCL, p. 6.

117. This figure is for married women with husbands present. The figures for 1881: 24.9 per cent for women with children under one, 24.4 per cent for children under five. Figures taken from the manuscript census samples for 1851, 1881.

118. If one examines those mothers with more than one child at home the percentages employed fall to 16 per cent for those with a child under one and 17 per cent for those with a child under five in 1851 and 22.7 per cent and 21.9 per cent in 1881.

119. In part this reflected the inability of the elite to admit its complicity in the wretched environmental conditions that plagued the city, a state of affairs quite profitable to some inhabitants of the town. For example, Henry Ripley earned £2000 a year from Ripleyville, a housing development he built for his employees. Ripley Documents, West Yorkshire Archives.

6 From Voluntarism to the Sanitary Gospel: The Family and Social Reform

1. 'The Mayor's Committee on the Moral Condition of the Town', photocopy of the original report printed in the *Bradford Observer*, March 7, 1850, BCL.

2. The belief in an evolutionary welfare state is a persistent one in British social history. For a discussion, see David Roberts, *Victorian Origins of the British Welfare State* (Hamden, 1969); Derek Fraser, *The Evolution of the British Welfare State* (New York, 1973).

3. Jane Lewis, *The Politics of Motherhood: Maternal and Child Welfare in England, 1900–1939* (London, 1980); Susan Pedersen, 'Gender, Welfare and, Citizenship in Britain during the Great War', *American Historical Review*, vol. 95, no. 4 (October 1990) pp. 983–1006.

4. Theodore Koditschek, *Class Formation and Urban Industrial Society: Bradford 1750–1850* (Cambridge, 1990) pp. 252–319.

5. Koditschek, *Class Formation*, pp. 66–8, 395–413; David Ashworth, 'The Treatment of Poverty', D. G. Wright and J. A. Jowitt, *Victorian Bradford* (Bradford, 1981) p. 84. One estimate puts the amount spent by private charities between 1837 and 1848 at £10,000. In the same time period the Poor Law Union of Bradford spent £220,000.

6. Koditschek, *Class Formation*, p. 382.

7. For a discussion of voluntary relief committees in the 1840s see Koditschek, *Class Formation*, pp. 398–403.

8. Bradford Female Refuge, Reports, 1861, 1871; Bradford Ladies Charity, Annual Reports 1870–1; Bradford Benevolent or Strangers' Friend Society Reports, 1844, 1865–6, 1866–7; Bradford Female Educational Institute, Rules, 1860; Orphan Girls Home for Industrial Training, 27th Annual Report, 1891. All BCL. Bradford Ragged School Minute Book, Letters, 1875–83, BA.

9. Reverend Jonathan Glyde, *Plea for a Park: A Lecture*, pamphlet (Bradford, 1853) BCL.

10. See John Eddowes, *The Poor Man's Church*, pamphlet (Bradford, n.d. (1860s?)) BCL; Reverend J.P. Chown, *Church Work in Large Towns*, pamphlet (Bradford, 1864) BCL.

11. For a discussion of the social work of churches see Jeffery Cox, *The English Churches in a Secular Society: Lambeth, 1870–1930* (Oxford, 1982).

12. See Leonore Davidoff and Catherine Hall, *Family Fortunes: Men and Women of the English middle class, 1780–1850* (Chicago, 1987) 140–8, 417–49; F. K. Prochaska, *Women and Philanthropy in Nineteenth Century England* (Oxford, 1980). For a discussion of these trends in France see Bonnie Smith, *Ladies of the Leisure Class* (Princeton, 1981).

13. Mrs Charles Garnett, *My Friends the Navvies*, pamphlet (Bradford, 1882) BCL.

14. Stephen Yeo, *Religion and Voluntary Organizations in Crisis* (London, 1976); E. P. Hennock, 'Poverty and Social Theory in England: the Experience of the Eighteen Eighties', *Social History*, vol. 1, no. 1 (January 1976) pp. 67–91. For more on Charles Booth see Kevin Bales, 'Charles Booth's survey of *Life and Labour of the People in London 1889–1903*', in Martin Bulmer, Kevin Bales and Kathryn Sklar, *The Social Survey in Historical Perspective 1880–1940* (Cambridge, 1991) pp. 66–110.

15. Jacob Behrens, *Memoirs* (Bradford, 1929) p. 73

16. Bradford Infirmary, Report, 1861 Bradford Female Refuge, Report, 1861, 1871; Bradford Ladies Charity, Annual Reports 1870–1. All BCL.

17. Ellen Ross, 'Hungry Children: London Housewives and London Charity, 1870–1918', in Peter Mandler, *The Uses of Charity: The Poor on Relief in the Nineteenth-Century Metropolis* (Philadelphia, 1990) p. 164.

18. Ashworth, 'Treatment', p. 85.

19. *History of Sunday Schools in Bradford*, pamphlet (Bradford, 1880) BCL.

20. The most visible sign of such disagreement was the active dispute between the Liberation Society and the Church Defence Association in the 1860s and 1870s.

21. *Bradford, a Review of Social Affairs*, February 29, 1896, BCL.

22. C. Richardson, *A Geography of Bradford* (Bradford, 1976) pp. 105–8. The creation of commuter rail services and other forms of public transportation from the 1870s on facilitated this process. See Richard Dennis, *English Industrial Cities of the Nineteenth Century* (Cambridge, 1984).

23. J. A. Jowitt, 'The Pattern of Religion in Victorian Bradford', in Wright and Jowitt, *Victorian Bradford*, pp. 37–61

24. Eddowes, *Poor Man's Church*; W. Walker, *The Church and Church Property, A Lecture*, pamphlet (Bradford, 1861) BCL.

25. *Census of Public Worship*, pamphlet (Bradford, 1882) BCL, p. 46.

26. Ibid., p. 48.

27. Jowitt, 'Pattern of Religion', pp. 48–52. The most important of these, the Salvation Army, had 6 per cent of the worshippers at services.

28. M. Cahill and J.A. Jowitt, 'The New Philanthropy: The Emergence of the Bradford City Guild of Help', *Journal of Social Policy*, vol. 9, no. 3 (1980) pp. 365–6.

29. See Celia Davies, 'The Health Visitor as Mother's Friend: a Woman's Place in Public Health, 1900–14', *Journal of the Social History of Medicine*, vol. 1, no. 1 (April 1988) pp. 39–59.

30. M. Paterson, who gave a lecture to the Association in April 1887, believed that doctors would be crucial in changing attitudes. M. Paterson, *Sanitary Conscience*, pamphlet (Bradford, 1888) p. 14, BCL.

31. The Bradford Sanitary Association, Annual Report, 1886, p. 9, BA.

32. For more on the development of health visiting see Davies, 'Health Visitor', pp. 39–59.

33. For this process in France see, Smith, *Ladies of the Leisure Class*, pp. 149–61.

34. Anne Summers, 'A Home from Home: Women's Philanthropic Work in the Nineteenth Century', in Leonore Davidoff, ed., *Fit Work for Women* (New York, 1979) pp. 41–6.

35. Susan Kent, *Sex and Suffrage in Britain 1860–1914* (Princeton, 1987).

36. Seth Koven and Sonya Michel, 'Womanly Duties: Maternalist Politics and the Origins of Welfare States in France, Germany, Great Britain, and the United States, 1880–1920', *American Historical Review*, vol. 95, no. 4 (October 1990) pp. 1076–1108.

37. See June Hannam, ''In the Comradeship of the Sexes Lies the Hope of Progress and Social Regeneration': Women in the West Riding ILP, *c.*

1890–1914', in Jane Rendall, ed., *Equal or Different: Women's Politics 1800–1914* (Oxford, 1987) pp. 214–238. For the WPPL see Rosemary Feurer, 'The Meaning of "Sisterhood": The British Women's Movement and Protective Legislation, 1870–1900', *Victorian Studies*, vol. 31, no. 2 (Winter 1988) pp. 233–60.

38. Koven and Michel, 'Womanly Duties', pp. 1107–108.
39. See Chapter 3.
40. Carolyn Steedman, *Childhood, Culture and Class in Britain: Margaret McMillan 1860–1931* (New Brunswick, 1990) pp. 42, 135; Patricia Hollis, *Ladies Elect: Women in English Local Government* (Oxford, 1987) pp. 178–185.
41. Hollis, *Ladies Elect*, pp. 135–6.
42. Steedman, *Childhood*, pp. 41–51. Joanna Bornat, 'Lost Leaders', pp. 221–3; Hannam, 'Comradeship', pp. 219–28.
43. Jane Lewis, 'The Working-Class Wife and Mother and State Intervention, 1870–1918', in Jane Lewis, ed., *Labour and Love* (Oxford, 1986) pp. 109–15; Judith Walkowitz, *City of Dreadful Delight: Narratives of Sexual Danger in Late-Victorian London* (Chicago, 1992) pp. 52–9.
44. The initial meeting of the NSPCC made this argument. NSPCC Bradford Branch, Annual Report, 1889, BCL.
45. Christopher Hamlin, 'Muddling in Bumbledown: On the Enormity of Large Sanitary Improvements in Four British Towns, 1855–1885', *Victorian Studies*, vol. 32, no. 1, (Autumn 1988) pp. 55–83.
46. Gareth Stedman Jones, *Outcast London* (London, 1971) pp. 241–80; Alan Kidd, "Outcast Manchester': Poor Relief and the Casual Poor 1860–1905', in Alan Kidd and K.W. Roberts, eds, *City, Class and Culture* (Manchester, 1985) pp. 48–73.
47. Marianna Valverde, ' "Giving the Female a Domestic Turn": The Social, Legal and Moral Regulation of Women's Work in British Cotton Mills, 1820–1850', *Journal of Social History*, vol. 21, no. 4 (Summer 1988) pp. 625–30.
48. Memo on Infant Care and Management in the Public Elementary Schools, Janet Campbell, Medical Department, Board of Education, July 1910, p. 10, BA.
49. For a discussion of the influence of eugenics and ideas of degeneration in this era see Dorothy Porter, ' "Enemies of the Race": Biologism, Environmentalism, and Public Health in Edwardian England', *Victorian Studies*, vol. 34, no. 2 (Winter 1991) pp. 159–78.
50. Bradford Sanitary Association, Annual Report, 1912, BA.
51. Female Sanitary Inspectors, Report, September 1910, p. 13, BCL.
52. Anna Davin, 'Imperialism and the Cult of Motherhood', *History Workshop Journal*, no. 5 (Spring 1978) pp. 9–65; Deborah Dwork, *War is Good for Babies and Other Young Children: A History of the Infant and Child Welfare Movement in England 1898–1918* (London, 1987).
53. Female Sanitary Inspectors, *Report*, September 1910, p. 12, BCL.
54. E. M. Evans, 'The Essential Qualifications of a Lady Health Visitor', Sanitary Conference, Bradford, July 7–11, 1903, p. 17, BCL.

55. Female Sanitary Inspectors, Report, March 1909, p. 7.
56. Bradford Sanitary Association, Annual Report, 1906, BA.
57. The Bradford Nest, Annual Report, 1885, BCL.
58. Ibid.
59. For more on the Society see George Behlmer, *Child Abuse and Moral Reform in England, 1870–1908* (Stanford, 1982).
60. By 1895, the Society investigated 1965 complaints of neglect, involving 511 children, and verified 1837. Of these investigations 1432 led to a warning to the offenders, 182 cases resulted in prosecution and 222 cases were dealt with in unspecified 'other ways'. Bradford Borough Police, Annual Report, 1889–1895, BCL.
61. *Bradford, a Review of Social Affairs*, November 29, 1895, BCL.
62. Bradford City Guild of Help, Case Books, BA.
63. Cahill and Jowitt, 'New Philanthropy', pp. 359–82.
64. Visiting and Finance Committee, Bradford Poor Law Union, Minutes, 1874, BA; Board of Guardians, Bradford Poor Law Union, Correspondence with the Local Government Board, 1881–2, PRO, Kew, MH 14 12/46.
65. Dwork, *War is Good*, p. 182.
66. Health Committee, Bradford Borough Council, Minutes, November 29, 1899 and December 4, 1899, BA.
67. Barbara Thompson, 'Population, Health and Social Change in an Urban Society: A Study of Demographic Change and the Impact of Municipal Intervention on the Health of the Population of Bradford, 1850–1925', PhD. dissertation, University of Bradford, 1988, p. 310; Cahill and Jowitt, 'New Philanthropy', p. 379.
68. For more on the ILP see David Howell, *British Workers and the Independent Labour Party 1886–1906* (Manchester, 1983) and Keith Laybourn and Jack Reynolds, *Liberalism and the Rise of Labour 1890–1918* (London, 1984).
69. For example, Labour supporters attacked medical charities in 1899. Notes and letters of J. H. Bell, BA.
70. Keith Laybourn, '"The Defence of the Bottom Dog": The Independent Labour Party in Local Politics', in Wright and Jowitt, *Victorian Bradford*, pp. 223–44; Cahill and Jowitt, 'New Philanthropy', pp. 371–2.
71. Quoted in Laybourn, 'Defence', p. 223.
72. Steedman, *Childhood*, p. 110.
73. Dr Kerr, Notes and Letters of Dr J. H. Bell, n.d., BA.
74. Others date the club from 1890. Steedman, *Childhood*, pp. 110–111.
75. *Bradford, a Review of Social Affairs*, November 9, 1895, BCL.
76. Fenner Brockway, *Socialism After Sixty Years: The Life of Jowett of Bradford* (London, 1946) pp. 53–8; Laybourn, 'Defence', pp. 237–9.
77. Laybourn, 'Defence', pp. 239–41.
78. Figure based on the Registrar-General's vital statistics for the Borough of Bradford.
79. Return for the Medical Department of the Local Government Board, 'The Prevention of Infant and Child Mortality', November 21, 29, 1913. PRO, Kew, MH 48/196.

80. Ibid.
81. Board of Guardians, Bradford Poor Law Union, Minutes, February 5, 1879; Children's Committee, Bradford Poor Law Union, Minutes, May 17, 1898 and April 26, 1899. Both BA.
82. Visiting and Finance Committee, Bradford Poor Law Union, Minutes, November 25, 1874, BA; Report of Dr Fuller on Feeding of Infants in the Provinces, PRO, Kew, MO 32/107.
83. Female Sanitary Inspectors, Report, December 1910, p. 13.
84. Health Committee, Bradford Borough Council, Minutes, July 6, 1900, BA; Board of Guardians, Bradford Poor Law Union, Correspondence with the Local Government Board, February 26, 1881, PRO, Kew, MH 14 12/46; Female Sanitary Inspectors Report, March 1909, p. 10.
85. Board of Guardians, Bradford Poor Law Union, Minutes, February 26, 1879, BA; Board of Guardians, Bradford Poor Law Union, Correspondence with the Local Government Board, January 24, 1881, PRO, Kew, MH 14 12/46.
86. Female Sanitary Inspectors, Report, September 1909, p. 6.
87. Bradford City Guild of Help, Case Number 1942, March 1908, BA.
88. For the conditions attached to relief see Pat Thane, 'Women and the Poor Law in Victorian and Edwardian England', *History Workshop*, no. 5 (Spring 1978) pp. 41–4.
89. For example, the parents of Patrick Leeson had to marry to ensure his return. Report of the Superintendent of the Bradford Children's Home, January 18, 1905, BA.
90. Ross, 'Hungry Children', in Mandler, *The Uses of Charity*, pp. 161–96; Lynn Lees, 'The Survival of the Unfit: Welfare Policies and Family Maintenance in Nineteenth Century London', in Mandler, pp. 68–91.
91. Superintendent of the Children's Homes, Bradford Poor Law Union, Report, May 24, 1905, BA.
92. This paragraph is based on the records of the Poor Law Union's Children's Committee, 1898–1906.
93. Superintendent of Bradford Children's Homes, Bradford Poor Law Union, Reports, 1903–6, BA; Children's Committee, Bradford Poor Law Union, 1898–9, BA.
94. Several children refused to return to their families when given the opportunity. Superintendent of Bradford Children's Homes, Bradford Poor Law Union, Report, November 23, 1904.
95. Hollis, *Ladies Elect*, pp. 256, 262, 274, 278–9.
96. Brockway, *Socialism*, p. 58. For Smith's views see E. J. Smith, *Race Regeneration* (London, 1918).
97. Brockway, *Socialism*, p. 55. One family was sued for the sum of 3d.
98. Evans, 'Qualifications', p. 14.
99. Superintendent of the Children's Homes, Bradford Poor Law Union, Report, March 15, 1905, BA.
100. Bradford City Guild of Help, Case Number 1933, September 1906–November 1908.
101. Ibid., Case Number 1946, February 1908–October 1912.
102. J. M. Winter makes this point in his *The Great War and the British People* (Cambridge (MA) 1986) pp. 213–45.

7 Family Limitation and Family Economy in Bradford 1851–81

1. *Cotton Factory Times*, April 24, 1885.
2. The most exhaustive study of fertility differences remains John Innes, *Class Fertility Trends in England* (Princeton, 1938). See also Michael Haines, *Fertility and Occupation: Population Patterns in Industrialization* (New York, 1979); Michael Teitelbaum, *The British Fertility Decline* (Princeton, 1984); George Boyer and Jeffery Williamson, 'A Quantitative Assessment of the Fertility Transition in England 1851–1911', *Research in Economic History*, vol. 12 (1989) pp. 193–217; R. I. Woods, 'Social Class Variations in the Decline of Marital Fertility in Late Nineteenth-Century London', *Geografiska Annaler*, vol. 66B (1984) pp. 29–38; R. I. Woods, 'Approaches to the Fertility Transition in Victorian England', *Population Studies*, vol. 41 (1987) pp. 283–311; R. I. Woods and C. W. Smith, 'The Decline of Marital Fertility in the Late Nineteenth Century: the case of England and Wales', *Population Studies*, vol. 37 (1983) pp. 207–25.
3. For a statement of this argument see E. A. Wrigley, *Population and History* (New York, 1969) pp. 190–3.
4. E. P. Thompson, *The Making of the English Working Class* (New York, 1966); David Cannadine, 'The Present and the Past in the Industrial Revolution', *Past and Present*, no. 103 (May 1984) pp. 131–72.
5. N.F.R. Crafts, *British Economic Growth During the Industrial Revolution* (Oxford, 1985) 89–114; Peter Lindert and Jeffrey Williamson, 'Reinterpreting Britain's Social Tables, 1688–1913', *Explorations in Economic History*, vol. 20 (1983) pp. 94–109; Jeffery Williamson, 'Was the Industrial Revolution Worth It? Disamenities and Death in Nineteenth-Century British Towns', *Explorations in Economic History*, vol. 19 (1982) pp. 221–45; Lindert and Williamson, 'English Workers' Living Standards During the Industrial Revolution: A New Look', *Economic History Review*, vol. XXXVI (1983) pp. 1–25.
6. Joel Mokyr, 'Has the Industrial Revolution Been Crowded Out? Some Reflections on Crafts and Williamson', *Explorations in Economic History*, vol. 24 (1987) pp. 293–319; Mokyr, 'Is Their Still Life in the Pessimist Case? Consumption during the Industrial Revolution, 1790–1850', *Journal of Economic History*, vol. 48, no. 1 (March 1988) pp. 69–92.
7. For a discussion of these issues see John Lyons, 'Family Response to Economic Decline: Handloom Weavers in Early Nineteenth-Century Lancashire', *Research in Economic History*, vol. 12 (1989) pp. 45–91; John Brown, 'The Condition of England and the Standard of Living: Cotton Textiles in the Northwest, 1806–1850', *Journal of Economic History*, vol. 50, no. 3 (September 1990) pp. 591–614.
8. Sara Horrell and Jane Humphries, 'Old Questions, New Data, and Alternative Perspectives: Families' Living Standards in the Industrial Revolution', *Journal of Economic History*, vol. 52, no. 4 (December 1992) pp. 849–880.
9. Maxine Berg and Pat Hudson, 'Rehabilitating the industrial revolution', *Economic History Review*, vol. XLV, no. 1 (1992) pp. 24–50

10. Jack Reynolds, *The Great Paternalist: Titus Salt and the Growth of Nineteenth-Century Bradford* (London, 1983) pp. 114, 125–129.

11. Report of Inquiry into the Condition of the Hand-loom Weavers, P.P. 1839, Report of H.S. Chapman, Assistant Commissioner, pp. 556–90.

12. D. G. Wright, 'Mid-Victorian Bradford 1850–1880', *Bradford Antiquary* (1982) p. 65. In 1882, the *Textile Manufacturer* stated that in the winter of 1847–8, 10 per cent of the entire population received parochial relief. *Textile Manufacturer*, January 1882. Recent Irish migrants were ineligible for relief and faced deportation if they applied. Select Committee on Poor Removal, P.P. 1854–5, Testimony of John Darlington, pp. 101–8.

13. Theodore Koditschek, *Class Formation and Urban Industrial Society: Bradford 1750–1850* (Cambridge, 1990) pp. 351–94.

14. Ibid., pp. 79–134.

15. Barbara Thompson, 'Public Provision and Private Neglect: Public Health', in D. G. Wright and J. A. Jowitt, eds, *Victorian Bradford* (Bradford, 1981) pp. 137–44.

16. Second Report of the Commission of Inquiry into the State of the Large Towns and Populous Districts, P.P. 1844, James Smith, 'Report on the Condition of the Town of Bradford', pp. 150–3.

17. See B. E. Supple, 'Income and demand 1860–1914', in Roderick Floud and Donald McCloskey, eds, *The Economic History of Great Britain Since 1700*, vol. 2, *1860–1970s* (Cambridge, 1981) pp. 121–43; David Greasley, 'British Wages and Income, 1856–1913', *Explorations in Economic History*, vol. 6 (1989) pp. 248–59; Charles Feinstein, 'What Really Happened to Real Wages?: Trends in Wages, Prices, and Productivity in the United Kingdom, 1880–1913', *Economic History Review*, vol. XLIII, no. 3 (1990) pp. 329–55.

18. Charles Feinstein, 'A New Look at the Cost of Living 1870–1914', in James Foreman-Peck, ed., *New Perspectives on the Late Victorian Economy: Essays in Quantitative Economic History 1860–1914* (Cambridge, 1991) pp. 151–79.

19. Feinstein, 'Cost of Living', pp. 163–7.

20. Bowley argued that large-shop prices may have differed from those of shops in working-class areas. Cited in Feinstein, 'Cost of Living', p. 162. For a sense of working-class shops see Robert Roberts, *The Classic Slum* (Manchester, 1971) pp. 78–93.

21. Supple, 'Income', pp. 128–36; Paul Johnson, *Saving and Spending: the Working-Class Economy in Britain 1870–1939* (Oxford, 1985).

22. For the differences in consumption among occupational groups see Lynn Lees, 'Getting and Spending: The Family Budgets of English Industrial Workers in 1890', in John Merriman, ed., *Consciousness and Class Experience in Nineteenth Century Europe* (New York, 1979) pp. 177–82.

23. For a discussion of this issue see A. Hall, 'Wages, Earnings and Real Earnings in Teeside: A Re-assessment of the Ameliorist Interpretation of Living Standards in Britain 1870–1914', *International Review of Social History*, vol. 26, pt. 2 (1981) pp. 202–19. For another measure of variation see Paul Johnson, 'Small Debts and Economic Distress in

England and Wales, 1857–1913', *Economic History Review*, vol. XLVI, no. 1 (1993) pp. 65–87

24. Feinstein, 'Cost of Living', pp. 151–3.
25. A. L. Bowley, 'Wages in the Worsted and Woolen Manufactures of the West Riding of Yorkshire', *Journal of the Royal Statistical Society*, Series A, vol. 65 (March 1902) pp 103–111; G. H. Wood, 'Real Wages and the Standard of Comfort since 1850', *Journal of the Royal Statistical Society*, Series A, vol. 72 (March 1909) pp. 102–3. Sidney Pollard found a similar pattern in Sheffield. Sidney Pollard, 'Real Earnings in Sheffield, 1851–1914', *Yorkshire Bulletin of Social and Economic Research*, vol. 9, no. 1 (May 1957) pp. 54–62. Feinstein argues that the Wood index of the cost of living appears more accurate than that of Bowley and it stretches back to 1850. Feinstein, 'Cost of Living', pp. 173–4.
26. Reynolds, *Great Paternalist*, p. 65; Inland Revenue, 2nd Report, P.P. 1855–6 and 12th Report, P.P. 1866–7. For the occupational structure of Bradford, see Chapter 1, pp. 16–20.
27. 'Bradford and the Yorkshire Worsted Manufacture', *Bulletin of the National Association of Wool Manufacturers*, no. 25 (1895) pp. 374–5.
28. Royal Commission on Labour, Group C., 'Textiles', vol. 2, P.P. 1892, Testimony of Edward Forster, p. 2.
29. D. T. Jenkins and K.G. Ponting, *The British Wool Textile Industry 1770–1914* (London, 1982) pp. 135–65; Eric Sigsworth, *Black Dyke Mills: A History* (Liverpool, 1958) pp. 45–74. For a discussion of the issue of fluctuations in income see Hall, 'Wages', pp. 209–19. Both Bowley and Wood fail to consider the impact of such fluctuations on absolute standards of living.
30. Ian Gazeley argues that the assumed differential improvement for poorer workers after 1886 diminishes if one factors in family size. Ian Gazeley, 'The Cost of Living for Urban Workers in Late Victorian and Edwardian Britain', *Economic History Review*, vol. XLII, no. 2 (1989) pp. 214–16.
31. Standish Meacham, *A Life Apart: The English working Class 1890–1914* (Cambridge, MA., 1977) pp. 128–34.
32. Koditschek, *Class Formation*, pp. 366–74.
33. As late as 1890, density in some parts of Bradford remained over 300 per acre. C. Richardson, *A Geography of Bradford* (Bradford, 1976) p. 98; Eighth Report of the Medical Officers to the Privy Council, P.P. 1866, Dr Hunter, 'On the Housing of the Poor in Towns'.
34. Dr Hunter found some areas where as many as fifty to one hundred persons shared a privy.
35. Fourteenth Report of the Medical Officers to the Privy Council, P.P. 1873, J. Nettien Radcliffe, 'Defects in the Sanitary Administration of Bradford', pp. 6–9. Despite this, work had not begun on a sewage system before 1863.
36. Bradford's infant mortality rate averaged over 200 per 1000 for the entire borough and reached considerably higher levels in inner city districts, Bradford Medical Officer of Health, Annual Report, 1876–84, BCL; Barbara Thompson, 'Infant mortality in nineteenth-century Bradford', in Robert Woods and John Woodward, eds, *Urban Disease*

and Mortality in Nineteenth-Century England (London, 1984) pp. 146–64; Richardson, *Geography*, pp. 117–19; Nettien Radcliffe, 'Defects', p. 3.

37. For a discussion of the division of labor in the industry, see Chapter 2.
38. *Textile Manufacturer*, July 1876; US Consul in Bradford, letter June 1878; *Bradford Observer*, June 13, 1878.
39. Notes of G. H. Wood, Huddersfield Polytechnic Library Archives; Royal Commission on the Depression of Trade and Industry, P.P. 1886, testimony of Henry Mitchell, p. 126. Wood calculated that wages in the worsted trade in 1883 were equal to those paid in 1871 and that wages declined further between 1883–1886. Mitchell concluded in his testimony that the general level of wages in 1884 was 10 per cent below that of 1874, the peak year for wages.
40. See note 25.
41. 5.5 per cent of the adult male work force listed itself as having a trade, but being out of work in the 1881 census. Manuscript Census of Great Britain, 1881, Borough of Bradford, West Yorkshire.
42. Manuscript Notes of G. H. Wood, CB 93, 2304–2566, Huddersfield Polytechnic Library Archives.
43. The annual reviews of trade in the *Observer* for these years made clear that all industries suffered from the slump and that they pinned their hopes on a revival of the worsted industry. For example the number of homes built dropped from 1700 in 1878 to 700 in 1879. *Bradford Observer*, January 1, 1880.
44. *George Hodgson, Maker of Power Looms for Weaving, Origin and Growth of the Firm*, pamphlet (Bradford, 1898) BCL.
45. *Bradford Observer*, January 19, 25, 1878.
46. United Pattern Makers Bradford Branch, Records, 1873–81; National Union of Woolsorters, Cashbook, 1863–81; National Union of Dyers, Branch 1, Records, 1878–82; Power Loom Overlookers Bradford Branch no. 2 Records, 1862–81; Power Loom Overlookers Bradford Branch no. 1 Records 1870–85. All BA.
47. *Bradford Observer*, June 13, 1878.
48. Chief Constable of the Borough of Bradford, Annual Report, 1870–81, BCL.
49. Bradford Poor Law Union, Correspondence with the Local Government Board, June 13, 1877 and March 15, 1878, BA.
50. Bradford Poor Law Union, Yearbook, 1872 and 1879, BCL.
51. For a discussion of the Poor Law in Bradford, see David Ashworth, 'The Treatment of Poverty', in Wright and Jowitt, *Victorian Bradford*, pp. 81–100.
52. The US market made up one-third of Bradford exports. 'Bradford and Yorkshire', p. 363.
53. Sigsworth, *Black Dyke Mills*, pp. 100–14.
54. Richardson, *Geography*, pp. 72–3.
55. Fenner Brockway, *Socialism After Sixty Years: The Life of Jowett of Bradford* (London, 1946) p. 53; Keith Laybourn, ' "The Defence of the Bottom Dog": the Independent Labour Party in Local Politics', in Wright and Jowitt, *Victorian Bradford*, p. 231.

56. See Arnold Evans, 'Back-to-Back Houses', *Transactions of the Epidemiological Society*, vol. 15, 1896, pp. 87–99; Thompson, 'Infant Mortality', pp. 146–64.

57. Richard Price, *Labour in British Society* (London, 1986) pp. 93–134; Meacham, *Life Apart*, pp. 134–55.

58. John Lee, *A Handy Guide to Bradford*, pamphlet (Bradford, 1873) BCL, p. iii.

59. Michael Anderson, *Family Structure in Nineteenth Century Lancashire* (Cambridge, 1971); Lyons, 'Family Response', pp. 45–91; Elinor Accampo, *Industrialization, Family Life and Class Relations, Saint Chamond 1815–1914* (Berkeley, 1989); David Kertzer and Dennis Hogan, *Family, Political Economy and Demographic Change, The Transformation of Life in Casalecchio, Italy, 1861–1921* (Madison, 1989); Mark Stern, *Society and Family Strategy, Erie County, New York 1850–1920* (Albany, 1987); David Levine, *Family Formation in an Age of Nascent Capitalism* (London, 1977); John Holley, 'The Two Family Economies of Industrialism: Factory Workers in Victorian Scotland', *Journal of Family History*, vol. 6, no. 2 (Spring 1981) pp. 57–69.

60. Louise Tilly and Joan Scott, *Women, Work and the Family*, New York, 1978; Ellen Ross, ' "Fierce Questions and Taunts": Married Life in Working-Class London', *Feminist Studies*, vol. 8 no. 3 (Fall 1982) pp. 575–602; Laura Oren, 'The Welfare of Women in Labouring Families: England 1860–1950', *Feminist Studies*, vol. 1, no. 1 (Winter-Spring 1973) pp. 107–125; Elizabeth Roberts, *A Women's Place – An Oral History of Working-Class Women 1890–1940* (Oxford, 1984); Jane Lewis, ed., *Labour and Love – Women's Experience of Home and Family 1850–1940* (Oxford, 1986).

61. Jane Humphries and Jill Rubery, 'The Reconstitution of The Supply Side of the Labour Market: the Relative Autonomy of Social Reproduction', *Cambridge Journal of Economics*, vol. 8, no. 4 (December 1984) pp. 333–46.; Jane Humphries, 'Class struggle and the persistence of the working class family', *Cambridge Journal of Economics*, vol. 1, no. 3 (September 1977) pp. 241–58; Nancy Folbre, 'Exploitation Comes Home: a Critique of the Marxian Theory of Family Labor', *Cambridge Journal of Economics*, vol. 6, no. 4 (December 1982) pp. 317–29.

62. See Gary Becker, *A Treatise on the Family* (Cambridge, 1981); Boyer and Williamson, ' Fertility Transition', pp. 93–117; Richard Easterlin, 'A Socio-Economic Framework for Fertility Analysis', *Studies in Family Planning*, vol. 6, no. 3 (March 1975) pp. 54–63.

63. Nancy Folbre, 'Of Patriarchy Born: The Political Economy of Fertility Decisions', *Feminist Studies*, vol. 9, no. 2 (Summer 1983) pp. 276–7. For an analysis that explicitly accounts for the differential burden of childcare and domestic work in assessing the desire for children see Warren Robinson, 'The Time Cost of Children and Other Household Production', *Population Studies*, vol. 41, (1987) pp. 313–23. For a discussion of generational differences see Harry Hendrick, *Images of Youth: Age, Class, and the Male Youth Problem, 1880–1920* (Oxford, 1990).

64. For a critique of the new home economics see Steve Ruggles, *Prolonged Connections* (Madison, 1987) pp. 13–29.

65. Tilly and Scott, *Women*, pp. 170–1 and David Levine, *Reproducing Families* (Cambridge, 1987) pp. 188–94. Levine argues that the family wage economy, in which all members worked to insure family subsistence, was supplanted by a consuming family dependent upon a single adult male wage earner.
66. J. A. Banks, *Victorian Values* (London, 1981) pp. 33–6.
67. Keith McClelland, 'Masculinity and the "Representative Artisan" in Britain, 1850–80', in Michael Roper and John Tosh, eds, *Manful Assertions: Masculinities in Britain Since 1800* (London, 1991) p. 76.
68. David Mitch, *The Rise of Popular Literacy in Victorian England* (Philadelphia, 1992) p. 190.
69. In Bolton, Oldham, Blackburn, Preston and Bradford the employment rate for all workers under twenty exceeded 30 per cent as late as 1911, compared with a national rate of 22 per cent. When children ten to fourteen are examined, the difference is more striking. The rate for England in 1911 was 4.6 per cent, while in the cities listed above it ranged from 13.6 to 16.8 per cent. Despite this, general marital fertility ranged from 68 to 98 per cent of the English national mean from 1906 to 1910. Census of England and Wales, 1911, *Ages, Occupations and Civil Condition of the People*; Registrar General, *Annual Summary of Births, Deaths and Marriages in the Great Towns*, 1906–10; Registrar General, *Annual Report of Births, Deaths and Marriages*, 1906–10.
70. 57 per cent of children aged ten to fourteen years worked compared with only 30 per cent in England and Wales. A majority of women over the age of fifteen worked in Bradford in 1851, compared with 39 per cent for England as a whole. These differentials remained throughout the mid-Victorian period and up until the First World War. E. H. Hunt, *British Labor History 1815–1914* (Atlantic Highlands, 1981) pp. 9–25.
71. To trace the evolution of the family economy, I use four samples of Bradford's population taken from the 1851, 1861, 1871 and 1881 censuses. These samples provide information about both fertility and family work patterns that highlights their mutual dependence. The size of each sample is as follows:

	1851	1861	1871	1881
Households	1,318	1,370	1,319	1,850
Total persons	7,102	5,743	5,732	8,961

72. The figures for 1881 are: 81.0 per cent husband, wife, child; 7.8 per cent kin; 0.7 per cent visitors; 1.2 per cent servants; 9.8 per cent lodgers (of whom 4.2 per cent lived as kin while lodging with another family)
73. The marginalization of adult men by mechanization shifted many men from domestic textile work to other casualized forms of employment in the worsted industry such as general laboring, machine combing, and warehousing. These occupations constituted over 23 per cent of the adult work force in 1881.
74. In 1881 women constituted 60 per cent and persons aged 10–25 over 50 per cent of the textile work force.
75. In 1881, 61.6 per cent of all households had at least one textile worker in the family.

76. Another factor that affected participation rates was the raising of the minimum age of half-time labor to ten in the mid-1870s.

77. Reports of the Inspectors of Factories, Alexander Redgrave, October 31, 1865, pp. 37–8. Mitch argues that this was the case in cotton textiles as well. Mitch, *Rise*, pp. 171–2.

78. Committee of Council on Education, P.P. 1871, Rev R. Wilden, 'Report on the Church of England Schools, Bradford District', p. 240.

79. Royal Commission on the Working of the Factory and Workshop Acts, P.P. 1876, Testimony of Charles Stead, p. 616.

80. Jane Bornat, '"What About that Lass of Yours Being in the Union?": Textile Workers and Their Union in Yorkshire, 1888–1922', in Leonore Davidoff and Belinda Westover, eds, *Our Work, Our Lives, Our Words* (Totowa, 1986) p. 79.

81. This occurred throughout the country after 1871. Mitch, *Rise*, pp. 162–3.

82. See Chapter 4.

83. Karl Ittmann and Barry Bergen, 'Half-Time Child Labor in Edwardian England', unpublished paper, 1981.

84. Lynn Lees, 'The Survival of the Unfit: Welfare Policies and Family Maintenance in Nineteenth-Century London', in Peter Mandler, ed., *The Uses of Charity: The Poor on Relief in the Nineteenth-Century Metropolis* (Philadelphia, 1990) pp. 68–91; E. H. Hunt, 'Paupers and Pensioners: Past and Present', *Ageing and Society*, vol. 9, pt. 4 (December 1990) pp. 407–30. For a differing view see David Thomson, 'Welfare and the Historians', in L. Bonfield and R.M. Smith, eds, *The World We Have Gained: Histories of Population and Social Structure* (Oxford, 1986) pp. 355–78.

85. Ruggles found that a majority of elderly people lived with their extended kin in 1871 Lancashire and that the numbers of elderly people who needed support grew throughout the nineteenth century. Ruggles, *Prolonged*, pp. 56–7, 106–26.

86. Eilidh Garrett found a similar pattern for children nine to thirteen and fourteen to nineteen in Keighley. Eilidh Garrett, 'The Trials of Labour: Motherhood Versus Employment in a Nineteenth-Century Textile Centre', *Continuity and Change*, vol. 5, no. 1 (May 1990) p. 131. For a discussion of adolescent labor see Michael Childs, 'Boy Labour in Late Victorian and Edwardian England and the Remaking of the Working Class', *Journal of Social History*, vol. 23, no. 4 (Summer, 1990) pp. 783–802, and Hendrick, *Images of Youth* pp. 33–47.

87. Given the prevailing pattern of in-migration of young people into Bradford, it is unlikely that large numbers of children below twenty left home to work outside Bradford or within the city.

88. Bornat, 'Textile Workers', p. 84–7.

89. Michael Anderson argues that assuming a complete sharing is problematic in the case of older children. See Anderson, *Family*, pp. 123–32.

90. Barbara Thompson, 'Population, Health and Social Change in an Urban Society: A Study of Demographic Change and the Impact of Municipal Intervention on the Health of the Population of Bradford, 1850–1925', PhD dissertation, University of Bradford, 1988, p. 282

91. David Vincent, *Literacy and Popular Culture* (Cambridge, 1989) pp. 133–4.

92. For more on family expectations see Bornat, 'Textile Workers', pp. 78–80.
93. Only a minority of married women worked for wages throughout this period. The percentages by year for married women's work age 30–49 are:

    1851 1861 1871 1881
    24.9   27.1 30.2 33.8

    Garrett found a similar pattern of declining participation with age in Keighley, but detected a fall in married women's work from 1871 to 1881. (Garrett, 'Trials of Labour', p. 130).

94. The statistics are:

		1851	*1881*
Age of wife 15–19		*(13)*	*(18)*
Living as	Kin	40.1%	38.8%
	Boarders	23.1%	11.2%
		20–24	*(109)*
		(161)	
	Kin	22.3%	23.9%
	Boarders	21.1%	9.2%
		25–29	*(168)*
		(238)	
	Kin	11.1%	11.9%
	Boarders	10.9%	16.1%
		30–34	*(166)*
		(234)	
	Kin	3.9%	7.9%
	Boarders	6.9%	4.2%

95. In 1851, 83.7 per cent were unemployed, in 1881, 77.9 per cent.
96. Anderson makes this point in his work, noting particularly the presence of grandmothers as potential helpers in the family. Anderson, *Family*, pp. 71, 141–4. Ruggles, however, discounts this factor in his study of extended family relationships. Ruggles, *Prolonged*, pp. 47–9.
97. One of the difficulties in determining the role of lodgers is the inconsistent manner in which they were enumerated. In 1851, they tended to be included in the household in which they lived. In 1861, 1871, 1881, they were sometimes included with households, sometimes counted as separate households. This makes exact analysis of their status problematic.
98. In 1851, women headed 23.8 per cent of lodging households and in 1881, they headed over 36 per cent. This compares with female headship of 14.6 per cent (1851) and 20.5 per cent (1881) for all households. For a discussion of lodging see Leonore Davidoff, 'The Separation of Home and Work? Landladies and Lodgers in Nineteenth and Twentieth Century England', in Sandra Burman, ed., *Fit Work for Women* (New York, 1979) pp. 64–97.
99. 75 per cent of mothers were unemployed compared to 65 per cent for all households in 1881. Lodging households had a mean of 0.613 children working per family compared with 0.988 for all families with a husband present.
100. John Lyons reported that handloom weavers in 1851 in Preston were no more likely than others to take in lodgers, but that they had twice the

number of lodgers, and that the wives of weavers were more likely to work outside the home. Lyons, 'Family Response', p. 67.

101. 35 per cent unemployed in lodger households compared to 25 per cent in all households in 1851.

102. Because of difficulties in linking procedures, this does not include the contribution of kin or lodgers.

103. This differs from the pattern found by John Holley in his study of Scottish textile communities. Holley, 'Two Family Economies', pp. 57–69.

104. Lees, 'Getting', pp. 175–7.

105. Using Registrar General figures, the total decline was some 50 per cent. Karl Ittmann, 'Child Labor and Fertility Decline in Seven English Cities, 1851–1911', unpublished paper, 1981.

106. The inability in this study to link fertility to infant mortality at the family level makes it difficult to assess the impact of lower infant and child mortality upon fertility. Aggregate data show only a weak correlation between the two, but John Knodel's family level data suggest a relationship. John Knodel, *Demographic Behavior in the Past* (Oxford, 1988) pp. 393–442; Etienne van De Walle and John Knodel, 'Demographic Transition and Fertility Decline: The European Case', *International Union for the Scientific Study of Population*, Contributed papers (Sydney, 1967) pp. 47–55

107. Thompson, 'Infant Mortality', pp. 134–38.

108. This reflects the higher rates of marital fertility for women 15–19 in the 1860s and probably the early 1870s, which may have resulted from the increased opportunities for work in the worsted trade and thus for marriage. Knodel uncovered a similar rise in the underlying level of fertility during the initial stages of family limitation, which he linked to better nutrition and a decline in breast feeding. Knodel, *Demographic Behavior*, pp. 284–5.

109. Accampo, *Industrialization*, pp. 117–123; Knodel, *Demographic Behavior*, pp. 291–3; Stern, *Society*, pp. 58–9.

110. These are two measures computed by Coale and Trussell to test for the level of both 'natural' fertility (not subject to conscious control) and fertility control. M is the ratio between the observed fertility in the 20–24 age group of women in any population and the fertility of the 20–24 age group in Coale and Trussell's standard natural fertility scale. m is the difference between the cumulative fertility of women 20–49 in any population and women 20–49 in Coale and Trussell's standard natural fertility scale. Coale and Trussell argue that a level of m of 0.2 or higher is indicative of deliberate fertility control. See A. J. Coale and J. T. Trussell, 'Finding Two Parameters That Specify a Model Schedule of Marital Fertility', *Population Index*, vol. 44 (1978) pp. 203–13. Woods and Hinde question the use of Coale and Trussell's index for Britain, arguing that regional variations in natural fertility were significant enough to warrant a separate schedule for Great Britain. The disparity between the two schedules (in addition to the randomness of smaller populations) may explain the poor fit of the Bradford data to the Coale-Trussell index. Woods and Hinde also believe, along with Knodel, that a level of 0.3 should be used as the threshold value of m. See P. Hinde and

R. Woods, 'Variations in Historical Natural Fertility Patterns and the Measurement of Fertility Control', *Journal of Biosocial Science*, vol. 16 (1984) pp. 309–21; Knodel, *Demographic Behavior*, p. 297.

111. Knodel and others argue that this increase in M reflects the elimination of factors that previously controlled fertility in a less systematic and conscious manner such as breast-feeding.

112. Dov Friedlander argues that the rising age of marriage in late nineteenth century England was the product of economic uncertainty and fear of unemployment. Dov Friedlander, 'The British Depression and Nuptiality: 1873–1896', *Journal of Interdisciplinary History*, vol. XXIII, no. 1 (Summer 1992) pp. 19–37.

113. Singulate mean age at marriage is a summary statistic that tracks changes in average age at marriage using proportions married at different ages (John Hajnal, 'Age at Marriage and Proportions Marrying', *Population Studies*, vol. 7 (1953) pp. 111–36).

Nuptiality measures for women	1851	1861	1871	1881
Bradford SMAM	26.41	26.47	25.68	26.09
England and Wales SMAM	25.77	25.39	25.13	25.30
Proportions Never Married 45–54				
Bradford	5.30	5.30	6.70	9.00
England and Wales	12.36	12.07	12.18	12.05

The source for English nuptiality figures is E. A. Wrigley and Roger Schofield, *The Population History of England 1541–1871: A Reconstruction* (Cambridge, MA., 1981) p. 437.

114. For a discussion of how fecundibility (probability of conception) varies by age see Maxine Weinstein *et al.*, 'Components of Age-Specific Fecundibility', *Population Studies*, vol. 44 (1990) pp. 447–67.

115. The child-woman ratios calculated here are not the same as those calculated for aggregate populations. In this case, only children linked to mothers are included, so in effect all illegitimate children are excluded. In addition, only married women with husbands present are included. The result is both fewer children and fewer mothers than in a conventional child-woman ratio. It might by more accurate to refer to this as a marital child-woman ratio.

116. J. A. Banks, *Prosperity and Parenthood* (London, 1954).

117. Peter Sterns, *Be A Man! Males in Modern Society* (2nd edition, New York, 1990) pp. 145–9; John Gillis, 'Gender and Fertility Decline among the British Middle Classes', in John Gillis, Louise Tilly and David Levine, eds, *The European experience of declining fertility, 1850–1970* (Cambridge, MA., 1992) pp. 31–47.

118. The increase in women twenty-five to thirty-four living as boarders or daughters/daughters-in-law reflects this decline in the position of married women in the 1870s.

119. Elinor Accampo argues that the domestic concerns of mothers, especially the need to balance their dual roles as workers and mothers, helped lead to family limitation. Accampo, *Industrialization*, pp. 123–4.

120. Ethel Elderton, *Report on the English Birthrate* (London, 1914) p. 236.

121. Indeed one measure of this is the greater likelihood of young children of working mothers to be at home rather than at work or school.
122. David Vincent makes this point in reference to the value of education to workers, Vincent, *Literacy*, pp. 125–6.
123. McClelland, 'Masculinity', p. 84.
124. One can detect the survival of older forms of collective punishment for violation of community norms. In May of 1875, neighborhood youths with the approval of adults (and apparently the police) ransacked the home of a neighbor who kept a disorderly house and whose dogs attacked a young child. Report of the Solicitor, Riot in Bradford, Quarter Sessions of the West Riding of Yorkshire, West Yorkshire Archives, Wakefield, QD/4/182.
125. For one statement of this see Ellen Ross, '"Not the Sort that Would Sit in the Doorstep": Respectability in Pre-World War I London Neighborhoods', *International Labor and Working-Class History*, no. 27 (Spring 1985) pp. 39–59.
126. Levine, *Reproducing*, pp. 212–14; Roberts, *Woman's Place*, pp. 83–4.
127. *Waddington's Pictorial Magazine*, 1858, BCL; *Lancashire and Yorkshire Penny Almanack*, 1860; *Denton's Year Book and Parlour Almanac*, 1875–82, BCL.
128. *Bradford Observer*, December 29, 1877.
129. Robert Baker, *The Present Condition of the Working Classes Generally Considered*, pamphlet (Bradford, 1851) p. 28.
130. Rev. Charles Best Robinson, *Christian Diligence – A Sermon to the St Peter's Lodge of Independent Order of Oddfellows (Lund)*, pamphlet (Bradford, n.d.) BCL, p. 8.
131. *Bradford Review*, December 28, 1867.
132. Ibid., September 14, 1867.
133. Thompson, *Making*, pp. 776–9; Angus McLaren, *Birth Control in Nineteenth-Century England* (New York, 1978) pp. 43–89.
134. Cited in Thompson, *Making*, p. 777.
135. McLaren, *Birth Control*, pp. 107–22.
136. George Cooper, *Eight Letters to Young Men of the Working Classes*, pamphlet (London, 1850) pp. 7–8.
137. Gaskell was a member of the Land and Labour League, the Socialist League, and a charter member of the ILP. See Brockway, *Socialism*, for an early photograph of Gaskell and other Bradford socialists.
138. He reported on his activities in a letter to *The Malthusian* in February 1879. Gaskell claimed he was well received. Cited in Thompson, 'Infant mortality', footnote 86.
139. One of Gaskell's collaborators was Jane Clapperton, a socialist and eugenicist, who wrote in favor of both birth control and communal domestic life in her book *Scientific Meliorism* (London, 1885). She quoted Gaskell extensively in the book.
140. *The Malthusian*, November 1880, p. 174.
141. G. A. Gaskell, *The Futility of Pecuniary Thrift*, pamphlet (London, 1890) p. 7.
142. *Bradford Observer*, March 11, 1880.

143. Ibid.
144. Ibid.
145. *The Malthusian*, November 1880, p. 173. This was one in a series of meetings held in the early 1880s reported by the *Malthusian*.
146. Norman Himes, *The Medical History of Contraception* (New York, 1970) pp. 251–6.
147. *British Medical Association Journal*, November 26, 1887, p. 1163.
148. H.A. Albutt, *The Wife's Handbook*, pamphlet (London, 1886) pp. 107–211.
149. *British Medical Association Journal*, November 26, 1887, p. 1164.
150. The trade carried some risks with it and *The Malthusian* reported several instances of individuals arrested for selling Albutt's pamphlet. *The Malthusian*, November 1886.
151. A large printing industry that published a wide variety of pamphlets and journals flourished in Bradford. Jack Reynolds, *The Letter Press Printers of Bradford* (Bradford, 1971) pp. 5–6.
152. Elderton, *English Birthrate*, pp. 97–8.
153. Ibid. pp. 97–8.
154. Bradford Medical Officer of Health, Annual Report, 1881, p. 7.
155. Bradford Medico-Chirurgical Society, Minutes, February 1882 and February 1884. BA.
156. For the attitude of the medical profession see McLaren, *Birth Control*, pp. 116–140.
157. *The Malthusian*, October 1879, p. 72.
158. For the opposition to birth control see Richard Soloway, *Birth Control and the Population Question in England 1877–1930* (Chapel Hill, 1982).
159. J. A. Banks, *Prosperity and Parenthood* (London, 1954).
160. Not coincidentally, these two areas were known for their higher fertility and a reliance upon domestic industry.
161. For more on Irish domestic life see Lynn Lees, *Exiles of Erin* (Manchester, 1979) pp. 123–63.
162. In 1851 only 29 per cent of women 15–49 were born in Bradford, by 1881 this rose to over 41 per cent.
163. This is a point emphasized by Nancy Folbre in her analysis of fertility decline. Folbre, 'Political Economy', pp. 273–278.
164. Sterns, *Be A Man*, pp. 80–107; McClelland, 'Masculinity', pp. 80–7.
165. J. B. Priestley, *Margin Released*, p. 63
166. Bornat, 'Textile Workers', pp. , 82–3, 87–9.
167. For adolescence see John Gillis, *For Better, For Worse: British Marriages, 1600 To The Present* (Oxford, 1985) pp. 267–79 and Hendrick, *Images of Youth*.
168. Priestley, *Margin*, p. 61.
169. Baker, *Present Condition*, p. 47.
170. Meacham, *A Life Apart*, pp. 62–3.
171. See note 113.
172. Gillis, *For Better*, pp. 231–41; Ellen Ross, 'Not the Sort', pp. 49–51; Roberts, *Woman's Place*, pp. 68–80.
173. Priestley, *Margin*, p. 63.
174. Bradford Town Mission, Report, 1851–2, BCL.

175. The parents of one child were required to marry before the Guardians would release him. Superintendent of Bradford Children's Homes, Report, January 18, 1905

176. Jeffery Weeks, *Sex, Politics and Society: The regulation of sexuality since 1800* (2nd edition, London, 1989) pp. 72–6.

177. See Note 94.

178. B.L. Hutchins, 'Yorkshire', in Clementina Black, ed., *Married Women's Work* (London, 1983, reprint of 1915 edition) p. 135.

179. Ibid., p. 137.

180. Anonymous, *Hints to Parents*, pamphlet (Bradford, n.d.) BCL.

181. Brockway, *Socialism*, p. 17.

182. Hutchins, 'Yorkshire', p. 136.

183. The Nest, Annual Report, 1885, BCL; *Bradford: a review of social affairs*, November 16, 1895.

184. Royal Commission on Labour, Group C, Textiles, vol. 1, P.P. 1892, testimony of William Drew, p. 227.

185. Commission on Popular Education, P.P. 1859, J. S. Winder, Assistant Commissioner, 'The State of Popular Education in the Specimen Manufacturing Districts of Rochdale and Bradford', pp. 182, 220.

186. Drew, Labour Commission, p. 227.

187. Brockway, *Socialism*, p. 18–19.

188. Bornat, 'Textile Workers', p. 81.

189. Brockway, *Socialism*, p. 17; Hutchins, 'Yorkshire', p. 136.

190. Richardson, *Geography*, p. 98.

191. Brockway, *Socialism*, p. 16.

192. Meacham, *Life Apart*, pp. 60–2; Carl Chinn, *They Worked All Their Lives: Women of the Urban Poor in England, 1880–1939* (Manchester, 1988) pp. 12–83; Ellen Ross, 'Labour and Love: Rediscovering London's Working-Class Mothers, 1870–1918', in Jane Lewis ed., *Labour and Love* (Oxford, 1986) pp. 73–96; Roberts, *Woman's Place*, pp. 125–168.

193. James Burnley, *Phases of Bradford Life* (Bradford, 1887) p. 24.

194. Hutchins, 'Yorkshire', pp. 140, 144, 147.

195. For women's networks see Ross, 'Not the Sort', pp. 51–5; Roberts, *Woman's Place*, 169–200; Chinn, *They Worked*, pp. 34–5. Meacham, *Life Apart*, pp. 52–9.

196. One mother left her child with a neighbor for 5s. per week. Superintendent of Bradford Children's Homes, Report, January 20, 1904. In another case, a woman living in Manchester arranged to pay 6s. a week to a former neighbor to look after her children, Superintendent of Bradford Children's Homes, Report, February 24, 1904. In a more extreme case one couple left their two children with a grandmother and left for America and sent 12s. a week back for the children. Often relatives could not afford to adequately house the children given to them, as was the case with the brothers and sisters of two young children brought to the workhouse. Superintendent of Bradford Children's Homes, Report, May 25, 1904.

197. One Poor Law visitor inquired about the respectability of a woman requesting the return of her grandchildren, Bradford Poor Law Union,

Children's Committee, December 5, 1899. In another case the neighbors of a woman accused her of being a drunk and attempting to break into their homes while they were gone. Superintendent of Bradford Children's Homes, Report, January 20, 1904.

198. Ellen Ross, "Fierce Questions and Taunts': Married Life in Working-Class London, 1870–1914', *Feminist Studies*, vol. 8, no. 3 (Fall 1982) pp. 575–602. For the distribution of food within the family and its relationship to the control of money, see Oren, 'Welfare of Women', pp. 107–25.

199. Pat Ayres and Jan Lambetz, 'Marriage, Relations, Money and Domestic Violence in Working-Class Liverpool, 1919–1939', in Lewis, *Labour and Love*, pp. 195–219.

200. Nancy Tomes, 'A Torrent of Abuse: Crimes of Violence between Working-Class Men and Women in London, 1840–1875', *Journal of Social History*, vol. 11, no. 3 (Spring, 1978) pp. 328–45.

201. Burnley, *Phases*, p. 172.

202. One case in January 1878 was dismissed because the victim had been drunk.

203. Chief Constable of Bradford Borough, Report, 1870–1883. The number of assaults prosecuted went from twenty to thirty per year in the 1870s to over seventy per year in the early 1880s.

204. *Bradford Observer*, November 7, 1882.

205. Anonymous, *The Improvident Marriage*, pamphlet (Bradford, 1865) BCL.

206. Robinson, *Christian Diligence*, p. 10.

207. B.K. Hanson, *Poems and Tales of Social Life*, pamphlet (Bradford, 1868) BCL.

208. Elderton, *English Birthrate*, p. 98

209. McLaren, *Birth Control*, pp. 215–53; Patricia Knight, 'Women and Abortion in Victorian and Edwardian England', *History Workshop Journal*, no. 4 (Autumn 1977) pp. 52–70; R. Sauer, 'Infanticide and Abortion in Nineteenth Century England', *Population Studies*, vol. 32, (1978) pp. 81–93.

210. *British Medical Association Journal*, November 26, 1887, p. 1163; Albutt, *Wife's Handbook*, pp. 27–8.

211. *Bradford Observer*, February 4–6, 1879.

212. Ibid., July 18, July 25, July 29, August 7, 1883.

213. Only a handful of cases made it into the court records during this era. The assize minute books showed only ten cases from Bradford in the assize docket from 1850 to 1889. Assize of Yorkshire, 2nd Court, 41/21–31, 1850–89, PRO, Chancery Lane.

214. Elderton, *English Birthrate*, pp. 97–8.

215. Wally Seccombe, 'Starting to Stop: Working-Class Fertility Decline in Britain', *Past and Present*, no. 126 (February 1990) pp. 173–8; Levine, *Reproducing*, pp. 174–6.

216. Quoted in Clapperton, *Scientific Meliorism*, p. 339.

217. H.A. Albutt, *Disease and Marriage*, pamphlet (London, 1891) preface.

218. 'X', *Bradford Review*, May 11, 1867.

219. Priestley, *Margin*, p. 63.

220. Weeks, *Sex, Politics*, pp. 249–72.

221. Diana Gittens, *Fair Sex: Family size and structure in Britain, 1900–1939* (New York, 1982) pp. 95–156.

222. Ross, 'Fierce Taunts', pp. 578–81; Roberts, *Woman's Place*, pp. 110–24; Meacham, *Life Apart*, pp. 64–6.

223. Roberts, *Woman's Place*, p. 119.

224. 'Haworth', *Cotton Factory Times*, June 17, 1885.

225. Wally Seccombe, 'Men's "Marital Rights" and Women's "Wifely Duties": Changing Conjugal Relations in the Fertility Decline', in Gillis, *et al.*, *European Experience*, pp. 66–84.

226. Knodel found evidence of a desire to stop rather than delay in the changing birth intervals, especially of the penultimate and last births. Knodel, *Demographic Behavior*, pp. 298–314.

227. Accampo argues for a just such a mix of stopping and spacing strategies. Accampo, *Industrialization*, pp. 120–2, 136–7.

228. Evidence from historical European populations suggests that the average age of last birth was about forty years prior to the onset of family limitation. When one considers the relatively steeper decline among this age group and the range in age at last birth that occurs naturally, the distinction between stopping and spacing for these women grows less certain. Knodel, *Demographic Behavior*, pp. 291–5; Michael Flinn, *The European Demographic System 1500–1820* (Brighton, 1981) pp. 29–30, 44–5, 83–5.

229. Paul Johnson makes this point in connection with patterns of savings in the period after 1870. Johnson, *Saving*.

230. Assuming that abstinence would eventually break down.

231. Michael Anderson, 'The social implications of demographic change', in F.M.L. Thompson, ed., *The Cambridge Social History of Britain 1750–1950, vol. 2* (Cambridge, 1990) p. 52.

Conclusion

1. Gareth Stedman Jones, 'Working-Class Culture and Working-Class Politics in London, 1870–1900: Notes on the Remaking of a Working Class', *Journal of Social History*, vol. 7, no. 4 (Summer 1974) pp. 462–508; Eric Hobsbawm 'The Making of the Working Class 1870–1914', in *Worlds of Labour, Further Studies in the History of Labour* (London, 1984) pp. 194–213.

2. Richard Price, *Labour in British Society* (London, 1986) pp. 96–8; Joseph Melling, '"Noncommissioned Officers": British Employers and their supervisory workers, 1880–1920', *Social History*, vol. 5, no. 2 (May 1980) pp. 183–221; Eric Hobsbawm 'The Formation of Working-Class Culture', in *Worlds of Labour, Further Studies in the History of Labour* (London, 1984) pp. 176–93; Derek Aldcroft, ed., *The Development of British Industry and Foreign Competition, 1875–1914* (London, 1968); Standish Meacham, *A Life Apart: English Working-Class Life 1890–1914* (Cambridge, MA., 1977) esp. pp. 116–55; Royden Harrison and Jonathan Zeitlin, eds, *Divisions of Labour: Skilled Workers and Technological Change in Nineteenth Century Britain* (Chicago, 1985).

3. Hobsbawm argues that as much as forty per cent of the British working class lived at or below the poverty line at the end of the nineteenth century. See Hobsbawm, 'Making', p. 184.
4. This is a counterpoint to the idea that the increasing costs of child-rearing brought a reduction in family size. Instead of consumerism precipitating fertility decline, I see fertility decline helping to spur on consumerism. See David Levine, 'Industrialization and the Proletarian Family in England', *Past and Present*, no. 107 (1984) pp. 188–95.

Appendix

1. Lee-Jay Cho *et al.*, *The Own-Children Method of Fertility Estimation* (Honolulu, 1986).
2. The sample was collected using a sampling program developed by Mike Strong of the Population Studies Center at the University of Pennsylvania. This allowed the direct keying of census data as it was written into a micro-computer. Once the data was collected, it was transferred from micro-computer to the main-frame computer. It was then compiled and dictionaries were generated for each variable. These dictionaries, which listed all the responses for each variable, were used to create numeric codes, which were then matched to the data set using a SAS program. Once the data was in this form, both SPSSx and FORTRAN datasets could be generated from the coded data.
3. Michael Haines, *Fertility and Occupation: Population Patterns in Industrialization* (New York, 1979) pp. 117–23, 182–4; R. Woods and C. W. Smith, 'The Decline of Marital Fertility in the Late Nineteenth Century: The Case of England and Wales', *Population Studies*, vol. 37 (1983) pp. 207–25. For a somewhat different approach see Eilidh Garrett, 'The trials of labour: motherhood versus employment in a nineteenth-century textile centre', *Continuity and Change*, vol. 5, no. 1 (May 1990) pp. 121–54.
4. The census categories used for this were children enumerated as the child of the head and the child of a boarder. The results varied between 87% to 91% for each of the four censuses. Haines assumed a figure of 95% at home with their mothers. Woods and Smith assumed that the figure was 100%.
5. D. V. Glass, 'A note on the underregistration of births in Britain in the nineteenth century', *Population Studies*, vol. 5 (1951) pp. 70–88. Wrigley and Schofield also estimated similar factors, but they only covered the period 1841–71 in this era; see E.A. Wrigley and Roger Schofield, *The Population History of England 1541–1871: A Reconstruction* (Cambridge, MA., 1981) pp. 588–91. The figures derived by Glass were:

	Male	Female
1851	1.048	1.042
1861	1.033	1.030
1871	1.027	1.026
1881	1.027	1.021

6. Barbara Thompson, 'Infant Mortality in Nineteenth Century Bradford', in Robert Woods and John Woodward, eds, *Urban Disease and Mortality in Nineteenth Century England* (New York, 1984) pp. 120–47.
7. It was also assumed that such age-heaping remained relatively constant over time and thus affected the results in a consistent manner.
8. See Wrigley and Schofield for this problem and methods used to correct for it: Wrigley and Schofield, *Population History*, pp. 113–18.

Bibliography

PRIMARY SOURCES

Manuscript Census Schedules

1851 – HO 107/2305, 2307, 2308, 2309.
1861 – RG 9/3313–23, 3225–336.
1871 – RG 10/4441–51,4460–64, 4474–82.
1881 – RG 11/4443–44, 4448–52, 4459–62.

Parliamentary Papers

Select Commission on Bleaching and Dyeworks,
    1st Report, P.P. 1854–5, XVIII.
    2nd Report, P.P. 1857–8, XI.
Census of England and Wales-Reports and Tables
    1851 – P.P. 1852–53 LXXV–LXXXVIII.
    1861 – P.P. 1863 L–LIV.
    1871 – P.P. 1873 LXVI–LXXI.
    1881 – P.P. 1883 LXXVIII–LXXX.
Committee of Council on Education. W. Bailey, 'Report on Bradford District Schools', P.P. 1874, XVIII.
Royal Commission on Depression in Trade and Industry. P.P. 1886, XXI–XXIII.
Education Department, Return of Detailed Statistics of Inspected Schools 1896–97, P.P. 1898, LXX.
Report of the Committee on Establishing Equitable Councils of Conciliation (Masters and Operatives). P.P. 1856, XIII.
Royal Commission on Friendly Societies and Benefit Societies. Report of Assistant Commissioner, E. L. Stanley. P.P. 1874, XXXIII, Pt. 2.
Report of Inquiry into the Condition of the Handloom Weavers. Report of H.S. Chapman, Assistant Commissioner, West Riding. P.P. 1840, XXIII.
Inland Revenue, Annual Report
    Second Report, P.P. 1857–8 XXV.
    Twelfth Report, P.P. 1868–9. XVIII.
Reports of the Inspectors of Factories, Report of Alexander Redgrave. 31 October, 1865. P.P. 1866, XXIV.
Royal Commission on Labour. Group C, Textiles, vol. 1, vol. 2. P.P. 1892, XXXV.
Local Government Board. Annual Report, 1873. J. H. Bridges and T. Holmes. 'Report on the Proposed Changes in Hours and Ages of Employment in Textile Factories'. P.P. 1873, XV.
——. Annual Report, 1880–81. Medical Officers to the LGB. John Spears. 'Report on Anthrax in Bradford'. P.P. 1881, XLVI.

Medical Officers of the Privy Council. Eighth Report. Dr. Hunter, 'On the housing of the poor in towns'. P.P. 1866, XXXIII.
——. Fourteenth Report. J. Nettien Radcliffe. 'Defects in the sanitary administration of Bradford'. P.P. 1873, XXVIII.
Interdepartmental Committee on Partial Exemption from School Attendance, vol. II. P.P. 1909, XVII.
Select Committee on Poor Removal and Irremovable Poor. P.P. 1854–55, XIII.
Commissioners Appointed to Inquire into the State of Popular Education in England (Newcastle Commission). 'Report of H.S. Winder on Bradford (Yorks) and Rochdale (Lancs)'. P.P. 1861, XXI.
Royal Commission on Population. *Report*, 1949, Cmd 7695.
Royal Commission on the Best Means to Prevent Pollution of Rivers (Rivers Pollution Commission)
1st Report, P.P. 1867, XXXIII.
2nd Report, P.P. 1873, XXXVI.
Registrar General. Annual Report on Births, Deaths and Marriages, 1842–1882.
Report of the Departmental Committee Appointed to Inquire into the Condition of School Attendance and Child Labour, P.P. 1893–94, LXVIII.
Select Committee on Scientific Instruction, P.P. 1867–8, XV.
Secondary Education Commission, Yorkshire, P.P. 1895–6, XLVIII.
Second Report of the Commission of Inquiry into the State of Large Towns and Populous Districts. James Smith, 'Report on the Condition of Bradford'. P.P. 1845, XVIII.
Royal Commission on Technical Instruction. P.P. 1884, XIX-XXI.
Eleventh and Final Report of the Royal Commissioners Appointed to Inquire into the Organization and Rules of Trades Unions and other associations. Appendix J. P.P. 1868–69, XXXI.
Report of the Royal Commission on the Working of the Factory Acts. P.P. 1876, XXX.

Newspapers and Journals

Bradford Observer
Bradford Review
Bradford Weekly Telegraph
Cricket Journal
The Malthusian

Bradford Central Library

Ackroyd, Edward. *The Yorkshire Penny Bank – A Narrative*, pamphlet, 1872, Empsall Collection.
Affleck, W.B. *How to Live*, pamphlet, n.d., Federer Collection.
The Age of the Long Chimneys or the Rule of the Factory Lords, pamphlet, n.d., Empsall Collection.
Allot, G.D. *A Pint of Beer*, pamphlet, n.d., Federer Collection.

Anonymous. *A Few Thoughts on the Sabbath Question*, pamphlet, 1856.

——. *A Few Hints to Parents*, pamphlet, n.d., Federer Collection.

——. *Bradford Park Movement: A Few Words of Appeal to the Public*, pamphlet, n.d. (1850s) Empsall Collection.

——. *Bradford Dram Shops*, pamphlet, 1871, Federer Collection.

——. *The Dispute in the Iron Trade: Freedom or Slavery in the Balance*, pamphlet, 1864, Empsall Collection.

——. *Foreign Competition and the Nine Hours Bill*, pamphlet, 1872, Empsall Collection.

——. *Home Lessons*, pamphlet, 1884, Federer Collection.

——. *Improvident Marriage*, pamphlet, n.d., Empsall Collection.

——. *Lord H. W. Ripley, Commander of the Forces and His Generals*, pamphlet, 1868, Empsall Collection.

——. *A Midnight Tour of the Common Lodging Houses of the Borough of Wakefield*, pamphlet, n.d., Empsall Collection.

——. *A Peep Behind the Scenes at the Bradford School Board*, pamphlet, n.d.

——. *Practical Hints to Young Men*, pamphlet, n.d., Empsall Collection.

——. *Questions Addressed to Parents and Masters on Their Conduct at the Times of Fairs and Feasts*, pamphlet, n.d.

——. *Remarks on Popular Education*, pamphlet, 1861.

——. *The Salvation Army: A Great Humbug and Delusion*, pamphlet, n.d., Empsall Collection.

——. *Some Account of the Life of Elizabeth Kenning*, pamphlet, n.d., Federer Collection.

Ashes, J. E. *Monarchy and A Republic*, pamphlet, 1873, Federer Collection.

Bailey, T. *The Managers and Overlookers' Assistant*, 1882.

Baines, Edward. *A Letter to the Earl of Shaftesbury on the Value of the Sabbath to the Working Classes*, pamphlet, 1855, Empsall Collection.

Baker, Robert. *The Present Condition of the Working Classes Generally Considered*, pamphlet, 1851, Dickons Collection.

Balme, M. and Burnett J. *A Letter to the Ten Hours Committee*, pamphlet, 1850, Dickons Collection.

Band of Hope Union. *Report*, pamphlet, 1867, Federer Collection.

Banks, J. W. 'The Progress of Engineering in Bradford', *Journal of the Bradford Engineering Society* 27th Session (1925–26).

Bartley, James. *The Eight Hours Movement: The 'Points' of the Parliamentary Committee of the TUC Considered and Replied To*, pamphlet, 1887, Dickons Collection.

Bell, Dr J. H. *On Woolsorters' Disease*. n.d.

Behrens, Jacob. *Cooperation in Germany*, pamphlet, 1867, Empsall Collection.

Bickerstreth, Rev. *The Physical Condition of the People in its Bearing upon Their Social and Moral Welfare*, pamphlet, 1860, Empsall Collection.

Binns, J. A. *Notes on Building Societies*, pamphlet, 1898, Federer Collection.

Bird, W. *Theatrical Amusements*, pamphlet, 1852, Empsall Collection.

Bradford Auxiliary of the Alliance for the Suppression of the Liquor Traffic, *Report*, 1872, pamphlet, Federer Collection.

Benevolent or Stranger's Friendly Society. Annual Reports 1844, 1865–6, pamphlet, Federer Collection

Bradford Building Society. *Rules and Tables*, pamphlet, 1870, Federer Collection.

Bradford Charity Organization. Report 1880–1.

Bradford Church Defence Association. *Proceedings, Nov 21, 1861*, pamphlet, 1861, Dickons Collection.

Bradford Club. *Rules and Members*, pamphlet, 1866, Federer Collection.

Bradford Corporation. Chief Constable of the Borough of Bradford. Annual Report 1870–81.

Bradford Corporation. Committees of Council. Reports 1853–1914.

Bradford Corporation. Medical Officer of Health. Annual Report 1874–95.

Bradford Female Educational Institute. Rules, 1860.

Bradford Female Refuge. Reports 1861, 1871.

Bradford Female Sanitary Inspectors. Annual Reports.

Bradford Friendly Society Medical Aid Association. Pamphlet, 1872, Empsall Collection.

Bradford Hospital. Reports of the Infirmary and Dispensary 1861–2, 1865, 1873–5, 1877–80. Pamphlet, Federer Collection.

Bradford Ladies Association for the Care of Friendless Girls. Reports 1882–6. Pamphlet, Federer Collection.

Bradford Ladies Charity. Annual Reports. 1870–1.

Bradford Mechanics Institute. Annual Reports. 1854–81.

Bradford Medico-Chirurgical Society. *Report of the Commission on Woolsorters' Disease*, pamphlet, 1882.

Bradford Mechanics' Institute. *The Jubilee Celebration*, pamphlet, 1882, Federer Collection.

The Bradford Nest, Annual Report, 1885.

Bradford Nursing Institution. Annual Reports 1875–99. Pamphlet, Empsall Collection.

Bradford Observer. 'Moral Condition of the Town 1849–1850', Bradford Central Library Collection.

Bradford Poor Law Union. Outdoor Relief 1878.

Bradford Poor Law Union. Yearbook.

Bradford Sanitary and Burial Committee. *Report on Smoke Nuisance*, pamphlet, 1862, Empsall Collection.

Bradford and District Teachers Association. *Memorial*, pamphlet, 1880.

Bradford Sunday School Union. Reports 1861, 1876, 1878, pamphlet, Federer Collection.

Bradford Sunday School Union. Report 1888, pamphlet, Empsall Collection.

Bradford Temperance Advocate and Advertiser, pamphlet, 1867, Federer Collection.

Bradford Temperance Society. Reports 1852–69, 1871–5, 1877–83, pamphlet, Federer Collection.

Bradford Town Mission. *Occasional Paper March 1857*, pamphlet, Federer Collection.

Bradford Town Mission. *Lecture*, pamphlet, 1858, Federer Collection.

Bradford Tradesmen's Home. Annual Reports 1874–93, pamphlet, Empsall Collection.

Bradford Tradesmen's Benevolent Institution. *Fourth Annual Report, Rules and List of Donors*, pamphlet, 1861, Federer Collection.

Bradford Union Club. Rules, Regulations and Bye-Laws, pamphlet, 1879, Federer Collection.

Bradford Woolsorters Society. *Rules and Orders*, pamphlet, 1839, Empsall Collection.

Bridges, Dr. J.H. *Health, with Remarks on the Death Rate of Bradford and Other Towns*, pamphlet, 1862, Empsall Collection.

Brown, J. *Home Thoughts on the 1868 Election*, pamphlet, n.d., Federer Collection.

Buckton, Catherine M. *Two Winters Experience in Giving Lectures to my Fellow Townswomen of the Working Classes*, pamphlet, 1873, Empsall Collection.

Burfield, H.J. *The Present Crisis – Our Duties and Dangers*, pamphlet, 1853, Empsall Collection.

Byles, Andrew. *Reciprocity and Free Trade*, pamphlet, 1879, Federer Collection.

Campbell, Reverend James. *Lessons in Social Science*, pamphlet, 1859, Dickons Collection.

——. *Our Niches: The Role of the Mechanics' Institute in the New Era of National Education*, pamphlet, 1870, Empsall Collection.

Catlow, Z. *Friendly Societies*, pamphlet, 1875, Dickons Collection.

Chester, G.J. *Statute Fairs: Their Evils and their Remedy*, pamphlet, 1856, Empsall Collection.

Chown, J.P. *A Sermon on Behalf of the Widows and Orphans Fund of the Bradford Oddfellows*, pamphlet, 1852, Empsall Collection.

——. *The Excelling Daughter – A Sermon to Young Women*, pamphlet, 1861, Empsall Collection.

——. *Church Work in Large Towns*, pamphlet, 1864, Federer Collection.

——. *England and America*, pamphlet, 1864, Dickons Collection.

Claradge, W. *Conditions of Educational Progress*, pamphlet, 1885, Dickons Collection.

Clarke, Dr. *Political Considerations for Workingmen*, pamphlet, 1870, Federer Collection.

Coffee Tavern Ltd. *Opening of the Old Mechanics' Institute Branch no. 18, Oct 29, 1881*, pamphlet, 1881, Dickons Collection.

Collinson, Edward. *The History of the Worsted Trade and Historic Sketch of Bradford* (Bradford 1854).

Conder, George. *Lectures to the Working Classes on Christianity*, pamphlet, 1850, Empsall Collection.

Cooper, Thomas *Eight Letters to Young Men of the Working Classes*. Pamphlet, 1850, Empsall Collection.

Cudworth, William. *The Mechanics' Institute A Brief History*, pamphlet, 1877, Dickons Collection.

——. *Methodism in Bradford*, pamphlet, 1878, Federer Collection.

——. *Worstedopolis*, pamphlet, 1881.

——. *Census of Public Worship in Bradford 1881*, pamphlet, 1882, Dickons Collection.

——. *The Ten Hours Bill: Was It Passed by a Liberal or Tory Government?* pamphlet, 1886, Dickons Collection.

——. *A Sketch History of the Town and Trade of Bradford*, pamphlet, 1888.

Curry, John. *Catholicity, Liberty, Allegiance*, pamphlet, 1875, Dickons Collection.

Dibb, John Edward. *The Fallacies of the Liberation Society*, pamphlet, 1874, Empsall Collection

Dissenters' Defense League. *Report of Meeting December 12, 1860*, pamphlet, Empsall Collection.

Ecroyd, W. F. *A Speech in Reply to the Attack upon the Policy and Advocates of Fair Trade by W. E. Gladstone*, pamphlet, 1879.

——. *The Policy of Self Help: Two Letters to the Bradford Observer*, pamphlet, 1879.

Eddowes, Rev. John. *The Church of England, The Poor Man's Church: A Lecture*, pamphlet, n.d., Empsall Collection.

——. *Leisure Hours*, pamphlet, 1855, Federer Collection.

Ellis, William H. *A Few Observations on So-Called Woolsorters' Disease*, pamphlet, 1874, Dickons Collection.

Evans, John. *Essay on the Progress of Intemperance*, pamphlet, 1848, Empsall Collection.

Evans. E. M. 'The Essential Qualifications of a Lady Health Visitor'. Sanitary Conference, Bradford, July 7–11, 1903.

Fairbain, A. M. *The Church and the People*, pamphlet, Empsall Collection.

Female Educational Institute. Rules, pamphlet, 1860, Federer Collection.

Female Refuge. *Report*, 1861, 1871, pamphlet, Dickons and Federer Collection.

Field, George. *Historical Survey of the Bradford Temperance Society*, pamphlet, 1897, Empsall Collection.

Field, Martin. *Yorkshire Band of Hope Union Historical Sketch*, pamphlet, n.d., Dickons Collection.

Firth, James. *One of the Principle Causes of Vice Ruling Predominant*, pamphlet, 1865, Empsall Collection.

Fison, F. W. *Report on the International Congress of Commerce and Industry, Brussels September 1880*, pamphlet, 1880, Federer Collection.

Forbes, Henry, *Rise, Progress and Present State of the Worsted Manufactures in England*, pamphlet, 1852, Dickons Collection.

Ford, Reverend James. *The Present Position of the Country*, pamphlet, 1879, Empsall Collection.

Forster, William. *The Movement for the Advancement of the British Wool Industries*, pamphlet, 1881, Empsall Collection.

Friends Provident Institution. Rules and Regulations, pamphlet, 1871, Empsall Collection.

Fudge or the Bradford Oracle (pseud.). *A School Board Discussion*, pamphlet, n.d., Dickons Collection.

Garnett, Mrs Charles *My Friends the Navvies*, pamphlet, 1882, Empsall Collection.

Glyde, J. *Plea for a Park*, pamphlet, 1853, Empsall Collection.

Godwin, John. *The Bradford Mechanics' Institute: A Paper*, pamphlet, 1859, Empsall Collection.

Gott, Charles. *Election Manifesto of 1875*, pamphlet, Empsall Collection.

Hallen, J. *Co-operation, A Poem Addressed to Working Men*, pamphlet, 1855, Empsall Collection.

Hanson, B. K. *Poems and Tales of Social Life*, pamphlet, 1868, Federer Collection.

Hanson, James. *Why Houses Are So Scarce and Rents So High*, pamphlet, 1865 Dickons Collection.

——. *Free Libraries: Their Nature and Operations*, pamphlet, 1867, Empsall Collection.

Harris, Alfred. *Technical Education A Lecture on Industry and Art*, pamphlet, 1883.

Holden, Isaac. *The Holden-Illingworth Letters*, B920/HOL.

Holmes, Isaac. *From Hand Industry to the Factory System: The Effects of the Transition upon the Working Class of Bradford*, 1914.

Holmes, John. *The Advantages of Cooperation Substantiated, A Letter Addressed to the Rev Norman MacLeod*, pamphlet, 1860, Federer Collection.

Household Words Almanac 1850–1858, pamphlet, Empsall Collection.

Hudson, W.H. *Health of Bradford*, pamphlet, 1859, Federer Collection.

Illingworth, Alfred. *Fifty Years of Politics*, pamphlet, 1905, Federer Collection.

Illingworth, J.T. *Progress of Oddfellowship in Yorkshire*, pamphlet, 1866, Empsall Collection.

Illingworth, Thomas. *A Sixty Years Retrospective of the Bradford Trade, Indicative of Some of the Causes of the Present Depression*, 1883.

——. *Distributional Reform*, pamphlet, 1885.

Kell, S.C. *Attitude of the Law-Making Classes Towards the Unenfranchised*, pamphlet, 1860s, Dickons Collection.

——. *Trade Unions-Their Proper Sphere of Action*, pamphlet, 1868, Empsall Collection.

Lambert, Hannah. *Friendly Letter to the Bradford Branch of the Girls Friendly Society*, pamphlet, 1886, Empsall Collection.

The Law of Wages: Four Essays by Workingmen, pamphlet, 1859, Empsall Collection.

Leach, Henry. *The Irish Church*, pamphlet, n.d., Federer Collection.

Lee, John. *A Handy Guide to Bradford*, pamphlet, 1873.

Lepper, Captain. *Right Road to a Bull's Eye*, pamphlet, 1863.

Letter about Proceedings of the late Brewster Sessions, pamphlet, 1858, Federer Collection.

Lewis, J.H. *Safety of Doing Right: Thoughts on the Crisis*, pamphlet, 1878, Federer Collection.

Lister, S.C. *American Tariffs*, pamphlet, 1879, Empsall Collection.

——. *Free Trade in Corn and Protection to Labour*, pamphlet, 1880, Empsall Collection.

——. *Mr. Forster and Free Trade*, pamphlet, 1881, Empsall Collection.

Lyon, George Edward. *Church of England – The Church of the People*, pamphlet, 1874.

Managers and Overlookers Society. *Fiftieth Anniversary of the Amalgamation of the Managers and Overlookers Society*, pamphlet, 1927.

Managers and Overlookers Friendly Society. Rules, pamphlet, 1873, Federer Collection.

McKechnie, Rev. A. *Sugar Candy for Spoiled Husbands – Wife at Home*, pamphlet, n.d., Federer Collection.

McLaren, Walter S. *Spinning Woolen and Worsted*, 1884.

Marshall, J.H. *Our Great Work and How to Do It*, pamphlet, 1859.

——. *The Social Evil In Bradford*, pamphlet, 1859.

Mitchell, Henry. *Report on the Paris Exhibition, together with those of artisans and others*, pamphlet, 1876, Dickons Collection.

——. *The French Treaty, 2 letters to the Bradford Morning Chronicle*, pamphlet, 1877.

——. *Trade and Fashion*, pamphlet, 1881, Dickons Collection.

Mundella, A.J. *Arbitration as a Means of Preventing Strikes: A Lecture at Mechanics Institute 5/2 1868*, pamphlet, Dickons Collection.

National Association for the Advancement of Social Science. *Extracts from Bradford Meeting*, 1859, Bradford Central Library Collection.

National Society for the Prevention of Cruelty to Children. First Annual Report, 1889. Pamphlet, Federer Collection.

Naylor, E. *The Evolution and Development of Bradford Building Societies*, 1908. Bradford Central Library Collection.

Neill, A. *The Bradford Building Trade*, 1859, Bradford Central Library Collection.

The Nonconformist. The Suffrage, A Series of Articles, pamphlet, n.d.

Oastler, Richard. *Letter on Factory Reform*, pamphlet, 1855.

Oddfellows. Report. Pamphlet, 1874, Federer Collection.

——. Rules of the Bradford District, pamphlet, 1872.

Operative Spinners and Weavers of Idle and Eccleshill. *An Appeal to Ministers and the Religious Public*, pamphlet, 1850, Federer Collection.

Parkinson, H.W. *Illegal Riches*, pamphlet, n.d., Federer Collection.

Paterson, M. *Sanitary Conscience*, pamphlet, 1888, Federer Collection.

Popular Amusements: Four Essays by Working Men on Rational Recreation, pamphlet, Dickons Collection.

Publics, B. *Sanitary Reform: Four Letters*, pamphlet, n.d., Empsall Collection.

Rand and Sons. *Sentiments Given to the Workmen*, pamphlet, 1850, Empsall Collection.

Rayner, George. *Address to the West Ward Conservative Association*, pamphlet, 1869, Federer Collection.

Rayner, Joseph. *Municipal Savings Banks for Working Men*, pamphlet, Dickons Collection.

Independent Order of Rechabites. Annual Report, 1871, pamphlet, Federer Collection.

Robinson, A.W. *Address to the People of England*, pamphlet, n.d., Dickons Collection.

Robinson, Rev. Charles. *Christian Diligence: A Sermon to St. Peters Lodge of the Independent Order of Oddfellows*, pamphlet, 1860, Empsall Collection.

Room, Rev. J. *Notes from the Logbook of a Late Worsted Inspector*, pamphlet, 1882, Federer Collection.

Ross, Malcolm *An Address to the Trades Unionists on the Question of Strikes*, pamphlet (1860s) Empsall Collection.

Russell, Rev. A.G. *Drinking and Disease*, pamphlet, 1869, Empsall Collection.

Saltaire Club and Institute. Rules, pamphlet, 1870, Federer Collection.

Savage's Bradford Family Almanac and Medical Companion, pamphlet, 1888, Empsall Collection.

Scoresby, Rev. William. *Report and Resolution Adopted at a Public Meeting Held at the Mechanics Institute*, pamphlet, 1846, Dickons Collection.

Second Equitable Bradford Building Society Rules and Tables pamphlet, 1870, Federer Collection.

Smith, A. *Lines Composed on the Occasion of the Overlookers Festival*, pamphlet, 1863, Empsall Collection.

Smith, Swire. *Educational Comparisons: Remarks on Industrial Schools*, pamphlet, 1873, Empsall Collection.

——. *Technical Education and Foreign Competition*, pamphlet, 1887, Dickons Collection.

Society of Stone Masons. Rules, pamphlet, 1865, Federer Collection.

Stanley, C. L. *Technical Education Necessary for England's Future Welfare*, pamphlet, 1887.

Students of the Bradford Technical School. *Report on the Weaving Schools of Germany*, pamphlet, 1879.

Timothy Tappitnose (pseud.). *Technicomania and its Cure*, pamphlet, 1878.

Temperance: Facts and Figures for the Working Man, pamphlet, n.d., Federer Collection.

Temperance Lighthouse, 1871–3, pamphlet, Empsall Collection.

Third Equitable Bradford Building Society. Report. Pamphlet, 1857, Federer Collection.

Third Equitable Bradford Building Society. *Rules and Tables*. 1865–72, 1875–6, 1886, pamphlet, Federer Collection.

US National Archives and Record Services. US Consulate at Bradford. Dispatches December 1865–July 1906.

Waddington's Pictorial Magazine no. 1–7, 1858, pamphlet, Federer Collection.

Wallace, Alexander. *The World's Greatest Benefactor: A Lecture Delivered to the Working Classes of Bradford*, pamphlet, 1853, Dickons Collection.

Wightman, J. *How I Joined A Building Society*, pamphlet, 1880.

Willcock, Joseph. *On the History, Progress and Description of the Bowling Ironworks*. 1873.

——. *Vote by Ballot: Three Essays by Working Men of Bradford*, pamphlet, 1860s, Empsall Collection.

Wood, Rev. Ben. *The Weaver's Shuttle; A Spiritual Allegory*, pamphlet, 1868, Empsall Collection.

A Working Man. *Reply to the Rev Brewin Grant's Half-Penny Letter*, pamphlet, 1853.

The Working Men's Paliamentary Reform Association. Manifesto and Address to the Electors, *To the Fore!* pamphlet, Empsall Collection.

Workingman's Committee Set up to Protest Against the Establishment of a General Destructor near Peel Park pamphlet, n.d., Empsall Collection.

Working Man's Mutual Improvement Society. *Program of Annual Trip*, pamphlet, 1875, Federer Collection.

Wrigley, Joseph and Bousfield, Charles E. *Report on the Woolen Cloth Manufacture of France*, pamphlet, 1877.

Lancashire and Yorkshire Penny Almanck, pamphlet, 1860, Federer Collection.

Young, Rev. Robert. *The Church and the Children*, pamphlet, 1860.

Bradford District Archives

Amounts of Income Tax Paid in Bradford 1879–80, Deed Box 30 Case 23.
Ash Grove Building Society. Rules of Agreement, Dec, 1860, pamphlet, 1860.
Bell, Dr. J. H. Records and Letters. Deed Box 16/19–20.
F.H. Bentham Ltd. West End Comb Works Bradford.
Bradford Chamber of Commerce. Minutes and Annual Reports. 1851–84
   71D80 1/1–5, 16/1 2/1, 17/1–2.
Bradford City Guild of Help. Case Books.
Bradford Conservative Association. Minutes December 1870–May 1876, June
   1876–April 1886. Special Collection no. 1 1–2.
Bradford Borough Council. Health Committee. Minutes.
Bradford Corporation. Improvement Commissioners. Minute Book 1843–9
   66D79.
Bradford Corporation Town Clerk Miscellaneous Records 40D80
Bradford Homeopathic Dispensary. Records 1859–1881 and Register of
   Patients 1861–2. Deed Box 17, Case 22, Deed Box 4 Case 3/2.
Bradford Liberal Club. List of Members 1867–71. Deed Box 16 Case 36/3.
Bradford Medico-Chirurgical Society. Minutes, 1882–1906.
Bradford Mechanics' Institute. Records. Deed Box 16
Bradford Observer. Circular on the State of the Textile Trade, 1846 Deed Box
   30 Case 34.
Bradford Poor Law Union. Children's Committee. 1898–9.
Bradford Poor Law Union. Letters, Orders and Minute Books. Welfare
   Department Records Special Collections no. 2.
Bradford Poor Law Union. Superintendent of Bradford Children's Homes.
   Reports, 1903–6.
Bradford Poor Law Union. Visiting and Finance Committee, Minutes. 1874.
Bradford Ragged School. Minute Book 1875–83. Deed Box 17 Case 4/11.
Bradford Branch of National Reform. Union Records 1850s,1860s. Deed Box
   17 Case 19/6
Bradford Reform Societies. Records. Deed Box 4 Case 1/1–22.
Bradford Reform Union. Members and Minutes 1840–50. Deed Box 4.
Bradford Sanitary Association, Annual Report, 1886, 1912.
Bradford School Board. Minutes 1870–83. 52D75 1/1–5.
Bradford School Board. Attendance Sub Committee 1873–85. 7/1–2.
Bradford School Board. School Management Committee 1871–83. 9/1–4
Bradford School Board. Log Books. Wibsey Wesleyan School, 1871–81;
   Wesleyan Day School, 1874–81; Horton Bank Top Board School 1874–81.
Bradford Short-time Committee. Letter n.d. Deed Box 16 Case 3/18
Bradford Temperance Societies. Records. Deed Box 16.
Bradford Town Mission. Annual Reports 1850–1900. 32D80 1/2.
Bradford Town Mission. Minute Book 1850–81. 32D80 72–75.
Bradford Trades Council. Minutes 1867–89. 4D82, 56D80 1/1–2.
Bradford Typographical Society. Records. 1854–69.
Bradford Volunteers. Records. 49D81/1/1–5
Bradford Woolcombers' Aid Association. Accounts and Letters 1854–90. Deed
   Box 16 Case 35/1–2d.

Bradford Workingman's Conservative Association. Records 1866–68. 51D79 2–5.

A Broadside Fired into the Salvation Army, 1883. Deed Box 6 Case 34/9.

Amalgamated Union of Dyers and Bleachers, Finishers and Kindred Trades. Prices Book, Minutes 1866–1992. 126D77/55–6.

National Union of Dyers Records, Branch 1. Minutes, Contributors Book 1878–94. 5D82 1/10,19.

Election Materials-Bradford Deed box 13/2–36.

Great Horton Chartist Association. List of members and contributors 1840–66. Deed Box 4 Case 1/1

Great Horton Industrial Self-Help Society. Thirty-Eighth Report and Balance Sheet. Deed Box 12 Case 6.

Harney, George, ed. *The Friend of the People*. 12 editions Deed Box 16 Case 18/1.

History of Sunday Schools in Bradford, 1880. Deed Box 5 Case 28/6

George Hodgson, Maker of Power Looms for Weaving, Origin and Growth of the Firm, pamphlet, 1898.

Holden, Isaac. Letters 1845–96.

Oastler, Richard. 'The Working-Men Are Thinking'. Address, Feb, 1850 (Clipping from Bell's Weekly Messenger, March 4, 1850).

Orphan Girls Home for Industrial Training, 27th Annual Report, 1891.

United Pattern Makers. Bradford Branch, Records, 1873–81.

Power Loom Overlookers Branch no. 2. Records and Minutes 1862–81.

Power Loom Overlookers Bradford Branch no. 1. Records 1870–85.

Bradford and District Power Loom Overlookers Society. *Souvenir Brochure 1844–1944*, 56D80 13/1

Saturday Half-Day Closing Association. Records, 40D78/145.

Ten Hours Movement. Letters, Circulars and Records. Deed Box 69 Case 6/3, Deed Box 17 Case 25/4, Deed Box 27 Case 1.

National Union of Woolsorters. Records. 21D82 2–4/1–3 National Union of Woolsorters, Cashbook, 1863–81.

The Working Men of England, Poem, n.d. Deed Box 16 Case 15/18.

Worsted Committee Records. 1771–1951.

British Library

Albutt., H..A. *Disease and Marriage*, pamphlet, 1891.

Huddersfield Polytechnic Archives

McMillan, Margaret. *Child Labour and the Half-Time System*. Pamphlet, 1896.

Wood, G.H. *Record Book on Wages in Various occupations*, 1743 CB78.

Wood, G.H. *Wage Notes*, MSS CB79–CB100 1744–65, CB 93, 2304–2566.

Leeds Public Library

Albutt, H.A. *The Wife's Handbook*, pamphlet, 1886.

Public Record Office

Assize of Yorkshire, 2nd Court. 41/21–31, 1850–1889, Public Record Office, Chancery Lane.
Local Government Board. Correspondence with the Bradford Poor Law Union. Public Record Office, Kew, MH 14 12/46.
Local Government Board. Return for the Medical Department. 'The Prevention of Infant and Child Mortality'. November 21, 29, 1913. Public Record Office, Kew, MH 48/196.
Local Government Board, Report of Dr. Fuller on Feeding of Infants in the Provinces, Public Record Office, Kew, MO 32/107.

West Yorkshire County Archives – Wakefield

Ripley Family. Correspondence, deeds, wills. C325
Report of the Solicitor, Riot in Bradford, Quarter Sessions of the West Riding of Yorkshire, West Yorkshire Archives, Wakefield, QD/4/182.
James Tankard Ltd. Bradford Worsted Yarn Spinners. Accounts, etc. 1869–74. C357

University of Leeds Archives

Edward Ripley and Son Bowling Dyeworks Dyers and Finishers. Wages Books 1850–90.
Robert Jowett & Sons. Records, Book no. 63 1881, Ledger Book 1872–81.
Oates-Ingham Valley Dye Works. Letter Book 1864–74.

SECONDARY SOURCES

Accampo, Elinor. *Industrialization, Family Life and Class Relations, Saint Chamond 1815–1914* (Berkeley, 1989).
Alexander, Sally. 'Women, Class and Sexual Difference in the 1830s and 1840s: Some Reflections on the Writing of a Feminist History', *History Workshop Journal*, no. 17 (Spring 1984) pp. 125–49.
Anderson, Michael. *Family Structure in Nineteenth Century Lancashire* (Cambridge, 1971).
——. 'Sociological History and The Working-Class Family: Smelser revisited', *Social History*, vol. 1, no. 3 (October 1976) 317–35.
Ashworth, David. 'The Treatment of Poverty', in Wright and Jowitt, 81–99.
Baines, Edward. *Yorkshire Past and Present*, 2 vols (London 1871–7).
Bailey, Victor. *Leisure and Class in Victorian England* (London, 1978).
——. '"Will the Real Bill Bailey Please Stand Up?" Towards a Role Analysis of Mid-Victorian Working-Class Respectability', *Journal of Social History*, vol. 12, no. 3 (Fall 1979) 336–353.
Banks, J.A. *Prosperity and Parenthood* (London, 1954).
——. *Victorian Values* (London, 1981).

Bateson, William. *The Way We Came* (Bradford, 1928).

Becker, Gary. *A Treatise on the Family* (Cambridge, 1981).

Behrens, Sir Jacob. *Memoirs* (Bradford, 1929).

Berg, Maxine, Hudson, Pat and Sonenscher, Michael eds, *Manufacture in Town and Country Before the Factory* (Cambridge, 1983).

——. and Hudson, Pat. 'Rehabilitating the Industrial Revolution', *Economic History Review*, vol. XLV, no. 1 (February 1992) 24–50.

Biagini, Euginio. 'British Trade Unions and Popular Political Economy, 1860–1880', *The Historical Journal*, vol. 30, no. 4 (1987) 811–40.

——. *Liberty, Retrenchment and Reform: Popular Liberalism in the Age of Gladstone, 1860–1880* (Cambridge, 1992).

——. and Reid, Alastair. eds, *Currents of Radicalism: Popular Radicalism, Organized Labour and Party Politics in Britain, 1850–1914* (Cambridge, 1991).

Bolin-Hart, Per. *Work, Family and the State: Child Labour and the Organization of Production in the British Cotton Industry, 1780–1920* (Lund, 1989).

Bornat, Joanna. 'Lost Leaders: Women, Trade Unionism and the Case of the General Union of Textile Workers', in Angela John, ed., *Unequal Opportunities: Women's Employment in England 1800–1918* (Oxford, 1986) 207–233.

——. ' "What About that Lass of Yours Being in the Union?": Textile Workers and Their Union in Yorkshire, 1888–1922', in Leonore Davidoff and Belinda Westover, eds, *Our Work, Our Lives, Our Words* (Totowa, 1986) 76–98.

Bowley, A. L. 'Wages in the Worsted and Woolen Manufactures of the West Riding of Yorkshire', *Journal of the Royal Statistical Society*, Series A, vol. 65 (March 1902) 103–126.

Boyer, George and Williamson, Jeffery. 'A Quantitative Assessment of the Fertility Transition in England, 1851–1911', *Research in Economic History*, vol. 12 (1989) 193–217.

Brockway, Fenner. *Socialism Over Sixty Years: The Life of Jowett of Bradford* (London, 1946).

Brown, John. 'The Condition of England and the Standard of Living: Cotton Textiles in the Northwest, 1806–1850'. *Journal of Economic History*, vol. 50, no. 3 (September 1990) 591–614.

Burnley, James. *Phases of Bradford Life* (Bradford, 1875).

Busfield, Deirdre. 'Skill and the Sexual Division of Labour in the West Riding Textile Industry, 1850–1914', in Jowitt and McIvor, 153–170.

Cahill, M. and Jowitt, J. A. 'The New Philanthropy: The Emergence of the Bradford City Guild of Help', *Journal of Social Policy*, vol. 9, no. 3 (1980) 359–82.

Caldwell, John. *Theory of Fertility Decline* (London, 1982).

Cannadine, David. 'The Present and the Past in the Industrial Revolution', *Past and Present*, no. 103 (May 1984) 131–72.

Chapman, S. D. 'The Pioneers of Worsted Spinning by Power', *Business History*, vol. vii (1965) 97–116.

Childs, Michael. 'Boy Labour in Late Victorian and Edwardian England and the Remaking of the Working Class', *Journal of Social History*, vol. 23, no. 4 (Summer 1990) 783–802.

Chinn, Carl. *They Worked All Their Lives: Women of the Urban Poor in England, 1880–1839* (Manchester, 1988).

Clark, Anna. 'The Politics of Seduction in English Popular Culture, 1748–1848', in Jean Radford, ed., *The Progress of Romance: The Politics of Popular Fiction* (New York, 1986).

——. 'The Rhetoric of Chartist Domesticity: Gender, Language, and Class in the 1830s and 1840s', *Journal of British Studies*, 31 (January 1992) 62–88.

Clark, P. F. *Lancashire and the New Liberalism* (Cambridge, 1971).

Clawson, Mary Ann. *Constructing Brotherhood: Class, Gender and Fraternalism* (Princeton, 1989).

Coale, Ansley J. 'The Demographic Transition', in *International Population Conference* (Leige, 1973) 53–71.

——. 'Factors Associated with the Development of Low Fertility: an Historic Summary', in United Nations, *World Population Conference: 1965*, vol. 2 (New York, 1967) 205–9.

——. and Trussell, J. T. 'Finding Two Parameters That Specify a Model Schedule of Marital Fertility', *Population Index*, vol. 44 (1978) 203–13.

——. and Watkins, Susan. eds, *The Decline of Fertility in Europe* (Princeton, 1986).

Cox, Jeffery. *The English Churches in a Secular Society: Lambeth 1870–1930* (Oxford, 1982).

Crafts, N. F. R. *British Economic Growth During the Industrial Revolution* (Oxford, 1985).

Cross, Gary. *A Quest for Time: The Reduction of Work in Britain and France, 1840–1940* (Berkeley, 1989).

Crossick, Geoffrey. *An Artisan Elite in Victorian Society: Kentish London 1840–1880* (London, 1978).

Cunningham, Hugh. *The Volunteer Force* (London, 1975).

——. *Leisure in the Industrial Revolution* (New York, 1980).

Davidoff, Leonore. 'The Separation of Home and Work? Landladies and Lodgers in Nineteenth and Twentieth Century England', in Sandra Burman, ed., *Fit Work for Women* (New York, 1979) 65–97.

——. and Catherine Hall. *Family Fortunes: Men and women of the English middle class, 1780–1850* (Chicago, 1987).

Davidson, Roger. *Whitehall and the Labour Problem in Late-Victorian and Edwardian Britain* (London, 1985).

Davies, Celia. 'The Health Visitor as Mother's Friend: a woman's place in public health, 1900–14', *Journal of the Social History of Medicine*, vol. 1, no. 1 (April 1988) pp. 39–59.

Davin, Anna. 'Imperialism and the Cult of Motherhood', *History Workshop Journal*, no. 5 (Spring 1978) 9–65.

Delius, Clare. *Memories of My Brother* (London, 1935).

Dennis, Richard. *English Industrial Cities of the Nineteenth Century* (Cambridge, 1984).

Donajgrodzki, A. P, ed. *Social Control in Nineteenth Century Britain* (London, 1977).

Donnelly, J. F. 'Science, Technology and Industrial Work in Britain, 1860–1930: towards a new synthesis', *Social History*, vol. 16, no. 2 (May 1991) pp. 191–201.

Donnison, Jean. *Midwives and Medical Men* (London, 1977).

Donovan, James. 'Infanticide and the Juries in France, 1825–1913', *Journal of Family History*, vol. 16, no. 2 (1991) 157–176.

Driver, Cecil. *Tory Radical The Life of Richard Oastler* (New York, 1946).

Dwork, Deborah. *War is Good for Babies and Other Young Children: A History of the Infant and Child Welfare Movement in England 1898–1918* (London, 1987).

Dyhouse, Carol. 'Working-Class Mothers and Infant Mortality in England, 1895–1914', *Journal of Social History*, vol. 12, no. 2 (Winter 1978) 248–262.

Easterlin, Richard. 'An Economic Framework for Fertility Analysis', *Studies in Family Planning*, vol. 6, no. 3 (1975) 54–63.

Elderton, Ethel. *Report on the English Birthrate* (London, 1914).

Elliott, Adrian. 'The Incorporation of Bradford'. *Northern History*, vol. 15 (1979) 156–175.

——. 'Municipal government in Bradford in the Mid-Nineteenth Century', in Derek Fraser, ed., *Municipal reform and the Industrial City* (New York, 1982) 121–61.

——. 'Social Structure in the Mid-Nineteenth Century', in Wright and Jowitt, 101–13.

Eyler, John. *Victorian Social Medicine: The Ideas and Methods of William Farr* (Baltimore, 1979).

Farnie, D. A. *The English Cotton Industry and the World Market* (Oxford, 1979).

Feinstein, Charles. 'What Really Happened to Real Wages?: Trends in Wages, Prices, and Productivity in the United Kingdom, 1880–1913', *Economic History Review*, vol. XLIII, 3 (1990) 329–55.

——. 'A New Look at the Cost of Living 1870–1914', in James Foreman-Peck, ed., *New Perspectives on the Late Victorian Economy: Essays in Quantitative Economic History 1860–1914* (Cambridge, 1991) 151–79.

Fenn, Geoffrey. *The Development of Education in An Industrial Town During the Nineteenth Century*, University of Leeds Institute of Educational Researches and Studies (1952–1953).

Feurer, Rosemary. 'The Meaning of "Sisterhood": the British Women's Movement and Protective Legislation, 1870–1900', *Victorian Studies*, vol. 31, no. 2 (Winter 1988) 233–60.

Firth, Simon. 'Socialization and Rational Schooling: Elementary Education in Leeds Before 1870', in Phillip McCann, ed., *Popular Education and Socialization in the Nineteenth Century* (London, 1977) 67–92.

Folbre, Nancy. 'Exploitation comes home: a critique of the Marxian theory of family labour', *Cambridge Journal of Economics*, vol. 6, no. 4 (December 1982) 317–29.

——. 'Of Patriarchy Born: The Political Economy of Fertility Decisions', *Feminist Studies*, vol. 9, no. 2 (Summer 1983) 260–84.

Foster, John. *Class Struggle and the Industrial Revolution* (London, 1974).

Fraser, Derek. *The Evolution of the British Welfare State* (New York, 1973).

Fraser, W.H. *Trade Unions and Society* (Totowa, 1974).

Freifeld, Mary. 'Technological Change and the Self-Acting Mule: A Study of Skill and the Division of Labour', *Social History*, vol. 11, no. 3 (October 1986) 319–343.

Friedlander, Dov. 'The British Depression and Nuptiality: 1873–1896', *Journal of Interdisciplinary History*, vol. XXIII, 1 (Summer 1992) 19–37.

Garrett, Eilidh. 'The Trials of Labour: Motherhood Versus Employment in a Nineteenth-Century Textile Centre', *Continuity and Change*, vol. 5, no. 1 (May 1990) 121–54.

Gazeley, Ian. 'The Cost of Living for Urban Workers in Late Victorian and Edwardian Britain', *Economic History Review*, vol. XLII, 2 (1989) 207–21.

Gillis, John. *For Better, For Worse: English Marriages, 1600 to the Present* (Oxford, 1985).

——. 'Gender and Fertility Decline among the British Middle Classes', in John Gillis, Louise Tilly and David Levine, eds, *The European Experience of Declining Fertility, 1850–1970* (Cambridge, MA., 1992) 31–47.

Gittens, Diana. *Fair Sex: Family Size and Structure in Britain, 1900–1939* (New York, 1982).

Gosden, P.H.J.H. *Self-Help* (New York, 1974).

Gray, Robert. *The Labour Aristocracy in Victorian Edinburgh* (Oxford, 1976).

——. 'The Deconstructing of the English Working Class', *Social History*, vol. 11, no. 3 (October 1986) 363–73.

——. 'Medical Men and Industrial Labour and the State in Britain, 1830–1850', *Social History*, vol. 16, no. 1 (January 1991) 19–43.

——. 'Factory Legislation and the Gendering of Jobs in the North of England, 1830–1850', *Gender and History*, vol. 5, no. 1 (Spring 1993) 56–80.

Greasley, David. 'British Wages and Income, 1856–1913', *Explorations in Economic History*, vol. 26 (1989) 248–59.

Haines, Michael. *Fertility and Occupation: Population Patterns in Industrialization* (New York, 1979).

Hall, A. 'Wages, Earnings and Real Earnings in Teeside: A Re-assessment of the Ameliorist Interpretation of Living Standards in Britain 1870–1914', *International Review of Social History*, vol. XXVI, pt. 2 (1981), 202–19.

Hall, Catherine. 'The Tale of Samuel and Jemima: Gender and Working-Class Culture in Nineteenth-Century England', in Harvey Kaye and Keith McClelland, eds, *E. P. Thompson: Critical Perspectives* (Philadelphia, 1990) 78–102.

Hajnal, John. 'Age at Marriage and Proportions Marrying', *Population Studies*, vol. 7 (1953) 111–136.

Hamlin, Christopher. 'Muddling in Bumbledown: On the Enormity of Large Sanitary Improvements in Four British Towns, 1855–1885', *Victorian Studies*, vol. 32, no. 3 (Autumn 1988) 55–83.

Hanham, H. J. *Elections and Party Management* (London, 1959).

Hannam, June. ' "In the Comradeship of the Sexes Lies the Hope of Progress and Social Regeneration": Women in the West Riding ILP, c.1890–1914', in Jane Rendall, ed., *Equal or Different: Women's Politics 1800–1914* (Oxford, 1987) 214–38.

Hardman, Malcolm. *Ruskin and Bradford: An Experiment in Victorian Cultural History* (Manchester, 1986).

Harrison, Brian. *Drink and the Victorians* (Pittsburgh, 1971).

Harrison, Royden. *Before the Socialists* (London, 1965).

——. and Zeitlin, Jonathan. *Divisions of Labour* (Chicago, 1985).

Hendrick, Harry. *Images of Youth: Age, Class, and the Male Youth Problem, 1880–1920* (Oxford, 1990).

Hennock, E. P. 'Poverty and Social Theory in England: The Experience of the Eighteen Eighties', *Social History*, vol. 1, no. 1 (January 1976) 67–91.

Higgenbotham, Ann. '"Sin of the Age": Infanticide and Illegitimacy in Victorian London', *Victorian Studies*, vol. 32, no. 3 (Spring 1989) 319–39.

Himes, Norman. *The Medical History of Contraception* (New York, 1970).

Hinde, P. and Woods, R. 'Variations in Historical Natural Fertility Patterns and the Measurement of Fertility Control', *Journal of Biosocial Science*, vol. 16 (1984) 309–21.

Hobsbawm, Eric. *Labouring Men* (London, 1964).

——. *Worlds of Labour* (London, 1984).

Holley, John. 'The Two Family Economies of Industrialism: Factory Workers in Victorian Scotland', *Journal of Family History*, vol. 6, no. 2 (Spring 1981) 57–69.

Hollis, Patricia. *Ladies Elect: Women in English Local Government 1865–1914* (Oxford, 1987).

Holt, Richard. *Sport and the British* (Oxford, 1989).

Horrell, Sara and Humphries, Jane. 'Old Questions, New Data, and Alternative Perspectives: Families' Living Standards in the Industrial Revolution', *Journal of Economic History*, vol. 52, no. 4 (December 1990) 407–30.

Howell, David. *British Workers and the Independent Labour Party 1888–1906* (Manchester, 1983).

Hudson, Pat. 'Protoindustrialization: The Case of the West Riding Wool Textile Industry in the 18th and Early 19th Centuries', *History Workshop Journal*, no. 12 (Autumn 1981) 34–61.

——. 'From Manor to Mill: The West Riding in Transition', in Berg, Hudson, and Sonenscher, 124–44.

——. *The Genesis of Industrial Capital: A Study of the West Riding Wool Textile Industry c. 1750–1850* (Cambridge, 1986).

Humphries, Jane. 'Class Struggle and the Persistence of the Working Class Family', *Cambridge Journal of Economics*, vol. 1, no. 3 (September 1977) 241–58.

——. and Rubery, Jill. 'The Reconstitution of the Supply Side of the Labour Market: the Relative Autonomy of Social Reproduction', *Cambridge Journal of Economics*, vol. 8, no. 4 (December 1984) 331–46.

Hunt, E. H. *British Labour History 1815–1914* (Atlantic Highlands, 1981).

——. 'Paupers and Pensioners: Past and Present', *Ageing and Society*, vol. 9, pt. 4 (December 1990) 407–30.

Hurt, J. S. 'Drill, Discipline, and the Elementary School Ethos', in Phillip McCann, ed., *Popular Education and Socialization in the Nineteenth Century* (London, 1977) 167–92.

Hurst, Michael. 'Liberal Versus Liberal: The General Election of 1874 in Bradford and Sheffield', *The Historical Journal*, vol. 15, no. 4 (1972) 669–713.

Hurst, Michael. 'Liberal Versus Liberal, 1874: A Rebuttal', *The Historical Journal*, vol. 17, no. 1 (1974) 162–4.

Hutchins, B. L. 'Yorkshire', in Clementina Black, ed., *Married Women's Work* (London, 1983, reprint of 1915 edition) 128–60.

Inkster, Ian. 'Marginal Men: Aspects of the Social Role of the Medical Community in Sheffield 1790–1850', in Woodward and Richards, eds, *Health Care and Popular Medicine in Nineteenth Century England* (New York, 1977) 128–63.

Innes, John. *Class Fertility Trends in England* (Princeton, 1938).

Jaffe, James. *The Struggle for Market Power: Industrial Relations in the British Coal Industry, 1800–1840* (Cambridge, 1991).

James, David. 'William Byles and the *Bradford Observer*', in Wright and Jowitt, 115–36.

James, John. *The History of the Worsted Manufacture of England* (reprint of 1857 edition, London, 1968).

Jenkins, D. T. *The West Riding Wool Textile Industry 1770–1835: A Study of Fixed Capital Formation* (Edington, 1975).

—— and Ponting, K. G. *The British Wool Textile Industry 1770–1914* (London, 1982).

——. and Malin, J. C. 'European Competition in Woolen Cloth, 1870–1914: The Role of Shoddy', in Mary B. Rose, ed. *International Competition and Strategic Response in the Textile Industries since 1870* (London, 1991) pp. 66–86.

Johnson, Paul. *Saving and Spending: the Working-Class Economy in Britain 1870–1939* (Oxford, 1985).

——. 'Small Debts and Economic Distress in England and Wales, 1857–1913', *Economic History Review*, vol. XLVI, no. 1 (1993) 65–87.

Johnson, Richard. 'Educating the Educators: "Experts" and the State 1833–39', in A. P. Donajgrodzki, ed., *Social Control in Nineteenth Century Britain* (London, 1977) 77–107.

Jones, David. *Crime, Protest, Community and Police in Nineteenth Century Britain* (London, 1982).

Jones Gareth Stedman. *Outcast London* (London, 1971).

——. 'Working-Class Culture and Working-Class Politics in London, 1870–1900; Notes on the Remaking of a Working Class', *Journal of Social History*, vol. 7, no. 4 (Summer 1974) 459–508.

——. *Languages of Class* (Cambridge, 1983).

Jowitt, J. A. 'The Pattern Of Religion in Victorian Bradford'. in Wright and Jowitt, 37–62.

——. ed. *Model Industrial Communities in Mid-Nineteenth Century Yorkshire* (Bradford, 1986).

——. and McIvor, A. J. eds, *Employers and Labour in the English Textile Industries 1850–1939* (London, 1988)

Joyce, Patrick. *Work, Society and Politics: The Culture of the Factory in Later Victorian England* (New Brunswick, 1984).

——. ed. *The Historical Meanings of Work* (Cambridge, 1987).

——. *Visions of the People* (Cambridge, 1991).

Katzenstein, Ira. 'Working-Class Formation and the State: Nineteenth-Century England in American Perspective', in Peter Evans, Dietrich Rueschemeyer, Theda Skocpol, eds, *Bringing the State Back In* (Cambridge, 1985) 257–284.

Kertzer, David and Hogan, Dennis. *Family, Political Economy and Demographic Change, The Transformation of Life in Casalecchio, Italy, 1861–1921* (Madison, 1989).

Kidd, Alan. 'Charity Organization and the Unemployed in Manchester c.1870–1914', *Social History*, vol. 9, no. 1 (January 1984) 45–66.

——. '"Outcast Manchester": Poor Relief and the Casual Poor 1860–1905', in Alan Kidd and K. W. Roberts, eds, *City, class and culture* (Manchester, 1985) 48–73.

Kirk, Neville. *The Growth of Working-Class Reformism in Mid-Victorian England* (Urbana, 1985).

Knight, Patricia. 'Women and Abortion in Victorian and Edwardian England', *History Workshop Journal*, no. 4 (Autumn 1977) 52–70.

Knodel, John. *Demographic Behavior in the Past* (Oxford, 1988).

Koditschek, Theodore. *Class Formation and Urban Industrial Society: Bradford, 1750–1850* (Cambridge, 1990).

Koven, Seth and Michel, Sonya. 'Womanly Duties: Maternalist Politics and the Origins of Welfare States in France, Germany, Great Britain, and the United States, 1880–1920', *American Historical Review*, vol. 95, no. 4 (October 1990) 1076–108.

Lambetz, Jan. 'Sexual Harassment in the Nineteenth Century English Cotton Industry', *History Workshop Journal*, no. 19 (Spring 1985) 29–61.

Laqueur, Thomas. *Religion and Respectability Sunday Schools and Working-Class Culture 1780–1850* (New Haven, 1976).

Lawrence, Jon. 'Popular Politics and the Limitations of Party: Wolverhampton, 1867–1900', in Biagini and Reid, 65–85.

Laybourn, Keith. '"The Defence of the Bottom Dog": The Independent Labour Party in Local Politics', in Jowitt and Wright, 223–44.

——. and Jack Reynolds *Liberalism and the Rise of Labour 1890–1918* (New York, 1984).

Lazonick, William. 'The Self-Acting Mule' *Cambridge Journal of Economics* vol. 3, no. 2 (September 1979) 231–262.

——. *Competitive Advantage on the Shopfloor* (Cambridge, MA., 1991).

Lees, Lynn. *Exiles of Erin* (Manchester, 1979).

——. 'Getting and Spending: The Family Budgets of English Industrial Workers in 1890', in John Merriman, ed., *Consciousness and Class Experience in Nineteenth Century Europe* (New York, 1979) 169–86.

——. 'The Survival of the Unfit: Welfare Policies and Family Maintenance in Nineteenth Century London', in Peter Mandler, ed. *The Uses of Charity: The Poor on Relief in the Nineteenth-Century Metropolis* (Philadelphia, 1990) 68–91.

Lesthaeghe, Ron and Wilson, Chris. 'Modes of Production, Secularization, and the Pace of the Fertility Decline in Western Europe, 1870–1930', in Coale and Watkins, 293–313.

Levine, David. *Family Formation in an Age of Nascent Capitalism* (London, 1977).

——. 'Industrialization and the Proletarian Family', *Past and Present*, no. 107 (1984) 168–203.

——. 'Production, Reproduction, and the Proletarian Family in England, 1500–1851', in David Levine, ed., *Proletarianization and Family History* (Orlando, 1984) 87–127.

——. *Reproducing Families The Political Economy of English Population History* (Cambridge, 1987).

Lewis, Jane. *The Politics of Motherhood: Maternal and Child Welfare in England, 1900–1939* (London, 1980).

——. ed. *Labour and Love: Women's Experience of Home and Family 1850–1940* (Oxford, 1986).

Lindert, Peter and Williamson, Jeffrey. 'Reinterpreting Britain's Social Tables, 1688–1913', *Explorations in Economic History*, vol. 20 (1983) 94–109.

——. 'English Workers' Living Standards During the Industrial Revolution: A New Look', *Economic History Review*, vol. XXXVI, no. 1, (1983) 1–25.

Lown, Judith. *Women and Industrialization: Gender at Work in Nineteenth-Century England* (Minneapolis, 1990).

Lumb, Francis. *Second Thoughts – A History of the Bradford Second Equitable Benefit Building Society* (Bradford, 1951).

Lyons, John. 'Family Response to Economic Decline: Handloom Weavers in Early Nineteenth-Century Lancashire', *Research in Economic History*, vol. 12 (1989) 45–91.

McClelland, Keith. 'Time to Work, Time to Live: Some Aspects of Work and the Reformation of Class in Britain, 1850–1880', in Joyce, *Historical Meanings*, 180–209.

——. 'Masculinity and the "Representative Artisan" in Britain, 1850–80', in Michael Roper and John Tosh, eds, *Manful Assertions: Masculinities in Britain since 1800* (London, 1991) 74–91.

McKibbin, Ross. 'Working-Class Gambling in Britain, 1880–1939', *Past and Present*, no. 82 (1979) 147–178.

MacKinnon, Mary. 'English Poor Law Policy and the Crusade Against Outrelief', *Journal of Economic History*, vol. 47, no. 3 (September 1987) 603–25.

McLaren, Angus. *Birth Control In Nineteenth Century England* (New York, 1978).

Mark-Lawson, Jane and Witz, Anne. 'From "Family Labour" to "Family Wage"? The Case of Women's Labour in Nineteenth-Century Coalmining', *Social History*, vol. 13, no. 2 (May 1988) 151–74.

Meacham, Standish. *A Life Apart: The English Working Class 1890–1914* (Cambridge, MA., 1977).

Melling, Joseph. ' "Non-Commissioned Officers": British Employers and their Supervisory Workers, 1880–1920', *Social History*, vol. 5, no. 2 (May 1980) 183–221.

Mitch, David. *The Rise of Popular Literacy in Victorian England: The Influence of Private Choice and Public Policy* (Philadelphia, 1992).

Mokyr, Joel. 'Has the Industrial Revolution Been Crowded Out? Some Reflections on Crafts and Williamson', *Explorations in Economic History*, vol. 24 (1987) 293–319.

——. 'Is Their Still Life in the Pessimist Case? Consumption during the Industrial Revolution, 1790–1850', *Journal of Economic History*, vol. 48, no. 1 (March 1988) 69–92.

Moorhouse, H.F. 'The Incorporation of the Working Class', *British Journal of Sociology*, vol. 7, no. 3 (September. 1973) 341–59.

——. 'The Marxist Theory of the Labour Aristocracy', *Social History*, vol. 3, no. 1 (January 1978) 61–82.

——. 'The Significance of the Labour Aristocracy', *Social History*, vol. 6, no. 2 (May 1981) 229–33.

More, Charles. *Skill and the English Working Class 1870–1914* (London, 1980).

Morgan, Carol. 'Women, Work and Consciousness in the Mid-Nineteenth Century English Cotton Industry', *Social History*, vol. 17, no. 1 (January 1992) 23–41.

Morris, R.J. 'Voluntary Societies and British Urban Elites, 1780–1850: An Analysis', *The Historical Journal*, vol. 26, no. 1 (1983) 95–118.

——. *Class, Sect and Party: the Making of the British Middle Classes, Leeds, 1820–1850* (Manchester, 1990).

Moscucci, Ornella. *The Science of Women: Gynecology and gender in England 1800–1929* (Cambridge, 1990).

Musson, A.E. *British Trade Unions* (London, 1972).

——. 'Class Struggle and the Labour Aristocracy', *Social History*, vol. 1, no. 3 (October 1976) 335–56.

National Union of Dyers, Bleachers and Textile Workers. 'Research Notes on the History of the National Union of Dyers, Bleachers and Textile Workers', Bulletin no. 2 (November 1979).

Neal, Frank. *Sectarian Violence: the Liverpool Experience, 1819–1914* (Manchester, 1988).

Notestein, Frank. 'Population: the Long View', in T.W. Schultz, *Food for the World* (Chicago, 1945) 36–57.

Oren, Laura. 'The Welfare of Women in Labouring Families: England 1860–1950', *Feminist Studies*, no. 1 (Winter-Spring 1973) 107–25.

Ostrogorski, M. *Democracy and the Organization of Political Parties* (London, 1902).

Pankhurst, K. 'Investment in the West Riding Wool Textile Industry in the Nineteenth Century', *Yorkshire Bulletin of Economic and Social Research*, vol. 7, no. 2 (September 1958) 93–116.

Peacock, A.J. *Bradford Chartism 1838–1840*, Borthwick Papers no. 36 (York, 1969).

Pearce, Cyrill. *The Manningham Mills Strike, Bradford December 1890–April 1891*, University of Hull Occasional Papers in Economic and Social History (1975).

Pedersen, Susan. 'Gender, Welfare and, Citizenship in Britain during the Great War', *American Historical Review*, vol. 95, no. 4 (October 1990) 983–1006.

Pelling, Henry. *Popular Politics and Society In Late Victorian Britain* (London, 1968).

Penn, Roger. 'Trade Union Organization and Skill in the Cotton and Engineering Industries in Britain, 1850–1960', *Social History*, vol. 8, no. 1 (January 1983) 37–55.

Pickstone, John. *Medicine and Industrial Society* (Manchester, 1985).

Pinchbeck, Ivy. *Women Workers and the Industrial Revolution* (London, 1981 edition).

Plumb, J.H. 'The New World of Children in 18th Century England', in N. McKendrick, J. Brewer and J.H. Plumb, eds, *The Birth of a Consumer Society: the Commercialization of the 18th Century England* (Bloomington, 1982) 286–315.

Pollard, Sidney. 'Real Earnings in Sheffield, 1851–1914', *Yorkshire Bulletin of Social and Economic Research*, vol. 9, no. 1 (May 1957) 54–62.

——. 'Nineteenth-Century Co-operation: From Community Building to Shopkeeping', in Asa Briggs and John Saville, eds, *Essays in Labour History* (London, 1960) 74–112.

Porter, Dorothy. '"Enemies of the Race": Biologism, Environmentalism, and Public Health in Edwardian England', *Victorian Studies*, vol. 34, no. 2 (Winter 1991) 159–78.

Price, Richard. *Masters, Unions and Men* (Cambridge, 1980).

——. 'The Labour Process and Labour History', *Social History*, vol. 8, no. 1 (January 1983) 57–75.

——. 'Structures of Subordination in Nineteenth-Century British Industry', in Thane, Crossick and Floud, 119–142.

——. *Labour in British Society* (London, 1986).

Priestley, J. B. *Margin Released* (New York, 1962).

Prochaska, F. K. *Women and Philanthropy in Nineteenth Century England* (Oxford, 1980).

Pykett, Lyn. *The Improper Feminine* (London, 1992).

Randall, Adrian. *Before the Luddites: Custom, Community and Machinery in the English Woolen Industry, 1776–1809* (Cambridge, 1991).

——. 'Work, Culture and Resistance to Machinery in the West of England Woolen Industry', in Pat Hudson, ed. *Regions and Industries: A Perspective on the Industrial Revolution in Britain* (Cambridge, 1989).

——. 'Peculiar Perquisites and Pernicious Practices: Embezzlement In The West of England Woolen Industry, c. 1750–1840', *International Review of Social History*, vol. XXXV, no. 2 (1990) 193–219.

Reynolds, Jack. *The Letter Press Printers of Bradford* (Bradford, 1971).

——. and Laybourn, Keith. 'The Emergence of the ILP in Bradford', *International Review of Social History*, vol. XX, pt. 3 (1975) 313–46.

——. *The Great Paternalist Titus Salt and the Growth of Nineteenth-Century Bradford* (London, 1983).

Richardson, C. 'Irish Settlement in Mid-Nineteenth Century Bradford', *Yorkshire Bulletin of Social and Economic Research*, vol. 20, no. 1 (May 1968) 40–57.

——. *A Geography of Bradford* (Bradford, 1976)

Roberts, David. *Victorian Origins of the British Welfare State* (Hamden, 1969).

Roberts, Elizabeth. *A Women's Place – An Oral History of Working-Class Women 1890–1940* (Oxford, 1984).

Robinson, Warren. 'The Time Cost of Children and Other Household Production', *Population Studies*, vol. 41 (1987) 313–23.

Rose, Sonya. '"Gender at Work": Sex, Class and Industrial Capitalism', *History Workshop Journal*, no. 21 (Spring 1988) 113–31.

——. 'Gender Antagonism and Class Conflict: Exclusionary Strategies of Male Trade Unionists in Nineteenth-Century Britain', *Social History*, vol. 13, no. 2 ((May 1988) 191–208.

——. *Limited Livelihoods: Gender and Class in Nineteenth-Century England* (Berkeley, 1992).

Ross, Ellen. '"Fierce Questions and Taunts": Married Life in Working-Class London', *Feminist Studies*, vol. 8, no. 3 (Fall 1982) 575–602.

——. '"Not the Sort that Would Sit on the Doorstep": Respectability in Pre-World War I London Neighborhoods', *International Labor and Working-Class History*, no. 27 (Spring 1985) 39–59.

——. 'Labour and Love: Rediscovering London's Working-Class Mothers, 1870–1918', in Lewis, *Labour and Love*, 73–96.

——. 'Hungry Children: London Housewives and London Charity, 1870–1918', in Peter Mandler, ed. *The Uses of Charity: The Poor on Relief in the Nineteenth-Century Metropolis* (Philadelphia, 1990) 161–96.

Rothenstein, William. *Men and Memories* (London, 1931).

Ruggles, Steven. *Prolonged Connections* (Madison, 1987).

Rule, John. *The Experience of Labor in English Eighteenth-Century Industry* (New York, 1981).

——. 'The property of skill in the period of manufacture', in Joyce, *Historical Meanings*, 99–118.

Russell, David. 'The Pursuit of Leisure', in Wright and Jowitt, 199–221.

Samuel, Raphael. 'Workshop of the World: Steam Power and Hand Technology in Mid-Victorian Britain', *History Workshop Journal*, no. 3 (1977) 6–72.

Sauer, R. 'Infanticide and Abortion in Nineteenth Century England', *Population Studies*, vol. 32 (1978) 81–93.

Schwarzkopf, Jutta. *Women in the Chartist Movement* (New York, 1991).

Scott, Joan. 'Men and Women in the Parisian Garment Trades: Discussions of Family and Work in the 1830s and 1840s', in Thane, Crossick and Floud, 67–93.

——. *Gender and the Politics of History* (New York, 1988).

Seccombe, Wally. 'Marxism and Demography', *New Left Review*, no. 137 (Jan–Feb. 1983) 20–46.

——. 'Patriarchy Stabilized: the Construction of the Male Breadwinner Wage Norm in Nineteenth-Century Britain', *Social History*, vol. 11, no. 1 (January 1986) 53–76.

——. 'Starting to Stop: Working-Class Fertility Decline in Britain', *Past and Present*, no. 126 (1990) 151–88.

——. 'Men's "Marital Rights" and Women's "Wifely Duties": Changing Conjugal Relations in the Fertility Decline', in Gillis *et al.*, 66–84.

Shiman, Lilian Lewis. 'The Band of Hope Movement: Respectable Recreation for Working-Class Children', *Victorian Studies*, vol. 18, no. 1 (Autumn, 1973) 49–74.

Sigsworth, E. M. *Black Dyke Mills: A History* (Liverpool 1958).

——. and Blackman, J. M. 'The Woolen and Worsted Industries', in Derek Aldcroft, ed., *The Development of British Industry and Foreign Competition, 1875–1914* (London, 1968) 128–57.

Smelser, Neil. *Social Change in the Industrial Revolution* (Chicago, 1959).

Smith, Bonnie. *Ladies of the Leisure Class* (Princeton, 1981).

Smith, Jonathan 'The Strike of 1825', in Wright and Jowitt, 65–79.

Smith, Richard. 'Fertility, Economy, and Household Formation in England Over Three Centuries', *Population and Development Review*, vol. 7, no. 4 (December 1981) 595–622.

Soloway, Richard. *Birth Control and the Population Question in England, 1877–1930* (Chapel Hill, 1982).

Spain, Jonathan. 'Trade Unionists, Gladstonian Liberals, and the Labour Law Reforms of 1875', in Biagini and Reid, 109–33.

Springhall, John. *Coming of Age: Adolesence in Britain 1860–1960* (Dublin, 1986).

Steedman, Carolyn. *Childhood, Culture and Class in Britain: Margaret McMillan 1860–1931* (New Brunswick, 1990).

Stephens, W. B. *Education, Literacy and Society, 1830–1870: The Geography of Diversity in Provincial England* (Manchester, 1987).

Stern, Mark. *Society and Family Strategy, Erie County, New York 1850–1920* (Albany, 1987).

Sterns, Peter. *Be A Man! Males in Modern Society* (2nd edition, New York, 1990).

Storch, Robert. 'The Plague of Blue Locusts: Police Reform and Popular Resistance in Northern England, 1840–1857', *International Review of Social History*, vol. XX, pt. 1 (1975), 61–90.

——. ed. *Popular Culture and Custom in Nineteenth-Century England* (London, 1982).

Styles, John. 'Embezzlement, Industry and the Law in England, 1500–1800', in Berg, *et al.* 173–205.

Summers, Anne. 'A Home from Home: Women's Philanthropic Work in the Nineteenth Century', in Burman, 41–6.

Supple, B. E. 'Income and Demand 1860–1914', in Roderick Floud and Donald McCloskey, eds, *The Economic History of Great Britain since 1700, vol. 2, 1860–1970s* (Cambridge, 1981) 121–43.

Taylor, Barbara. *Eve and the New Jerusalem* (New York, 1983).

Taylor, George. 'Bradford and the Worsted Manufacture', *Practical Magazine* (October 1873).

Teitelbaum, Michael. 'Birth Underregistration in the Constituent Counties of England and Wales, 1841–1910', *Population Studies*, vol. 28 (1974) 329–43.

——. *The British Fertility Decline* (Princeton, 1984).

Thane, Pat. 'Women and the Poor Law in Victorian and Edwardian England', *History Workshop*, no. 5 (1978) 29–51.

——. 'The Working-Class and State "Welfare" in Britain, 1880–1914', *The Historical Journal*, vol. 27, no. 4 (1984) 877–900.

——., Crossick, Geoffrey and Floud, Roderick, eds. *The power of the past: Essays for Eric Hobsbawm* (Cambridge, 1984).

Tholfsen, Trygve R. *Working-Class Radicalism in Mid-Victorian England* (New York, 1977).

Thompson, Barbara. 'Public Provision and Private Neglect: Public Health', in Wright and Jowitt, 137–64.

——. 'Infant Mortality in Nineteenth Century Bradford', in Robert Woods and John Woodward, eds, *Urban Disease and Mortality in Nineteenth Century England* (New York, 1984) 120–47.

Thompson, Dorothy. *The Chartists: Popular Politics in the Industrial Revolution* (New York, 1984).

Thompson, E. P. 'Homage to Tom Maguire', in Asa Briggs and John Saville, eds, *Essays in Labour History* (New York, 1960) 276–316.

——. *The Making of the English Working Class* (New York 1966).

——. 'Time, Work-Discipline, and Industrial Capitalism', *Past and Present*, no. 38 (1968) 57–97.

——. 'On History, Sociology and Historical Relevance', *British Journal of Sociology*, vol. 27, no. 3 (September 1976) 387–402.

Thompson, Noel. *The People's Science: The popular political economy of exploitation and crisis 1816–1834* (Cambridge, 1984).

Thomson, David. 'Welfare and the Historians', in L. Bonfield, R. M. Smith and K. Wrightson, eds, *The World We Have Gained: Histories of Population and Social Structure* (Oxford, 1986) 355–78.

Tilly, Louise and Scott, Joan. *Women, Work and Family* (New York, 1978).

Tomes, Nancy. 'A Torrent of Abuse: Crimes of Violence between Working-Class Men and Women in London, 1840–1875', *Journal of Social History*, vol. 11, no. 3 (Spring, 1978) 328–45.

Tranter, Neil. *Population and Society 1750–1940* (New York, 1985).

Tylecote, Mabel. *The Mechanics Institutes of Lancashire and Yorkshire Before 1851* (Manchester, 1957).

Valverde, Marianna. ' "Giving the Female a Domestic Turn": The Social, Legal and Moral Regulation of Women's Work in British Cotton Mills, 1820–1850', *Journal of Social History*, vol. 21, no. 4 (Summer 1988) 619–34.

van de Walle, Etienne and Knodel, John. 'Demographic Transition and Fertility Decline: The European Case', *International Union for the Scientific Study of Population*, Contributed Papers (Sydney, 1967).

Vincent, David. *Literacy and Popular Culture in England 1750–1914* (Cambridge, 1989).

Vincent, John. *Formation of the Liberal Party 1857–1868* (London 1966).

Walkowitz, Judith. *Prostitution in Victorian Society* (Cambridge, 1980).

Wall, Richard. 'Work, Welfare and the Family: An Illustration of the Adaptive Family Economy', in Bonfield, Smith and Wrightson, 261–94.

Walton, John and Poole, Robert. 'The Lancashire Wakes in the Nineteenth Century', in Storch, 100–24.

Ward, J. T. *Chartism* (London 1973).

Webb, Igor. 'The Bradford Wool Exchange: Industrial Capitalism and the Popularity of the Gothic', *Victorian Studies*, vol. 20, no. 1 (Autumn 1976) 45–68.

Weeks, Jeffery. *Sex, Politics and Society* (London, 1989).

Weinstein, Maxine, *et al.* 'Components of Age-Specific Fecundibility', *Population Studies*, vol. 44 (1990) 447–67.

Wharton, Ronald. *History of Boxing in Bradford* (Bradford, 1980).

Williamson, Jeffery. 'Was the Industrial Revolution Worth It? Disamenities and Death in Nineteenth-Century British Towns', *Explorations in Economic History*, vol. 19 (1982) 221–45.

Winter, J. M. *The Great War and the British People* (Cambridge, MA. 1986).

Wood, G. H. 'Real Wages and the Standard of Comfort since 1850', *Journal of the Royal Statistical Society*, Series A, vol. 72 (March, 1909) 91–103.

Woods R. I and Smith, C. W. 'The Decline of Marital Fertility in the Late Nineteenth Century: The Case of England and Wales', *Population Studies*, vol. 37 (1983) 207–25.

Woods, R. I. 'Approaches to the Fertility Transition in Victorian England', *Population Studies*, vol. 41 (1987) pp. 283–311.

Woodward, John and Richards, David, eds, *Health Care and Popular Medicine in Nineteenth Century England* (New York, 1977).

Wright, D. G. 'A Radical Borough: Parliamentary Politics in Bradford', *Northern History*, vol. 4 (1969) 132–66.

——. 'Liberal Versus Liberal, 1874: Some Comments', *The Historical Journal*, vol. 16, no. 4 (1973) 597–603.

——. 'Mid-Victorian Bradford 1850–1880', *Bradford Antiquary* (1982) 65–86.

Wright, D. G. and J. A. Jowitt, eds, *Victorian Bradford* (Bradford, 1981).

Wrigley, E. A. and Schofield, R. S. *The Population History of England 1541–1871: A Reconstruction* (Cambridge, MA. 1981).

Yarmie, Andrew. 'Employers' Organizations in Mid-Victorian England', *International Review of Social History*, vol. XXV, pt.2 (1980) 209–35.

Yeo, Stephen. *Religion and Voluntary Organizations in Crisis* (London, 1976).

Dissertations and Unpublished Papers

Collins, Malcolm. 'Drink, Temperance and Prostitution in Victorian Bradford', MA Thesis, University of Leeds, 1971.

Donnelly, James. 'The Development of Technical Education in Bradford 1825–1900', MEd Thesis, University of Leeds, 1984.

Garnett, Colin. 'Irish Immigration and the Roman Catholic Church in Bradford 1835–1880', PhD dissertation, University of Bradford, 1984.

Laybourn, Keith. 'Yorkshire Trade Unions and the Great Depression', PhD dissertation, University of Manchester, 1976.

Macleod, Stella. 'The changing Face of the Bradford Borough Bench 1848–1980', BA Thesis, University of Bradford, 1980.

Mortimore, Michael. 'Urban Growth in Bradford and Its Environs, 1800–1960', MA Thesis, University of Leeds, 1963.

Roberts, John. 'The Bradford Textile Warehouse 1770–1914', PhD dissertation, University of Bradford , 1976.

Roper, Norman Brian. 'The Contribution of Non-Conformists to the Development of Education in Bradford in the Nineteenth Century', MEd Thesis, University of Leeds, 1976.

Russell, David. 'The Popular Musical Societies of Bradford', PhD dissertation, University of York, 1979.

Thompson, Barbara. 'Population, Health and Social Change in an Urban Society: A Study of Demographic Change and the Impact of Municipal Intervention on the Health of the Population of Bradford, 1850–1925', PhD dissertation, University of Bradford, 1988.

West, Bob. 'Water and Worstedopolis', Unpublished paper, 1982, Bradford Central Library.

Wright, D.G. 'Politics and Opinion in Nineteenth Century Bradford', PhD dissertation, University of Leeds, 1966.

Index